This book is an account of an almost completely neglected archaeological epic, the uncovering and restoration of all the classical monuments of Rome during the French occupation (1809–14). This was the first large-scale archaeological programme in the city. Based on archives in Rome and Paris, the archaeology of these five years is placed against its essential background: the fate of the monuments since antiquity, and the contemporary Napoleonic political and cultural history. Dr Ridley describes the enormously complicated organisation which carried out the work, and identifies the leading administrators, archaeologists and architects. The bulk of the work is a detailed account of the excavation and restoration work on the Forum Romanum, the Colosseum, and the Forum of Trajan, the main classical monuments. There are numerous illustrations of the monuments both before and after the French intervention, as well as unpublished plans from the archives, and an extensive specialist bibliography.

The book is intended for anyone interested in archaeology, in Napoleonic Europe, and, above all, in Rome.

The eagle and the spade

The eagle
and the spade

Archaeology in Rome during the Napoleonic era

RONALD T. RIDLEY

Reader in History,
University of Melbourne

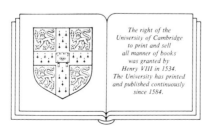

The right of the
University of Cambridge
to print and sell
all manner of books
was granted by
Henry VIII in 1534.
The University has printed
and published continuously
since 1584.

CAMBRIDGE UNIVERSITY PRESS

Cambridge
New York   Port Chester   Melbourne   Sydney

Published by the Press Syndicate of the University of Cambridge
The Pitt Building, Trumpington Street, Cambridge CB2 IRP
40 West 20th Street, New York, NY 10011–4211, USA
10 Stamford Road, Oakleigh, Victoria 3166, Australia

First published 1992

Printed in Great Britain at The Bath Press, Avon

British Library Cataloguing in publication data

Ridley, Ronald T.
The eagle and the spade
1. Italy. Rome. Antiquities. Classical. Excavation of remains
I. Title
937

Library of Congress Cataloguing in publication data

Ridley, Ronald T., 1940–
The eagle and the spade
Ronald T. Ridley.
p.   cm.
Includes index.
ISBN 0 521 40191 7
1. Rome (Italy) – Antiquities – Conservation and restoration –
History – 19th century.   2. Excavations (Archaeology) – Italy – Rome –
History – 19th century.   I. Title.
DG63.R54   1992
937′ .6 – dc20   90–43070   CIP

ISBN 0 521 401917 hardback

for
Piero Treves
great scholar and generous friend

Contents

Illustrations

FIGURES

Acknowledgements

My sincerest thanks are due to the staff of the following places, for allowing me to have access to their resources and treasures, and for the constant kindness they extended to me while I was working there: Prof. Carlo Pietr-angeli, Director of the Vatican Museums; L'Archivio dello Stato, Rome; Les Archives Nationales, Paris; Istituto Nazionale di Archeologia, Rome; Il Museo di Roma; The American Academy, Rome; L'Ecole Française, Rome; La Biblioteca Nazionale, Rome; La Biblioteca Casanatense, Rome; The British Library, London. And a special place is owed to Anne Pottage, of the University's graphics department, who so brilliantly redrew the maps of the main areas of French activity from the originals in the Archives Nationales. The above institutions and Dottoressa Carla Maria Amici also generously granted permission to include precious illustrations in this book. I should like finally to express my gratitude to the readers and editors of Cambridge University Press, who suggested so many improvements in regard to clarity and consistency, and, as always, to my wife, for her unlimited expertise.

Abbreviations

Ann. Ist.	Annali dell'Istituto di Corrispondenza Archeologica
ASL	Accademia Nazionale di S. Luca
ASR	Archivio dello Stato, Rome
Atti Accad. Arch.	Atti della Pontificia Accademia Romana di Archeologia
BCAR	Bollettino della Commissione Archeologica di Roma
BG	Buon Governo (Archivio dello Stato)
Bull. Ist.	Bollettino dell'Istituto di Corrispondenza Archeologica
Bull. Soc. Hist. Art. Fr.	Bulletin de la Société de l'Histoire de l'Art Française
Bull. Soc. Nat. Antiq. Fr.	Bulletin de la Société Nationale des Antiquaires de France
CIL	Corpus Inscriptionum Latinarum
CRAIBL	Comptes-Rendus de l'Academie des Inscriptions et Belles-Lettres
CT	Codex Theodosianus
DBF	Dictionnaire de biographie française
DBI	Dizionario biografico degli italiani
Diss. Accad. Arch.	Dissertazioni della Pontificia Accademia Romana di Archeologia
DNB	Dictionary of national biography
ILS	Inscriptiones latinae selectae
JDAI	Jahrbuch des Deutschen Archaeologischen Instituts
MEFR	Mémoires de l'Ecole Française de Rome
Mél. Arch. Hist.	Mélanges d'Archéologie et d'Histoire
Mem. Accad. Arch.	Memorie della Pontificia Accademia Romana di Archeologia
NS	Notizie degli scavi
PBSR	Proceedings of the British School in Rome

Abbreviations

RAL	*Rendiconti dell'Accademia dei Lincei*
Rend. Accad. Arch.	*Rendiconti della Pontificia Accademia Romana di Archeologia*
Rev. Arch.	*Revue Archéologique*
Rev. Etudes Nap.	*Revue des Etudes Napoléoniennes*
Rev. Etudes Ital.	*Revue des Etudes Italiennes*
Rev. Inst. Nap.	*Revue de l'Institut Napoléon*
RM	*Römische Mitteilungen*

Prologue

By universal agreement, Rome is one of the most important archaeological sites in the world. Some would say that the Roman Forum was the most 'sacred' of all such sites.

The Roman monuments had been subject to decay and destruction since the end of antiquity, then to endless plundering from the Renaissance.[1] A systematic excavation and restoration of the main classical remains of the city was undertaken for the first time during the French occupation, 1809–14. Although the work was motivated by political and economic considerations, this was the beginning of archaeology in Rome. The French instituted a huge programme at enormous expense, centring on the Forum. This vast undertaking has, however, been ignored, save for two general works, one Italian and one French, on Rome under Napoleon, and one specialist work in Swedish, which devotes one chapter to the subject.

By way of prologue, a survey is offered of basic bibliography, to demonstrate how little attention has been paid to this crucial subject by precisely the works where one would expect to find it. Three categories of published writings are considered: contemporary travellers, both English and French; works on the Napoleonic period; and specialist archaeological studies.

There are few French travellers to Italy during the French occupation, and little mention is made of archaeology. Stendhal (Henri Beyle) was in Rome from 30 September to 3 October 1811 and from 13 to 15 October. Apart from his obsession with the Colosseum, he mentions the French operations only in connection with Martial Daru's excavations in the Forum of Trajan.[2] The first impressions of his visit appear in a letter to his sister, dated 2 October, and *Journal d'Italie*.[3] There is nothing about Daru in *Rome, Naples et Florence en 1817*. Stendhal's interest began with his *Vie de Rossini*, 1823, and Daru was especially praised in the second edition of *Rome, Naples et Florence*, 1826.[4] The simple key to these comments is the fact that Daru was Stendhal's cousin. The writer stated that it was he who gave him the idea of going to Italy.[5]

Another visitor in 1811 was Alfonse de Lamartine, who arrived in Rome about October. He concentrates in his memoirs on the friends he met in the coach from Florence, including a singer, on Baron von Humboldt, the Prussian ambassador, and on a woman painter, with whom he fell in love. There is the usual casual reference to monuments, but more surprisingly, in the very midst of the Embellisements which must have been at fever pitch all around him, Lamartine writes with studied vagueness: 'On voyait le matin les moines traîner la brouette, au pied du temple contigu, pour en déblayer la poussière.'[6]

In April 1813 arrived Jeanne Françoise Récamier. She spent the summer at Canova's apartment at Albano and met antiquarians such as Aubin-Louis Millin, also visiting, and Jean-Baptiste Dagincourt. Despite a claimed interest in antiquities, Mme Récamier's only note of the current situation was the obligatory visit to the Colosseum. In December she went off to Naples, where she stayed until Easter 1814, and the usual show excavation was made for her at Pompeii. The most amusing anecdote of her stay in Rome, in fact, is her mentioning *Corinne* to the Governor, General Miollis, who thought it was an Italian town![7]

Two notable French writers had the benefit of two visits to Rome, one before and one after the French occupation. Here, if anywhere, one might expect the contrasts to be noted. Germaine de Staël left Switzerland for Italy in December 1804. She was in Rome 3–17 February 1805 and from about 13 March to 11 May. Her letters reveal that her major interest in monuments was in St Peter's and (once again) moonlight visits to the Colosseum. The contrast between past greatness and present insignificance was compelling: 'Tant de grandeur dans les souvenirs and tant de petitesse dans ce qui nous reste.'[8] The main antiquarian results of this visit may be found better in *Corinne*, 1807, where the heroine leads Lord Nelvil on a guided tour.[9] They visit the Pantheon, Castel Sant'Angelo, the Pyramid of Cestius, the Via Appia, the monuments of the Palatine, Aventine and Esquiline, and, of course, the Forum. All the remains bear their traditional names and exhibit their appearance just before the French intervention.

Mme de Staël made a second visit to Italy from late 1815 until mid 1816. She was in Rome very briefly. The visit was for two purposes: the health of her husband Albert Rocca and to obtain a Papal dispensation for the marriage of her daughter.[10]

The other visitor who came twice was Chateaubriand, first as secretary to the French embassy in 1803, then as ambassador, 1828–9. In his *Mémoires d'outre tombe*, he mentions very summarily at the end of his account the main undertakings of the French: the clearing of the Temple of Vespasian, of Saturn, of part of the Via Sacra, the stairs of the Colosseum and its arena, repairs to 'seven or eight rooms' of the Domus Aurea, and exploration of the Forum of Trajan.[11]

Of English visitors to Italy during the French period, there were, of course, few. Italy was closed to the English, in fact, from 1795 until 1815, save for the brief period of the Peace of Amiens (27 March 1802 until the end of the year). Thereby hangs an interesting story. A young Scotsman, Joseph Forsyth, was one of perhaps a number who took advantage of the lull in hostilities, which doubtless was expected to be more permanent. With the resumption of war, he was arrested and held prisoner until 1814. When many representations on his behalf proved unsuccessful, he finally descended to a literary appeal to Napoleon, publishing his travel notes.[12] The author was justifiably unhappy with the shortcomings of his work, and his notes on Rome are extremely poor. Even the Forum is hardly mentioned.

Such works of English travellers could be decidedly deceitful. John Chetwood Eustace visited Italy in 1802. His account was not published until 1813, but attained at least eight editions by 1841. As late as the third, 1815, the text recorded Rome as he saw it originally, with a postscript which the inattentive might miss, where some more up-to-date, albeit second-hand, 'information' was given. English prejudice in those years knew no bounds: 'The French under the pretext of beautifying the city, but in reality to discover and seize the treasures of art still supposed to be buried under its ruins, have commenced several excavations, and of course made some discoveries.'[13]

Examples of the French clearings are the Column of Phocas, seemingly ascribed to a 'Greek exarch in the seventh century'; the Basilica of Maxentius, where nothing was found but 'remnants of marble shafts and capitals'; the Colosseum, where Eustace takes up the arena debate,[14] unfortunately on the wrong side; the temples in the Forum Boarium; the temples of Saturn and Vespasian, which 'now exhibit a most majestic appearance' (far and away his most generous tribute); and Trajan's Column. On the other hand, Pius 'perfected and commenced' many of the excavations and improvements; the museums were plundered, the Vatican library robbed of all its manuscripts, and the population reduced from 180–200,000 to 90,000!

One of the first visitors after Napoleon's fall was the Irish barrister, John Mayne, in Rome from October 1814 until January 1815. He mentions various classical monuments, but all in passing: the columns of Trajan and Aurelius, triumphal arches, the Colosseum, the Pantheon, the Palatine, the Mausoleum of Augustus, the Pyramid of Cestius, the Baths of Caracalla, the Tomb of the Scipios and of Caecilia Metella. Of the Forum he says only: 'I wish the Forum had not got the name of Campo Vaccino. It sounds mighty unpoetical. They who gave it did not feel the "magic of the name".'[15] Mayne was not antagonistic to the French, but had little interest in antiquities, and so was unable to recognise what they had done. He seems to have been more interested in finding strings for his violin.

Another Irish lawyer, Sylvester Douglas, Baron Glenbervie, was in Rome from November 1815 until March 1816. Despite his reputedly being a classics

scholar, and having the most authoritative guide, he reveals in his diary
nothing of the classical remains. His guide was none other than the Papal
Commissario delle Antichità, Carlo Fea, and he records a precious picture
of the antiquarian (although the ignorant editor has made an egregious error
with the name):

The Avocato Fece [sic] sat with me above three hours yesterday morning, and gave
me much interesting information concerning some of the principal remains of antiquity here. He has an office which Winckelmann once had, and afterwards I believe
Venuti, viz. President of Antiquities, and being also a 'legale', or lawyer, what he
told me partook of antiquarian and legal knowledge. He is the editor of an edition,
with notes and additions by himself, of the Italian translation of Winckelmann's
History of Art. He is a man of acknowledged learning, but splenetic and satirical,
and has brought upon himself much animosity and abuse from his fellow antiquarians
by combating the hitherto received opinions concerning the Colosseo, the Pantheon
etc.[16]

Here is an excellent characterisation of Fea who will play a leading part
in the following pages. It is undoubtedly significant, and a great pity, that
Glenbervie did not choose to share Fea's information with his readers.

   The most famous English visitor after the French period was Byron. His
letters reveal his presence in Rome from 29 April until 20 May 1817, but
they are singularly uninformative. He was mostly taken up with his divorce.

I am delighted with Rome – as I would be with a bandbox – that it is a fine thing
to see – finer than Greece ... I have been riding my saddle horse every day – and
been to Albano – it's [sic] lakes – and to the top of the Alban mount – and to
Frascati – Aricia – etc. etc. – with an etc. etc. etc. about the city and in the city
– for all which – vide Guide-book – As a whole – ancient and modern – it beats
Greece – Constantinople – every thing – at least that I have ever seen – but I can't
describe because my first impressions are always strong and confused ...[17]

He mentions to everyone his most exciting experience: the sight of a live
Pope and a dead Cardinal (Bracchi was lying in state).

   There were also guidebooks. One of the most popular was *Rome in the
nineteenth century*, which appeared anonymously in 1820, ran to a fourth
edition by 1826, and reappeared in a fifth as late as 1849 in Bohn's Library.
It was in fact by Charlotte Waldie (Mrs Eaton), who was in Rome in 1817.
The work is remarkable for its anti-Papal sentiments and a refusal to name
any contemporary antiquarian, although reference is constantly made to their
views. The French undertakings are also often mentioned, but most ungener-
ously.[18]

   The Rev. Edward Burton devoted a book to the antiquities of Rome,
after his visit in 1818–19, a *Description of the antiquities and other curiosities
of Rome*, 1821. Although purportedly specialising in notes on the classical

remains, the only credit given to the French is for the Domus Aurea. Other monuments are noted as 'lately' cleared, but the French are nowhere mentioned. There are other disquieting elements: although Burton knows that the Temple of Concord has recently been found, the discovery of the Column of Phocas inscription is ascribed to the Duchess of Devonshire in 1816, Fea's identification of the Temple of the Dioscuroi in 1817 is unrecorded, and Nibby's correct identification of the Basilica of Maxentius is credited to Vasi![19]

So much for French and English visitors and guidebooks in the early nineteenth century. In these one gains only an erratic, prejudiced and entirely unreliable picture of the great undertakings so often carried out before these visitors' very eyes. We turn to general works on the French occupation.

In the first place, and rightly so under all heads, is the account by none other than the Prefect himself, Count Camille de Tournon. His *Etudes statistiques sur Rome* saw two editions (1831, 1855). Book 5, chapter 10 is devoted to 'Des travaux exécutés par l'administration française, pour la restauration et la conservation des monumens'. Tournon describes the monuments one by one as they were in 1809 and then the French clearances and restoration. The accounts are succinct but comprehensive. The book has been justifiably the main source for most modern writers wanting to give a brief but reliable account, without resort to the archives. This book will be cited throughout the third chapter on the individual monuments.

Of more recent general works, the classic study is by Louis Madelin, *La Rome de Napoléon*, 1909. Despite its length, however, it devotes only a few pages to archaeology.[20] These are based solely on French archives, which Madelin had consulted exhaustively. The only 'Italian' source is the *Giornale del Campidoglio*. It is for this reason that Madelin completely ignored the two commissions of 1810 and 1811.

The monumental study of Edouard Driault, *Napoléon et l'Europe* in five volumes, devotes a chapter to Rome.[21] His sources are essentially Madelin and Tournon. Valadier and Camporese, the two main architects of the works, are hardly mentioned: Stern, Gisors and Berthault[22] are the creative geniuses.

André Fugier's *Napoleone e l'Italia*, 1970, has only one or two pages on the Embellisements, derived from Madelin and Boyer. More recently there is Fiorella Bartoccini's *Roma nell'Ottocento*, 1985. The French work receives quite unreliable notice.[23] The monuments singled out are the Forum Boarium, the Temple of Vespasian and that of Jupiter Tonans (the same thing), the Colosseum, the Arch of Titus (on which little was done), and the Forum of Trajan. There is mention of a 'vast archaeological park' from the Forum to the Via Appia (nowhere known to me). Creation of 'open spaces' is illustrated by projects for the Pantheon, the Portico of Octavia, the Mausoleum of Augustus and the Forum of Trajan but, as is well known, the French quite neglected the portico and mausoleum. The architects mentioned are

Berthault – but where is the much more important Gisors? – and Valadier – but where is the equally important Camporese?

Our third and final category of published sources is specialist archaeological studies, where surely one might count on reliable and detailed information, as well as proper care to place the French undertakings in their historical context, namely treatment of the monuments and archaeological investigation in Rome, both before and after the first decade of the nineteenth century.

It is extraordinary that the proceedings of the Pontificia Accademia Romana di Archeologia, which begin in 1821 and reprint papers delivered in the Accademia from its refounding in 1810 by the French, contain only one contribution on the archaeological work 1809–14: Bianchi and Re's paper on the Colosseum.[24]

In 1829 began the *Bollettino* of the Istituto di Corrispondenza Archeologica (later the German Archaeological Institute). In the first volume is a paper by Karl Bunsen on excavations in the Roman Forum, celebrating the resumption in 1827 of the grand plan, talked of by the French, for the total excavation of the Forum. He includes discussion of excavations going back to the beginning of the century, with a chronological table of excavations. This is both inaccurate (many dates are wrong) and so summary as to be quite inadequate. No special credit, certainly, is given to the French administration for having made the most important contribution up until 1814 to the recovery of the whole Forum area.[25]

A French archaeologist visited Italy in 1811 and 1812: Louis Charles François Petit-Radel. In his *Voyage historique ... dans les principales villes de l'Italie*, 1815, scattered through its pages, are only the most fleeting and general allusions to the French achievements. He knows nothing, for example, of the Forum of Trajan, the clearing of the Colosseum seems to be ascribed to Pius VII, and work on the Temple of Vesta had barely begun.[26]

One of the most famous Italian archaeologists and topographers of the early nineteenth century was Antonio Nibby. His *Del Foro Romano*, 1819, hardly mentions the French.[27]

It would have been of the greatest interest to have Rodolfo Lanciani's *Storia degli scavi* for the nineteenth century. The Istituto di Archeologia in Rome possesses what exists of a sketch of the later volumes, never completed, but they are only the barest notes, virtually all culled from *CIL*, and so listing only the main inscriptions found. We do, however, have his *Ruins and excavations of ancient Rome*, 1897. The French work is frequently mentioned but often can be detected only by those already conversant with these accomplishments, because the French are not named and sometimes dates are not given. These references, scattered as they are throughout the volume, cannot give any coherent idea of what was achieved between 1809 and 1814.[28] There is, however, a brief passage in another of Lanciani's books, which in fact excited my interest in this whole question. It is succinct, but at least lists in one place the main monuments to which the French paid attention, so that the extent of their work becomes apparent:

Under the wise administration of Count de Tournon not less than one million dollars were spent in works of public utility, and in excavating and laying bare to archaeological investigation such monuments as the temples of Vespasian, of Castor and Pollux, of Antoninus and Faustina, of Venus and Rome, of the Mater Matuta, of the Fortuna Virilis, the basilica of Constantine, the Colosseum, the Golden House of Nero, the Janus of the Forum Boarium, the Basilica Ulpia, the Forum of Trajan, etc.[29]

The great archaeological era opened by the work of Giacomo Boni at the very end of the nineteenth century stimulated many new guides to classical Rome. One of the standard works is by Christian Hülsen, *Das Forum Romanum*, 1904. Hülsen was a student of the history of archaeology, so it was only fitting that he devoted some pages to the history of that subject in the Forum. Credit is given first to Fea, who proposed the complete excavation of that area, and although the French did not carry this out, they turned 'their attention' to the Forum. Hülsen credits them with demolition of the houses around the temples of Saturn and Vespasian, the freeing of the Tabularium, the restoration of the Temple of Vespasian, and the identification of the Column of Phocas (but seemingly dated to 1811). The first exact plan of the area was attributed to Caristie in 1811, published in 1821.[30]

The Italian student Orazio Marucchi, *The Roman Forum and Palatine*, 1906, stated simply that the work of Pius VI was 'continued by the French government from 1811 to 1814', but specified only work on the Clivus Capitolinus (which should have been dated to 1817) and the discovery of the base of the Column of Phocas.[31]

The most detailed book on the Forum is by Ettore de Ruggiero, *Il Foro Romano*, 1913. He similarly provided the briefest – even misleading – allusions. The French are mentioned as such only once, excavations of that time are grouped with later work, and the only person named is Fea. The vainglorious abbot could not have asked for more.[32]

Not unexpectedly the book by Henri Thedenat, *Le forum romain*, 1904, paid attention to the French. Chapters 4–6 discuss the history of the excavations, and the Napoleonic period is at least given its due.[33] His source is, however, simply Tournon.

One might have expected a detailed account of the French contribution in Adolf Michaelis, *A century of archaeological discoveries*, 1908, an otherwise excellent account of nineteenth-century archaeology. The second chapter, in fact, is devoted to the Napoleonic period, and discusses in detail Egypt, Pompeii and the Museum in Paris – but there is not a word about Rome. The great expedition to Egypt with its army of savants was truly the opening of Egyptian antiquities to the modern Western world, and the energy displayed at Pompeii gave the work its first great impetus, but the

French literally uncovered the major classical remains of Rome and made the first serious excavations. All of that was neglected by Michaelis.

More specialist archaeological discussions are extraordinary. Some might turn with great expectations to A. Ladolini's study of the excavations in the Forum from 1800 to 1836, only to find that the detail commences only in 1817, from which time the account is most valuable.[34]

There are, indeed, two books on Napoleonic activities in Rome, particularly archaeology and town-planning, one in Italian and one in French. Attilio La Padula's *Roma e la regione nell'epoca napoleonica*, 1969, is virtually a reprint of his *Contributo alla storia dell'urbanistica Roma 1809–1814*, 1958. Whole pages are taken over word for word. The later version is, however, soundly based on Roman archival material and well illustrated. It gives the main story of the organisation of the programme of works, but almost no details on the individual monuments.

Ferdinand Boyer's *Le monde des arts en Italie et la France de la Révolution à l'Empire*, 1969, is again mostly a reprint, this time of the many articles Boyer published previously. This book is based on French archives. It sets out to give a complete survey of each area of work, and is more complete than La Padula, but still very summary, as will be demonstrated.

In sum, an Italian writer has used Italian sources, and a French writer used French archives. Since the various archival sources are divided between Paris and Rome, the central bureaucracy and the provincial administration, each tells half of the story. It is one of the archival worker's greatest enjoyments to be able to recognise in one archive the letter to which he or she has already seen the answer in another. One might also note that La Padula and Boyer persist in using the almost universally erroneous names given to the main monuments of Rome in the French period.

There is, finally, one specialist account of these excavations and restorations by Marita Jonsson, *Monumentvardens Begynnelse*, 1976. This work in Swedish tells of clearances from 1800 until 1830. It is an admirable book, based on archives and well illustrated. The main difficulty of the work's accessibility has now been overcome by a well-deserved Italian translation.[35] The French period is, however, covered in only one chapter of sixty pages. Most fundamentally, anyone acquainted with the archives will be taken aback by the deadeningly impersonal account, when the story of these years is so full of striking and conflicting personalities.

THE PLAN OF THE PRESENT WORK

Various parts of the story of the French archaeological work in Rome have already been told, mostly very summarily. The major problem is how to organise the narrative to make it connected and at the same time to allow easy consultation under the main monuments.

The book is therefore set out as follows:

1. A prologue offers some survey of preceding bibliography, demonstrating the paucity of existing references.

2. An introduction traces the background to the French occupation through a sketch of Roman influences on French culture in the eighteenth century and a thematic discussion of Rome 1809–14.

3. The first chapter is the essential prelude, the condition and history of the monuments from the end of antiquity until the arrival of the French. This vast story is given only in its main lines. The discovery and digesting of all the archival documents were too much even for the genius of Rodolfo Lanciani, whose *Storia degli scavi* reaches only to 1600. My account divides the matter into two fundamental sections: the theory of Papal legislation and the reality.

4. The second chapter is the history of the French antiquities and embellishments organisations. Here the various commissions, the main plans, the work-force and the fascinating gallery of administrators, architects and antiquarians are all introduced.

5. The third chapter discusses the major monuments in turn in alphabetical order. In this way, information about French work on any of them is instantly and completely accessible. The monuments, it should be noted, are without exception given their modern names, in contrast to all other writers, who persist in using the early nineteenth-century ones, which are today unintelligible and create confusions. Most modern discussions combine and confuse, moreover, what is here divided into two chapters.

6. A final chapter describes the bitter controversies which arose as a result of the archaeological work: the interpretation of the Colosseum arena, and of the podium.

7. A conclusion puts the French work into perspective, by listing major later work on the most important monuments and other archaeological discoveries, at least to the end of the nineteenth century, and the beginning of the 'Boni era'.

THE ARCHIVES

The bibliography reveals an extensive already-published array of sources, although most of them are either very general or devoted to matters of detail. The most fundamental sources are the archives in Paris and Rome. Work on archives, as its devotees know well, can be the epitome of frustration or of exhilaration: either what you seek cannot be found or the answers to all your questions are there, and perhaps some treasure trove which you never expected. It is very different from reading books: archives cannot be borrowed, there is usually only one copy, the text may be illegible rather than clearly printed, and conditions are often crowded, dusty and noisy.

I must say, however, that I found the research for this book a memorable experience. I was shown great courtesy by all staff, but the most unforgettable part was to hold in one's hands the letters written by some of the most important and famous people in Europe of the time. This experience increasingly will be unknown to later generations. Archival material is, for good reasons, being transferred to microfilm. Documents will not be held in the hand any more. I am glad to have known the thrill of the old system.

A major concern is legibility. I can state categorically that with one exception all the documents I used were easily readable. People from many different social classes, with varying degrees of education, all had clear hands. The one almost inscrutable exception was Antonio Canova.

As an historian, finally, my use of these documents produced a reassuring and strengthening conviction. After reading thousands and thousands of letters, reports and so on, I came to realise that an historian even hundreds of years after the events can know such leading characters and many simple people better than almost any of their contemporaries. Most of the latter saw only one side of each person, whereas the historian reading extensive archives can study people from many points of view. I soon came to make a character estimate of the main people in my story, to see them, for example, as honest, hard-working, civilised and thinking of others – or the opposite. I make not the slightest excuse for my partisanship: it rests, as just explained, on the most extensive evidence and long acquaintance with it, under conditions which require commitment.

ILLUSTRATIONS

Very great care has been taken in choosing illustrations which serve the vital purpose of showing the monuments both before and after the French work. In the eighteenth century, when little work was being undertaken, the problem is not very pressing. In the nineteenth century, however, preference must be given to those which can be precisely dated, for so much changed so quickly after the French had given the lead.

Introduction

At the end of the eighteenth century, French life and culture were permeated with classical influences. France's 'political thought, her symbols and institutions were mainly Roman'.[1] The list of classical symbols in Revolutionary France is fascinating: laurel wreaths, the fasces, the eagles of the army, and names of institutions such as the Consulate and Tribunate, not to mention the veneration of classical heroes of liberty such as Camillus, Cincinnatus, Fabius, the Gracchi and Brutus. Revolutionary oratory was wholly modelled on that of Cicero.[2]

Roman influence was seen in more tangible ways. In architecture, Napoleon's attitudes were notorious: 'Une architecture grandiose symétrique devait chercher ses modèles chez les anciens: lorsqu'on lui proposait d'élever des monuments commémoratifs, colonnes, arcs de triomphe, trirème ou même éléphants, il les voulait toujours à la manière des Romains. Son empire devait être le continuateur de cet empire qui s'était étendu de l'Egypte aux îles Britanniques.'[3]

The two leading architects of the time, Pierre Fontaine (1762–1853) and Charles Percier (1764–1838), were deeply imbued with a passion for Rome, where they both had been students for many years, although many of their contemporaries were more influenced by Greek styles.[4] There was indeed a whole school of architects who drew their inspiration from 'the simplicity of the Greeks and the grandeur of the Romans': Poyet, Duforny, Vaudoyer, Clavareau, Beaumont, Gisors the Younger and others.[5]

The Column of Trajan was the inspiration for all French commemorative columns – there had even been talk of buying it – but especially for that of the Place Vendôme.[6] The archetypal dome was that of the Pantheon. As for triumphal arches, imitations of the characteristic Roman form had been standard for city gates in France since the eighteenth century, but the Arch of the Carrousel by Percier and Fontaine (1808) was consciously modelled on that of Severus in the Forum.[7] The Pyramid of Cestius was regarded as the archetypal funerary monument.[8]

As examples of classically inspired work we may mention the transformation of the church of Ste Géneviève into the Panthéon, begun by Soufflot and Rondelet in 1791 and completed only under the Restoration;[9] Vignon's Madeleine (1806-), Roman Corinthian, octostyle peripteral; and even grander, Brogniart's Bourse (1808-), a gigantic Corinthian peristyle, with fourteen columns across the front and twenty on each side in the style of an enormous unpedimented Roman temple.[10]

In art, the most famous painter of the Revolution and Empire was Jacques Louis David (1748–1825), who first made his name and marked a turning-point with his *Horaces*, 1784, followed by *J. Brutus, premier consul, de retour à sa maison après avoir condamné ses deux fils*, 1789, *Bélisaire*, 1791, and *Les Sabines*, 1799. His work has been described as responsible for a change in art fashions from Homeric mythology to the 'melodramas' of Livy.[11] Jean Drouais in the 1780s painted *Le gladiateur mourant*, 1785, *Marius à Minturnes*, 1786, and *C. Gracchus partant de sa maison*.

The dramatic presentations in Paris between 1800 and 1804 under the Consulate are known. They included Porta's *Les Horaces*, Voltaire's *La mort de César*, d'Arnault's *Marius à Minturnes*, Legouve's *Epicharis et Néron*, and Hoffmann's opera *Adrien*.[12]

Perhaps, however, the most stunning classical manifestation in Napoleonic France was women's clothing. 'The essential of women's costume, which was no longer made only in light stuffs, was a very high-waisted sheath, generally with a square, low-cut neckline covering the shoulders, girdled below the bust with a narrow belt. It fell in straight folds to the knees for the tunic, to the feet for the skirt ...' Hair was cut short, 'à la Titus' or 'à la Caracalla'.[13]

What had stimulated all this interest in the classical world, and Rome in particular? It is customary to mention the discovery of Pompeii (1748) and Herculaneum (1738). The excitement caused by the uncovering of the two buried cities with the art and other treasures discovered there was enormous. These discoveries were not, however, at all necessary to explain this phenomenon.[14] There had always been interest in Rome among the French since the Renaissance: collections of antiquities and excavations were important. The remains of the cities of Magna Graecia had been known much earlier and it must be remembered that the excavations at Pompeii and Herculaneum were intermittent and the discoveries kept notoriously secret.[15]

There had long been famous guidebooks such as François Misson, *Voyage d'Italie*, 1691 (6th edn, 1743), François Deseine, *L'ancienne Rome*, 1713, *Rome moderne*, 1713, and Charles Cochin, *Voyage d'Italie*, 1758. And the wonders of Rome, in particular, had long been familiar through the works of artists. Besides the engravings of Giambattista Piranesi, *Le vedute di Roma*, c. 1748-

78, there were the views of his predecessor, Giovanni Paolo Panini (1691–1765),[16] of his friend, Hubert Robert (1733–1808), 'Robert des Ruines',[17] and of his contemporary, Giuseppe Vasi, *Le magnificenze di Roma*, 10 vols, 1747–61. The Académie de France in Rome, moreover, had been founded for artists by Louis XIV as long ago as 1666.

In architecture, as early as the 1750s the defenders of the ancients had reacted against the 'Jesuit style' of Borromini and Bernini and demanded a return to Vitruvius and Palladio. The leaders in France were Jean-François Blondel (*Architecture française*, 1752), Marc-Antoine Laugier (*Essai sur l'architecture*, 1753) and Jacques Antoine (*Traité d'architecture*, 1768). In art, similarly, there had been a return to the antique as models in the Académie Royale, among other European academies, from the mid eighteenth century, under the influence of Winckelmann and others.[18] This antiquarian inspiration for painters was derived from the Renaissance, Pompeian frescoes, Roman reliefs and Greek vases, although it was not so much particularly Roman as Greek. Joseph-Marie Vien[19] copied a Herculaneum wall-painting in his famous *Cupid-seller*, 1763. Jean-Baptiste Greuze showed *L'Empereur Sévère reprochant à son fils Caracalle*, 1769, and Nicholas Lépicié painted *Le dévouement de Porcia*, 1777, *Le départ de Régulus*, 1779 and *La piété de Fabius*, 1781.

It is even more notorious that classical influences had triumphed in French literature even from the seventeenth century, after the famous 'Battle of the Books', providing not only many of the most common stories but even the literary forms in which they were presented. Corneille (1606–84) had produced *Cinna, Horace, La mort de Pompée, Sertorius, Othon*, and *Titus et Bérénice*. Greek-inspired drama, on the other hand, dominated Racine (1639–99), but much in Molière's comedies (1622–73) was derived from Terence.[20]

Fascination with the classical world, and Rome in particular, had been a feature of French life and culture even before the Revolution. The political concerns of that Revolution and the succeeding Consulate and Empire and France's expansion in Europe were, however, to give that interest a new, heightened meaning.

THE PAPAL STATES DURING THE REVOLUTIONARY AND NAPOLEONIC PERIODS

From 1780 all eyes, including French, were on Rome, the capital of the Arts. Travellers contemplated the ruins and meditated on mortality. There was a great increase in guidebooks, hotels improved, and tourists – from England and Germany as well as France – poured in. The number of French from the higher classes vastly increased on the outbreak of the Revolution, but then the situation was reversed in 1793 with the murder of the French agent, Hugo de Bassville, and the French had to flee.

Revenge came in 1797 with Napoleon's declaration of war on the Papal States. On 19 February, to avert invasion, the Peace of Tolentino was signed. The conditions were the surrender of Bologna, Ferrara and the Romagna, a huge increase in indemnities, and the handing over of one hundred major works of art and five hundred manuscripts.[21] Disaster had been only postponed. On 27 December, the French emissary, General Duphot, was shot in Rome. The city was occupied by the French army under General Berthier, on 10 February 1798 the Pope was deposed, and a Republic proclaimed. Pius VI left Rome, to die in exile in France. The French were, however, forced out of Rome by the Neapolitans, first briefly and then on 30 September, 1799, not to return for almost a decade. Pius VII, elected in Venice in March 1800, entered Rome in July.

Rome was simply one of the Italian states radically affected by the Napoleonic wars. As early as the campaign of 1796–7, the north came under French control: the Lombard Republic was established in May 1796 and the Cisalpine Republic in June 1797. The kingdom of Piedmont was conquered by 9 December 1798. It was then the turn of Naples, whence Ferdinand fled and where the Parthenopean Republic was set up on 23 January 1799. Florence was occupied on 25 March. A series of French reverses, however, overthrew these Republics, as at Rome, in 1799.

Napoleon himself was occupied in Egypt in 1798–9, but by the new constitution of December 1799 was appointed Consul. The capture of Milan on 2 June 1800 ensured the restoration of the Cisalpine Republic. French attention then turned to Austria, but among the terms of the Treaty of Lunéville was the conversion of the Grand Duchy of Tuscany into the Kingdom of Etruria. In 1801, a Concordat was made with the new Pope, Pius VII, recognising him in the Papal States. In 1804, however, Napoleon was crowned Emperor[22] and named next year King of Italy. Although the French lost control of the seas at Trafalgar (21 October 1805), the Russians and Austrians were defeated at Austerlitz on 2 December, after which the latter gave up all her Italian territories to France, and the Bourbons of Naples were deposed. Joseph Bonaparte became King of Naples. After victories at Jena (1806) and Friedland (1807) over Prussia and Russia, Napoleon's attention turned to the Iberian peninsula. With the occupation of Spain in March 1808, Joseph Bonaparte was transferred to become king there and was replaced in Naples by Napoleon's brother-in-law, Joachim Murat.

The above brief outline of Napoleon's victories makes abundantly clear that, within a decade, the Papal States were hemmed in by French-occupied territories on all sides. Pius VII, supported by his Secretary of State, Cardinal Consalvi,[23] one of the ablest diplomats of the period, stoutly refused to enter the 'Napoleonic system', or break neutrality by closing his ports to the English, or to recognise the King of Naples. On 2 February 1808, French troops under General Miollis occupied Rome.

The classic study of this period of Rome's history remains Louis Madelin's *La Rome de Napoléon*, 1906. This work is based on a vast array of documents in archives in Paris and Rome. Madelin was certainly a Frenchman, but gave credit where it was due and drew the character of the main actors in the drama with convincing complexity. This is not to say that he did not have his heroes (Napoleon, Tournon and Miollis) and his villains (notably Joachim Murat, and most of the Roman aristocracy).

The parlous state of Rome in the early nineteenth century could hardly be denied by any historian. The population was about 130,000, of whom Madelin estimated one quarter lived off the state.[24] The same historian calculated that six-tenths of the wealth was owned by the church and another three-tenths by the nobility. A total of 1,463 monks and 1,131 nuns lived in some 145 monasteries and convents, although the monks' income was less than one million francs a year. There is little to be said in favour of any aspect of the administration. Madelin singled out 'justice' for its corruption, incompetence, chaos and laziness. On the other hand, it was admitted that the hospital system was excellent and indeed that the religious with their charity supported the entire poor population. The city of Rome was notoriously violent and dangerous[25] while the countryside was infested with a banditry infamous throughout Europe. To top everything off, the state was bankrupt. Reforms had been attempted, especially by Cardinal Consalvi, but had run into immovable opposition.

The French ruled Rome for six years. There may have been some who expected widespread improvement and modernisation. The administration was characterised, however, by many mistakes. First was the long period of indecision after the military occupation when the Romans were left uncertain of their future, which only hardened their resistance to the annexation when it came. There was a bizarre interregnum of sixteen months during which the Papal government continued to function under a French military occupation. This ended in June 1809 when the Papal States were incorporated into France and a Consulta Straordinaria was set up. The very name of this 'comité de démolition' shows that it was only an interim arrangement. When the Consulta came to an end in 1810, the effective administration was really only a continuation of the same. Despite its grandiose title as 'second city of the Empire', it must be remembered that Rome never had a governor. Napoleon on 3 June 1810 named to the post of all people Fouché, Duc d'Otranto, only to rescind the order on 1 July. General Miollis remained therefore for four years as military ruler, although technically only Lieutenant-Governor, second to a non-existent governor. The civil head was a Prefect, Camille de Tournon, who arrived in November 1809.

The second and most fatal mistake of all was the kidnapping and deportation of the Pope. This outrageous and brutal action on the night of 6 July, 1809 shocked Europe and turned a frail man aged sixty-seven into a martyr and saint, making him invincible to Napoleon and removing any last shred of hope that the population of Rome could be won over to the occupiers. The Romans spent the next five years longing for his return. The French administration, admittedly, had been impossible while he remained; it was even more so after his removal.

The third mistake was connected with the second, a continuation of Napoleon's religious 'policies', although his contradictory attitudes to the Church hardly merit that term. By decree of 17 April 1810 religious corporations were declared dissolved. The 13,000 religious in the Papal States were thus made homeless, and the convents and monasteries confiscated to the state. Italy was filled with an army of dispossessed and embittered monks, and the poor lost their sustenance. A brutal blow destroyed a fragile system of cooperation, fundamental to the social fabric. The French were to find to their cost what economic and social disruption they had caused.[26]

Along with this went the usual device of despotic regimes: an oath of loyalty. It was first applied to all the clergy. Of the twelve bishops left in Rome, ten signed (there is a famous story of Tournon's subterfuge to help them),[27] but most canons and more than two hundred priests refused. They were deported. The oath was then extended to all secular officials. Fifty mayors resigned. The whole administration was put to needless anxiety, and people of integrity, it should be noted, were most likely to be the ones to suffer. The last and most vicious application of this obsession with 'loyalty' was the decree of 4 May 1812 that all officials who had refused to take the oath were to be exiled and have their property confiscated.

To ensure that the French administration was hated by almost everyone, conscription was imposed, after the union with France in 1810. Not even the pleading of Tournon could fill the required lists. The few boys who could be torn away from their mothers mostly deserted as soon as they marched out of Rome and joined the brigands. And from 1811, Napoleon had the idea of summoning the sons of the nobility to Paris for their 'education'.

By 1813 the government was a fiction. Napoleon's reputation had been destroyed in Russia in 1812 and then at Leipzig on 18 October 1813. By late summer, the English fleet began to raid the coastal forts and even burned Anzio. The man who thought he might turn the situation to his own advantage, albeit at the cost of high treason, was none other than the Emperor's brother-in-law, the King of Naples. On the pretext of marching north to defend the Po, he began to occupy Rome in November. On 19 January, 1814 his agent, General le Vauguyon, took possession of the city. Most of the administrators had to leave within a few days, for fear of their lives, but General Miollis rose to the occasion and solemnly occupied Castel Sant'Angelo, where he held out until allowed to leave with all honours on

10 March. Within a month Napoleon had abdicated, and on 24 May Pius VII returned from exile in France.

From the above narrative, it is hard to imagine that any Roman supported the French government. The aristocrats were in the forefront of the collaborators, seemingly influenced by the example of Duca Braschi, Pius VI's nephew and mayor, because they were rewarded with office and attracted by the European links now open to them. The upper bourgeoisie followed suit, especially the commercial classes, for obvious reasons. The main opposition came from the mass of the population: the lower bourgeoisie, which had benefited from clientship or was faithful to the Church, and the poorest.[28]

What did the French achieve? The perspectives of historians vary: how else can it be? At the beginning of this century, the Frenchman Madelin spoke of the 'astonishing and edifying' list of projects which his countrymen mostly realised and in such a short time. He asked us to imagine twenty or thirty French administrators in the middle of a people who, he admitted, did *not* love them, served badly by their subordinates, and facing constant political resistance on all sides. They set up the whole complicated new administration. They attempted to improve agriculture and create industry and commerce. Grain cultivation increased by 50%, and there was some redistribution of land, by satisfying creditors with Church lands. On the other hand, drainage of swamps, and the introduction of cotton and soda were not successful. Bad seasons in 1811 and 1812 were a heavy blow. Attempts to establish new industries, such as the great cotton factory in the Baths of Diocletian (!), failed, mainly because of attachment to old-fashioned methods of production, despite sending people abroad to learn and the setting up of a Società Romana di Agricoltura, Arti e Manifatture in 1810. In addition there was a general economic collapse in 1811, ruining the petite bourgeoisie, caused by a vast scaling down of public debts and enormous increases in taxation.[29] There was to be 'no Eldorado on the banks of the Tiber'.

On the other hand, the French cultivated the Arts, organised schools, refounded academies, created art galleries, cleared the ancient monuments, restored palaces, made streets, built cemeteries and gardens, and banked rivers.[30]

The Italian historian, Fiorella Bartoccini, instead of Madelin's materialist categories, acknowledges a revolution in attitudes, the beginning of, or stimulus to, ideas which were to come to fruition fifty years later. She contrasts the Napoleonic period, naturally, with the earlier Jacobin Republic.

Ugualmente non incise in profondità qualche anno dopo il dominio napoleonico, maggiormente ricco di propaganda e di sollecitazione, di coinvolgimento e di coopta-zione, con premesse e basi più sicure, con tendenze conciliatrici, con aperture di sviluppo sul terreno sociale e di miglioramento su quello materiale, con anni più lunghi di impegno ... Sembra più nel giusto Stendhal quando dice che i Romani avevano 'intravisto' la civiltà: significava, per essi, l'insolito apprendimento, attraverso inoltre un contatto diretto, del fatto che esisteva un 'mondo esterno', una 'diversità' e una 'alternativa', una 'novità' di condizioni e di leggi che rendevano più facile e organizzata la vita collettiva, una 'possibilità' di maggiore partecipazione e presenza nella gestione del potere. L'apprendimento non significava comunque accettazione, limitata a quegli elementi che si vedevano nuovamente sbarrata la strada della fortuna economica e della ascesa sociale dal mondo pontificio della Restaurazione, o che avevano maturato consapevolezze e programmi politici. Molto più importante, e irreversibile, la trasformazione materiale dei costumi e delle abitudini ai più alti livelli della popolazione.[31]

Of all the transformations, there is one as important as any other, unmentioned in the above summary: the classical and archaeological aspect of Rome. The present study is devoted to the French contribution to the history of Roman archaeology. It cannot be understood except in the context of the political and social background outlined above. Nor can it be understood without narrative and analysis of the preceding treatment of Rome's classical monuments.

1

The protection and destruction of classical Rome before 1809

There can never be a simple, definitive answer to the question how well or how ill treated the Roman monuments had been before the nineteenth century, because the evidence is held in an enormous mass of archival sources and because the historian cannot work outside an incubus of prejudice regarding institutions such as the Papacy and concepts such as the Renaissance. For the purposes of this introductory chapter, necessary to put the French work into context, we may rely on two fundamental and famous works of very different approach. One is the essay on the ruins of Rome, by the young Carlo Fea in 1784 which served as an appendix to the Italian translation of Johann Winckelmann's *Geschichte der Kunst des Althertums*;[1] Fea, sixteen years later, was to become Papal Commissioner for Antiquities. The second work is one of many by the most famous archaeological historian of his time, Rodolfo Lanciani: *The destruction of ancient Rome*, 1899. These will naturally be supplemented by standard works. How could one overlook the Catholic Ludwig Pastor, or the Protestant and Ghibelline Ferdinand Gregorovius?

One begins inevitably with the barbarian sacks of Rome by the Goths in AD 410 and the Vandals in 455. Fea played down Alaric's damage, but relied too much on Christian sources (Augustine, *City of God* 1.7; Orosius 7.39), who were themselves anxious to compare the three days' sack favourably with earlier disasters. Lanciani detailed the widespread evidence for destruction of wealthy houses on the Aventine. Gaiseric's fourteen days' plunder was similarly discounted by Fea by reference to praise of Rome's monuments by Cassiodorus (for example, *Variae* 7.15, comparing Rome with the seven wonders of the world). Lanciani, following Procopios (3.5.3–4), tended to agree with Fea that Rome was plundered rather than destroyed. Both placed considerable emphasis on Procopios' description (8.21) of the Forum of Peace and the many statues of Phidias and Lysippos still existing in this quarter. This, however, does not give due weight to the context:

an omen occasioned by the transit of a herd of cattle through this forum – shades of Campo Vaccino rather than the glories of old Rome.[2]

In his preface to the discussion of Christian treatment of the pagan monuments, Fea rightly stressed the importance of natural causes of ruin. Fire had been an eternal enemy of the monuments. Tiber flooding, sometimes up to 12 feet deep and strong enough to sweep away buildings, was another scourge: Fea listed the floods of 589, 685, 725, 791 and 797. Even more devastating were earthquakes. To these must be added political considerations: the move of the emperors to Constantinople, and neglect of Rome. There may have been as well civil disturbances, as referred to in the restoration of Constantine's baths in the fifth century (*ILS* 5703: 'civilis vel potius feralis cladis vastatione vehementer adflictas') and the restoration of the statue of Minerva damaged by fire in a 'tumultus civilis' in the same century (*ILS* 3132).[3]

What Fea treated summarily was the effect of the establishment of Christianity on attitudes to the monuments of paganism. Constantine and his successors protected ancient monuments. The cult was to cease, but the buildings were not to be destroyed.[4] It is Gregorovius who drew our attention to the edict of Majorian in AD 458, however, in which it was admitted that public buildings *were* being destroyed at the instigation of the Urban Prefect. Building materials were being taken from 'beautiful ancient structures' to repair others, even private ones. Majorian therefore explicitly banned the destruction of ancient temples and other monuments (*Nov. Maj.* 4). 'The state of barbarism to which this edict bears witness had set in under Constantine, since whose days the populace had continued to wage destruction to the monuments of antiquity ... The building of Christian churches since the time of Constantine had given an irresistible impulse to the pillage of ancient monuments.'[5]

Theodoric (493–526) is admitted by Fea to have found Rome in ruins, but he also undertook important repairs: to the theatre of Pompey (Cassiodorus, *Variae* 4.51), the Colosseum (*ILS* 5635), and officials were appointed to care for aqueducts, sewers, baths and harbours.[6] Yet Fea suggested that by the seventh century only the strongest buildings were surviving, because of the natural disasters he had listed.

That century saw a major innovation in Christian attitudes towards the pagan monuments. As far as we know, for the first time a temple was converted into a church. The Pantheon became S. Maria ad Martyres under Boniface IV in 609 by permission of the emperor Phocas. This set a precedent for many other such 'conversions'.[7] Otherwise the seventh century was marked by two major depredations: Honorius I in 629 removed the gilt-bronze roof-tiles of the Temple of Venus and Rome.[8] Better known is the similar removal by the emperor Constans II in 663 of the bronze tiles of the Pantheon – despite its recent conversion into a church.[9]

Both Fea and Lanciani pointed to the Einsiedeln Itinerary of the ninth century as showing that much of classical Rome still survived.[10] With the end of Lombard rule in the eighth century, however, Rome fell prey to civil wars among the nobility. By the tenth century aristocratic families were busy turning ancient monuments into forts: the Orsini in the Mausoleum of Hadrian and Theatre of Pompey, the Colonna in the Mausoleum of Augustus and Baths of Constantine, the Conti on the Quirinal, the Savelli in the Theatre of Marcellus and the Tomb of Caecilia Metella, and the Frangipani in the Colosseum. Fea naively suggested that these ancient buildings were granted by the Popes to such 'rich and powerful families to look after them'![11]

In the long-standing struggle between the emperor Henry IV and Pope Gregory VII, Rome was besieged in late 1082 and captured. Henry retreated only on the appearance of the Norman, Robert Guiscard. The latter, according to Fea, burned the city from Porta Flaminia to the Campus Martius, and from the Lateran to the Colosseum, destroying two-thirds of the city. Lanciani stressed the damage on the Caelian, evident in the destruction of S. Clemente and SS Quattro Coronati, and on the Oppian and the intervening valley, but claimed that the 'larger monuments, such as temples, theatres and baths, were not much damaged by the fire'. The two antiquarians thus disagree, with Fea's estimate of the damage being paradoxically much greater.[12]

For the classical remains of Rome in the twelfth and thirteenth centuries, both Fea and Lanciani made much of the *Mirabilia Urbis Romae* and the *Ordo Romanus* of Benedict (later Celestinus II, 1143–4). Fea here showed critical sense, admitting that many monuments seem to have survived, but that we have no evidence concerning their state. As Lanciani pointed out, what is interesting is that so many monuments had lost their classical names.[13]

By the twelfth century many more classical monuments had been converted into Christian churches. Fea cited S. Nicola near Trajan's Column, three churches in the Circus Flaminius, three in the Baths of Severus Alexander near the Pantheon, and the Benedictine monastery of Aracoeli on the Capitol.[14] The mention of this last reminds us that it was now a collection of nameless ruins, possession of which was granted by Anacletus II (1130–8) to S. Maria in Aracoeli.[15]

There is no more bitter satire on all the most exalted things of earth than the fact that Rome knew a time when her Capitol was given into the possession of the monks who prayed, sang psalms, scourged their backs with whips and planted cabbages upon its ruins. Anaclete II ratified the abbot of S. Maria in Aracoeli in possession of the Capitoline hill: and his Bull throws a passing light on this labyrinth of grottoes, cells, courts and gardens, houses or huts and on the ruinous walls, stones and pillars with which it was covered.[16]

At the same time, political power was returning to this spot: a place for assemblies, the seat of the prefect, the palace of the senators; the main market of Rome was held there until its removal to the Piazza Navona in 1477. And in 1348, the staircase of Aracoeli was built from the ruins of the Temple of Quirinus on the Quirinal.[17]

Fea was right to call our attention to the abandonment of Rome by the Popes (1306–76), which left the classical remains in peace. In his famous letter to Giovanni Colonna, Petrarch recalled their walks in Rome, with a wealth of antiquarian detail, but how many monuments he mentioned still existed? He recalls the various hills, the Campus Martius, the Via Sacra, the Sublician Bridge, the Capitol with its various temples, the Column of Trajan, the Pons Aelius, Hadrian's Mausoleum, the temples of Tellus (on the Esquiline?), of Fortune (in the Forum Boarium?) and of Peace (the Basilica of Maxentius), the Pantheon, the Column of Marcus Aurelius, the Septizonium, and some bogus monuments such as the arches of Pompey and Marius (*Fam.* 6.2).

At the same time, in 1349, Rome was struck by a disastrous earthquake which damaged many important churches and unspecified 'ancient buildings' (*Fam.* 11.7).[18]

PAPAL LEGISLATION TO PROTECT THE MONUMENTS: THE THEORY

A selection of these fundamental documents may be found, for the fifteenth and sixteenth centuries, in Fea's *Relazione di un viaggio ad Ostia*, 1802, and, for the seventeenth and eighteenth centuries, in Filippo Mariotti's *Legislazione delle Belle Arti*, 1892. These texts must be read with the greatest care and in full if they are to be of any use. We shall find often that the respect for the monuments enjoined upon others was not observed by the very Pope issuing the decree.

The question of the protection of monuments must first be placed in a wider perspective.[19] Among the first nations to protect their antiquities were Sweden and Denmark. In the former, a Royal Antiquary was established in 1630, and all monuments came under the Crown from 1666. In Denmark laws to protect monuments were passed by Christian IV (1610–48). Anything connected with the tradition and history of the country was declared national property in 1848. In Germany, no alterations were allowed to historical buildings without government permission from 1815, and all important exports were prohibited in 1818. Austria similarly set up a central commission to investigate and maintain artistic and historical monuments in 1825. In Greece, all ancient objects were declared state patrimony and excavations were made a public monopoly in 1834 with the foundation of the monarchy.

Other countries were surprisingly late to take such action. It was only in 1883 that England passed the Ancient Monuments Protection Act, and it had very limited application. In France only from 1887 were monuments protected.

In Italy, concern was early and strong – naturally so, given the richness of the inheritance. Only Naples and Rome had complete legislation, however. In 1755 Naples banned the export of ancient objects and in 1822, influenced by the Pacca edict,[20] set up a Commission of Antiquities and Fine Arts.

It will be seen, then, that Roman attempts to protect antiquities, going back to at least 1462, make that government the first to pass such laws. The only difficulty was enforcement, and the horrible paradox was that the main infringer was the very government which had passed the laws.

It is highly ironic that Pius II issued a very severe prohibition against damaging ancient buildings in April 1462.[21] The reasons expressed are not entirely artistic or historical: the buildings are an ornament to Rome, and also an illustration of ancient virtue and an encouragement to imitation, but most importantly they show the fragility of the human condition! Pius was, in fact, confirming earlier papal decrees which established unspecified fines. No one was to 'demolish, destroy, weaken, break, or convert into lime' the remains of any ancient building above ground in the city or in its district. The whole operation was then undercut by the provision that the Pope by a Bull or Apostolic Brevia could make exceptions.

On 1 August 1514 Raphael was appointed to succeed his uncle, Bramante, as architect of St Peter's. By a letter of Cardinal Bembo a year later (26 August 1515), to facilitate the supply of stone, it was laid down that any discovered in Rome and up to one mile outside the city had to be reported to Raphael within three days, subject to a fine of between 100 and 300 gold pieces (the latter sum was Raphael's salary). In conclusion, Bembo noted that important inscriptions were being destroyed, and he forbade stone cutters to harm any inscription without Raphael's permission.[22]

The appointment of Latino Manetti as Commissario delle Antichità on 28 November 1534 by Paul III reveals interesting papal self-criticism.[23] One of the pontifical cares, states Paul, was that of the seat of the 'first universal empire and then the holy Christian religion'. It was now a matter of pride that the capital of Christianity was the same as that of the Roman Empire. The city had, of course, to be cleared of idolatry, and the old temples rededicated to God and the saints. It was thus painful that after the barbarians, 'our carelessness and fault and even greed and deceit' had done so much damage: trees were allowed to take root in ancient buildings, ignoble modern ones were built in and around them, and all kinds of stone and metal were carried off to other countries. Most criminal of all was the reduction of ancient stone to lime, sometimes even harming the monuments of the martyrs. After suitable praise of the qualifications of Manetti, he was given control over all monuments, and was to clear them of 'brambles, bushes and trees, and especially ivy and wild fig', and to prevent any building being put up against them, any damage to them, the use of them for lime, or any export of them. Offenders were subject to excommunication and fines.

Despite this decree, little was done. Manetti was often absent on diplomatic missions, and papal building projects required materials: permission was given on 22 July 1540 for the Fabbrica di S. Pietro to extract stone from anywhere inside and outside the city. A remarkable exception to the rule was the preservation of the fragments of the consular fasti and lists of triumphs, rescued by Cardinal Farnese in 1546.[24]

On 20 December 1556 Paul IV appointed as Superintendent and Keeper of Antiquities Mario Frangipani, to prevent the removal from the city and its district of any 'ancient buildings, antiquities or statues, or fragments there-of' even at the instance of the cardinals, with very extensive powers of arrest and detention in the customs and ports such as Civitavecchia and Ostia. No motives were given, save inspiration by similar orders of Eugenius III (1145–53).[25]

Pius IV in July 1562 appointed two cardinals, Marco Antonio Emilio and Alfonso Gesualdo, as Prefects and Keepers of Antiquities for life. The motives were explained very briefly: to preserve the decoration of her antiquities for the queen of all cities, and to prevent anyone who visited it from despoiling it. In more detail, it was noted that people removed whatever they liked of the marbles, statues, capitals, gems, coins, vases, pottery, inscriptions and metalwork; some copied antiquities and sold them as originals; and those indifferent to Rome's beauty carried out excavations without licence. The two prefects were given very wide powers of action, instruction and jurisdiction, with the usual penalties, even to excommunication, in addition to fines and corporal punishment. A new concern of the legislation seems to be falsification of precious objects as well as their exportation: sculptors, goldsmiths, stone-cutters and gem-makers were not to 'export, sculpt, cut, cast, or make others in their likeness, or in any way alter or change' any ancient object.[26]

It was among the duties of the Conservatori, the municipal councillors, to protect the ancient monuments. The situation was calamitous, as shown by their petition in 1580 to Gregory XIII to prevent excavation of *pozzolana* under and near public buildings, which caused their collapse. They instanced the Palazzo Maggiore, which had been saved only by the Conservatori re-inforcing the foundations.[27]

Ippolito Aldobrandini, Camerlengo (Papal Treasurer) to Urban VIII, in 1624 reissued earlier prohibitions[28] on the export from the Papal States of all antiquities, under penalty of their confiscation, a fine of 500 scudi and possible corporal punishment. No motive was given save the fact that pre-vious edicts were not being observed.

That they had little power is shown by the renewal of 1646 under Innocent X. The protection of antiquities was justified by damage to buildings and the loss to Rome and their owners of 'beautiful' things, both ancient and modern. The penalty for illegal export had now risen to 500 gold ducats. There was to be no dealing without permission in antiquities worth more than one scudo. Equally subject to penalties were workmen who made cases, customs officials and porters (obviously those crucial to illicit exports). Those who already had licences to excavate had to report within ten days or lose them. If they wished to sell any stone, it was to be examined by the Commissioner, who also had full access to any stores of antiquities. The impression given is that the overriding concern was with building materials and works of art rather than relics of antiquity for their own sake. This edict was reissued in 1686 under Innocent XI: its effectiveness was obviously slight.[29]

A new era seems to appear in the eighteenth century. Cardinal Spinola, Camerlengo to Clement XI, issued an edict in 1704 to protect pictures, stucco, pavements, mosaics, monuments and tombs. The motives expressed were to conserve the ancient remains which increased appreciation of the city's magnificence among foreign nations and which illustrated sacred and secular history. Inscriptions especially were protected as important for 'learning'; they were not to be damaged or moved. Finally, no manuscripts were to be bought or sold without permission.[30]

Attention turned to excavations in 1726. Cardinal Albani's edict under Benedict XIII forbade excavations without licence or even, where necessary, supervision by the Commissario delle Antichità. No buildings were to be damaged. Any finds were to be reported immediately to the Commissario. No inscription or relief was to be harmed, and fragments of column were to be preserved to see if a whole one could be reconstructed. The penalty, however, was light: three lashes and 25 scudi.[31]

The same cardinal in 1733 under Clement XII attempted to make detection and conviction of illegal exporters easier. Justification was becoming more concerned with antiquities for intellectual reasons. Those who contravened such orders

Sapendosi tuttavia che più d'uno ardisce trasgredire gl'Ordini sudetti in grave pregiudizio del pubblico decoro di quest'Alma Città, a cui sommamente importa il conservarsi in essa le Opere illustri di Scoltura, e Pittura, e specialmente quelle, che si rendono più stimabili, e rare per la loro antichità, la conservazione delle quali non solo conferisce molto all'Erudizione si sagra, che profana, ma ancora porge incitamento ai Forastieri di portarsi alla medesima Città per vederle, ed ammirarle, e dà norma sicura di Studio a quelli, che applicano all'esercizio di queste nobili Arti, con gran vantaggio del pubblico, e del privato bene.

Concern was also expressed for cameos, intaglios, medals of all sorts and figured bronzes which rendered the museums of Rome so famous. The 500 gold ducats penalty was now to be divided in three, with one third going to the accuser. Officials who did not act on denunciations were to be deprived of their posts. Accessories to the export, such as carpenters and sailors, who turned accuser were pardoned and could share the fine. Investigations were specially the task of the Commissario, but extensive powers of search were given to many officials. Finally, all foreigners, whether ecclesiastical or secular, were subject to the law after being in Rome for fifteen days.[32]

It is significant that Cardinal Valenti in 1750 could only repeat his predecessor's motivation almost word for word.[33] Previous edicts had to be reinforced, however, by Benedict XIV 'to remove those infinite abuses produced both by time and by the indolence of subaltern ministers'. The edict of 1701 was cited as precedent once, that of 1717 five times, of 1726 the same, and 1733 thrice. The major innovation was the realisation that the existing staff could not cope with the surveillance required – or the increased activity of collectors – and so the Commissario gained three assistants or Assessors: one for painting, one for sculpture, and one for 'cameos, medals [i.e. coins], engravings, and any other kind of antiquity'.

What can be said of four centuries of papal legislation to protect the antiquities of Rome? In the very first place, the endless repetition of the same general restrictions shows their utter ineffectualness. Second, the actions of the very Popes who issued them contradicted these edicts, as we shall see. Third, attention has been paid to the motives expressed for such papal concern. They vary from Pius II's interest in the demonstration of human frailty to Leo X's monopoly of building materials, to Paul III's sense of Christian Rome as heir of the pagan past, to Innocent X's desire to prevent damage to buildings by excavations, to Clement XI's concern to maintain foreign interest in Rome. Only in the eighteenth century do we find any awareness of the irreplaceable historical evidence constituted by the monuments, and their contribution to learning.

The most famous papal law on antiquities was that issued by the newly elected Pius VII on 2 October 1802 through the pro-Camerlengo, Cardinal Doria Pamphilii. Its real author, however, was the newly appointed Commissario, Carlo Fea.[34] It contains some seventeen clauses. Export of all antiquities was, as always, banned. The penalty was the now standard 500 gold ducats, with the addition – according to the status of the contravener – of up to five years in the galleys. Sale within Rome was expressly allowed, and within the Papal States with permission, and export beyond was allowed for any work by modern artists. To reform the Assessors, they were given the modest honorarium of twenty scudi per month, instead of a percentage of their valuations. No ancient building was to be damaged, unless the Inspector or Commissario deemed it of no importance. All owners of antiquities were to give a list of them within one month, under pain of having them confiscated. Anyone who, while moving earth, found antiquities had to declare them. Even on private land, excavations required a licence and supervision by the antiquities service; the penalty for contravention was 500 gold ducats.

The motives were given more extensively than for any of the preceding edicts we have analysed. They are also expressed in different terms from those of the preceding century: the preservation of monuments and art is for artists and the encouragement of the Arts. Alongside the preservation of existing examples, however, is a new concern: the discovery of 'new rarities which in part may compensate for the loss of those of which the vicissitudes of time have robbed us'. In short, Pius VII sought to refill the museums of Rome to compensate for the confiscation of treasures by France after the Treaty of Tolentino. It was for this reason that in the last clause he urged every effort to repair these losses and, despite the treasury crisis, set aside 10,000 scudi for purchases.

THE TREATMENT OF THE MONUMENTS OF CLASSICAL ROME: THE REALITY

No discussion of medieval and Renaissance Rome would be complete without consideration of the lime-burners and stone-cutters. In the Popes' building activities, mainly churches, of course, Fea admitted that much ancient material was used, but he refused to believe that the Popes damaged anything: they used only 'ruins'! He admitted the existence of the infamous lime kilns, but claimed that only 'the useless ruins of so many statues' were consumed. If abuses had to be admitted, they were excused by the 'calamity and barbarism' of the times. Lanciani's discussion, to the contrary, cited the destruction for churches and palaces of the Basilica Julia, the Tomb of Alexander Severus, half the Colosseum, the Arch of Lentulus, and the Circus Maximus.[35]

For the fifteenth century, such apologetics are totally outmoded. An exhaustive study of Vatican archives was conducted by Eugene Müntz in his *Les arts à la cour des Papes pendant le XV et le XVI siècle*, 1878–82, on which all later work relies.

Eugenius IV (1431–47) used travertine from the Colosseum for S. Giovanni in Laterano, but also repaired the roof of the Pantheon.[36] Nicholas V (1447–55) is usually held up as the perfect Renaissance prince, founder of the Vatican Library. 'Quelque sympathie que l'on éprouve pour lui on a de la peine à l'absoudre du reproche de vandalisme. Ce pape qui commença la démolition de la primitive basilique du Vatican fut aussi celui qui causa le plus de ravages dans la région située entre le Célius et le Capitole.'[37] Müntz listed his plundering of the Colosseum, the Forum (the Basilica of Maxentius and Temple of Venus and Rome), the Circus Maximus and the Aventine. More than 2,500 cart-loads of stone were carried away from the Colosseum alone in one year.

It is often claimed, however, that such charges of vandalism are anachronistic. Müntz dealt firmly with this misunderstanding. The Middle Ages respected classical Rome, and such actions in the Renaissance were castigated by Poggio Bracciolini and Flavio Biondo.[38]

Pius II (1458–64) will be remembered as the formulator of the early law to protect the monuments. The attentive reader of Müntz will find contradictory judgements on his actions: 'Nous ne ferons pas à Pie II l'injure de croire qu'il a lui-même violé les prescriptions de sa bulle. Lorsque dans les comptes de ses bâtiments il est question de travertins retirés du Colisée, de St Cosme et Damien, du Capitole, du Pont de S. Spirito, et d'autres quartiers couverts de ruines antiques, il faut croire qu'il agit de blocs gisant à terre ou bien enfouis dans le sol.' Compare: 'Au quinzième siècle . . . l'amphithéâtre Flavien ne sera jamais considéré que comme une immense carrière. Nicolas V, Pie II malgré sa fameuse bulle, y ont puisé sans scruples.'[39]

Paul II (1464–71) continued this policy: 'Le Colisée a payé la rançon de tant d'autres chefs d'œuvre antiques restaurés par Paul II.' Vasari accused him of being a principal cause of the destruction of the Colosseum for the building of his palace and the church of S. Marco. On the other hand, small repairs were made to the Pantheon portico and the Arch of Titus, and a leading medallist, Cristoforo Geremia of Mantua, was commissioned to restore the equestrian statue of Aurelius for 300 gold florins.[40]

Another Pope, to whom much credit is usually given, Sixtus IV (1471–84), is also roundly condemned by Müntz:

Quelle indifférence pour l'antiquité toutes les fois que la vanité du pape n'est pas directement en jeu! Il ouvre le musée du Capitole, mais disperse celui du palais Saint-Marc [of Paul II]; il achève la restauration de la statue de Marc Aurèle, mais démolit une demi-douzaine de temples ou d'arcs de triomphes; il défend l'exportation des marbres, mais autorise ses architectes à prendre partout les matériaux nécessaires aux constructions nouvelles . . . La longue martyrologie de Rome antique enregistre son règne comme un des plus néfastes.[41]

The text of the volume fills out the details: the decree allowing the Vatican architects to take stone from anywhere is dated 17 December 1471. The Colosseum was plundered for the Ponte Sisto, the Pons Sublicius for cannon balls, while the Temple of Hercules in the Forum Boarium and the triumphal arch near the Palazzo Colonna were both razed. Some repairs, on the other hand, are noted for the Temple of Vesta, while restoration of Aurelius' statue by the goldsmiths Nardo Corbolini and Leonardo Guidoccii in 1473–4 cost 675 florins.[42]

The admission of Fea is eloquent. He must have known much of this evidence: the great building programmes of Nicholas V and Sixtus IV meant the final destruction of the ancient monuments.[43] Sixtus IV should be remembered, on the other hand, as the founder of the Capitoline Museum, the first public collection in Europe.[44]

Alexander VI (1492–1503) destroyed the pyramid in the Borgo, plundered the frieze and casing of Hadrian's Tomb, and destroyed part of the Baths of Diocletian and the Forum Transitorium. The Palazzo Torlonia (1496–1504), Lanciani reminds us, was built with the stone of the Basilica Julia, while the Palazzo della Cancelleria (*c.* 1486–1517) depended similarly on stone from the Colosseum and the triumphal arch of Gallienus.[45] Alexander also allowed stone workers to work anywhere in the Forum and Colosseum, paying a 'rent' of one third of their production.

The most famous description of the ruins of Rome in the fifteenth century is found in the first book of Poggio Bracciolini's *de varietate fortunae* of the 1430s. There is some grouping of monuments by categories, but this is not followed strictly. Poggio mentions the Tabularium (by his time a salt-store, as is shown in many early engravings), Tomb of Publicius, the Pons Fabricius, the Arch of Lentulus on the Aventine (now lost), the Pyramid of Cestius, the Pantheon, an arch of Augustus near the Tiber (perhaps repairs to the Cloaca Maxima), the 'Temple of Peace' (Basilica of Maxentius), the Temple of Romulus (SS. Cosma e Damiano), the Temple of Antoninus and Faustina, the Temple of 'Castor and Pollux' (Venus and Rome), the Temple of Vesta in the Forum Boarium, the Temple of Minerva in the Forum of Nerva (with lime-works, note, in the portico), the Temple of 'Concord' (Saturn – almost complete when he first came to Rome; Poggio thought the temple of Saturn was S. Adriano), the portico of the Temple of Mercury (the portico of Octavia?), the Temple of Apollo on the Vatican (S. Petronilla), 'Jupiter Stator' (S. Nicola in Statera between the Palatine and Aventine),[46] the Baths of Diocletian, of Caracalla, of Constantine (ruins on the Quirinal), of Alexander Severus ('extensive, fine' ruins near the Pantheon), and of Domitian, the arches of Severus, Titus, Constantine, Gallienus, the 'Arch of Portogallo' (destroyed in 1662) and another on the Via Flaminia, the Colosseum ('reduced in large part to lime through the Romans' stupidity'), the Theatre of Marcellus, columns of the portico of the Temple of Jupiter (Apollo?), the Amphiteatrum Castrense, part of the Theatre of Pompey, the mausoleums of Augustus and of Hadrian, the columns of Trajan and Aurelius, the tombs of Caecilia Metella and of Antonius Lupus, the Vatican Pyramid (destroyed by Alexander VI), some obelisks, and the three columns each of the temples of Vespasian and the Dioscuroi.

It is striking that most of the classical remains were already in the sad state and reduced to the number we know today. Poggio also commented on the Capitol as deserted and reduced to a rubbish heap, the Palatine in ruins, and the Forum as the haunt of animals.

A collection of inscriptions (unpublished) formed by Ludovico Agnelli, archbishop of Mantua (d. 1499), has a dedicatory letter by Fra Giocondo da Verona, who served as architect in Naples, France and Venice before being appointed shortly before his death in 1515 to help Raphael design the new St Peter's. In this letter[47] he complained that Rome was full of ruins

and that new ones were being created daily. Anything not firmly anchored
was moved about: what was today in the Circus Flaminius would be tomor-
row on the Tarpeian Hill, unless it finished in the lime kiln or embedded
in some rustic building. Giocondo gave an exhaustive list of kinds of buildings
so destroyed that no part remained and whose locations were no longer
known. He forbore to specify any, to save him and Agnelli from bursting
into tears. He mentioned only huge heaps of fragments of inscriptions and
the boast of some that the foundations of their houses were completely composed of statue fragments.

Leo X (1513–21) was the recipient of the famous letter, whether by Castig-
lione or Raphael, appealing for protection for the monuments.[48] The author
stressed his efforts in studying antiquity, seeking out the ruins, measuring
them, and comparing the written sources. Yet the city once the Queen of
the World is piteously damaged; more, Rome is the 'universal fatherland
of all Christians'. The enemies of Rome's past glories are listed: Time, the
barbarians, and – the Popes:

Quanti hanno comportato, che solamente per pigliar terra pozzolana si sieno scavati
dei fondamenti, onde in poco tempo poi gli edifici sono venuti a terra! Quanta
calce si è fatta di statue, ed altri ornamenti antichi! che ardirei dire, che tutta questa
Roma nuova, che ora si vede quanto grande ch' ella si sia, quanto bella, quanto
ornata di palagi, chiese, e altri edifici, che la scopriamo, tutta è fabbricata di calce
di marmi antichi. Nè senza molta compassione posso io ricordarmi, che poi, ch'io
sono in Roma che ancor non è l'undecimo anno, sono state ruinate tante belle
cose, come la Meta, che era nella via Alessandrina, l'Arco mal avventurato, tante
colonne, e Tempi, massimamente da M. Bartolommeo delle Rovere.

The ruins must be preserved as a witness to the bravery and virtue of the
'divine souls' whose memory encourages imitation. They are the ruins of
Italian greatness.[49]

The Forum was a major source of building stone for new constructions
precisely in the days of Julius II and Leo X. Architects of the first rank,
such as Bramante, availed themselves of this quarry. Raphael's glorious
appeal was by an individual, powerless against widespread abuse. In the
first decades of the sixteenth century were destroyed the remains of the Basilica Aemilia, and a great part of the Basilica Julia, while the temples of
Vesta, Saturn and Vespasian provided marble and travertine.[50]

The sixteenth century saw yet another sack of Rome, by Charles of Bourbon in 1527. The city was pillaged for eight days, a calamity compared by
Lanciani only with the Gallic sack of 390 BC and the Norman sack of 1084.
As his narrative makes clear, however, it was mainly the treasures of churches
and palaces which were looted; ancient monuments seem to have suffered
little.[51]

It is interesting to compare two versions of Paul III's (1534–49) concern for the monuments. In 1534 he appointed Manetti as Commissario, to enforce very strict regulations.[52] Fea credits him with the massive clearing programme for the entry of Charles V in 1536 (Plate 1), the collection in the Palazzo Farnese of all the statues found in his reign in the Baths of Caracalla, and (by mistake) the disinterment of the Column of Trajan, which was the work of Sixtus V.[53] Lanciani's rejoinder was laconic. He cited only the Bull of 22 July 1540, which 'officially sanctioned and encouraged the destruction of classic remains', handing over to the Fabbrica di S. Pietro the monuments of the Forum and Via Sacra.[54] As for the Palazzo Farnese (1540–), its building material did not come from the Colosseum, but the blocks of travertine from Tivoli and the marbles from the Temple of the Sun on the Quirinal and from the Baths of Caracalla. The marbles of the Sala Regia in the Vatican were drawn over ten years from some enormous and rich monument on the Caelian near the station of the fifth cohort of the Vigiles and from the Forum of Trajan.[55] 'Das Jahrzehnt von 1540–1550 hat den antiken Monumenten Roms vielleicht mehr Schaden zugefügt, als die vorhergegangenen beiden Jahrhunderte.' The stone seekers haunted the Forum.[56] Here one of the most venerable monuments was destroyed in 1543: the Regia, office of the chief priest of classical Rome, the Pontifex Maximus. Nearby in 1546 fragments appeared of the consular fasti and the lists of triumphs, which came, as was realised only this century, not from the Regia but from the Arch of Augustus. These very foundations of the chronology of Roman history were saved from destruction only by the intervention of Cardinal Alessandro Farnese.

The same man also saved another invaluable document, once again in fragments, the marble plan of ancient Rome set up under the Severi in the third century in the Templum Sacrae Urbis, and discovered under Pius IV (1559–65). Onofrio Panvinio, the famous antiquarian, could make sense of only the larger fragments. Hundreds of smaller ones were placed in a cellar and then used in the garden wall of the Farnese palace, where they were rediscovered in 1888–9.[57] Pius also transformed, through Michelangelo, part of the Baths of Diocletian into S. Maria degli Angeli (1563–6).[58]

Things came close to disaster with the Dominican Pius V (1566–72), who wanted pagan remains neither about him in the Vatican nor in the city to distract pilgrims. He gave away part of the Belvedere collection to the Capitol, and it was feared he might destroy monuments.[59]

The work of completing St Peter's under Gregory XIII (1572–85) is admitted to have involved a 'reckless destruction' of both Christian and pagan remains (Plate 2). Of care for monuments there is cited only restoration of the Column of Aurelius in 1574.[60] The Palazzo Caffarelli (1576–1610) was built on the remains of the temple of Jupiter Capitolinus.

It is well known that Sixtus V (1585–90) destroyed the Septizonium on the Palatine,[61] but he also created the first piazza around the Column of

Plate 1 Martin Heemskerck (1498–1574) was in Rome in the 1530s, working with Antonio da Sangallo and others for Charles V's visit. There is little evidence here for the famous clearing in the Forum for that occasion, unless the arches of the Arch of Severus have been cleared. The level of debris in general is not high (note the base of the Column of Phocas). The Forum is, however, a clutter of modern buildings. The cattle fountain is not yet to be seen.

Trajan, buying houses for 10,000 scudi and then demolishing them.[62] He similarly repaired the Column of Aurelius for the same sum.[63] Not so well known are the sanctioning of the destruction of the Tomb of Caecilia Metella and of the Arch of Janus, and the destruction of much of the hitherto intact Claudian aqueduct. The papal architect, Fontana, mentions demolitions at the Baths of Diocletian, and plans to turn the Colosseum into a cloth factory to promote industry and provide lodging for beggars. On the other hand, Sixtus also re-erected no fewer than four obelisks.[64]

One of the most cultured visitors to Rome in the sixteenth century was Michel de Montaigne, the famous essayist, who arrived on 30 November 1580 and left on 19 April 1581. His diary is full of wonderful pictures and impressions, such as his audience with Gregory XIII, a Jewish circumcision and an exorcism. The only reference to the ruins of classical Rome is a long lament for their loss:

il disoit, qu'on ne voyoit rien de Rome que le Ciel sous lequel elle avoit esté assise et le plant de son gite; . . . que ceus qui disoint qu'on y voyoit au moins les ruines de Rome en disoint trop: car les ruines d'une si espouvantable machine rapporteroint

Plate 2 Etienne du Perac, *I vestigi delle antichità di Roma*, 1575. Du Pérac was one of the most famous Roman illustrators of his time (c. 1535–1604). The view shows the temples of Saturn and Vespasian deeply buried and so are the classical foundations of the Tabularium. The Forum is crossed by laden animals, bearing salt which is being carried in sacks into the Tabularium. The legend stresses the few remains of antiquity then to be seen.

plus d'honneur et de reverence à sa mémoire; ce n'estoit rien que son sepulcre. Le monde ennemi de sa longue domination, avoit premieremant brisé et fracassé toutes les pieces de son corps admirable, et parce qu'encore tout mort, ranversé et desfiguré, il lui faisoit horreur, il en avoit enseveli la ruine mesme ... Mais qu'il estoit vraisemblable que ces mambres desvisagés qui en restoint, c'estoint les moins dignes, et que la furie des ennemis de cette gloire immortelle, les avoit portés, premieremant, à ruiner ce qu'il avoit de plus beau et de plus digne.[65]

Montaigne mentions, in fact, only the Testaccio, Forum of Peace, the Forum ('duquel on voit encore, la chute toute vife, comme d'une grande montaigne, dissipée en plusieurs horribles rochiers'), and the Theatre of Marcellus.

In general, Fea confessed amazement at the barbarities committed during the sixteenth century, a period he characterised as one of good taste, the century of Michelangelo among artists, and a time of avid collectors of antiquities. Lanciani for once was more hopeful: 'The systematic demolition of the remains of ancient Rome ends with the sixteenth century.'[66]

History does not bear out his optimism. The seventeenth century provided its own share of desecrations. Paul V (1605–21) demolished the Baths of Constantine to build the Rospigliosi palace, and the Temple of Minerva in the Forum of Nerva for the Borghese chapel in S. Maria Maggiore and the Aqua Paola.

Urban VIII (1623–44) destroyed the Secretarium of the Senate House in the Forum (see Plate 3), and some of the Mausoleum of Hadrian but most notoriously removed the bronze beams of the portico of the Pantheon not for Bernini's Baldacchino in St Peter's but for cannon for Castel Saint Angelo.[67] It is proper to call attention to the paradox that the same Pope restored the missing column on the left-hand corner of the portico.

Alexander VII (1655–67) demolished the Arco di Portogallo to widen the Corso in 1662 and removed the bronze doors from the Senate house in the Forum to provide the central door of S. Giovanni in Laterano. On the other hand, he repaired the Pyramid of Cestius, and replaced the two columns still missing from the left-hand side of the Pantheon portico.[68]

Neither Fea nor Lanciani paid much attention to the eighteenth century. Following the great earthquake of 1703, Clement XI (1700–21) allowed the stone from the Colosseum to be used to build the Porto di Ripetta. The beginning of a long story dates from the excavation of the column of Antoninus Pius in the Campus Martius in 1703.[69] Clement also deserves credit for his stimulus to the preservation of antiquities in museums. He initiated the Galleria Lapidaria in the Vatican, and founded the museum of Christian antiquities. He took measures to protect the Belvedere statues and bought and donated to the Palazzo dei Conservatori the statues of the Cesi collection.[70] The century was to see remarkable activity by Popes in founding museums.

Clement XII (1730–40) restored the Arch of Constantine.[71] He also reorgan-

Plate 3 Claude Lorrain, *Campo Vaccino, c.* 1636. The famous cattle fountain can be seen by the Dioscuroi. The columns at the right must represent the Temple of Vespasian. The Arch of Severus is buried to the top of the lateral arches. The portico of the Temple of Antoninus and Faustina stands out on the left, its columns filled with modern structures. Columns lie about everywhere.

Plate 4 Giuseppe Vasi, *Magnificenze di Roma*, 1747–61, pl. 12, Campo Vaccino. The carefully numbered details show: 1 the Arch of Severus, with the lateral arches now turned into stores or dwellings; 2 the Temple of Saturn; 3 the almost totally buried columns of the Temple of Vespasian; 4 the Column of Phocas, with modern houses very close; 5 the Capitol. Note the accuracy of the inscription on the Arch of Severus.

Plate 5 G. Vasi, *Magnificenze di Roma*, 1747–61, pl. 13. A view of the Forum in the other direction, towards the Colosseum. 1 'Ancient columns' is all he offers for the remains of the Temple of the Dioscuroi; 2 the Temple of Antoninus and Faustina, well buried and with the portico filled in; 3 next to it, the church and convent of SS. Cosma e Damiano, with only the door of the Temple of Romulus to be seen; 4 Church of S. Maria Nuova (now S. Francesca Romana) in the apse of the Temple of Venus and Rome; 5 at the rear left, the three great arches of the 'Temple of Peace' (Basilica of Maxentius). Not just cattle, but oxen and carts dominate the foreground and a road runs towards the Arch of Titus, bordered by a few trees.

Plate 6 Giambattista Piranesi, *Vedute di Roma*, 1740s–70s, pl. 15. Although
the artist has adopted a much steeper perspective from the Capitol than previous views, his detail is very useful. Two modern buildings near the Column
of Phocas, a third under the Capitol, and another alongside the Temple of
Saturn are very clear. One side of the Arch of Titus is supported by buildings
extending to the convent of S. Francesca. The avenue of trees is growing.

ised the Capitoline art and antiquities collections, which had been housed
in the Palazzo dei Conservatori. The new museum opposite was inaugurated
in 1734. The nucleus of the collection was the Albani collection, featuring
imperial busts and acquired by the Pope for 60,000 scudi.[72]

Benedict XIV (1740–58) excavated the Obelisk of the Sun in the Campus
Martius in 1748, which was restored by his successor. The 'enclosing walls'
of the Colosseum were restored; it had been neglected since the 1703 earthquake. The collections of the Capitoline Museums were enormously
expanded.[73] (Plates 4, 5)

Clement XIII should be remembered for his appointment of Winckelmann
as Commissario delle Antichità in 1763.[74] Clement XIV (1769–74) was the
founder of the Museo Clementino in the Vatican (1771) to house the most
precious archaeological finds.[75] The proceeds of the state lottery went to
buy sculpture and other works of art and to finance excavations.[76]

It is not inappropriate, finally, to recall as an indication of attitudes to classical finds that when the incomparable Esquiline silver treasure was discovered in 1793, Pius VI sold it, which is why it is today in the British Museum. To his credit, however, between 1783 and 1794 he re-erected no fewer than three obelisks (those of the Quirinal, Monte Citorio, and Trinità dei Monti).

The only specialist study of archaeology in late eighteenth-century Rome is Carlo Pietrangeli's *Scavi e scoperti di antichità sotto il pontificato di Pio VI*, 1958. As the Museo Clementino was expanding in the 1770s, artists decorated it with precious marbles, mosaics, stuccoes and paintings, and 'squadre specializzate di scavatori percorrevano lo Stato Pontificio, esploravano il sottosuolo delle vie, delle piazze, degli orti di Roma alla ricerca degli oggetti antichi che occorrevano per completare la collezione del nuovo museo'. As well as these initiatives by the Camera Apostolica, 'pullulano infatti a Roma gli antiquari italiani e stranieri, i quali, mediante regolare permesso (o anche senza) vanno alla ricerca delle antichità che poi offrano in vendita al Pontifice o ai collezionisti privati, specialmente inglesi, che non badavano a spese per assicurarsi nuovi pezzi per loro raccolte d'arte.'[77]

A vast increase in excavations, therefore, came about with the accession of Pius VI in 1775. Pietrangeli lists 130 between 1775 and 1780. The major director was the Cameral Architect, Guiseppe Pannini, but they were limited 'alla sola ricerca e al ricupero delle opere d'arte'.[78]

For the last years of the eighteenth century, Pietrangeli lists[79] as the most important excavations:

> Ludovico Mirri's discovery of the painted rooms in the Domus Aurea, 1774;[80]
> the excavation of the Bacchic sarcophagus while digging the foundations of the Vatican sacristy, 1776;[81]
> Cardinal Casali's excavations on the Via Appia, 1776–7 (which produced sarcophagi for the Vatican and Copenhagen);
> Cardinal Pallotta's excavations in the Conservatorio dei Mendicanti near the Basilica of Maxentius, 1776–9;[82]
> Nicola d'Azara's excavations in the Villa Peretti near S. Maria Maggiore, 1777;[83]
> the discovery of the Ustrinum Augustorum, during building operations in the Campus Martius, 1777;[84]
> Gavin Hamilton's excavations on the Palatine, 1777, which produced the Apollo Sauroctonos of Praxiteles;[85]
> the discovery of the cippolino column in Piazza di Campo Marzo, 1778, now in the Piazza di Spagna;
> the clearing of the vineyard of Cardinal Muti near S. Vitale, 1779–81;[86]
> the tomb of the Scipios (see below), 1780;
> Giovanni Volpato's excavations in the Piazza S. Marco, 1780;[87]

excavations in the Villa Palombara on the Esquiline, 1781, which produced the Discobolos of Myron;[88]
the rediscovery of the Augustan obelisk from his mausoleum by Nicola
Forti, 1782.[89]
Baron von Fredenheim's excavations in the Basilica Julia, 1788;[90]

In all his invaluable *Ruins and excavations of ancient Rome*, Rodolfo
Lanciani singles out two acts of vandalism beyond all others: the sacking
of the Palatine by Francesco, Duke of Parma, in the 1720s[91] and the mutilation
of the Tomb of the Scipios:

The brothers Sassi, owners of the vineyard in which the discoveries of 1614 had
taken place, while enlarging their wine cellar in May 1780, came once more across
the hypogeum, and laid bare its precious contents. In reading the accounts left by
Morcelli, Marini, Visconti and Amaduzzi, we cannot understand how such acts
of wanton destruction as the brothers Sassi perpetrated on the most venerable of
Roman historical tombs could have been permitted or left unpunished by Pius VI,
whose love for antique monuments certainly cannot be questioned . . . The sarcophagi
were broken to pieces; their inscribed fronts removed to the Vatican; the aspect
of the crypts altered; the movable objects dispersed; the facsimiles of the original
epitaphs affixed to the wrong places; the signet ring of one of the heroes, with
the image of Victory, given away to a Frenchman, Louis Dutens, who in turn gave
it or sold it to Lord Beverley. And lastly, the very bones of the illustrious men,
which had been respected even by the so-called barbarians, would have been dispersed
to the four winds, but for the pious interference of Angelo Quirini, a senator of
Venice, who rescued the relics of L. Cornelius Scipio, son of Barbatus, and placed
them in a marble urn in the Villa dell'Alticchiero, near Padua.[92]

We have already alluded to foreign collectors. Pietrangeli singled out Gavin
Hamilton[93] and Thomas Jenkins.[94] English collectors, who led the field for
classical antiquities, began to descend on Italy in the eighteenth century.
The extraordinary purchases came largely from the sale of the great Italian
collections owing to 'the increasing pecuniary embarrassment of the noble
families of Rome'. The Giustiniani collection went in part to the Earl of
Pembroke; the Odescalchi collection in 1724 to Spain; the Chigi collection
in 1728 to the King of Poland. By 1740 the Barberini, Sacchetti and Ottoboni
collections were on sale. The Villa Medici collection was lost to Florence
in 1769, the Farnese collections to Naples in 1787. So much invaluable art
and antiquities could be exported often only by fraud, claiming it had been
purchased, for example, not by a private person, but by the King of England.[95]
One example of the plundering of Rome will suffice. Charles Tatham
wrote to Henry Holland on 25 October 1795:

And now that you have in all a collection amounting to 180 articles, I believe that
Rome has been sacked [sic], for among the best enquiries and no small acquaintance,

I do not know of a single article of the kind remaining which is worth buying up ... it is the opinion of many that I have been successful in my pursuit, the which is attributable mostly to the French artists having been so long banished from the Roman State, who for the most part bought up everything of the kind ...

And when the French confiscated all English property at Leghorn in 1796, Tatham could boast that his eight cases were all safe at Rome with the Venetian ambassador.[96]

We may conclude our survey of the eighteenth century and return to the monuments through the eyes of one of the most famous and intelligent visitors of the time, Goethe. He was in Rome from 1 November 1786 until 21 February 1787, and from June 1787 until April 1788. He came admittedly for the sake of his writing (principally *Egmont*) and his art, but among his many associates were the archaeologists Johann Fr. Reiffenstein and Karl Philip Moritz. Of classical monuments he mentions the Pantheon (9 November 1786), the Pyramid of Cestius and the Palatine (10 November), the monuments along the Via Appia (11 November), the Colosseum (2 February, 1787, a night visit), the Mausoleum of Augustus (16 July), the Column of Trajan (which he climbed, 23 July), the Column of Aurelius (24 July, another night visit), the Circus of Maxentius, called the Stadium of Caracalla (December). Goethe was conversant with old drawings, presumably Renaissance, of antiquities, and had seen at an exhibition two paintings showing ancient and modern Rome. The only monument, however, which gains more than a passing line is the Colosseum, and that not for itself but the impression created by the fire of the monks who lived there.

Most remarkably, there is no fascination with the Forum. Goethe looked out over it once when visiting the Palazzo del Senatore for a reception (February 1788) and noted the Arch of Severus, the Temple of Minerva (i.e. of Antoninus and Faustina, a medieval misnomer), the Temple of Peace (Basilica of Maxentius), the Colosseum and the Arch of Titus. Only the most conspicuous and well-known buildings thus attracted his attention.

THE ADMINISTRATION OF ANTIQUITIES UNDER THE PAPAL GOVERNMENT

We are well informed about the Papal antiquities organisation of the early nineteenth century, because the new French administrators in 1809 made endless enquiries about it as they attempted to set up their own system. Well might they ask questions, for the old arrangements were complex. The man on whom fell the main burden of providing the answers was Carlo Fea. It is appropriate here to introduce the first of the major figures in the history of the archaeology of Rome under the French.

Carlo Fea (Plate 7) was born in Liguria in 1753, and had taken a degree

CAROLVS FEA AB AMICIS

Plate 7 Carlo Fea (1753–1836), by Giambattista Wicar, 1813. The portrait
shows Fea in his floruit, precisely during the French period. The caption was
satirised by Juan Masdeu as meaning that Fea's full name was Fea de Amici.

in law at the Sapienza. He then turned to antiquities, largely as a result
of producing a new edition of Winckelmann's history of ancient art (1783–4);
crucial also was the gaining of the patronage of the Chigi, through employment in their library. After amazing vicissitudes, including various imprison-
ments, during the time of the French Republic (1798-9), in 1801 he was
appointed Commissario delle Antichità as successor to Filippo Visconti, an
office he was to hold the longest of all incumbents, for thirty-six years until
his death. Although notorious for his egotism and unprincipled style of controversy, he was to play a leading part in the work of the French, and always
to be the leading champion of the protection of Rome's classical heritage.

As early as 18 August 1809 he sent a description of the papal antiquities
service to Baron de Gérando, member of the Consulta with special care
for cultural matters.[97] He described recent work on the Pantheon, the Colos-

seum, and the Arch of Constantine which had been undertaken at the initiative of the Pope or the Commissario. Convicts had been used for economic reasons and to give them employment ('quella gente oziosa e disperata'). The work on the Colosseum Fea especially recommended for continuation: for the honour of the government and as an object of admiration both in Rome and abroad. The Forum Boarium also, he suggested, should be cleared between the two temples. Ostia, incidentally, he considered ruined forever by the man who had conducted the excavations (Giuseppe Petrini).

The Popes had assigned 10,000 scudi for these repairs and acquisitions, over and above the salaries of the officials, which were paid from the Cassa dell'Impresa de' Lotti. The monthly salaries were:

> the Commissario (Fea): 20 scudi, plus 2 scudi per day when out of Rome, and a carriage at his disposal;
>
> assessors of painting and sculpture (Stefano Piale and Giambattista Monti):[98] 20 scudi each;
>
> their assistant: 6 scudi;
>
> the president and first custodian of the Capitoline Museum (Fea): 7 scudi;
>
> assistant to the Commissario (Agostino Toffanelli): 11 scudi;
>
> the keeper of paintings in the Capitoline (Clemente Cittadini): 8 scudi;
>
> the keeper of the Palazzo dei Conservatori (Giuseppe Emmanueli): 15 scudi;
>
> the architect (Giuseppe Valadier): unpaid, but provided with a carriage and 2 scudi per day out of Rome.[99]

This was plainly insufficient for the arch bureaucrat. Within days he had submitted a list of seven questions to Fea – at least, we have his answer in a report of seventeen pages dated 27 August.[100] The first question concerned the duties of the Conservatori (municipal councillors). They cared for the ancient walls, made repairs to buildings such as the Colosseum, Pyramid of Cestius, Arch of Janus, and Columns of Trajan and Aurelius. These Conservatori were now abolished. Finance had come from the Camera Capitolina and after 1801 from the Camera Apostolica. Work was decided upon by ministers, the Commissario, and the Architetto Camerale, Giuseppe Valadier. Now it was the responsibility of the Minister of the Interior through the Commission of Antiquities.

The second question concerned the use of convict labour, in answer to which Fea referred de Gérando to his book, *Relazione di un viaggio ad Ostia*.

The third question was about income from art exports. Fea gave the total *value* of such exports for 1800–3 as

modern paintings	65,177 scudi
ancient paintings	16,768
modern marble	68,318
ancient marble	21,911
bronzes	1,095
mosaics	500
	173,769 scudi (i.e. 929,644 frs).

The significance of these startling figures was to be revealed to the Consulta.

As for the present state of the accounts (question four), Fea replied that there never were separate accounts for Antiquities and Fine Arts. Expenses were simply described as 'infinite', and divided among many officials. Those who know de Gérando's character may imagine his near apoplexy at this.

He next asked who were the architects employed. On the Colosseum, Fea told him, they were Camporese, Palazzi and Stern. Everything else came under Valadier, who could manage, Fea assured de Gérando.

Question six asked what excavations should continue. Fea promised to send a separate memoir. The last question concerned the Forum Boarium.[101]

Arrangements for the export of antiquities were explained to the Consulta on 20 December, probably by Fea.[102] All exports were subject to licence, issued by the Commissario, assisted by the two assessors. The tax on exported ancient paintings was 15% of the estimated value, on ancient sculpture 18%. The income from such taxes between 1800 and 1804 averaged for paintings, 3,424 frs (on an annual average value of 22,470 frs) and for sculpture, 5,296 frs (annual average value 29,425 frs). All other exported art, averaging in value 181,900 frs per year, was tax free. On the export of art works, therefore, valued on average at nearly a quarter of a million francs, the income from tax averaged less than 9,000 francs.

A similar report of the same date[103] explained how excavations were controlled. Since Leo X (1513–21), the Popes had tried constantly to protect the monuments. Fea made the startling admission, however, that many of them wanted only to perpetuate their own names and so they pillaged the antiquities to build their own monuments. This was 'une sorte de barbarie qui accusait la négligence du gouvernement'. It was revealed that for discoveries made on public land, the Papal government had claimed only one third of the objects discovered.

A final report of Fea was made as late as 15 March 1811 to Camille de Tournon.[104] Here Fea admitted that paintings and marbles were being acquired for small amounts and sold abroad at vast profit, notably in England. By the time of this report, however, by contrast with the considerable income from export taxes 1800–10, for the second half of 1810 it was 194 scudi (about 1,028 frs) and the work of the Commission (cleaning monuments, draining water, making casts and so on) amounted to the pittance of 34 scudi.

In sum, one can only be amazed at the 'system' which had a sizable income (10,000 scudi or more than 50,000 frs), but which carried out so little work and allowed, by the Commissioner's own admission, the export at budget prices of so many art treasures, to enrich the pockets of foreign dealers and the collections of other countries.

It is important to realise that this old Papal system survived in part alongside the new French organisation. Fea remained Commissario delle Antichità in particular and complained to de Gérando that his salary had been reduced to 20 scudi per month because employees were not allowed to be paid for more than one job. With the suppression of the Conservatori, all their duties now fell on him, he grumbled, and he always refused to claim rises or rewards for extraordinary labours.[105]

THE ARCHAEOLOGICAL ACTIVITY OF PIUS VII FROM 1800 UNTIL 1809

Mention may be found, scattered in older antiquarian works, of the attention devoted to the monuments by Pius VII in the few years before his exile. Details and documentation are, however, very difficult to trace. It is necessary to examine these undertakings as a prelude to the French period, and they demonstrate an unprecedented concern for the major remains of classical Rome. It was no coincidence that Carlo Fea had been appointed Commissario delle Antichità in 1801.

The most famous reference to the activity of the new Pope is by Giuseppe Guattani:

Dopo l'esaltazione del felicemente regnante Sommo Pontifice Pio VII, molti scavi si sono intrapresi a beneficio dell'architettura, le più sotterranee ed ignote parti de' capitali vetusti edifici, trascurati (chi lo crederebbe?) nei tempi più luminosi de' Giuli e de' Leoni. Per tacere di meno recenti, fatti al Tempio di Vesta sul Tevere, alle Terme Dioclezianee, agli archi di Settimio Severo e di Costantino, alle Terme di Nerone, al Pantheon, al Colosseo.[106]

Not so well known but equally authoritative is the summary provided by Cardinal Consalvi, Secretary of State 1800–6:

On déblaya, on restaura les plus fameux des monuments antiques, comme les arcs de Septime Sévère et de Constantin, qui furent déterrés jusqu'au niveau du pavé romain. On débarrassa le Colisée des pierres et des monceaux de terre qui depuis tant de siècles encombraient ses issues. Ces heureux recherches démontrèrent la fausseté de ce qui jusqu'alors avait été accrédité. On inaugura ainsi de semblables travaux dans l'arène et à l'extérieur, afin de rendre ce gigantesque monument à son état primitif; mais les crises qui se succédèrent ne permirent pas de mener cette œuvre à bonne fin. Pour empêcher la chute imminente d'un des côtés qui menaçait ruine et qui pouvait occasioner celle de la plus notable partie de l'édifice, on construisit le grand éperon (il grande sperone), et au témoignage de tous, ce grand éperon est digne du Colisée qu'il soutient . . .[107]

This account is prefaced by Consalvi's admission that excavations were undertaken in order to compensate for the loss of the one hundred master-pieces seized by France under the terms of the Treaty of Tolentino.

We turn now to consider in more detail these early works of Pius VII.

The Arch of Constantine

The sure attribution of this arch to the first Christian emperor did little to protect it. Someone removed the heads of the Dacian prisoners.[108] On the other hand, there had been an attempt to clear the arch in the time of Gregory XV (1621–3): the earth was all cleared away, a wall built around it, and a 'bridge' built under the main arch to allow the whole to be seen. Fearing, however, that it would become simply a rubbish dump, the Pope abandoned the plan and restored the earth.[109] A major restoration was under-taken by Clement XII (1730–1740): the eight missing heads of the statues were replaced by Pietro Bracci, using ancient models, some thirteen heads were restored on the reliefs, and the columns which had been taken away for S. Giovanni in Laterano were replaced.[110]

Immediately before the French work came the isolation under Pius VII (see Plate 8). In 1805 the architect Tommaso Zappati excavated around the arch and then built a retaining wall. Contemporary accounts claim that nothing of importance was found in the excavation, save the triumphal way in polygonal slabs, twelve palms (2.6 m) down. It rained very heavily during the work, but the water disappeared very quickly, revealing the presence of efficient ancient drains.[111] The wall was removed when Leo XII undertook excavations between the Capitol and the Colosseum in 1829.[112]

The Arch of Septimius Severus

It has been suggested that this arch was well preserved because in the Middle Ages it belonged in part to the Church of SS. Sergio e Bacco.[113] This is not to say that it remained exposed. Its proximity to the slope of the Capitol meant that it was constantly being buried. From the Renaissance various attempts were made to clear it[114] but the first concerted attempt was under Pius VII.

The arch was found buried to approximately half the height of the lateral arches, a depth of nearly 4 m. The area around for a small space was cleared

CES · TRIVMPHALES · SEVERIANVS · ET · CONSTANTINI
BASIM · DETECTI · ET · OPERE · NOVO · CIRCVMCLVSI

Plate 8   The commemoration of the clearing of the arches of Constantine and
Severus in the frescoes of the deeds of Pius VII in the Vatican.

and a retaining wall built. The commemorative inscription was dated 1803:
'Pius VII P.M. ruderibus circum egestis arcum restituendum et muro sepien-
dum curavit anno MDCCCIII.'[115] Amongst other things, shops in the lateral
arches had to be removed. The ancient level revealed the paving formed
by huge blocks of polygonal basalt. The road through the central arch
divided, becoming the Clivus Capitolinus in one direction and running to
the Tullianum in the other. The lateral arches were discovered to have steps,
and the doors between these and the central arch were uncovered. The drain
for water coming down from the Capitol was found, which forced a deviation
in the surrounding wall to allow it to empty outside it.[116] A vital note on
the work is provided by Fea: it was carried out by convicts in the summer
of 1802 and 1803, when there was no work at Ostia.[117]

   The most interesting question remains to be solved. Who was the antiquarian or architect supervising this undertaking? The answers offered are
as contradictory as possible. Angelo Uggeri ascribed the clearing and walling
to Tommaso Zappati. Gasparoni in his biography of Giuseppe Camporese
claimed that he was responsible for the clearing and walling of the arches
of both Constantine and Severus. Antonio Nibby in his most famous book
referred to an unpublished text of Fea's excavations. And finally in her biography of Stern, Eva Brues ascribed the excavations to both Giuseppe Camporese
and Tommaso Zappati. The archives show that the work was carried out

by the Inspector Giuseppe Petrini, supervised by Zappati, with some consultation of Camporese.[118]

The Colosseum

The great Flavian amphitheatre is the most imposing ruin of classical Rome, but its survival has often been in doubt. The last games were held there in the sixth century. By the twelfth it was being used as a fortress, notably by the Frangipani family, sometimes by the Annibaldi, until it passed under the control of the senate and people in the fourteenth century. By later in the same century it was a stone quarry. Material from it contributed to buildings such as the Palazzo Venezia, the Cancelleria, and the Ponte Sisto. Sixtus V (1585–90) had plans to clear the accumulated earth, but they were cut short by his death. In 1700 Clement XI closed the outer arches to exclude 'malviventi'; these arches were henceforth until 1811 used as manure deposits! An earthquake in 1703 brought down a western arch, which was used for the Porto di Ripetta. In 1714 Clement XI erected the chapels in the arena, and in 1749 Benedict XIV consecrated it to the Passion and the martyrs.[119] One might have thought the building now well protected, or what remained of it. The hermit supposed to be looking after the chapels, however, was instead growing hay in the arena.

In 1800 Angelo Uggeri issued his famous appeal: 'Cette superbe masse est maintenant si ruinée qu'elle ne présente à la vue qu'un objet pittoresque aussi défiguré à l'extérieur qu'à l'intérieur, et les siècles à venir n'auront pas même l'avantage de le voir dans l'état où elle est à présent, si l'on n'apporte le plus grand soin à prévenir le progrès de la destruction dont elle est menacée.'[120] The position up to this time was summarised by Fabio Gori: 'i papi sino a tutto il secolo XVIII non hanno fatto altro che daneggiare questo insigne monumento'.[121]

A major question, obviously, is when the Colosseum suffered the enormous damage on the Caelian and Forum sides. Luigi Canina suggested that it was half ruined by the sixteenth century, so that the main damage must have occurred between the ninth and fifteenth centuries. His main evidence was the depictions by Marliani, Kock and du Pérac.[122] The question was dealt with at greater length by Rodolfo Lanciani. The Vatican archives confirm Flaminio Vacca's claim that the monument was protected by Eugenius IV (1431–47). For the destruction on the Caelian side, Lanciani nominated the earthquake of 422 (*CIL* 6.1763), or before 508 (6.1716). Once the collapse began, it would have been hard to arrest; he properly notes the condition of the arches near Pius VII's buttress.

As for the fall of the southern porticoes, Lanciani suggested that this must be dated after Bede ('Quamdiu stat Colysaeus, stat et Roma: Quando cadet Colysaeus, cadet et Roma: Quando cadet Roma, cadet et Mundus')[123] and before 1386, when the arms of the senate and S. Salvatore were put up in the inner sections. Games are supposed to have been held in the Colosseum in 1332 (Muratori), but by 1362, the Frangipani were wrangling over the stone. Lanciani therefore suggested 'Petrarch's earthquake' of 1349 as the culprit.[124]

What work was carried out by Pius VII before 1809? Published sources offer the usual contradictions. It is preferable to resort immediately to the authority: Carlo Fea in his report to de Gérando.[125] The architect Carlo Fontana in 1705 had asked for the clearing and buttressing of the building. This request was finally granted a century later! It was agreed to clear the Colosseum inside and out by means of convicts, removing the manure stores and the rubble, clearing the vaults and all interior porticoes, excavating down to the ancient level on the outside, removing the modern accretions such as hay-stores, and surrounding the whole building with a retaining wall.

Work began on 1 October 1805 under the direction of Giuseppe Camporese, Giuseppe Palazzi and Raffaele Stern, assisted by Carlo Lucangeli.[126] Between ninety and one hundred and sixty workers were employed. The operations were suspended in 1808 because of the cost. The poor workers toiled for ten hours a day for three bajocchi. The overseer Lucangeli received 15 scudi per month. The total cost was about 268 scudi per month.

Further archival insight comes from an undated memorandum,[127] telling that the work proceeded with zeal for some time until the architects' enthusiasm cooled because they were not paid and could not be present every day. As well as earthquake damage in 1804, which necessitated the buttress (see below), the main problem was drainage. It was claimed that there was no money, but this was untrue. Money which should have been spent on the Colosseum was spent on the road outside the Porta del Popolo, the main northern entrance to Rome.

Further details are given by Giuseppe Guattani.[128] The excavators discovered the 'secret passage' from the Caelian, and cleared the two principal *ambulacra* and found their drainage system. Many fragments of decoration were recovered, proving the richness of the building. Under the stairs from the second *ambulacrum* to the upper floors were found rooms thought to be lavatories or brothels (which excited a long digression on the latter!). The drainage system is described in detail: circular in the third *ambulacrum*, with seventy-two smaller transverse channels leading to another circular drain in the second *ambulacrum*, whence another twenty canals led to the largest circular drain under the outside steps. Lucangeli is noted as having published detailed measurements of the whole building.

The outstanding memorial to the work of Pius VII is, of course, the great buttress towards S. Giovanni in Laterano. The commission of the three architects (Palazzi, Camporese and Stern) made proposals to combat the imminent

Plate 9 Raffaele Stern (1774–1820), no date, by Nuvoli (S. Luca).

collapse of this section. Some had suggested demolishing it, to which the architects replied that this would be to excel even the barbarians. A second plan was also rejected: to cut the edges of the weakened section on the oblique to strengthen them and to wall in the fragile arches. Too much would be lost, the architects said. They refused to sacrifice even one stone. The result was the buttress. The final report was signed by Stern (see Plates 9 and 10). The design of the buttress may therefore be credited to him.[129] The commemorative inscription dates the work to Pius' seventh year (March 1806 to 1807).

Stern was so proud of his work that he declared that it was the only modern brick which could stand comparison with ancient work! Not everyone was convinced even at the time. The French architect Guy Gisors, reporting on the restoration still needed in 1813, noted the buttress and sarcastically suggested that if this method were adopted every time some section was in danger, the Colosseum would soon be buried under a mass of supporting walls.[130]

Paolo Marconi puts this restoration in a wider context.[131] 'Rispetto dell'an-

EATRVM · FLAVIVM · MARTYRVM · CRVORE · R

Plate 10 The commemoration of the Colosseum buttress in the frescoes showing the main events of the reign of Pius VII in the Vatican.

tico, cultura impregnata del filone tardo-manierista romano, predisposizione
romantica al rovanismo' are all combined here in this work by Stern. He
remarks, as anyone must, the way the falling stones are caught as if by
some giant hand; it would obviously have been possible to put them neatly
back in place.

The Pantheon

This glorious testimony to Roman architectural genius is one of the few
classical buildings to have been cared for by the Popes. In AD 609 it had
been transformed into a Christian church. This did not prevent the emperor
Constans II removing the bronze roof-tiles in 663. Gregory III in c. 735 repaired
it with lead and various succeeding Popes, especially in the seventh to ninth
centuries, carried out minor restorations. By 1400, three columns of the
eastern portico were missing, however, and the portico was being buried
under rubbish. Both Martin V (1417–31) and Nicholas V (1447–55) repaired
the roof. Eugenius IV (1431–47) cleared the portico of sellers and rubbish.
Pius IV (1559–65) cleaned and repaired the bronze doors. The most notorious
vandal, however, was Urban VIII (1623–44), who removed the bronze roof
beams of the portico,[132] but who also constructed the two campanili (Bernini's
'ass's ears', demolished finally in 1883) and replaced one of the three missing

Plate 11 Carlo Fea, *L'integrità del Pantheon revendicata*, 1820, the Pantheon
before the restorations of Alexander VII. Note the modern buildings crowded
around it on every side, the booths in the portico, the three missing columns
on the left, and the much higher ground level.

columns (see Plate 11). The Pantheon portico was fully restored by Alexander
VII, who replaced the last two missing columns (those with the Chigi star)
on the left-hand side, and cleared it of hovels and booths. He planned to
extend the Piazza della Rotonda by pulling down houses between the Via
del Seminario and the Via del Sole.[133] The architect Paolo Posi wrecked
the inside classical attic in 1747. Repairs were carried out to the covering
of the cupola by the Commune in 1681 (499 scudi) and 1689 (3067 scudi).
In 1756 Benedict XIV placed the building's maintenance under the Palazzi
Apostolici.[134]

The main work under Pius VII before the French period was the excavation
by Carlo Fea and Giuseppe Valadier in 1804 (see Plate 12), motivated by
the planned new edition of Antoine Desgodetz, *Les édifices antiques de Rome*,
1682. The sounding on the right-hand side of the building was to check
its plan and elevation. Just below the modern level was found the ancient
travertine pavement, extending 10 feet from the wall, like a wide footpath.
Checking if the rotunda was supported by buttresses, Fea found only small
barrel vaults extending from a wall parallel to the curve of the temple. No

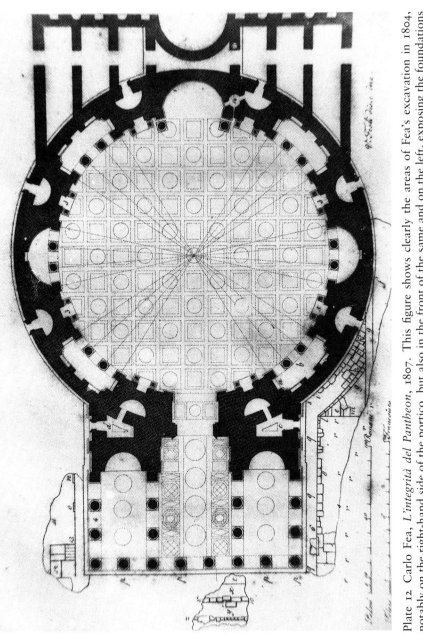

Plate 12 Carlo Fea, *L'integrità del Pantheon*, 1807. This figure shows clearly the areas of Fea's excavation in 1804, notably on the right-hand side of the portico, but also in the front of the same and on the left, exposing the foundations of the building and the ancient pavements.

great substructures were found: 'stat mole sua'. One of the main drains to take away water during construction was also uncovered. This was enough, as Fea's title indicates, for him to ascribe the whole building to Agrippa.[135] The steps in front of the portico were subsequently found. There was a difference of 4 feet in the height of the portico and the paving, joined by steps 1 foot high and 1¼ feet wide.[136]

One of the most famous sagas of the early years of Pius VII concerned the baker who had established his oven against the Pantheon. This modern building had belonged to Duca Bonelli, who sold it to the baker. After severe floods in February 1806, he began to rebuild it, contrary to law, severely damaging the Pantheon in the process. Attempts by Fea, Valadier and Camporese to have him removed were unsuccessful. The building must have been substantial, being valued in 1803 at 5,839 scudi. In truth, Camporese had valued it for repairs in September 1806, talking glibly of doing no damage to 'such precious remains' (i.e. the Pantheon). He was bold enough to express the wish of all 'intelligent people' to see the Pantheon freed of houses, but admitted that this was incongruous with his activities as valuer. Fea told the baker in October 1804 during the excavations and in the presence of Valadier not to undertake any repairs.[137]

Attempts to remove the fish market in and around the Pantheon were equally unsuccessful. We have noted Alexander VII's good work and plans. In 1662 he decreed that the fish market be removed to the Piazza di Pietra. The benches, tables and booths were cleared, not just those of fish merchants, but for goats, fruit and vegetables, birds and bread. The ineffectiveness of this action is clear: the bans had to be reissued in 1711, 1725 and 1752.[138]

The Temple of Antoninus and Faustina

Work was carried out here from 1807, but this was by the Académie de France in Rome, not the Papal government.[139]

The Temple of 'Vesta' in the Forum Boarium

In his *Roma descritta*, 1805, Giuseppe Guattani reported on recent excavations in this temple, without naming the director. The purpose was to examine the foundations. Under the base of the columns was found no plinth, but a marble step 8 inches high, with substructures of tufa 6 feet deep and 'becoming ever wider, finally extending 9 feet'. This was obviously originally covered with marble steps. The archives of the Académie de France in Rome reveal that this investigation was carried out by J. A. Coussin for the Académie.[140]

Most importantly, we have Fea's report to de Gérando.[141] Work was begun in 1804 to clean and repair the temple, which was covered up to the base of the columns. These in turn were out of line and threatening collapse, a danger increased by the weight of hay piled up inside by the prior! Another hazard from the hay was, of course, fire.

Fea reported all this to the Pope, the Cardinal Camerlengo, and Prince Giustiniani, the patron of the church, who ordered the prior, Canon Petrarca, to clear away the hay and give the key to Fea. The last was given permission to make repairs. Work commenced on clearing the portico, but ceased for 'economic reasons' and the prior filled it again with wood, damaging the columns.

Apart from these major undertakings, the notes prepared by Rodolfo Lanciani for the continuation of his *Storia degli scavi* in the nineteenth century[142] mention the following work, based mainly on *CIL*, his first thesaurus for survey.

1801: Domenico Crescentini asked permission to excavate in the Forum near the Basilica of Maxentius.

A necropolis was found near the Porta Latina.

Giuseppe Petrini was allowed to excavate on the Via Portuensis.

A cameo was found on the Aventine and sold to a Polish princess for 900 piastres. When Fea visited the excavations he found some rooms with painted walls and mosaic pavements.

1803: Fea's excavations in front of S. Cosimato in Trastevere, discovering a dedication to Gordian from Colonia Heliopolitana (*CIL* 6.432) (April).

Inscriptions in S. Priscilla (*CIL* 6.8398, 9706).

In the Forum, a large round base was discovered.[143]

Fea discovered the *milliarium aureum*.[144]

1804: Another inscription from S. Priscilla (*CIL* 6.1577).

1805: Fea's excavations in the Piazza S. Susanna, near the Osteria dei Tre Gigli, finding fragments of granite column and selciata. Under the osteria were found substructures from the Baths of Diocletian (January–February).

Towards Testaccio, excavations by Marianna Dionigi, finding broken vases and pottery and a small room with reticulate walls (November).

An inscription from S. Lorenzo in Lucina (*CIL* 6.9063).

1806: At Quattro Fontane, the discovery by the monks of the statue of Augustus' physician, Antonius Musa.

Inscriptions from the cemetery of Comodilla (*CIL* 6.2190) (April).

1807: Tombs in the Vigna Moroni near Porta S. Sebastiano (*CIL* 6.2323, 2330, 2340) (December).

1808: An ancient bath at the Badia delle Tre Fontane.

Another inscription from S. Callisto (*CIL* 6.15043) (13 January).

Very much aware of the limitations of Lanciani's notes, we can say that there is nothing here to add to the main areas of activity already noted for the first nine years of Pius VII. Not without mention, finally, should be 1808: Valadier's work in the Forum Holitorium, occasioned by repairs to the church. This led to excavations in the three temples, under which were found what were presumed to be the remains of a prison.[145]

2

Commissions, commissions, commissions: the administration of antiquities under the French

The following story has never been told, although many people have already turned over the multitude of documents in the Roman and Parisian archives. There are, of course, allusions to the main events in the works of writers such as La Padula and Boyer, but on only the most summary scale. There is now one chapter in Marita Jonsson's book. For those willing to spend more time there are many fascinations.

First, there is the incredible activity of the handful of leading administrators in Rome, men for the most part utterly different in temperament, often bitterly at odds but, in two cases at least (Tournon and Miollis), deeply imbued with a love of Rome's classical past. The various organs they set up in order both to reveal Rome's monuments and to provide employment for the poor meant an enormous increase in their administrative burdens, which they gladly undertook. These Frenchmen were fully supported by the leading Roman architects, notably Valadier and Camporese, and antiquarians, of whom Fea was Commissario delle Antichità.

The complexity of this antiquities organisation, and the conflicts within it, have never been explained. There were, in fact, three bodies working side by side. The Commission des Embellisements is the only one usually to have received any attention. Its work was phenomenal, but the Accademia di S. Luca also played an outstanding part in restoring and maintaining the monuments under Antonio Canova. Martial Daru, Intendant des Biens de la Couronne at Rome, was the third figure, entrusted with excavations to find works of art. To distinguish these three operations is often very difficult, as the Accademia especially found to its cost, and therein lay endless confusion and friction.

Second, 700 miles away lay the Parisian bureaucracy, with a variety of ministries claiming control over the archaeological and town-planning work in Rome. As will be revealed, the fatal flaw was that these bureaucrats who claimed the right to control everything had never been to Rome, and relied on impressions from their classical education! They finally sent two agents in 1813, who could not speak Italian and who grandly revised all the plans drawn up over many years by the leading Roman architects. The revisions did not, of course, matter, since time was now up for the French in Italy. One of the two visitors, however, was later revealed as utterly corrupt. That, again, is a story which has never been told.

Desire to control from so far away was one thing, and endless bickering over who had the competence was another, but in reality the very worst result was the holding to ransom every week of the Roman administrators and the poor workers, when the funds for pay had not been approved from Paris.

Third, and not least fascinating, is the vast human canvas: ministers, governors, prefects, presidents, intendants, architects, even the more lowly inspectors at work. They are revealed as honest, tireless, concerned for those who depended on them, harassed, and driven to the ends of their patience. Some, on the other hand, have not escaped the light of history; they are shown to be ruthless, incompetent and even appallingly dishonest.

The wonder is that so much was accomplished in such a short time. That, in the last analysis, was only partly due to the organisers we have just named. More than to anyone else, it was due to the thousands of unemployed of all classes who toiled for little more than a franc a day, together with a midday bowl of soup. The laying bare of Rome's classical past was carried out under the French, but the human resources were Roman.

THE COMMISSION OF 1809

The Consulta set up on 10 June 1809 as a temporary measure to prepare Rome for a new, unspecified government was composed of General Miollis, Joseph-Marie de Gérando (Plate 13), Laurent-Marie Janet, Ferdinando dal Pozzo, and Cesare Balbo as secretary. One of its first decrees, dated 21 June 1809, began:

La consulte extraordinaire désirant donner à la ville libre et impériale de Rome un premier gage de la haute protection de Sa Majesté l'Empéreur et Roi pour la conservation des monuments anciens et modernes que renferme cette cité célèbre, arrête:
1. il sera formé une commission chargée de l'inspection et de la conservation spéciale des monuments anciens et modernes de la ville de Rome et des états romaines.[1]

Article 2 laid down that the commission was to prepare reports on the conservation and restoration of the monuments. Article 3 specified that the first particular tasks were the protection of St Peter's from lightning strikes and the paintings of Raphael from air. Article 4 named the members: Luigi Martorelli, Director of Imperial Archives, Gaetano Marini, Director of the Vatican Library, Antonio Canova, the famous sculptor, and Vincenzo Camuccini, a leading painter (the last name in a different hand). Marini

Plate 13 Joseph-Marie de Gérando (1772–1842). As a virtual Minister of the Interior in Rome, he was the Consulta member most responsible for archaeological matters.

was to be replaced on 10 August by the antiquarian Filippo Aurelio Visconti, because he had never attended a meeting![2]

The operations of this Commission were never very reassuring. Martorelli reported to the Consulta that it should look after all monuments previously under the care of the Cardinal Camerlengo and the Capitol (i.e. the municipal administration). He noted that road works were accustomed to take stone from wherever they could find it, including ancient monuments. It was further recommended that all 'sepulchral stones' be gathered in one place, such as a corridor of the Belvedere (but we have seen that Clement XI founded the Galleria Lapidaria in the Vatican). These suggestions seem rather undercut, however, by the admission that of the four members, Marini had returned home, Canova had declined, and Camuccini was about to depart on a long journey, so that only Martorelli was left. He went so far as to offer a list of replacements including Carlo Fea and Filippo Aurelio Visconti.[3]

By July, the Consulta itself was trying to remove the fish markets and other disfigurements from the Pantheon, a matter which, as we have seen, had already exercised a number of Popes. Otherwise the records of the Consulta for 1809 show activity – using convict labour – centring on the Colosseum.[4]

On 5 November the man who was to be the inspiration for the archaeo-

Plate 14 Camille de Tournon, Prefect of Rome, by Mlle Hortense Lescot, 1810. Behind him is a capriccio: a column on the right and the famous Horse-Tamers of the Quirinal, where he first had his office and dwelling. In his hand he holds a map of the Department of Rome.

logical and town-planning achievements of the French period arrived in Rome to take up his post. He had just turned thirty-one. This was the Prefect, Camille de Tournon (Plate 14), who had been appointed on 6 September. The only previous major post he had held had been as Intendant at Beirut, which he perhaps owed to the fact that he spoke German, in 1806. He had been captured, however, by the Austrians in June 1809 and freed only in August. There was considerable nervousness over Napoleon's reaction to this clumsiness, but all had been dispelled by his speedy nomination to Rome, probably due in the main to the support of the Minister of the Interior, Montalivet. He was at this time the youngest prefect in the Empire, and Montalivet called him affectionately his 'Benjamin'.[5] He was to remain the Prefect in Rome until the evacuation in January 1814 and to be the most popular by far of all the French administrators in the capital.

Important regulations were drawn up on 20 December, governing both the export of antiquities and excavations. Responding to Fea's report on the papal organisation,[6] the Consulta decreed that no article termed an antiquity was henceforth to be exported (an antiquity was defined as a column, inscription, coffin, vase, statue, relief or painting). On the other hand, no licence was required for the export of the work of any living artist. As in the edict of 1802, a very clear distinction was made between ancient and modern works of art. It seems, however, that some antiquities might be exported, for it was then stated that licences would be refused for any item essential for the study of ancient art, and on items eligible for export the same tax would apply as previously. It was, of course, expected that attempts would be made to smuggle out prohibited exports. In this case, the item would be confiscated, and a fine double its value imposed. The objects confiscated would go to the museum. Taxes levied would be used to pay the jury and assist artists (clauses 1–7).

This jury was to be established to evaluate items and issue licences, all of which had to be approved by the Prefect. The jury was to be composed of nine members drawn from names submitted by the Accademia di S. Luca. The Chirografo of 1802 was specifically to remain in force (clauses 8–17).

On the matter of excavations and protection of monuments, it was laid down that all excavations had to be authorised. The authorisation could be given by the senate or the jury at Rome, and the prefects in the departments. The excavator had to specify the 'system of work' and the means to be employed, and the distances from roads and public buildings were to be laid down. The president of the jury might require that the site be visited, and excavations could be closed for reasons of public safety or health. Finds were to be declared weekly, and even articles discovered by chance had to be declared (clauses 1–9).

There followed protection of the monuments: all were to be preserved at public expense. There was to be no demolition, destruction or removal of material for any other building. Private persons were obliged to maintain the monuments on their land. There was to be no digging for *pozzolana* closer than 10 m to any ancient monument. And finally it was suggested that the government be empowered to buy property for excavation, but this clause was crossed out in the original draft (clauses 10–16).[7]

These were the strictest regulations laid down in the history of attempts to protect the classical remains. Would their enforcement be any more successful than all the preceding laws?

The budget drawn up for 1810[8] showed a total income for the state of 4,834,910 frs and expenses of 3,949,950 frs. Salaries were more than 400,000 frs, education 300,000, hospitals 300,000, police 100,000, 'embellishments' 360,000, assistance to the poor 150,000 and provision of cemeteries 210,000. The most expensive item was, in fact, 'public monuments', costing 500,000 frs.[9]

Various authorities such as antiquarians were consulted on the priorities of work to be carried out on the classical buildings. Visconti suggested[10] that the most urgent repairs were to the Temple of Antoninus and Faustina, to the so-called Minerva Medica, and to the Fountain of Egeria, because it was known to 'cultivated visitors' and was 'dear to Romans'. He thoughtfully stated that Valadier could provide details of all expenses involved (the first instance, perhaps, of the architect's endless estimates). Visconti's list was singularly unimaginative, and quite out of keeping with the grandiose plans the French had in mind. The way things were going to be tackled at this early stage is indicated by de Gérando's letter to Olivetti, Director of Police, calling for regulations for the work of convicts, so far used in different ways on different tasks. A great number were now employed, and many more would be shortly, de Gérando assured the Director.[11]

On 22 April, Tournon wrote to de Gérando, telling him that the government would carry on the 'honourable task' of preserving the ancient monuments, and that he had called a meeting on the Capitol for Wednesday 25 April, to be attended by the Mayor (Duca Braschi Onesti) Carlo Fea, the most distinguished members of the Accademia di S. Luca, and leading architects and craftsmen.[12]

Early in 1810, the Consulta was paying for work carried out by convicts at the Colosseum, the Temple of Vesta, and the Domus Aurea.[13]

THE COMMISSION DES MONUMENTS, 1810

It was on 9 July 1810 that the Consulta drew up the most extensive regulations for excavations and protection of monuments and established another commission to see to both.[14] The prelude listed all the major papal regulations since 1622 as precedents. We may assume that Carlo Fea was the main drafter, just as he had been the instigator of the Chirografo of 1802. The new decree naturally expanded the regulations of the previous December.

The first nine articles concerned excavations: there was to be no work without authority, which was granted by the Prefect. The exact work proposed and its means were to be detailed and weekly reports of finds made to the Prefect. He had authority to fix proximity of public roads and houses, and to close the work if it endangered public health or safety.

Articles 10–13 dealt with the preservation of monuments. No damage whatsoever was allowed; private individuals who owned them had to maintain them, and if they did not, the Prefect would see to it at their expense.

The third and fourth sections established the Commission des Monuments et Bâtiments Civils. It was part of the prefecture of Rome, and numbered thirteen members under a President (the Prefect) and Vice-President (the Mayor). Four of the thirteen members were to be the assistant to the Mayor, the Chief Engineer of the Department, the Director of the Accademia di S. Luca, and the Professor of Antiquities at the University. The other nine were to be three antiquaries, three architects, two sculptors and one painter. The Commission was to meet once a week. Its functions were (clause 19):

i) D'inspecter, de surveiller la conservation de tous les monuments, bâtiments civils, ouvrages d'Art, et en général tout ce qui peut intéresser l'Histoire, les Arts, et l'Antiquité, de provoquer toutes les mésures d'autorité qui seraient nécessaires pour assurer le respect qui leur est dû, ou pour faire punir conformément aux lois ceux qui y auraient porté atteinte.

ii) De proposer le genre et la nature de travaux nécessaires à leur conservation, réconstruction ou entretien.

iii) D'approuver les plans, devis, dresser sur la proposition, et d'en surveiller l'exécution.

iv) De régler les comptes des entrepreneurs des dits travaux, de fixer et de régler toutes les dépenses d'entretien, de garder les dits monuments et bâtiments civils.

v) D'accorder la faculté de faire exécuter des fouilles, d'inspecter les travaux de cette nature, soit sur les propriétés particulières, soit dans les lieux appartenant à l'Etat ou à la Couronne, et de faire observer les règlements qui y sont relatifs.

One wonders that anyone dared to be nominated to enforce such a set of obligations!

The first tasks were to make a detailed list of all monuments important for 'science or art' whose care fell under the government, and another for those under the care of the Commune or the Department. These lists were to describe the present state of the monuments, the repairs necessary and the costs. The Commission's priorities for repairs were to be sent by the Prefect to the city architects to draw up plans. Members of the Commission could not under any circumstances decide upon the plans or estimates, but could carry out excavations or repairs using convicts. Requests for permission to excavate or export works of art were to be addressed to the Prefect, who delegated one of the Commissioners to make an inspection and advise him. The Prefect also was to delegate Commissioners to inspect public works and private excavations.

The burdens of the Commissioners were obviously great, but those of the Prefect as President were awe inspiring and time consuming. It has rightly been emphasised that the new arrangements guaranteed the preservation of the monuments better than the preceding Papal regulations. Excavations, repairs and restorations were to be in accordance with a comprehensive plan and under the control of experts.[15]

We have a description of Rome just before these works began in a letter of Tournon: 'La ville antique est pleine de jardins, de vignes et de champs, mais au milieu desquels s'élèvent les ruines des temples, des palais, des thermes, des aqueducs. Ce mélange de ruines, d'arbres et de plantes fait un effet très gracieux, et rend plus inspirants ces beaux vestiges.'[16] Here, on the eve of the great transformation, is a totally Piranesi-esque view of Rome's antiquities. Tournon noted further that, within the walls, the northern and eastern parts of the city were abandoned, and that it was concentrated on the two banks of the Tiber.

The first meeting of the Commission was held on Saturday 8 September in Tournon's office in the Quirinal. Tournon asked every member to visit the monuments coming under his specialisation to plan expenses for 1811. The Commission was to meet every Tuesday evening at seven.[17]

Visconti made surveys of repairs to the Temple of Saturn, of Antoninus and Faustina, and to the Tabularium. Stern and Vici valued the granary by the Colosseum buttress. Principe Gabrielli began negotiations for the removal of the fish market from the Pantheon piazza.[18]

The main question was the work-force. Most of the labour in such under-takings previously had been provided by convicts. The original intention to continue in the same way had to be abandoned in favour of providing work for the poor and unemployed.[19] On 30 October, de Gérando wrote to Giacinto Pollani, Acting President of the Commissione di Beneficenza, asking how many of the poor could be employed during the winter (a slightly late start, one might think, but this was when the poor most needed support). The Baron described the work as 'very easy', simply the movement of earth, digging of ditches, and the like. It would be easy to earn 15 bajocchi a day for moving 3 cu m of earth. Every fifty workers were to have an assistant foreman, paid 5 paoli (50 bajocchi) and each hundred workers a foreman (*conduttore*), paid 6 paoli. Workers were to be further subdivided into squads of ten, led by a corporal. De Gérando was aware, however, that there might be obstacles to all these fine plans in 'the customs of the country' and the 'attitudes of the poor'.[20]

November 1810 is one of the best-documented months in the whole history of the French projects in Rome, with a flurry of letters from all sides as the vast work-force was organised and all kinds of problems with the 'easy' work arose.

The Commission met on Friday, 2 November, and planned six ateliers: the Forum Boarium with one or two brigades; the Temples of Saturn and Vespasian, and the Tabularium (three or four); the Temple of Antoninus and Faustina (one); the Colosseum (one or two); the Domus Aurea (one); and the Arch of Janus. On the same day, Valadier prepared a report, 'an economic plan for the work to be done on public monuments in the city of Rome'. He suggested that the whole work should be overseen by an engin-eer and that each atelier needed an experienced architect. All workers should be paid by the task (*a cottimo*).[21]

On Sunday, 4 November, a circular was sent out to all parishes, headed with the symbol of the imperial eagle, crowned and clutching thunderbolts (Plate 15). The Consulta, in accordance with the aims of the Emperor and aware of the problem of the 'needy poor', had informed the Commissione di Beneficenza that anyone who wished to be employed in excavation or similar work should report to his parish within twenty-four hours to be enrolled. The priest was to submit a list to the Commission, which would

LA COMMISSIONE
DI PUBBLICA BENEFICENZA

La Consulta straordinaria secondando le mire sempre benefiche di SUA MAESTA' L'IMPERATORE e RE, e facendosi carico della circostanza de' poveri bisognosi, che si trovano senza lavoro, e senza mezzo di sussistenza, ad oggetto di provedere sull'istante ad ogni classe d'Indigente, ha ordinato alla Commissione di Beneficenza di render noto quanto siegue.

Ogni Individuo che vorrà occuparsi in scavare o nell' interno della città, o nel circond...io delle Mura, o in altri lavori analoghi, dovrà presentarsi al proprio Parroco, nelle 24 ore dalla data del presente per essere ascritto in una nota che lo stesso Parroco rimetterà subito alla prefata Commissione, ad effetto che da questa venga formato il ruolo de' lavoranti, e possa in seguito intimarli ove dovranno ritrovarsi Martedì e Mercoldì prossimo sotto la direzione degli Architetti Valadier, e Camporesi. Il pagamento si farà in ragione del Metro Cubico, calcolando in circa baj. cinque per ogni Metro sino al terzo Metro fatto nel giorno inclusivamente, quattro bajocchi per il quarto, e tre per il quinto.

Tutti quelli poveri poi, che sono in grado di lavorare, e che amando piuttosto di vivere nell'ozio e nella miseria, non vorranno corrispondere alle benefiche mire del Governo, e si ricuseranno di farsi inscrivere nella già detta nota, non potranno giammai sperare de' soccorsi.

Con questa paterna misura e con un lavoro facile a chicchesia, il Governo provido fornisce i mezzi ai ben intenzionati di sussistere, e toglie i vani pretesti di mendicità agli oziosi.

La Commissione si lusinga, che i veri Poveri vorranno secondarne le mire, e daranno a conoscere col loro puntual servizio uno spirito di filiale riconoscenza.

Roma li 4 Novembre 1810.

Per il Presidente assente

GIACINTO POLLANI.

Nella Stamperia di. Luigi Perego Salvioni.

Plate 15 The call for workers (November 1810).

G.CAMPORESE·ARCH.

Plate 16 Giuseppe Camporese (1763–1822), artist unknown. Painted about
the time of his death.

make a roll of workers to begin next Tuesday and Wednesday under the
direction of the architects Valadier and Camporese. Payment was to be by
the cubic metre, 5 bajocchi each for the first three, 4 for the fourth, and
3 for the fifth. A solemn warning was then given to the poor who could
work but preferred to live in sloth and misery that they would receive no
further help. The proposal to provide work was described as 'fatherly' and
the tasks were 'easy'. The poor were therefore to show 'filial gratitude'.[22]

The thunderbolts clutched by the imperial eagle certainly symbolised the
hopes of the Commission. Pollani was ordered to have the first brigade at
the Bocca della Verità under Valadier at 7 a.m. on Tuesday, 6 November,
and the second at the Colosseum under Camporese on Wednesday (see Plates
16 and 17). It was only on the Tuesday that de Gérando sent a letter to
Camporese telling him that he had been selected to assist Valadier in the
direction of the works, with Fea as superintendent. He was therefore ordered
to go every morning at eight to the house of Defougères, Inspector of the
Division of Ponti ed Argini (Ponts et Chaussées), to give the necessary orders.

Plate 17 Giuseppe Valadier (1762–1839), by Giambattista Wicar, 1827. Valadier is here aged sixty-four. There is unfortunately no portrait contemporary
with the French period when he was about fifty.

The payment was now set out at 20 bajocchi for men twenty years and
older, 1 bajocco for each year of age for those between twelve and twenty,
and 12 bajocchi for women. Camporese and Valadier were to receive 200 frs
per month. The same letter was sent to Valadier[23] and presumably to Fea.
On the same day the Commission met and approved the plans for the proposed public garden in the Forum and around the Colosseum.

Pollani reported to de Gérando that the first brigade had reported to Valadier as required at the Bocca della Verità, and that he would see that the
second did the same for Camporese on the next day. On the 8th, however,
Defougères informed de Gérando that work had not begun, because the
announcements had not been published and the poor did not attend. He
hoped that work could begin next Monday, the 12th.[24]

The two architect directors, Camporese and Valadier, were indeed eminent
figures. They were almost exact contemporaries, being born in 1763 and
1762 respectively. Camporese had long been a pontifical architect, working
on the Museo Pio Clementino and the Sala della Biga in the Vatican, but

had also played a leading role during the French Republic of 1798–9 as one of the aediles and a decorator of the Altar of the Fatherland. He had made his peace, however, with the restored Pius VII and had participated in the most important archaeological work of the new reign: the clearing of the Arch of Severus and the buttress for the Colosseum. Valadier was also a papal architect, but his earliest works had been mainly various church restorations outside Rome (at Rimini, Urbino, Spoleto and Orvieto). Under Pius VII he had already made a name by his restoration of the Milvian Bridge and the design of the façade of S. Pantaleo. The two men were also linked by family ties: Valadier's eldest son married Camporese's daughter.

Apart from Camporese and Valadier as immediate directors of the work, as an intermediary between them and the Commission, Collicola was appointed as controller of works.[25] He was to oversee discipline and morale, and 'if one may say so, be a guardian of these numerous unfortunates'. On a more everyday level, Collicola was to arrange with the architects for the employment of each brigade and (a little confidentially, said de Gérando) see to the number of workers at the beginning and end of each day, their tools, and their lunch-time soup.[26]

Work was finally to begin. De Gérando wrote to Tournon on Sunday, 11 November, saying that it would commence on the morrow and that the workers had to be paid! Tournon was to arrange for this with the Mayor.[27] Here was the very beginning of one of the greatest problems with this most ambitious programme of public works, and Tournon was precisely the person to whom most anguish was caused by it. On the same day, Collicola informed de Gérando that he had consulted the two architects and they had agreed that work should begin with the temples under the Capitol (two brigades) and the Basilica of Maxentius (another two). Work would be impossible, however, without the acquisition of the buildings in the architects' report marked for demolition: the storerooms against the Tabularium for storage of tools, one or two rooms in the Capitol for offices, the house against the Temple of Saturn, and the garden of S. Francesca Romana.[28]

Not only workers, but tools were essential. Some contractor, almost certainly Andrea Lezzani, set out what was needed to employ 800 men:[29]

530 barrows at 2.2 scudi	1,166
maintenance for 5 months	72
wood and nails	36
280 *caravani*	336
maintenance	224
100 shovels	227.50
1,200 baskets	150
3 cables	60
4 sets of tackle	36

hoes, sieves, small shovels	50
6 men to distribute all these	300

2,658 scudi.

At its meeting on the 14th, the Commission, on Tournon's motion, decreed that the buildings under the Tabularium were to be demolished. De Gérando stated that he had visited the workers at midday and found the soup excellent: the poor had signalled their gratitude by their blessings. The buildings in the Forum to be demolished were worth about 20,000 frs. There were two dumps: in Stern's garden for the Colosseum, and behind the Temple of the Dioscuroi for the Forum. The ever-attentive de Gérando also noted that pay for women was higher than usual and might be inducing them to abandon other work. They were therefore to be paid by the task.[30] The Commissione di Beneficenza, in fact, agreed. Wages for men and boys were declared too high: 'useful arms' for agriculture and manufacturing were being lost. The parishes were to issue new tickets, and a model was included. It set out name, place of birth, civil status, health, attitude to work, previous work, length of time unemployed, the reason, degree of misery and moral condition![31]

The three 'directors' (Camporese, Valadier and Fea) reported that work was encountering all kinds of difficulties, such as drains and pavements. Payment by task was therefore impossible. The workers were, moreover, unskilled and taken on without order, and the same was true of the corporals. Pollani informed de Gérando on 18 November that the workers numbered 750, but that there was not enough work or soup. At its meeting on the 20th, the Commission decided to reduce the number of women and children workers, and to reduce their pay to 8 bajocchi per day. A check was to be made to see whether some men could not be employed elsewhere. Grandiose plans were clearly being outstripped by economic realities and an over-hasty organisation.

A happier light is thrown on the situation by Collicola. He had the highest praise for the vigilance and intelligence of the two architects who were the linchpin of the whole operation. He was also very pleased with the contractor, Andrea Lezzani. Work was progressing at the Colosseum, the Temple of Antoninus and Faustina, of Vesta, and the Capitol. 'We are still children', he predicted, 'but we will become giants.'[32] Despite this, Valadier and Camporese received a very peevish letter from de Gérando demanding an answer to his long-requested information on the value of the cubic metre in order to set new wages. They were established, and the reductions caused the resignation of many women and boys. The new tickets, on the other hand, produced better workers.[33]

Wages may have been reduced, but the work was ever expanding in scope (see Plates 18 and 19). There were eight brigades by 29 November, ten by

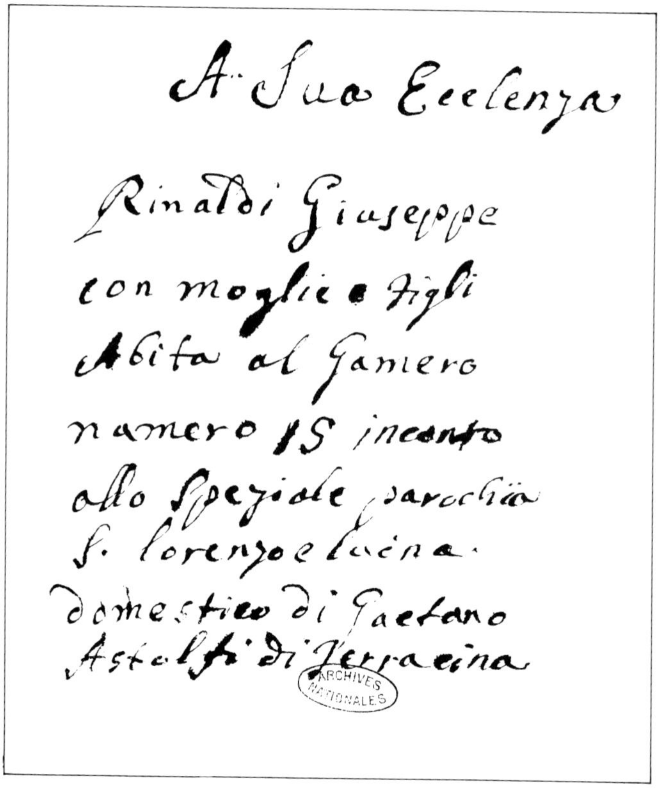
A Sua Eccelenza

Rinaldi Giuseppe
con moglie e figli
Abita al Ganiero
numero 15 inconto
allo Speziale parocchia
S. lorenzo e lucina.
domestico di Gaetano
Astolfi di Terracina

Plate 18 Petition for work by one of the unemployed (F le 137.1), directed to de Gérando. On the back is 'petition no. 3510'.

1 December, twelve by the 4th, thirteen by the 6th, and no fewer than fifteen by the 12th. Ovens were provided for the midday meals, to make them more economical. A doctor visited the workers twice a week to check for scabies and scurvy. He found seven or eight infected one morning and they were dismissed until cured. (One wonders how this was to be effected. Were they put under treatment?) The buildings blocking the Temple of Saturn were being demolished. Collicola boasted that there had already been much improvement for 'the eye of the lover of the beautiful', especially at the Temples of Antoninus and Faustina and of Saturn, while 'the eye of the man who is a friend of men' would rejoice at the improvement in the health of the workers.[34] Collicola was, like Tournon, deeply interested in the condition of the poor. Demolitions, however, became more urgent every day, as he warned de Gérando, for the 800 men had to be kept occupied. The Baron had other concerns. He told Tournon that it was time to total expenses so far, to check the way accounts had been kept, and to see if the architects had drawn up plans![35]

A fateful dispute began on 21 December. Collicola wrote to de Gérando

Plate 19 Achille Pinelli, *La beneficenza al Pincio.* What must have been the rather characteristic chaos of the working sites is superbly captured here, with some men digging, others carrying away debris in barrows, and others resting. Apparently a foreman, with book and cane, stands under the tree.

objecting to the presence of Carlo Lucangeli in the Colosseum, where he had 'no special superintendence' over works. He was simply one of the foremen of one hundred workers clearing the exterior, but he was breaking all the rules. De Gérando replied that Lucangeli was preparing a cork model of the building, a work 'of the greatest importance'. For this he had to examine the internal and subterranean structures. He had previously employed convicts; now he had to use the poor. Collicola answered that he wanted to make some private observations and de Gérando agreed to this, but told him to follow instructions in the meantime. Soon after, Collicola transferred to Monte di Pietà, and on 4 January 1811 de Gérando wrote to Ippolito Gérard, appointing him Collicola's successor.

Demolitions could no longer be postponed. The first five buildings considered were the monastery of S. Francesca, the houses in the Forum belonging to the church of S. Chiara di Gallese, the house of the Orientalist Fathers against the 'Temple of Fortune' in the Forum Boarium, the wooden structures on the Ponte Sisto belonging to the Marchese Massimi, and the granaries near the Colosseum owned by Sig. Diotallevi. On 28 December, the Consulta decreed that all be bought by the city and demolished.[36]

The endemic problem of shortage of money appeared for the first time in a more serious form in the same month. On 26 December, Mayor Braschi wrote to Tournon asking for at least 7,000 frs to pay the workers who were threatening a riot. A second letter on the same day told the Prefect bluntly that the government, not the municipality, had authorised the work.[37]

The new year revealed continuing problems with the organisation of the workers. One of the last reports of Collicola suggested a plan to reduce their number.[38] The country dwellers, he recommended, should be the first to be dismissed, having regard to those who could most easily make their living in the country but retaining the most useful. The brigades numbered sixteen, each of fifty men divided into squads of ten. Collicola suggested reducing the squads to three men, since smaller groups were easier to control. The total would thus be reduced from 800 to 240 men, not counting women and boys, corporals, foremen and soldiers.

In January we hear for the first time of the 'Commission du Rétablissement du Forum', of which Tournon was a member.[39] Work was concentrated on the Colosseum, the Temple of Antoninus and Faustina, the Capitol and the Forum Boarium. An alternative plan to reorganise the work-force was to reduce the number of brigades. They were to be reduced to eight, by dismissing two on each of 15 and 30 January and 15 and 28 February. The workers were to be told a week in advance and receive a week's rations. These decrees were signed by the Consulta. Reduction of expenses was obviously increasingly urgent. Tournon wrote at the end of January to Gérard, the new Inspector, explaining that Lezzani's commissions were too high. He received 2½ bajocchi per worker and 3½% of the total weekly wage bill. This was to be reduced to 1 bajocco per worker. Gérard was simply ordered to make a new contract on these terms.

We have, in fact, the weekly accounts of Lezzani from the time the work began, on 12 November, until the middle of January 1811:

	No. of brigades	Expenses
12–24 Nov. (1st and 2nd weeks)	6 then 7	632 scudi
26 Nov.–1 Dec. (3rd week)	10	768
3–7 Dec. (4th week)	13	651
10–15 Dec. (5th week)	15	930
17–22 Dec. (6th week)	16	1,124
24–9 Dec. (7th week)	16	1,310
31 Dec. –5 Jan. (8th week)	16	877
7–12 Jan. (9th week)	16	1,601
14–19 Jan. (10th week)	16	1,535

9,428 scudi = 50,440 frs.

With 800 men employed, the expenses could not be slight. One can only feel that the contractor, Lezzani, was profiting rather handsomely.[40] By April, his accounts from the beginning of work totalled 89,809 frs. The Consulta paid him 40,000, leaving the other half as a debt on the Municipality.[41]

At the beginning of May, Tournon sent Montalivet a plan of the Forum and two plans of Rome to illustrate the works proposed in the budget. The Parisian archives reveal a secret: within two months, Neuville, head of the third division of the Ministry of Interior, admitted to Montalivet that they had been lost as they were sent from department to department![42]

On 25 March 1811, Napoleon's son, the King of Rome, was born. The celebrations in the capital were finally organised by 8 June, and were very impressive:

A la nuit, tout le Capitole, le Forum, le Colisée furent illuminés et entourés d'une foule immense de spectateurs, qui, grâce aux travaux exécutés dans cette belle partie de Rome, pouvaient jouir de tout l'effet de ces antiques monuments, sortis des ruines qui les environnaient, et rendus plus brillants par le goût qui avait présidé à leur illumination. Le Colisée surtout attirait les regards par sa masse prodigieuse, et la hardiesse avec laquelle on en avait dessiné en traits de feu les formes majestueuses et la belle architecture. Les arcs de Septime, de Constantin, les temples d'Antonin et Faustine, de la Concorde [i.e. Saturn], de la Paix [the Basilica of Maxentius], les colonnes de Jupiter Stator [Castor and Pollux] éclairés avec le même discernement offraient un coup d'œil que peut présenter la seule ville de Rome.

So they were described by the most discerning observer, the Prefect himself.[43] The archaeological works could obviously already be used to great political advantage by the regime. This may, indeed, be the first use of such an archaeological setting in this way, the earliest use of 'Lumière', with the great crowd described by Tournon providing the 'Son', as they gasped in amazement at the illuminations.

Despite the excessive costs and the troubles with Paris, the excavations progressed so well that in July the two Architect Directors proposed to publish them, and who better equipped than themselves to do it? The plan was that each four months a fascicule of about nine pages of plans, sections and views would appear. That on the Temple of Antoninus and Faustina had, in fact, already been published. Like all vast enterprises, however, it needed government support. The architects proposed to Tournon that 200 copies be taken on standing order by the schools of Fine Arts.[44]

THE COMMISSION DES EMBELLISEMENTS, 1811

The whole scope and nature of the work in Rome were transformed by the imperial decree of 27 July, setting up a new commission. This decree laid down the main programmes in Rome for the rest of the French occupation. The projects and their budgets were as follows:

Navigation of the Tiber	100,000
Ponte Orazio	50,000
Ponte Sisto	50,000
Piazza di Traiano ⎫	
Piazza del Pantheon ⎭	50,000
Piazza del Popolo	150,000
Garden of the Capitol	100,000
Markets	50,000
Abattoirs	100,000
Botanical Garden	50,000
Reserve	300,000
	1,000,000 frs.

Although most of the budget was for town-planning and facilities, almost half the 700,000 francs allotted was devoted to archaeological or classical sites: the Garden of the Capitol, stretching from the Capitol through the Forum to the Colosseum, and the areas around the Column of Trajan and the Pantheon. What is immediately striking is how totally unrealistic were the sums assigned, as was to become immediately apparent. And where were the million francs to come from? Half was drawn from the 'Domaine Extraordinaire' and half from the Municipality.[45]

More importantly, whence came the inspiration for this list? The answer was discovered in 1927, when a letter of Tournon to Montalivet in July 1811 was published.[46] The young Prefect was, in fact, in Paris at the time. He had been given leave for his wedding with Mlle Adèle de Pancemont, and he left Rome on 27 June.[47] In his letter to his Minister, Tournon divided the necessary works into two categories: (i) restoration of ancient monuments; (ii) clearing and beautification.

For the first, the centre of attention was naturally the Forum. Tournon could point to great advances already made in clearing the Colosseum, the Temples of Antoninus and Faustina, of Saturn, of Vespasian, and of the two in the Forum Boarium. It was suggested that 100,000 frs could complete this work and occupy 600 workers for three months. Daru, Intendant de la Couronne in Rome, was noted as engaged in discovering works of art, not in restoration of monuments. As for the various projects for clearing the Forum to its ancient level, Tournon declared it flatly to be an impossibility; the monuments should be connected by 'an irregular promenade', which must include the Palatine. The cost of earth removal, filling and demolition would not exceed 100,000 frs and would provide work for two seasons (six winter months in all) for another 600 workers.

The other monuments suggested for attention by Tournon were the Forum of Nerva, the Column of Trajan, the Portico of Octavia, and the Porta

Maggiore. The portico and the column also came under the heading of beauti-fication, by opening up piazze.

Under his second heading, Tournon went on to list widening of roads (the approach to St Peter's, and from Naples through the Forum), cleaning the Tiber, a new fourth bridge across the river to be named after Horatius Cocles, abattoirs, markets, promenades (as well as the Forum and the Piazza del Popolo), and cemeteries. He finally explained his motives: not only the beautification of the second city of the Empire, but also the need to give work to those deprived of all sustenance by the suppression of the convents.[48]

The inspiration for the great imperial decree was therefore a report by the young Prefect, fortunately on leave in Paris for personal reasons and able to consult closely with the Minister of the Interior. At the same time we must recognise once again 'l'énorme surcroît de labeur que pareil pro-gramme allait ajouter à une administration déjà écrasante'.[49]

The contribution of Tournon, however, answers the question of inspiration for the Embellisements in only the most immediate sense. What those who have paid attention to these schemes so far have quite overlooked is a more universal rationale. Rome was, of course, to be the 'second city' of the Empire. That was rhetoric and romanticism. The real purpose is revealed by compar-ing parallel schemes of public works in Paris:

Pour Napoléon les travaux ont une autre utilité: donner aux Français des hôpitaux, des abattoirs, des fontaines, des marchés, des rues plus larges, des places plus vastes, des ponts plus nombreux, c'est manifester l'intérêt du Gouvernement, les attacher au régime et compenser par les facilités accrues de la vie, toutes les libertés dont il les privait et les sacrifices militaires qu'il leur imposait.[50]

The correspondences are remarkable. Hardly a word need be changed save 'Romans' for 'French' to put the Embellisements in their true light. The list of public works is almost identical with those proposed in Rome, and no subject population felt more politically alienated than the Romans whose head of state had been kidnapped and for whom, after that, the most resented aspect of the occupation was precisely the 'military sacrifices' imposed by conscription.

By the last day of July Tournon informed Montalivet that copies of the decree were in his hands and that projects were being drawn up. He thought that the first operations should be the Jardin du Grand César (400 workers), demolitions on the Palatine, and clearing of the Forum Romanum and Forum Boarium (another 400). On 4 August, he wrote again. Demolitions were to begin immediately with the Convento del Popolo and the convent of S. Bonaventura on the Palatine. By 16 August four work-sites were to be estab-lished, each employing 200 people: the Basilica of Maxentius, the Arch of Janus, the Colosseum, and the Forum Boarium. These groups were to be augmented so that by October there would be 2,000 workers in companies of 100 and brigades of ten. The rates of pay laid down were, for men 1.25 frs per day, for women 75 centimes, for boys 50. They were to provide their own tools, but to receive 'une soupe économique'. This letter was, in fact, a decree drafted for sending on to Rome. It is marked 'approuvé' and signed by Montalivet. At the same time, Tournon made an interesting admission: he was anxious to begin work on Napoleon's birthday (15 August). No sooner said than done! Another decree of the same date, 4 August, laid down that on 15 August at midday, the Mayor and Councillors and a detachment of gendarmes were to proceed to the Forum and Palatine, to read the Emperor's decree, and to take possession of those buildings and land which now belonged to the city.[51] Here are all the grand hopes for the beginning of the great archaeological campaigns in Rome. It was soon to be discovered that even one million francs for all these projects was only a fraction of the cost. And despite Tournon's hopes for a ceremonially appropriate beginning for the work on 15 August, it did not commence until 28 September, after his return from Paris. We may justly suspect that, without the Prefect's intelligence and zeal, little could be done.

The meetings of the new Commission are preserved in the first register of its records in the Archivio dello Stato in Rome. At the first, on Tuesday, 17 September 1811, two of the three members were absent. Marini represented the still-absent Tournon, Gabrielli attended for Mayor Braschi, but Martial Daru was present. They drew up a list of staff:

an accountant	1,200 frs per annum
a secretary	600
an Inspector (Pietro Fortuna)	1,800
two architects (Camporese and Valadier)	80 per month
a surgeon for the workers' health	600 per annum.

At the very next meeting, the derisory pay of the architects was raised to 200 frs per month, and Fortuna was replaced as Inspector by Giulio Camporese, the architect's son.[52] It was decided to meet every Monday at 7 p.m. at the Prefecture. Giulio Camporese was given 10,000 frs to pay the workers and was directed to submit a daily and a weekly report. On 28 October, a basic division of competence was suggested between the two architects: Valadier was to supervise the Jardin du Grand César, while Camporese had control of the Jardin du Capitole. This division was not observed in practice.

Camporese and Valadier reported to Principe Gabrielli on 5 October on the slowness and inexperience of the workers, and the difficulty of fixing a rate of pay (see Plate 20). To avoid unrest, it had been decided to pay a daily rate, but only for that week; from next week the pay would be, as resolved, by the cubic metre of earth removed (*a cottimo*).[53] Tournon was, in fact, reproved by Montalivet for paying 1.25 frs per day together with soup, because workers in Rome usually received 1 fr. Under these circumstances, all other public works had been unable to attract labour. He

Plate 20 Angelo Uggeri, *Vues pittoresques*, workers of the Commission des
Embellisements (detail of Plate 49). The characteristic methods of work are
shown: the man with a barrow, the woman and child with a basket, all carrying
away the excavated debris, in this case from the Forum of Trajan. Note that
the woman, as well as her own basket, supports a babe in arms, not to mention
the child by her side.

demanded that the pay be 'modified' and that Tournon explain his motives.[54]
The traps for the young, well-meaning Prefect were manifold. The detested
Janet had informed on Tournon, who replied to his Minister that the pay-rate
had been approved by him and that only the best workers received as much,
which was in fact less than could be gained even in the fields.[55]

Sustenance for the workers was another problem. They were given the
famous soup at lunch-time. The furnisher of this, Antonio Quattrochi,
charged 1½ bajocchi per plate, and claimed that the servings were not small.
There had been some delay in the service, for which he was penalised, but
he affirmed that the soup was of the best quality. Valadier would attest that.

The major concern was, of course, money, as it had been with the old
Commission des Monuments. By November, 26,190 frs had been spent. The
Mayor received 10,000 frs to pay the workers on 3 December, the same
on 11 December, and 20,000 on 20 December. No wonder: by the end of
October there were 700 workers, by 12 November, 1,000.[56]

In 1812, on 7 January and again on the 21st, another 20,000 frs were
paid out. Montalivet received accounts, showing that up to 8 January, 91,000
out of the first 200,000 frs allotted had been spent, and that now 1,500
workers were busy. Tournon asked for another 200,000 frs on 7 January

and again on 1 February.[57] At the meeting of the Commission on 8 February, it was admitted that excavations so far, in the Forum Boarium, Temple of Antoninus and Faustina, Basilica of Maxentius and at the Arch of Janus, had used a considerable part of the 100,000 frs allotted for the Jardin du Capitole. Eight hundred workers were employed here. On the same day, Montalivet announced a further grant of 200,000, making a total of 400,000 frs.[58] Two days later, Tournon sent to Paris the lists of acquisitions indispensable for the two 'Gardens' and the Forum of Trajan, with plans and a corresponding key. Prices had been agreed upon already between the Mayor and the owners, in accordance with the architects' estimates. The Prefect asked for urgent approval. The total cost was 367,691 frs.

Increases in costs by the end of February, in fact, necessitated some forward planning, 'tableaux de répartition des exercices 1811–1812'.[59]

Allotted July 1811		Already spent	Needed to complete
Jardin du Capitole	100,000	134,523	165,476
Forum of Trajan	50,000	15,021	124,978

The original estimates were thus shown to be seriously short.

On 6 March, Tournon informed Montalivet that the first 200,000 frs had been spent. On the same day Braschi told the Prefect that funds to pay the workers were exhausted and that there was danger of 'grave disorder'.[60] Where were the other 200,000 already approved by Montalivet?

Nature then intervened. At 3.15 a.m. on 22 March, disaster struck. The most severe earthquake of the century hit Rome, registering 7–8 on the scale. Part of the Colosseum collapsed, and many churches and palaces were damaged. The work of care for the classical remains was enormously increased, with the burden falling especially on the Accademia di S. Luca.[61]

In March, Montalivet had been sent the plans for the Jardin du Grand César and for the Jardin du Capitole. Tournon then received the surprising and doubtless frustrating demand that all plans were to be submitted in various colours, with letters and numbers corresponding to the legend. Once again the bureaucrats in Paris, who knew nothing of Rome save what they had learned at school, could not follow the plans. And what was happening to the vast sums of money allotted? The explanation for this brusqueness is revealed, as usual, by the Parisian archives. Neuville had written to Montalivet admitting that he could not understand the plans and wickedly suggesting that a great deal of money was involved.[62]

Scandal was, in fact, looming in Rome. At its meeting on 7 April, the Commission discussed the finding that some workers were missing at roll-call and that six company chiefs had been sacked. It is obviously not unconnected that a week later the Commission announced that Giulio Camporese had resigned as Inspector and had been replaced by Clemente Giardini.[63] The new Inspector issued strict instructions for the foremen and corporals. The first is amusing: that all workers were to be 'active'; dead men were excluded under any pretext! Second, no replacements were allowed after the formation of the squads each Monday. Third, the hours of work were to be publicly displayed, so that everyone knew them. Fourth, lateness of up to one hour meant the loss of one-third of a day's pay for foremen and corporals and a quarter for others. After one hour, the worker was not admitted. Fifth, foremen and corporals had to have written permission to be absent.[64] It is obvious that there had been considerable corruption over the pay sheets. Giulio Camporese had at the least been held guilty of lack of strict supervision.

Tournon replied to the questions from Paris about the spending of the million francs for 1812, which now became important. He admitted that nothing had so far been spent on the navigation of the Tiber, the bridge of Horatius, the abattoirs and markets (although the plans had been submitted) or the botanical garden. The Forum of Trajan, allotted 50,000 frs, had already taken 125,000 and would need another 75,000.[65] He began to become desperate, or exasperated. Montalivet was demanding plans of the Jardin du Capitole before acquisitions could be approved but plans for the Forum of Trajan had been sent months before and had not yet been approved.[66] Montalivet replied that he had approved expenditure to a total of 440,000 frs, and was alarmed that the million francs allotted each year was not being spent in accordance with the imperial decree, especially since Tournon estimated that an additional 75,000 frs were needed for the Forum of Trajan.[67] Meanwhile, on 19 May, the Commission had assigned another 26,566 frs to pay the workers.

It is from the middle of 1812 that a striking evocation of the Forum was provided by Tournon. Out of a population of 120,000, 13,000 families were registered for charity, mainly employees of the old papal government. 'On voit des peintres, des hommes de loi, des marchands aux travaux du Forum, gagnant, la pioche à la main, 16 sous par jour.'[68]

By 1 July, the two main archaeological projects had cost, for the Jardin du Capitole, 203,105 frs with another 196,894 needed, and for the Forum of Trajan, 40,647, with another 84,352 needed.[69] Writing to Montalivet on 20 July, Tournon announced that the million francs for 1811 were now spent. The new million for 1812 would be spent as follows:

Jardin du Capitole: 100,000 frs (only 200,000 of the 300,000 allotted had been spent)
Jardin du Grand César: 50,000 would complete it
Forum of Trajan: 75,000
acquisition of land and buildings: 250,000 (out of total needed 379,000)
enlarging the approach to St Peter's: 100,000
Tiber navigation: 100,000

the piazza of the Fontana Trevi: 50,000
Piazza del Pantheon: 100,000.[70]

The suspicions aroused in Paris about money not being spent in accordance
with imperial wishes, compounded by ignorance of the topography and distance, were nothing compared to the frontal attack in Rome made by Martial
Daru, one of the three Commissioners. In August he wrote to the Commission
complaining about 'ill-advised projects' which had been ridiculed by the public. He approved of the clearing of the Pantheon, the Piazza Trevi, the widening of the Corso by the demolition of part of the Palazzo Venezia, the
cemeteries, abattoirs and markets. He did not approve, on the other hand,
of 'precipitous gardens' ('jardins escarpés'), and was supported by another
member of the Commission (since there were only three this could only
be Braschi), by Montalivet and the Commission des Bâtiments in Paris (with
both of whom he must have been in contact). How many years would be
needed before the plantations disguised the irregularity of the gardens? Daru
then turned to the Jardin du Grand César, where more than 1,000 workers
had been employed for months, he claimed, making a garden most contemporaries would never enjoy. He similarly objected to the Jardin du Capitole
in 'an unhealthy quarter where no one will go'. Nothing was more important,
he admitted, than clearing the ancient monuments, but they should not be
masked with palisades and plantations.[71]

Tournon had other more practical concerns always before him. When
money was not available to pay the workers, what was to be done? General
Miollis told him that he heartily approved of the device to which he was
now compelled to resort, namely forcing the Municipal Treasurer to advance
60,000 frs on the 100,000 promised by Montalivet. The Municipality, after
all, was supposed to contribute half the costs. And with 800 workers
employed, the weekly pay could amount to 7,000 frs.[72]

So much work depended on demolitions. At the end of September, Tournon
was still begging Montalivet for approval of those submitted in February.
Of the 367,691 frs total, 82,532 would suffice for this season's work in the
Forum of Trajan, 121,361 on the Palatine, and 50,000 in the Forum Romanum.[73] The same month Montalivet authorised another 100,000 frs, but
Tournon, in acknowledging it, informed the Minister that more than half
had to be paid to the Municipality to cover advances made as far back
as 1810 and that after paying the workers what was owed them, there was
not enough left to cover the month.[74] Despite the financial crisis, it was
still proposed at the end of November to add two new companies of workers.
The situation could not be allowed to continue as it was. Montalivet seemed
finally to have realised that Tournon needed help. He informed him that
100,000 frs was to be constantly at his disposal from the 500,000 due from
the Domaine Extraordinaire for 1812.[75] And then perhaps the most bizarre

episode of all came to light. It was realised that although the Domaine had paid its 500,000 frs share for 1811, the Municipality, to which the Commission had been busily repaying advances and thus consuming its funds, had paid only 100,000 frs of its share. And it was now almost the end of 1812!

Two interesting letters crossed on 5 December. Montalivet finally approved the demolitions requested to a value of 367,691 frs, to come out of the million for 1812. (The grant for the year could clearly not cover any such vast expense.) The details were as follows:

Forum of Trajan	77,216
Palatine Garden	121,361
Forum	91,891
Colosseum	21,865
Forum Boarium	46,539
Piazza del Popolo	8,815
	367,691 frs.[76]

Tournon, on the other hand, wrote to say that the Commission had only 5,000 frs in the treasury, despite a request for another 100,000 on 23 October. Not even the approach of Christmas helped. On 8 December, the Commission told the treasurer to authorise payments, since it was a time of the year when the workers should be able to rely on the Emperor's munificence. The 20,000 frs owing at the end of the month was again temporarily covered by the Municipality.[77]

Clearly 1812 was a year of deepening crisis, as it was discovered that the funds allotted for each project were for the most part utterly inadequate and as Tournon fought to keep the work progressing and, more importantly, the poor in pay. He was being obstructed by an unwilling Municipality, which was not paying the contribution laid down by the imperial decree, and being betrayed by the other member of the commission, Daru, who was denouncing the work in Paris. No wonder that the Ministry there with its many divisions of bureaucrats decided to send out two agents to investigate the work of the Embellisements on the spot.

THE YEAR OF THE VISIT, 1813

On 12 December 1812 Montalivet informed Tournon that the Conseil des Bâtiments Civils could not decide about the great garden projects except on the spot. Two experts would therefore be sent to Rome. Guy Gisors, commended for his ability to reconcile grandeur with economy, was to review plans for the Pantheon, the Forum of Trajan, and the cemeteries, abattoirs and markets. Louis Berthault was described as very skilled in decorating pleasure gardens: he was the creator of Malmaison and was working on Compiègne. Both were to be put in touch with Roman artists. They would stay about six weeks. Montalivet in a postscript admitted the great embarrassment in his Conseil, since the members had to rely on 'ancient memories' of Rome.[78] More than one reputation was to be broken over this visit and the havoc created retarded the completion of many projects, so that the French never completed them.

The instructions for Gisors were very extensive. He was to see especially to the demolitions and the stability of monuments; to the cost of the Piazza del Pantheon (Tournon had sent the plans on 2 April 1812 without estimates) and the Forum of Trajan (what was happening with the demolition of the two convents?) and to the cost of demolition at all sites.

Tournon thanked Montalivet for sending the two men. (These seem to be his real feelings.) He had told Denon, when in Paris in 1811, of the need for an architect skilled in garden work. He admitted that considerations of economy did not always accord with the 'unrestrained grandeur' of the Roman architects, who did not always give a clear idea of what was to be undertaken, but only wanted to make their name with large projects. They gave free rein to their imagination. Gisors and Berthault would have to be on guard against this desire for the immense.[79] One may imagine what Camporese or Valadier would have thought had they seen these charges. Who was promoting these immense projects if not the French administration? Had Tournon fallen out with the architects? Or was he feeling so threatened or exhausted that, for once, he would use others to shield himself?

The plans had one slight drawback. Gisors was to reveal in his report on the Pantheon that he did not know Italian, and there is no reason to believe that Berthault was in a better situation. The bureaucrats in Paris complained that they could not follow the plans of a city they had never seen, so sent two experts who did not understand the language spoken there!

Berthault arrived on 5 February, and Gisors on the 14th. By 23 February, Gisors had already prepared his report on the Forum of Trajan,[80] but at the end of March Berthault was complaining that his work was taking much longer than he had anticipated. He had to make three copies of each plan; luckily he had four artists to help, whom he had brought with him. He would need another two months' leave, in addition to the two and a half granted. On 25 March, however, he issued his long report on the Jardin du Capitole.[81]

Characteristic of Gisors' mentality was a 'request' for information to Tournon. He suggested that demolitions required a report for each site in seven columns: houses to buy, those already bought, those paid for, those demolished, those under demolition, their present condition, and finally 'observations'. For material recovered, four columns would suffice: description of materials, quantity, price obtained, 'observations'. And for material in store, four columns: description, quantity, value, 'observations'. Furnishings of convents and churches, however, were more complicated – perhaps six columns: description, quantity, use, price obtained, value of items unsold, and the inevitable 'observations'.[82] One may imagine how Tournon, moving heaven and earth just to pay workers, reacted to this.

Gisors himself made a long report on the demolitions.[83] Montalivet, it will be remembered, had only in December approved demolitions to a value of 367,691 frs. Acquisitions of these buildings so far totalled a little more: 371,647 frs. Gisors was horrified to discover, however, that of this sum, only 18,271 frs had been paid to the owners. He was furthermore particularly concerned at the small returns from the sale of materials, and suspected Giardini's predecessor as Inspector (Giulio Camporese) of dishonesty. Again his mentality is fully revealed: he uselessly repeats documents and is obsessed with figures. How many cubic metres of earth had been dug out and cleared away until 1 April 1813? The stunning answer is 208,065.04. And how much had been paid in wages? A total of 491,909 frs 54 centimes. Gisors was then able to do a wicked sum. He divided the wages by the cubic metres and discovered that the cost per cubic metre had been not 1 franc or 1.25 francs, but 2.36 francs.

Before he left in May, Gisors made recommendations in two reports for far-reaching changes in the organisation of the Embellisements.[84] The two highest-paid members were the two architects, receiving 2,400 frs. Next came Clemente Giardini, the Inspector, paid 1,800 frs. Gisors stressed that he was not an architect, but made up for this professional shortcoming by his intelligence and zeal. He should be placed, Gisors recommended, in charge of administration and accounts. The Controller of Works should be a French architect who knew Italian (Gisors was obviously not to be an applicant). This man's tasks were to watch that the architects did not change plans approved by the Commission, to see that those plans were carried out, and to ensure that the architects behaved with 'zeal and integrity'. The architects, by contrast, were to be concerned with drawing up plans, always following the orders of the Commission, and assisted by 'hommes de bâtiments', not Italian counts and marquises as was the case. Between the architects and the contractors were to be inspectors. It is obvious that the main point of these recommendations was to institute stricter controls over the architects.

As for the labourers, Gisors was concerned that their wages should represent their various rates of work. The more difficult tasks were to be reserved for the stronger men, who would earn more. And the removal of debris could be improved by working in 20 m sections in relays, instead of sections of varying length. Gisors was also anxious to avoid injury to the women, by their being hit by the wheelbarrows. The carts taking away the rubbish should be identified by some sign, and a system of cards was to be used by controllers at the pick-up and delivery points, so that the trips made could be checked each day. Each company of seventy-five men, ten women and nine boys, with an overseer and six corporals should be able to clear

nearly 60 cu m each day, Gisors claimed. It is obvious that the French visitor
believed that he had found many possibilities at least for corruption and
incompetence.

   All these suggestions were approved by the Conseil des Bâtiments in Paris
– but too late. On 10 May, Gisors left Rome[85] and Berthault departed
about 20 May.[86] On 10 June, Tournon informed Montalivet that Gisors
had requested 5,000 frs towards his expenses, and Berthault 10,000. The
Commission des Embellisements approved these sums.[87] On the same day,
Montalivet wrote to Tournon that he should pay them 6,000 frs each. The
letter, of course, arrived too late.

   And here begins one of the most fascinating sagas in the whole story of
the French work in Rome, never before told, perhaps because of its scandalous
nature. On 5 December, Berthault submitted his total expenses for reimbursement:

travel	3,947
board for himself and an assistant (14 Jan.–14 June)	5,250[88]
salary for three artists at 300 frs per month	3,250
office expenses	500
hire of carriage in Rome	800
plans finished in Paris after his return	6,000
	19,747 frs

of which 10,000 had already been paid by Tournon.

   Gisors was called in by the Conseil des Bâtiments to assist and investigate.
His report to the Conseil is dated 27 March 1815. The travel expenses turned
out to be highly inflated. The ordinary route from Paris to Rome and return
was 445 posts, not 581: 2,673 frs instead of 3,486. And the horses cost 1.5 frs,
not 4.5: 105 frs instead of 315. In all, the total was 2,920 frs instead of 3,947
for travel. As for board, Gisors approved the 5,250 frs. Berthault did indeed
employ three artists in Rome, but their salary was too high. Gisors suggested
250 frs per month, giving 2,775 frs. Office expenses were approved, but the
carriage costs were inflated: 600 frs would suffice. The grand total should
therefore have been 12,045 frs rather than 19,737; for the 6,000 frs claimed
for the plans should have been taken out of the honorarium.

   It was in connection with the last that Berthault made his fatal mistake.
On 2 May 1815 he claimed an honorarium of 41,004 [sic] frs. This made,
be it noted, a total claim by Berthault of 60,000 frs! Gisors was again consulted. He suggested that 18,000 frs would be sufficient for the honorarium,
with the cost of the plans being covered by it.

   The Ministry of the Interior described the claim of 60,000 frs as 'exorbitant'. Expenses were paid according to the time spent, not the importance
of the project. It was even suggested that the main ideas for improvements

came from Gisors and that the drawings Berthault valued so highly did not require much effort. It was concluded that he should be paid 14,703 frs (in toto?). By the end of May Berthault knew that all was not well. He was writing to Maulnoir, Chef du Bureau des Bâtiments Civils, complaining that although he had often tried to see this man, the porter had strict instructions not to admit him. He begged again for payment of the honorarium and to be allowed to see Maulnoir to know what was happening.

Much was happening, and had already happened. A report of the Bâtiments Civils in August 1815 told the story so far: that in March they accepted Gisors' revision of the expenses, reducing them to 12,045 frs, but that his suggestion of 18,000 for the honorarium should be reduced to 16,000, making a total of 28,045 frs. Now, however, everything was to be further scaled down, on the grounds that Berthault had claimed for much that had been provided for him in Rome by Tournon:

travel	2,920
lodging	2,775
honorarium	16,000
	21,695
	− 10,000 already received
	11,695 frs.

Not only had there been a two-thirds reduction in Berthault's claim, but the payment was not forthcoming. He began writing plaintive letters. A change in the Ministry (Montalivet's resignation) produced new delays. On 8 March 1816 the Ministry made further reductions:

travel	2,670 plus 257
the three artists	2,775
lodging in Rome (105 days at 50 frs)	5,250
lodging en route (165 days at 25 frs)	4,125
	15,077 frs.

This was justified by the observation that Berthault received a salary as government architect at Compiègne; he could not claim loss of work, because acceptance of a government post meant the renunciation of other work. Berthault was informed of the new assessment on 19 March. He replied on 15 April, complaining that his carriage expenses had been omitted and that a carriage was essential in Rome's hot climate (he had been there, we may note from February to May). What piqued him most, it seems, was that his daily allowance was the same as architects attached to the Ministry: what a dishonour! Was he to be out of pocket by his mission for the government, and all his projects come to nothing as well?

The final letter in the dossier is the reply of the Minister, le Comte de

Vaublanc. It was stated that the number of posts from Paris to Rome is 221 (the Inspector-General had made the same journey). The cost of the carriage was omitted because Berthault had been paid 50 frs a day expenses, when the usual allowance was 35 frs. No change would be made to these decisions, Berthault was finally and firmly informed, because otherwise all architects sent on such missions would protest. No one had ever been more favourably treated than he.

One may assume therefore that he was finally paid the 5,077 frs outstanding, receiving thus just one quarter of what he had claimed. This is an astounding story, which the twentieth century will well understand. Modern parallels of inflated claims for expenses, especially when on government missions, are not unknown to us. Modern treasuries and taxation departments are equally as relentless as the Bâtiments Civils were when they scent a fraud.

There is one final irony. At some later date, Berthault asked permission to show the precious drawings and plans, for which he claimed such high recompense, to the Emperor of Austria, Franz I. He promised to return them within a few days. Permission was obviously granted. They have not been seen since.

TIME RUNS OUT

We must return to the more mundane narrative of the last year of French rule in Rome, the other side of 1813.

To open the new year, Tournon reported to Montalivet on 6 January. The main task of 1812 had been the Basilica of Maxentius. Part of the convent of S. Francesca had been demolished, and the garden made between the Colosseum and the Basilica. The Temple of Vespasian had been cleared, but work on the Tabularium was still in progress. Demolitions in the Forum of Trajan were complete.[89] The 100,000 frs promised by the Minister in November, however, had still not arrived, and the Municipality was still covering the wages. Montalivet approved a further 210,000 frs on 11 January.[90]

The next month, Daru made further criticisms of the Commission. He proposed many reforms in the recording of meetings and criticised wasted effort and insufficient attention to what was useful and necessary, as usual. The Jardin du Grand César and the demolitions were special objects of his criticism.[91]

As always, Tournon's main concern was paying the workers. On 6 March, he told Montalivet that the treasury of the Commission contained only 8,345 frs. Although he had received a draft for 160,000 frs at the end of January, he needed now another 200,000. He was still begging for this a month later.

The endless need for money caused alarm in Paris. On 7 April, the Minister directed Tournon to send the accounts as specified in November, with a separate sheet for each work-site. At the same time, Montalivet attempted his sums. Approving a further 200,000 frs, he claimed that the 910,000 spent so far did not add up:

Jardin du Capitole	296,622
Jardin du Grand César	147,138
Forum of Trajan	79,199
markets	4,638
wages	49,253
Tiber navigation	63,000
garden work	53,718
acquisition of houses	26,000
cemeteries	93,983
	813,554 instead of 910,000 frs.

Tournon was fortunately able to set the record straight. He had forgotten some delayed payments, notably 100,000 for the Ponts et Chaussées. Far from having 100,000 frs credit, the members of the Commission had been forced to borrow 60,000 frs on their personal credit.[92] Expenses for May were 56,332 frs.

On 12 April and 28 May, Montalivet approved a further 140,000 and 150,000 frs respectively from the Domaine Extraordinaire. Thus while the Domaine had paid its 500,000 frs share for 1811 and already paid 290,000 for 1812, it was again noted that the Municipality had contributed only 200,000 in 1811 and 60,000 frs so far for 1812. The Treasurer informed Tournon that the Municipal Treasury was bankrupt, owing to expenses for cavalry, advances to prisons, and the payment of 474,783 frs to the Caisse du Service, for which repayment although due had been refused.[93]

On 15 June, in conformity with the recommendations of Gisors (the two visitors had now left Rome), Pietro Bianchi, the architect famous for his collaboration with Lorenzo Re in the Colosseum arena debate,[94] was taken on as temporary Controller of Works with a salary of 2,400 frs, the same as the two architects. Within two months, for his 'zeal', he was made permanent. Expenses for June were 39,962 frs.

Payment of 32,423 frs for houses in the Forum Romanum and Forum of Trajan was approved by the Commission at its meeting on 13 July. Expenses for August were 58,093 frs. Paying the workers continued to be critical. The Commission decided again at the end of September to compel the Municipal Treasury to lend 20,000 frs. The Treasurer refused, because he had no authorisation. Tournon was instructed by the Commission to obtain 25,000 frs with the loan being personally guaranteed by the members. Montalivet was to be informed to what lengths they had been pushed. Workers at this time still numbered nearly 1,000.[95]

The situation improved markedly in October, when the Caisse du Service repaid 250,000 frs of its borrowing from the Municipal Treasury, and expenses for the month fell to 40,011 frs. The Ministry of the Imperial Treasury in Paris wrote a very strong letter to Tournon, reproving him for the improper measures adopted to obtain funds for the Commission. Montalivet intervened as well: 'Je regrette que vous ayez été forcé d'employer ce moyen contrairement aux règles établies. Je ne puis trop vous inviter à régulariser le plutôt possible toute l'opération.'[96] We can only be amazed at the bureaucratic fantasy of such people and their total incomprehension that what was at stake was not some administrative nicety but the subsistence of nearly 1,000 poor, who were only awaiting pay for work they had already carried out. Tournon replied that the total debts of the Commission by early November were 136,421 frs and that this could be covered by the 170,000 frs still owed by the Municipality from 1811. Expenses for December were 33,389 frs.

The last weeks approached. On 10 January 1814 Montalivet calmly assigned another 200,000 frs. The totals paid were now as follows:

1811:	500,000	from the Domaine Extraordinaire
	330,000	from the Municipality
1812:	380,000	from the Domaine Extraordinaire
	60,000	from the Municipality.

And now a further 200,000 frs.[97] In total, therefore, out of two million francs allotted over the two years, less than one and a half million francs had been paid out, although the Domaine had contributed its share.

Just four days after this last payment was authorised, the French administration fell before the coup of Joachim Murat.

'LA SICUREZZA DE' MONUMENTI, ANZI LA LORO
INTEGRALE ESISTENZA RIPOSA IN LEI':
THE ACCADEMIA DI S. LUCA AND THE MONUMENTS

The main lines of the Commission des Embellisements as told above are relatively well known. The other two thirds of the story are not.

Early in the French administration, in February 1810, Baron de Gérando of the Consulta wrote to Vincenzo Camuccini, the painter and at that time Principe of the Accademia di S. Luca, announcing that a commission of nine was to be established to look after the ancient monuments and advise on the export of works of art.[98] This was plainly the Commission des Monuments which was, in fact, established in July of that year. Although members of the Accademia would have expected to play a considerable role in this

Commission, they can have had no idea of just how fundamental the Accademia's responsibilities were soon to be.

On 6 November 1810, by imperial decree from Fontainebleau, it was decreed that the Accademia should be properly housed by December and that

Il lui sera donné en toute propriété un revenu de cent mille francs sur les biens du domaine dans le département du Tibre. Sur ces 100,000 francs, 25,000 francs seront spécialement affectés au service et à l'entretien de l'Académie et 75,000 francs aux réparations des Monumens d'Architecture antique, sous la surveillance de Notre Intendant de Rome. Nos Ministres de l'Intérieur et des Finances et Notre Intendant Général de la Couronne sont chargés de l'exécution du présent Décret.[99]

The maintenance of the Accademia meant notably the payment of salaries. The Intendant who was to have 'surveillance' of the decree was the Intendant des Biens de la Couronne, Martial Daru, who arrived in Rome in March 1811. The division of the execution of the decree among three important ministers in Paris was to be the source of endless confusion.[100]

The new statutes of the Accademia set out its composition, meetings, chairs, students and competitions, models and beadles, care of ancient monuments, endowment and expenses.[101] It is the sixth section which interests us, in six clauses: the Council of the Accademia was to look after ancient monuments and see to their preservation. It was to nominate an architect to report on all monuments and advise repairs. A commission was to verify the reports and authorise repairs. The architect's report was to include drawings and estimated costs. Each month he was also to report on the work and expenses, and separate accounts were to be kept. The Secretary was to keep a special archive for drawings, reports and decisions. As events were to show, however, the main burden of responsibility was to fall on the Principe of the Academy, Antonio Canova (Plate 21).

At the time of the imperial decree Canova was fifty-three years of age. His fame was already such that in his twenties he had been commissioned to sculpt the funerary statues of Clement XIII and XIV and had made a portrait of Napoleon during a visit to Paris in 1802. The same year he had been appointed Inspector-General of Fine Arts and Superintendent of the Vatican and Capitoline Museums. He had just finished his famous portrait of Pauline Bonaparte, and under the French was to be Director of Museums and Principe of the Accademia di S. Luca.

By May 1811 Daru, at least, was occupied around the Colosseum, the Temple of Vespasian and in the Forum Boarium. Because some of this work was restoration, the Accademia was probably involved. Daru also proposed to Canova that work should begin on the Domus Aurea. The same month Valadier reported to Tournon on repairs needed for the Pantheon and on 2 June the Accademia voted nineteen to six to demolish the campanili.[102]

As with the work of the various commissions, a major concern was finance.

Plate 21   Antonio Canova (1757–1822), by Thomas Lawrence, 1816.

Payment of the direction of the excavation and restoration absorbed most of it. Daru proposed that two architect directors were not needed. He suggested a much reduced staff, costing 350 frs per month rather than 842. Camporese and Valadier were thus alienated, and on 23 June 1811 both tendered their resignation. Daru favoured keeping on Camporese for the Accademia's work on the Pantheon and the Temple of Vespasian.[103] The architects must have been induced to withdraw these resignations, for from July they made regular reports to the Accademia.

The finances of the Accademia began to take shape, at least on paper. On 12 June, at St Cloud, it was decreed that it should have the rent of forty-two houses and 410 other properties, which were to provide an annual income of 101,473 frs 69 centimes from 1 January 1811.[104] The reality was not quite so simple.

By July, the major contributions of the Accademia were under way: the reconstruction of the Temple of Vespasian, and important repairs to the

Colosseum and Pantheon.[105] In fact, in August Camporese and Valadier compiled a list of all monuments under the care of the Accademia, classified according to the urgency of the work. There were eighty-eight in Rome alone! They included six obelisks, four theatres, twenty-two temples, nine baths, three aqueducts, one villa, eight arches, three tombs, three columns, two circuses, seven bridges, one palace, three porticoes, the Cloaca Maxima, the Pyramid of Cestius, and the ancient walls.[106]

At the same time, the Accademia began taking over the properties ceded to it by the Domaine.[107] The major problem for the Accademia appeared, however. Daru wrote to say that it was responsible for repairs to ancient monuments from 1 January. The 4,500 francs borrowed for these from the Royal Treasury had now to be repaid. The Accademia generously accepted this responsibility, but noted that not all excavations were relevant to repairs and cited the example of the Temple of Vespasian.[108] The ubiquitous contractor, Andrea Lezzani, was also claiming payment, and Pasquale Belli, Camporese and Valadier were commissioned to investigate whether these expenses fell within the time and competence of the Accademia.

Daru again harassed Canova in October, claiming that there was no cause for delay in payment of workers, since the Accademia's money had been available since January. The Principe replied bluntly that requests to the Director of the Domaine for the payment of the monies due to the Accademia had not even been answered. Second, the 75,000 frs were for the repair of ancient monuments, not for building retaining walls, drains and roads or for the supply of soup to workers. Of Lezzani's expenses for May and June, totalling 9,961 frs, only 3,171 was the Accademia's share. Of Inspector Giardini's expenses, 1,047 frs, only 664 fell to the Accademia, and 642 had already been paid. The meeting of the Accademia on 17 November complained of Daru's daily sending of creditors to be paid. Again it was determined to reply that they were not liable for expenses of the Beneficenza. On receipt of a written order justifying the amounts, the Accademia offered to pay what it could from the money in its account.[109]

Something also seems to have soured the relations of Camporese and Valadier with the Accademia. Academicians Andrea Vici, Virginio Bracci and Pasquale Belli were deputed to check regularly the diligence and exactness of the two architects in the direction of repairs. Such control of the architects was set out in the Accademia's statute, but it was proposed to reduce the two architect directors to one. Both wrote to Canova protesting. This, they assured him, had nothing to do with the poor pay they received: they were motivated by their 'love and enthusiasm' for the monuments, and had been busy for two years without fault and underpaid. The number of monuments under the Accademia's care made two architects a necessity. Their salary was absorbed by their travelling expenses alone.[110]

By the end of the year, the Accademia had spent 16,380 frs on restoration of monuments: 6,724 for the Temple of Vespasian; 6,259 on the Colosseum; 909 on the Pantheon; 17 on the obelisk in the Piazza Navona; 1,070 paid to Lezzani, and 1,400 to the architects.[111]

The great earthquake on 21–2 March 1812 only increased the Accademia's burdens, notably in the Portico of Octavia and the Basilica of Maxentius. Repairs in the wake of this, in fact, occupied much of 1812. The Accademia wrote to the Commission des Embellisements asking for material for these. Giardini replied they would have to pay for it, with six months' grace. Daru at least offered what he had in the Giardino Imperiale of Montecavallo and in the *ambulacra* of the Colosseum.[112]

The old confusion about areas of responsibility continued. There were a nasty series of demands on the Accademia by Lezzani. Canova received a 'final notice' from Daru on 31 March. In April a reply was drafted stating that these claims had nothing to do with maintenance or repair. On 25 May, Daru calmly sent the bills on to the Commission des Embellisements.[113]

Further disaster struck on the night of 18 November. During a storm, a pilaster of the Colosseum fell. Daru wrote a stinging letter to the whole Accademia. As well as the damage to the Colosseum, one of the arches of the Basilica of Maxentius was about to fall and all [sic] other monuments required attention. He reminded the Accademia of the decree of November 1810, and the endowment. (Could the Accademia forget? It must have wished it had never heard of 100,000 frs.) Daru demanded answers to the following questions. What sums from the endowment had so far been received? What use had been made of them? He required details, adding sarcastically that this meant not to confuse the Colosseum with the Temple of Vespasian! The collapse at the Colosseum had shown that the Accademia had failed in its appointed task, causing great expense for repairs, and even worse making a very bad impression on the public.[114]

As if these disputes at Rome were not enough, the Parisian bureaucracy became involved in the definition of the monuments which came under the Accademia's care. Tournon attempted to sort this out for Montalivet, by explaining that two classes were distinguished: those monuments which have 'more or less resisted time' (the Colosseum, temples, arches, baths and the Pantheon), which were henceforth to be looked after by the Accademia; and bridges, aqueducts, palaces and churches, which came under the Prefect and the Mayor. This answer obviously missed the whole issue, which was the confusion between the Accademia's maintenance of monuments and the Commission des Embellisements' programme, not to mention Daru's excavations. An unseemly battle, in fact, broke out in Paris among three ministries for control of the Accademia. The head of the third division of the Ministry of the Interior, Neuville, reported to his minister, Montalivet, that despite mention of three ministries in two decrees the Accademia claimed that it was dependent only on the Intendant de la Couronne. This was not, Neuville assured him, Napoleon's intention. Montalivet thereupon wrote to the Intendant Général, the Duc de Cadore, stating that the Minister of Finance had already played his part by deciding what properties were to constitute the endowment. Montalivet, on the other hand, was to organise the Accademia, its teaching and administration, and 'determine the principles of special arrangement which were to establish relations with the Intendant Général' for the maintenance of the monuments. The Intendant Général replied that the decree seemed to put the Accademia under the control of the Ministry of the Interior, except for the matter of monuments. Montalivet plainly approved this answer and wrote on the side of it: 'Ceci mérite beaucoup d'attention.'[115] Here is appalling evidence of bureaucratic disputes, as if the Accademia's situation were not desperate enough, being called upon to care for upwards of one hundred monuments with an income that would have been ridiculously insufficient, even had it been at its disposal. And to cap everything else, the Accademia was suspected of incompetence or worse. The Duc de Cadore reminded Daru that the Accademia had now had two years' income (150,000 francs). Had this been spent in accordance with the Emperor's wishes? What works had been carried out? Had Daru overseen them? Had the whole sum been spent?[116]

In an attempt to explain its situation, on 10 January 1813 the Accademia approved a report by the architects and antiquarians on the monuments to be repaired and sent it to Daru, stressing that the devastation at the Colosseum alone would not be covered by the endowment. By the end of the month, however, Daru demonstrated that he was interested only in regulations. The Accademia was responsible not only to him, but also to the Prefect and to the Minister of the Interior. (Here was the consequence of the correspondence in Paris at the end of the previous year.) Under Daru's control came all work for restoration of monuments, financed by the 75,000 frs. From now on, what he required was this: whenever repairs were necessary, instigated by the Accademia, the 'authorities', an artist or Daru himself, the Accademia was to meet, state why the work was necessary, what was to be done, how long it would take, and what it would cost. Opinions in favour and contrary were to be recorded. The Principe was to state the finances available.[117]

The dual control must have dismayed the Accademia. Tournon wrote to Canova stating that its organisation, administration and discipline came under his control. One improvement was supposed to be that henceforth it would receive the 75,000 frs in quarterly instalments. Amongst other minor details, Tournon asked for a list of the 452 properties which made up the endowment, with notes on their condition, a plan of the Accademia's building, and sums so far spent on the monuments (although that was outside his control). Canova noted in this dossier that the Accademia received, in fact, only 93,275 frs yearly instead of 100,000, and that repairs and rent collection cost 4,000 frs. Less than 90,000 frs were left, despite all the grand talk of imperial generosity.[118]

Daru's capacity for new regulations was bottomless. He next demanded that when the Accademia had decided on repairs he was to receive two copies and that no work was to proceed without his authorisation. On completion of the work, again two copies of the reports were to be sent to Daru. And each January he was to receive three copies of the report on the last year's work. Furthermore, the control of the revenues was to be removed from the Accademia to the Prefect, all for the better repair of the monuments. Daru explained this change generously: it was occasioned by no fault of the Accademia; it was simply a rule that the same people do not authorise and pay expenses. The artists were to see to the Arts, the administrators would attend to the administration.[119]

Canova replied in the strongest terms. The imperial decree of 1810 had given the Accademia control of its income. It had rendered accounts to Daru for 1811 and 1812. It was henceforth to meet to consider any repairs and report to Daru, but the architects had always made a weekly report, which Daru could see. The Accademia had always kept precise accounts. As for sending Daru two copies of any proposed repairs, Canova declared roundly that the Accademia alone should decide about such work. He cited the dangers of recent excavations at the Temple of the Dioscuroi, and the risk to the Arch of Titus from the demolition of adjacent buildings. The Accademia thus became involved with this monument.[120]

By July, Daru informed Canova of recent discoveries in the Forum of Trajan requiring work beyond the planned area. Daru wanted to consult the members of the Accademia about their value to art and history and about the methods to be followed.[121]

In the same month, to give some idea of the appalling load on the Accademia, Valadier and Camporese drew up a list of the monuments needing immediate attention ('pronto soccorso'). It included the obelisk at S. Giovanni in Laterano, the Baptistry of Constantine, the Amphitheatrum Castrense, the Baths of Helena, the Claudian aqueduct, the Pyramid of Cestius, the 'Temple of Cupid' near S. Croce (an apse in the Sessorium), the Minerva Medica, the Portico of Octavia, the Colosseum, the Baths of Titus, the obelisk of S. Maria Maggiore, the 'Trophy of Marius', the Arch of Gallienus, the Temple of Mars Ultor, the Forum of Domitian, the Baths of Agrippa, the obelisk in the Piazza del Popolo, the Arch of Janus, the Arch of the Argentarii, the 'Baths of Livia', the Temple of Camenae and Bacchus, and the Fountain of Egeria on the Via Appia.[122] How could anyone imagine that the Accademia had the staff or the money to attend to all these repairs?

And yet, at the same time, pressure was being brought to bear on it to care not only for monuments in Rome but also those outside the city! It was particularly the Mayor, Duca Braschi, who was trying to force the

Accademia to see to these extra-urban repairs.[123] Valadier was also caught in a dual position. He had replaced Camporese as director of excavations on behalf of the Crown, and wrote to Canova urging repairs to the Baths of Titus, the Colosseum and the Basilica of Maxentius. He could not, he said, do everything himself, and he stated formally that he would not be responsible for any disaster. The scaffolding he was continually erecting was only temporary and could not calm his fears. The details and costs of the repairs needed were defended by the architect as having been made by a special commission. He reminded Canova of the shame and criticism that would be visited on the Accademia in the event of any damage being sustained by them.[124]

It may be assumed that the famous debate over the method of consolidating monuments occasioned by Gisors' criticism of Stern's Colosseum buttress also dramatically affected the Accademia's work. Montalivet's approval of Gisors' principles meant that the 'original form' was to be restored, and what 'time or malevolence' had destroyed was to be replaced, brick by brick, stone by stone.[125]

Requests for repairs to the Colosseum were never ending. Canova finally explained the situation to Daru. The Accademia was insolvent, unable to pay its employees. Enormous sums had been spent on the Temple of Vespasian, the Basilica of Maxentius, the Colosseum, and the roof of the Pantheon. Not only was the endowment exhausted, but the Accademia was also in debt for thousands and unable to carry out even the most urgent repairs. Its only resort was to call on the government for help, especially in the case of the Pantheon, where all the craftsmen were demanding payment.[126]

The Intendant revealed the truth to Montalivet. In two and a half years the Accademia had received 134,133 frs, instead of 250,000. In Daru's opinion, this was not helped by the fact that the Academicians were not good administrators, and had to see to the collection of rents, suing of debtors and so on. To the Accademia, however, his reply was very different, a combination of threat and irony. Daru declared that it was 'displeasing to see that the beneficent provisions of His Majesty do not produce the benefits intended'. Napoleon had already done more than anyone ever did for archaeology, Fine Arts and the beautification of Rome, and at enormous cost. Now he claimed that the Accademia had in fact received 283,333 frs, of which 212,500 were for the maintenance of the monuments. Of this, he asserted, only one-third (78,519 frs) had been spent for this purpose. Changes were obviously needed in the administration. The Accademia must carry out its responsibilities as entrusted by the Emperor.[127] It is hard to imagine two more different letters on the same subject. The light thrown on Daru's character and administrative methods is not pretty.

On the last day of November 1813 he was even more blunt: the means had been voted, the public was not interested in reasons for delay. He expressed regret at having to repeat the same demands every letter, but winter was approaching, and the damage of last year had not yet been repaired.[128]

Within little more than a month, the Accademia was to be relieved of Daru's attentions. This whole story of the grand intentions for that body stemming from the imperial decree of late 1810 makes one wonder at the grasp of reality by Napoleon and his advisers, thinking that 75,000 frs would suffice to keep all the classical monuments of Rome in good repair. The Colosseum alone, of course, required more than that. The famous endowment turned out to be in part fanciful, since the Accademia had actually to collect rents and look after the properties, but more importantly, the gravest millstone ever placed around its neck. All this would have been vexing enough, but Canova in particular had his life made miserable by the endless harassment and arrogance of Martial Daru, under whose 'surveillance' the work on the monuments had been placed.

MARTIAL DARU AND THE WORK FOR THE CROWN

It was in October 1810 that Antonio Canova was summoned to Paris, where he had his famous breakfast meeting with Napoleon. He was ordered to live in Paris, but refused. When he complained about the removal of Italy's art treasures in 1797, Napoleon is reported to have said: 'Italy can recompense itself with excavations. I want to excavate in Rome. Tell me, has the Pope spent much on excavations?' Canova explained that the Pope had little money to spend but that he had built a new museum.[129]

By imperial decree of 6 November 1810, the Crown was ordered to undertake excavations in Rome, with a treasury of 200,000 frs. On precisely the same day the Accademia di S. Luca was given an endowment of 100,000 frs, of which three-quarters was for the maintenance and repair of monuments.[130] The proportions of the two grants are very revealing. Vivant Denon, Director of Museums in Paris, was to be consulted about the excavations.

One of the most remarkable documents of the French occupation is, in fact, Denon's declining of this duty.[131] He began by saying that he thought that there was little hope of finding anything of importance in Rome, since all the imperial baths and the Palatine had been explored. One would have to go to Ostia or Antium or the villas down to Naples. It was noted that Napoleon wanted to provide work for the poor. Denon observed that the main problem in Rome was the lack of fresh air: 'J'ai donc pensé qu'un des plus grands bienfaits que Votre Majesté pourrait répandre sur cette grande cité serait de lui procurer une promenade salubre assez spacieuse pour sa population et dont les magnifiques débris d'antiquités qu'elle possède feraient le plus bel et le plus digne ornement.' He therefore proposed that such a garden should include the Capitol, Forum and Palatine as far as the Oppian and Caelian hills. The cost would be 3 millions, but much less if the troops of the garrison as well as the poor were employed.

The direction of the excavations thus fell to Martial Daru, appointed Intendant des Biens de la Couronne in Rome on 12 March.[132] His elder brother, Pierre, was Intendant Général in Paris. The latter informed him that he had been nominated to carry out the work with a treasury of 200,000 frs. He was to seek help from the most famous antiquarians and academicians. The finds were to belong to the Emperor. Monthly accounts were to be sent to Paris for authorisation of payment.[133] Nothing more was said, unfortunately, about the identity or organisation of the workers, but we may assume that the model of the Commission des Monuments and the later Commission des Embellisements was followed. Raffaele Stern was appointed Architect of the buildings of the Crown on 25 February, and Canova was named Director of Museums. Although he at first begged off on the plea of being too busy, by April he had accepted.

Daru wrote to his brother at the beginning of May to inform him that the excavations were to commence sooner than expected. Tournon had told him that he had no more money for work in the Forum, but Miollis said that it had to continue. Daru stated that he had attempted to consult Denon before he left Paris but that the Director of Museums had admitted that he knew nothing about Rome. The Accademia di S. Luca, despite its endowment, had not yet received any monies. Daru had thus begun, and was paying his workers by provisional orders. The amounts were small: 200–300 frs a day.[134]

By the end of the same month, Daru reported on the work on the Commission des Monuments in the Forum. He calculated that about two months' work remained, on the northern side of the Colosseum, the Temple of Vespasian, and the Via Capitolina. (All this was to be transformed, of course, by the establishment of the Commission des Embellisements in just two months' time.) The funds of the Crown, he therefore suggested, would be better spent where there was hope of finding antiquities (which was, after all, the purpose of the work), in the Domus Aurea, for example.[135]

By June Daru was beginning his work there and in the Colosseum.[136] Almost immediately, the question of organisation arose. It was necessary to reduce the administration costs so that they did not absorb most of the budget. The Intendant wrote to his Inspector of Works, Ippolito Gérard.[137] The staff was to be one inspector (1,800 frs), one architect (1,200) instead of the previous two, one 'commis d'ordre' (480), where previously there had been two, one guard (360) and another 360 frs were calculated for office expenses. A surveyor was still to be employed, but in an honorary capacity, since he was already paid by the Crown. Pay for each worker was to be 1 fr a day, and the midday soup. Daru insisted that order be maintained in the excavations, otherwise he would stop the pay of the staff. (This implies that there had been some disorder.) On the other hand, we must acknowledge that Daru realised that the workers depended on their pittance and so he had them paid immediately, later regularising the provisional drafts.[138] The list of salaries identifies the staff. The new Inspector was Clemente Giardini, the Architect Giuseppe Camporese (replaced by Valadier in September 1813), and the Surveyor was Giuseppe Bernasconi, replaced after an apoplectic attack in November 1811 by Giovanni Rancioni.[139]

The reference to disorder explains, in fact, the replacement of Gérard by Giardini as Inspector, and the picture presented is very disturbing. Daru visited the work-sites on 22 June. Instead of the 206 workers listed, he could find only 116. Only one man was at the Domus Aurea. The others were all at the Colosseum, but doing nothing, or rather, what was worse than useless, namely clearing the galleries but dumping the earth outside instead of taking it to S. Giovanni in Laterano or S. Maria Maggiore. No objects had been transferred from the storerooms to the Vatican Museum. Daru was in one of his highest furies: he would stand this state of affairs no longer, and workers not present would not be paid.[140]

Since the object of the Crown's excavations was to find works of art, rewards were established for finds, up to 5 frs.[141] Daru's humanity to the poor, moreover, is attested by his general principle of continuing pay for seriously hurt workers. A foreman at the Colosseum, for example, 'fell under the ruins' and was given a month's sick-leave at 1.30 frs per day. A workman was given a month at 1 fr per day. Daru also paid his workers for 15 August, Napoleon's birthday, although it was a holiday.[142]

If his Inspector was soon replaced, Daru reported to his brother his great satisfaction with his architect, Camporese: 'il s'en acquitte fort bien'.[143] As work progressed, however, the old confusions we have already seen racking the work of the Accademia di S. Luca reappeared. Pierre Daru warned his brother not to confuse the restoration of the Temple of Vespasian with excavations. The latter was what the 200,000 frs were for.[144] And Daru was to suffer the same agonies as the Commissions. In July, on a Saturday pay-day, he did not have the 2,000 frs he needed. The number of workers varied from day to day, as they came and went from hospital (note the obvious perils for the unskilled workers or springing from the dangerous conditions under which they laboured), and because they were taken for other work by Miollis or the Director of Police. Daru was also concerned about the effects of heat as summer advanced. He wanted to distribute brandy, or at least vinegar, although it would have to be paid for by the workers.[145]

On 27 July 1811, the Commission des Embellisements was established, of which Daru was one of the three members, along with Tournon and Braschi. He was henceforth involved in the excavations in two guises. And on 14 September, Pierre Daru was replaced in Paris as Intendant Général by the Duc de Cadore.

Further squabbling about money broke out in December. The municipal treasury claimed reimbursement from the Crown for 49,422 frs, the cost of the excavations the municipality had carried out under the Consulta.[146] That same month Daru was employing 200 workers at the Colosseum and Domus Aurea, and their pay had been raised to 1.25 frs per day, to keep up with the pay of the Embellisements, although Daru thought their work was easier. Within a few days he would be employing fifty men in the Forum of Trajan.[147]

For 1812 and 1813 the archives of the Crown are devoted to the work in these three monuments.[148]

Martial Daru has the distinction of being the only French administrator in Rome to be celebrated in literature. In a footnote in his *Vie de Rossini*, 1823, Stendhal, Daru's cousin, claimed: 'Rome doit la plupart de ses embellisements sous Napoléon à M. Martial Daru, Intendant de la Couronne, amateur fort éclairé et ami intime de Canova.' In his *Rome, Naples et Florence*, in the second edition of 1826, he remarked, apropos of the Forum of Trajan, that this work was more important for posterity than that of the ten most active Popes.

WORKS OF ART ADDED TO THE VATICAN MUSEUM

Martial Daru was commissioned to carry out excavations expressly with the purpose of finding antiquities. The works of the Commissions, notably the Embellisements, were also bound to uncover works of art. The French archives preserve complete lists of these finds as they were transferred to the museum.[149] As paradoxical as it may seem, virtually nothing of importance was found, attesting above all to the vandalism of the lime-burners and the rapacity of earlier collectors. Samples may be offered of these museum records.

Embellisements de Rome

Aujourd'hui Premier Decembre Mille huit cent douze à onze heures du matin le Sieur Antoine d'Este Conservateur du Musée Impérial s'étant rendu au Bureau de la Commission des Embellisements à l'éffet de pouvoir retirer tous les objets dans le dit Bureau, et provenants des fouilles et travaux faites par la Commission susdite pendant les mois d'octobre et novembre, a choisi en présence de moi sousigné Inspecteur Général et pris possession des fragments qui ont été trouvés au Temple de la Paix pour les déposer dans le dit Musée Impérial, ainsi qu'il suit.

Savoir: *Temple de la Paix* [i.e. Basilica of Maxentius]

1. Tête de Bacchus grand comme nature.
2. Tête virile avec barbe plus grand que nature.
3. Fragment d'un Chapiteau de Pilastre.
4. Fragment de la main d'une femme tenant une vase.
5. Petit fragment d'ornement.
6. Portion d'une jambe.
7. Fragment d'une main Colossale.
8. Fragment d'une jambe de Mercur.

9. Fragment de corniche ornée.
10. Fragment d'empreinte en brique.
11. Lampe en terre cuite.

[Signed] L'Inspecteur Général: C. Giardini

Of the same date:

Maison de l'Empereur
Bureau de l'Intendance de la Couronne

Aujourd'hui premier Decembre 1812 à 10 heures du matin le Sieur Antoine d'Este Conservateur du Musée Impérial, s'étant rendu au Bureau de l'Administration des fouilles à l'effet de pouvoir retirer tous les objets existants dans le dit Bureau et provenants des fouilles faites à la charge de l'Intendant de la Couronne, pendant les mois d'Octobre et Novembre, a choisi en présence de moi, sousigné Controlleur aux fouilles et pris possession des fragments de Sculpture, qui ont été trouvés dans les Thermes de Titus, Colisée et dans le Forum de Trajan, pour déposer dans le dit Musée Impérial, ainsi qu'il suivit.

Savoir: *Aux Thermes de Titus* [i.e. Domus Aurea]
1. Colonne cannellée qui peut être servie de Candelabra.
2. Demi Colonne idem.
3. Fragment d'un Chapiteau d'ordre Ionique.
4. Fragment d'un Chapiteau d'un pilastre.
5. Fragment de plafond orné de sculpture.
6. No. 39 Fragments en terre cuite et avec des ornements.
7. No. 12 Empreintes de brique.
8. Fragment en marbre d'un feston de Laurier.
9. Portion d'un demi volute d'un Chapiteau.
10. Fragments d'un Corniche ornée de sculpture.
11. Fragment d'un Console avec une portion de Corniche ornée.

Colisée
1. Tête d'une Nymphe de grandeur naturelle.
2. Torse viril de grandeur naturelle.
3. Portion d'un Sarcophage avec la partie supérieure d'une figure qui paroît être une Muse.
4. Fragment d'un bas relief où on voit les jambes d'un enfant.
5. Empreinte en brique.
6. Fragment d'un Console.
7. Fragment d'un petit lion qui jettoit de l'eau.
8. Fragment de vase ornée de sculpture.
9. Fragment de petite Boîte avec une portion de drapperie.
10. Fragment d'une main avec une grappe de raisin et des fruits.

Forum de Trajan
Petite Tête de Junon en bas relief.

[Signed] Le Controlleur aux fouilles: C. Giardini.

Plate 22 Head of a Dacian from Trajan's Forum (Amelung I, pl. 21).

Plate 23 Woman's portrait bust, mid second century, from Trajan's Forum (Amelung I, pl. 23).

It is sadly evident that these lists are interested, in the first place, in recording only objects as such, items for the Musée Impérial, quite oblivious of their context. No details of any kind, save the most general, are given. I have consulted the Director of the Vatican Museums, Professor Pietrangeli, about them, and we agreed that it would be impossible in the vast storerooms to identify such objects, even if they still existed.

Second, it is equally obvious that finds of any artistic merit or importance were very rare. Despite excavations all over the centres of classical Rome, virtually nothing of importance was discovered.[150]

A careful check has also been made of the standard and invaluable catalogue of the Vatican Museums, W. Amelung's *Die Sculpturen des Vaticanischen Museums* (4 vols., 1903–8). For many items, admittedly, no provenance or date of discovery is given, but in the Braccio Nuovo there are two major pieces attributed to the French excavations. These are no. 127, the head of a Dacian in golden marble with brown flecks, which was found in Trajan's Forum (Plate 22). In the notes on this piece, we are told that no. 3 was found in the same place, although no note is given in the discussion of that item. This second object is a woman's portrait bust (Plate 23). The head

Plate 24 Head of Medusa, from the Temple of Venus and Rome (Amelung I, pl. 6).

is thought not to belong to the lower portion in stone or the quality of work. The head is of the generation of the Younger Faustina.

There is, furthermore, a head of Medusa (no. 27; Plate 24). This was found, according to tradition, in Hadrian's Temple of Venus and Rome. Amelung therefore ascribes it to the 'first' excavation in 1819. Among the finds in that very temple, however, transferred to the Musée Impérial in October 1813, is a 'tête colossale de Méduse en marbre'.

A statue of Atlantis, finally, now in the Belvedere collection, is stated to have been found near the Colosseum in 1811. That is all.[151]

THEFT OF ANTIQUITIES

In all the archives consulted there is hardly any reference to what one might have considered a very grave danger, the theft of any antiquities found by the workers. The only cases are as follows.

Rotoli, Commissioner of Police, wrote to Tournon on 17 March 1812 to report that workers had stolen forty-three gold coins which they said they had found in the work in the Piazza del Popolo. They were passed to a dealer in antiquities, Giuseppe Colangeli, surnamed 'il frascatano'. Giuseppe Patrizi also bought five coins but with a friend, Giuseppe Conte, had then threatened to denounce Colangeli to the authorities, and had extorted money from him.[152] The Commissioner reported further cases of theft to Clemente Giardini, the Inspector of Public Works, on 30 June, but the register does not record the sequel.

A report on the arrest of a worker, dated 27 December 1810, tells that Domenico Calzanera, worker no. 35 in the eighth brigade, had offered money to Girolamo Albenzi, who had found a piece of black glass with a white layer on top. He also paid Francesco Rossi for a silver medallion. He claimed that he did not know that everything found had to be handed in, although the regulation was published in every work-place. Calzanera was handed over to the police and forbidden further employment. The two items, the piece of onyx and the medallion, were later recovered from a silversmith opposite S. Carlo al Corso, who had bought them for 4.20 scudi.[153]

We may be sure, then, that theft was not a serious problem. This was because so little of value was found, and because obviously only the smallest items such as coins could be easily concealed by the workers.

3

Arches, fora, theatres and temples: the monuments cleared and restored by the French

THE ARCH OF DOLABELLA

This monument appears briefly in the archives in 1812 after the bad earthquake. In a report by Valadier, he stated that the tremor had dislodged one of the 'arcuations' and that the pylon towards S. Stefano Rotondo was detached and visibly out of line and needed a buttress.[1]

Another report, by the Commission of Antiquities, was signed by Guattani, Fea, Massimiliano, Ottaviani, Re and Visconti. They stressed the antiquity and importance of the arch (it is dated AD 12), commended Valadier's report, and urged the Mayor to undertake repairs quickly.[2]

The arch also appears in the records of the Accademia di S. Luca, entrusted from the end of 1810 with the maintenance of ancient monuments. In August 1812, Valadier and Camporese were instructed to repair the arch immediately, and in September to make another visit and prevent any further damage. Repairs were begun, but ceased by the end of the same month when the house owner underneath complained of material falling on his roof. They were, however, complete by 17 October.[3]

THE ARCH OF JANUS

Just by the Forum Boarium stands a strange, four-sided monument, traditionally associated with Janus. It is perhaps rather an arch of Constantine, dated to the early fourth century AD. On each of its four sides it is surrounded by two tiers of niches (12 on each side, 48 in all). The monument is hardly distinguished, but because of its survival and bulk (16 m high, 12 m square) and proximity to the two temples in the Forum Boarium and the Arcus Argentariorum it has always attracted attention.

In Mariano Vasi's *Itinerario istruttivo di Roma*, 1804, the arch is shown buried in debris up to the substantial cornice below the first tier of niches, and with medieval brick additions on top, deriving from the monument's service as a fortress of the Frangipani. Antonio Nibby recorded very briefly that it was excavated in 1812. When we turn to Camille de Tournon for details, we are told only that the arch was cleared of the earth surrounding it to a depth of 2 or 3 m.[4]

This was, indeed, one of the simpler clearances of the French administration. In August 1811 Tournon wrote to Montalivet, the Minister of the Interior in Paris, announcing that the second of the four working gangs of the Embellisements was to start work here soon.[5] The Commission met on 26 September and laid down that work was to start on the morrow with fifty workers. The earth was to be dumped in the garden of a certain Signor Gabella.[6]

Excavations began, in fact, on Saturday, 28 September. Thirty-four people started, but they were too many: they got in each other's way as they made for the dump. For this first day they were to be paid at the fixed rate of 1.25 frs, but from the following Monday they were to be paid according to the amount of earth moved ('a cottimo').[7] By 19 October, Tournon informed Montalivet that the work was half finished and that one hundred workers were employed.[8] A statement for the period 28 September to 21 December reveals that 6,747 man-working days had been spent, 5,143 cu m of earth removed, and 8,131 frs expended. The average per day was therefore 1.2 frs.[9] By 8 January 1812 the work was declared complete.

A different project then arose. The building had been excavated to its foundations. Now it had to be freed from various buildings such as granaries in Via S. Giorgio in Velabro and Via S. Giorgio Decollato, hay-lofts in the Via dei Cerchi, Via S. Giorgio in Velabro and Via S. Anastasia. With these demolitions, Valadier declared, 'there will be restored to public view a grandiose relic of antiquity interesting in all respects' – a somewhat generous assessment.[10]

As usual, it was Angelo Uggeri who provided a diverting comment.[11] Although the monument had been cleared of soil, vegetation was still luxuriant on top. Ivy, pellitory, holly, olive and fig had put down roots so deep and numerous that they endangered the monument. 'A beneficent hand will soon arrive to the great regret of painters, to stop the progress of the state of destruction.'

The remains of the Frangipani fortress were not removed until 1829 (Plate 25).[12]

THE ARCH OF TITUS

One of the simplest and most charming – save for Jews – monuments of the Forum is the arch commemorating the triumph of Titus, with the famous depiction of the seven-branched candelabrum in the relief inside the vault, and the less-noticed apotheosis of Titus in the roof. We are familiar with the monument in the form transmitted to us by the careful and restrained restoration by Valadier between 1818 and 1824.

Plate 25 One of a set of twenty watercolour illustrations, artist unknown, two of which are dated 1811. They show very precisely, albeit without great art, the main monuments in the middle of the French period. The Arch of Janus has been cleared to its foundations, but the medieval fortifications remain on top, and the foliage has not been cleared, exactly as Uggeri tells.

Some idea of the early nineteenth-century state of the arch may be gained from Vanderlyn's drawing,[13] which shows it in a tolerable condition, with a paved, curbed street passing under it. The preservation is, however, undoubtedly owed specially to the buildings on either side and a kind of buttress on the Palatine side (see Plate 26). Luigi Rossini shows both sides of the arch in 1817, with the medieval additions on top and virtually the total loss on the Forum side of all but the central opening with two truncated columns. There seems to be still some building against the northern side (see Plate 27).[14]

The work of the French in this case was limited to isolation, with dangerous results. Tournon in his *Etudes statistiques* mentions only that the arch was cleared and that this showed how badly it had previously been treated. He then needlessly mentioned the subsequent restoration, which 'some say' was in poor taste, and assured his readers that the French were not responsible for that![15]

The archives offer very little detail on the work. The general statement of the Embellisements of all works 28 September 1811 to 31 March 1813 gives a total of eighty-eight man-working days, to remove 49 cu m of earth,

Plate 26 John Vanderlyn, *The Arch of Titus*, 1805. The view before the French work shows a sloping buttress on the left, and on the right the enormous buildings between the arch and the church of S. Francesca Romana. The cornice is damaged and slipping. The medieval brickwork on the attic is festooned with vegetation.

Plate 27 Luigi Rossini, *Cinquanta principali vedute di Roma*, 1818, pl. 13, the Arch of Titus. From this side, little appears to have changed, despite French demolitions of supporting buildings which had seriously endangered the arch. This illustration dates from immediately before Valadier's restoration.

at a cost of 119 frs, a very modest amount. Contemporary published sources date the work to 1810.[16]

In the archives of the Accademia di S. Luca under February 1813 there is mention of reinforcement on the 'left side' of the arch to strengthen 'the great masses of travertine which rested vertically there'. The next month, Canova wrote to Daru, revealing that demolitions to the adjacent convent of S. Francesca Romana had endangered the arch. The ever-officious Intendant replied by inviting the Accademia to take steps to see that it did not suffer further. He mentioned two plans: to build brick buttresses on each side, or to take it down and rebuild it. In any case, the weighty medieval additions to the attic were to be removed. A commission nominated by the Accademia suggested strengthening the northern pylon and reinforcing the Palatine buttress, before re-attaching the outer marble with iron bolts (*spranghe*).[17]

In the meantime, Gisors and Berthault had arrived. Gisor's report is dated 31 March 1813. He complained about the supports for the arch on all sides as hideous and inadequate, so obviously the monument was so endangered that such intervention had already occurred. The French architect's proposal was to support the arch by scaffolding, take it down, and then reconstruct it. Piers which needed restoration were to be rebuilt in brick or stone rather than marble:

l'arc de Titus devrait d'abord être étayé et cintré de toute parte en charpente pour pouvoir démonter et remonter sans coup férir les parties des voussoirs gravitantes qu'on rétablirait le plus soigneusement possible sur les autres voussoirs inférieurs qu'on replacerait eux-mêmes, avant, dans leur position naturelle après avoir rétabli, soit en pierre, soit en briques, les masses des parties de piedroits dont l'arc est maintenant privé, en sorte que cet intéressant monument présentât de nouveau sa forme et ses proportions premières.[18]

It will be noted that this dismantling and rebuilding was a radical proposal but it was put into effect within a few years.

As with so many other projects, however, time ran out for the French administration. Work on the arch was undertaken in 1810, but apparently left in a more precarious state than before. By 1813 the need to intervene was dramatically obvious. The debate about which method to adopt was to be re-enacted, of course, in 1818.

THE BASILICA OF MAXENTIUS

Camille de Tournon painted a rather depressing picture of the remains of one of the most imposing monuments just outside the formal eastern boundary of the Forum before the French turned their attention to it. The vast halls, the remains of the three right-hand vaults of the originally three-aisled building, had been walled in and now housed only animals and carts. Rubbish buried the walls almost to the spring of the vaults.[19] This description is confirmed by contemporary illustrations (Plates 28 and 29). Vasi's engraving, looking directly at the vaults, shows the middle and right-hand ones more buried than that on the left (towards the Forum) and obscured by walls and houses. Everything is in ruins, shattered and about to fall, with vegetation covering all summits.[20]

Since its construction by Maxentius (AD 306–12) and completion by Constantine – whence a certain ambivalence in its naming, but the latter was all too fond of taking others' credit – little is known of its later history, save that it had been used as a cattle stall since the sixteenth century, and that it was also a cavalry school and a coach-builders.[21] The last remaining of the eight marble columns in the central nave was removed by Paul V in 1613 to Piazza S. Maria Maggiore, where it may still be seen. At the beginning of the nineteenth century, the vast remains were still known as the Temple of Peace, by confusion with the nearby (but vanished) Flavian complex. The Basilica was now to become 'the most considerable work' undertaken by the Commission des Embellisements.[22]

Plans for the clearing were being drawn up by late 1811. The earth was to be removed to the nearby vineyard of S. Francesca Romana,[23] an unfortunate choice, one might think. The last place that should have been considered for a dump was the Forum itself! Work was to begin on Monday, 30 September.[24] Pietro Fortuna, Inspector General, indeed informed Principe Gabrielli, assistant to Mayor Braschi, that 'this morning work began on the Temple of Peace with fifty men'[25] but the architects Camporese and Valadier found that the excavations immediately ran into masses of travertine and marble belonging to the mason Pietro di Lezze. Surely such obvious obstacles could have been foreseen! When told to remove all his materials, he replied that he could not undertake the slightest expense, because he was 'poor and sick'. What was to be done? Should the workers themselves remove the obstruction? As well, bramble walls had to be taken away (presumably serving as cattle pens) and small buildings belonging to the Conservatorio dei Mendicanti, for which permission was needed.[26]

These were very inauspicious beginnings, yet in October, although the building had been one-third buried, the work, relying on 300 labourers, was one quarter finished.[27] By December, 500 workers were employed. Column bases had been found, and the arm of a statue which could be judged to have been originally 12 feet high.

In January 1812 the pavement was being cleared, uncovering the lower pillars supporting the arches and vaults. Fragments of ancient art continued to appear: 'a mutilated statue' of very fine style, eight medals, the head of a chimera in *nero antico* with coral eyes, two arms belonging to a statue 16 feet high, half-effaced inscriptions, and the broken bases of columns.[28]

Plate 28 Giambattista Piranesi, *Vedute di Roma*. The parlous state of the Basilica of Maxentius is obvious, even allowing for artistic exaggeration. The three remaining vaults are in danger of collapse. The ground is littered with fallen masses, which were to require so much hard work by the labourers in 1812. On the left can be seen the grain-stores belonging to SS. Cosma e Damiano and private houses and storerooms.

Plate 29 One of the set of twenty watercolours, artist unknown, dated 1811, the Basilica of Maxentius. It is interesting to compare Piranesi with this much simpler view of the Basilica before the French work. The ruin is made to seem rather neat. The wall running across the right front cutting off two of the three vaults enclosed the courtyard and house belonging to the Mendicanti (compare the plan, Fig. 1).

As so often, great hopes of finding new works of art were to be sadly disappointed. The French excavations, despite the removal of such enormous quantities of earth, found hardly anything of importance in this category. The plunderers over the previous centuries had done their work too well.

The usual problems arose over compensation. The Commission des Embellisements agreed to pay Principe Colonna 200 scudi for the gardens he gave up for the dump.[29] It is fascinating how often in this work we shall see the greed of the Roman aristocracy as it sought economic advantage from the properties it held all over Rome in the path of the excavations. By March, the portico was being cleared, and painting had been discovered in the third vault, showing four figures 2 feet high. In general, precious light was beginning to be shed on the construction of the building.[30]

The same month, the disastrous earthquake struck Rome. Now, if not before, some restoration was necessary. A commission of the Accademia di S. Luca visited the building (see Fig. 1). It was found that the left-hand pilaster in the westernmost vault (A) needed reinforcing: it was completely disintegrating, probably as a result of the earthquake. The arches in the

Figure 1 The Accademia's repairs to the Basilica of Maxentius (ASL 171.61).

two levels above (DD, EE) had also suffered. The repair agreed upon was to close the left-hand lower arch (FG), at present used as a passage for carts, and use the middle opening (H) instead. This would both fortify the vault and produce symmetry, since the right-hand side opening (II) was already closed.[31] While mentioning the Accademia, it would be convenient to note that it also carried out repairs at another point, to the pylon and arch to the right of the entrance. Restorations here began in September, and these two works in the Basilica were a major preoccupation of the Accademia into 1813. As far as one can follow the details, the same work is often reported as finished, and is then subsequently found to be still in progress. They are both reported as complete, however, by May 1813. The Accademia also saw to repairs to the portico, and the setting up of a great block adorned with sculpture which had fallen down.[32]

To return to the main narrative, at the beginning of May 1812 work was slowed down by the enormous amount of debris from the fallen vaults. This was broken up and used to build a road across the Forum! The slowness and difficulty of the operation caused some anxiety either to Montalivet or to Tournon, for the latter in his regular progress reports was at pains to explain that this labour could only be appreciated on the spot. Two views were sent to the Minister, showing the ancient and present state of the Basilica. As if construction difficulties were not enough, in June, 200 labourers had to be sent away to the country to help fight a grasshopper plague![33]

By July, these workers had returned, and Tournon was again assuring his Minister that the work could not be judged until it was completed, and that the expense would probably not be regretted. Some more precious fragments had been found, as well as the pavement of *giallo antico* and a bas-relief. Three hundred workers were still employed. The fragments of art are listed in the objects given to the Vatican Museum: pieces of entablature, the bas-relief, some mosaic, a mutilated foot, part of an arm, a colossal man's head in poor style, a cameo of a Vestal's head, among others.[34]

The work was approaching completion by September because Valadier was able to present his plan for the tender for the construction of markers linked by iron bars to separate the Basilica from the Forum.[35] Next month the portico was still being cleared, but the great western semicircular niche was found. There were two in the building: the original one of Maxentius at the western end, and another built by Constantine on the middle of the northern side when he built an additional entrance on the south, on the Via Sacra.

At the beginning of 1813, Tournon could inform Montalivet that the Commission's main work of 1812, the clearing of the Basilica, was now complete (Plate 30). It remained only to close it off with chains to prevent further damage. Camporese's plan was to erect thirty-six small columns of travertine, a work costing in total 4,020 frs.[36]

Plate 30 Luigi Rossini, *Le antichità romane*, 1819–23, pl. 74, the Basilica of Maxentius, 1822. Rossini's view shows the Basilica as left after the French clearing, with the three vaults of the right-hand aisle free to the base of the arches. The portico appears on the right. There are still large masses left on the ground, and the edge of a modern building still on the very left, while some foliage on the roof may have grown there in the eight years since the French left Rome.

As usual, Gisors, now visiting Rome, had criticisms of the work on the Basilica. To support the weight of the earth banked up outside the northern vaults, three buttresses had been built, and to fortify the heads of the wall carrying the vaults, piers had been constructed thicker than the wall and so high that they penetrated the centre of the vaults.[37] These must have been a serious disfigurement, and for once we must agree with Gisors.

Further objects found in the Basilica were handed over to the Vatican Museum in April: a very damaged but colossal head, architectural elements, fragments of inscriptions and sculpture and of a sarcophagus, and seven brick stamps.[38] By June, Tournon reported that the repairs by the Accademia to the portico were finished, but he was still promising a month later that the clearing would be completed by the end of the month.[39]

The accounts of the Commission for the work on the Basilica make an impressive record. In the general statement of costs from 28 September to 31 December 1811 the total man-working days are given as 31,248; the earth removed, 12,593 cu m at a cost of 37,678 frs.[40] We have the monthly totals for the work throughout 1812. They show that the most intense month was January (17,000 frs) and the slackest months were, of course, in the summer (between 7,000 and 8,000 frs). The average monthly expenditure during the year was more than 10,000 frs.[41]

For the project, the grand totals were:

(i) clearing the Basilica: man-working days, 135,385; earth removed, 57,360 cu m; cost, 158,977 frs;
(ii) transport of the debris: man-working days, 6,834; cost 8,108 frs;
(iii) clearing the vestibule: man-working days, 6,665; earth removed, 2,663 cu m; cost 8,790 frs.[42]

In sum, 60,000 cu m of earth had been dug out and carted away at a cost of more than 175,000 frs. This was more than double the cost per cubic metre calculated by the Embellisements. The work had obviously been laborious and run into many obstructions.

The daily work reports confirm that the Basilica was the major site during 1812, with usually three or four companies working, a total of between three and four hundred workers, but sometimes as many as six or seven companies. Breaking up of the fallen masses from October required a further company, but by the beginning of 1813 activity was scaled down to one company, so that many workers could be transferred to the Colosseum.

Tournon summed up the French achievement as the clearing of the building down to the ancient pavement, the restoration of the three remaining vaults, and the consolidation of the remains, especially coating them to prevent water penetration.[43] 'Qu'il est imposant ce temple de la Paix, qui couvre de ses voûtes immenses un pavé de marbre, de porphyre et de granit, tandis que naguère de vils animaux souillaient ce parvis sacré, recouvert de vingt pieds de débris.'[44] So the proud words of the Prefect looking back on an enormous undertaking. On the important question of who was responsible for the work, the answer is clear. The Commission des Embellisements co-operated with the Accademia di S. Luca. The leading architects of both bodies, Camporese and Valadier, are shown by the archives as involved in the work.

One episode in the clearing of the Basilica is of such interest, both for the light it throws on the condition of the workers and the relations of the French administrators, that it deserves to be recounted by itself.

Workers' riot in the Basilica of Maxentius

When work began on the Basilica, as always with such clearances, a major problem was where to dump the debris. The original plan was, it will be remembered, to put it in the nearby grounds of S. Francesca Romana. This was apparently changed in favour of the Colonna gardens at the foot of the Esquiline.

In the light of this, the two architects, Camporese and Valadier, wrote to Pietro Fortuna, the Inspector General, on 11 October.[45] They were concerned at the nature of the earth and the distance it had to be transported. They suggested that the pay should be 2.5 frs per cubic m, considering the time and effort required by workers who were 'inexperienced and unused to such work'. 'Se questo apprezzo non corrisponderà al franco e 25/100 come viene prescritto nel decreto non sarà al certo nostro difetto, ma poca volontà e cattiva voglia degli operai che sono di opinione gli si debba passare una tel giornata, sebbene facciano un lavoro aggiatissimo e a loro arbitrio.' The rate suggested was, therefore, double the level already prescribed, but the architects were obviously concerned over the state of the labourers. The crisis struck sooner than they imagined.

The architects' recommendations were not followed. Three companies earned the maximum rate (1.25 frs per worker per cu m), but another two, admitted to have been badly directed, had averaged only 88 and 95 centimes each. Claiming the same pay as the others, these workers invaded the pay office of the Commission in the Forum and extorted it. Two company chiefs were dismissed; the corporals were reduced to the ranks; and five workers, regarded as the ring-leaders in the riot, were to be sent to prison.[46]

This incident throws a vivid light on working conditions in the excavations. The work was admitted to be arduous for untrained labourers. Even more important was the direction of the gangs. If not properly organised so that the workers did not get in each other's way and waste time and energy, they might receive only 70% of the already meagre pay. When some gangs did better, the loss was all too clear. The poor workers were now, however, to take second place as the dispute widened to involve the leading political figures.

The Commission was informed next that the Director General of Police had refused to arrest the five workers on the grounds that 'il n'était point tenu à recevoir des demandes de cette nature'. Faced with this crisis, Tournon, as President of the Commission, was delegated to write a letter to the Police Chief informing him that the police were bound to arrest workers who broke in and extorted money. The Commission roundly declared that it would not be responsible for any further disorders under these circumstances.[47] That is all that is to be found in the register of the Commission's meetings.

In the accounts, however, is found a letter of Giulio Camporese, inspector in the Basilica, to Mayor Braschi, explaining his part in the affair (on which we shall see further). He states that he looked for Pietro Fortuna, the Inspector of Public Works, the evening of 21 October, to obtain the addresses of the five men to be arrested. He found him finally at 10.30, but he had left the records in his office in S. Francesca Romana. Camporese went there to check them, only to find that the men had been replaced, and so were not entered. He thus could do no more and work had continued as normal on 22 October. He was making secret enquiries, however, about the men's addresses, so that they could be arrested that evening.[48]

For the conclusion of the story, we must turn to the final register of the Commission, the correspondence. On 23 October, Jacques Norvins, Director General of Police, replied to Tournon's letter, written at the insistence of the Commission. He expressed his regret that relations had taken a bad turn. He explained that Tournon had requested the arrest of the five workers, but without giving addresses of three, and offering as justification for the order their insubordination, but without giving any details. The Police Chief noted that he had undertaken to arrest the men when he had all their addresses, and that that had been conveyed to the courier who brought the letter from Tournon. When that man did not return, Norvins did nothing further. He had also offered to send a police inspector to make a round of the work-sites. He was as anxious as Tournon for good order and was highly offended that the Prefect had so officiously reminded him of his duties. Tournon's letter of 22 October claimed he refused the Commission's request to arrest the men. That, Norvins declared, was 'une malhonnêteté', 'faux et absurde'. No explanation had been given of the 'disorders'. If doors have been forced, one calls a judicial officer, who ascertains the crimes and sends an account to a procurator, who orders arrests. In future cases, Norvins assured Tournon, the foreman had only to ask the local commissaires to arrest the criminals in the act.[49]

Two days later, Martial Daru, Intendant de la Couronne, wrote to the Préfecture, informing the Secretary that Giulio Camporese had made an inexact report to the Commission. Norvins never refused to arrest the instigators of the riot. To the contrary, he had naturally asked for their addresses. The Commission had directed Camporese to give all details required, but he had not carried out these orders. It was suggested that in future, in case of disorders, the chief at the work-site could ask the local commissioner of police to make arrests, but Camporese was warned to use great circumspection in such demands.[50]

It seems that Giulio Camporese had been directed to cooperate with the police, but that the vital details could not be found, most importantly the addresses of the men. Equally mysteriously, the Police Chief was not given any details of what they had done, so naturally could not act. Within two days, the Commission reacted very sharply, but Tournon was finally the most compromised person, since he had been delegated to remonstrate with Norvins, without being in full possession of the facts. These prominent people, however, can be left to fend for themselves. The origin of the whole episode was the desperation of the poor workers, when they saw their meagre pay reduced through no fault of their own.[51]

THE COLOSSEUM

The work carried out here under the papal government has already been described.[52] Some internal clearing had been accomplished, the drainage system uncovered, and the great Stern buttress built. The enormous damage to the southern side was still unremedied. Rubbish was piled up both against the external walls and inside to a depth of three or four metres. The gaping vaults and cracked walls foretold imminent destruction. This was being hastened by the luxuriant vegetation which covered the ruins (see Plate 31).[53]

The main activity of the newly appointed Consulta for 1809, as revealed by its records, was directed to this monument. The work was carried out by convicts, and the sums paid out amounted to 158.65 scudi.[54] Early in 1810, Carlo Lucangeli wrote to the Consulta, explaining that he had been 'for a good many years' superintendent of restorations by the convicts, and had also worked on the buttress. Now he asked permission to resume work, especially in view of the planned new edition of Antoine Desgodetz's *Les édifices antiques de Rome*, 1682. As a testimony to his good faith, Lucangeli noted that he was still owed 70 scudi from when he was inspector of the convoy transporting the Borghese collection to Paris – but he was prepared to waive that![55] Olivetti, the Police Chief, was in favour of the employment of convicts on such works. There were 250 of them in the prisons of Castel Sant'Angelo.[56] The sum of 641 frs was paid for the work of the convicts at the Colosseum between 13 February and 24 March. Major work then ceased, when restoration of the Temple of Vesta was proposed.[57]

On 19 July, de Gérando wrote to Tournon asking his advice on the plan of the architects Palazzi, Camporese and Stern to demolish some granaries encumbering the Colosseum. The cost was estimated at 2,000 frs, which meant the work could not be undertaken until 1811.[58]

Plate 31 Antonio Canaletto (d. 1768), *The Colosseum*. The view from the Arch of Constantine shows the enormous destruction on the Caelian side, and the unsupported outermost portico where Valadier was to construct the second buttress.

Lucangeli's request to carry out further excavation had been approved, but nothing had been done. It transpires that he wanted to make a model of the building in cork. At the end of September, with the intervention of both de Gérando and Tournon he was assigned ten convicts. For October expenses were about 70 frs.[59]

The long-standing issue of the 'filthy hay-loft' of Domenico Diotallevi was to be one of the major episodes in the French attempts to restore the Colosseum. It blocked the view of the amphitheatre from the Lateran, and was therefore of considerable size. It was described as a hiding-place for thieves and all kinds of criminals. The owner had bought it from the Archeospedale di S. Giovanni, on condition that it should be ceded to the government when required. The compensation to be paid was the same as the purchase price (400 scudi, or 2,140 frs) in 1810, although there had been many improvements. Valadier recommended therefore that Diotallevi be given a bonus ('una buona uscita'). Demolition would occupy thirty convicts for fifteen days. Valadier's valuation was sent by the Commission of Monuments to de Gérando at the end of November, and Tournon reported to the Consulta at the end of the next month, stating that the removal of the building was indispensable for the programme of embellishments. The Consulta declared, however, that it was unable to act, and could only recommend the acquisition and await the decision of the courts, since private property was involved.[60] One begins to see the endless bureaucratic obstacles which could hamper archaeology and town-planning.

A more formal beginning to the work of the French at the Colosseum was clearly signalled by the decree of the Consulta on 11 January 1811. A programme was laid down: excavations were to be continued around the whole periphery from the gate opposite the Forum to that of S. Giovanni. When it rained, work was to be carried on in the interior galleries. Where the road skirted the amphitheatre, the earth would have to be supported, and a fence of painted wood was to be erected all around the excavations. And soon, compensation (73 scudi) was being paid to Principe Colonna, who lost part of his gardens in the works.[61]

In May, an important delegation visited the Colosseum: Daru, Camporese, (Giuseppe?) Bernasconi,[62] Canova, and Gérard, Daru's director of excavations. Their report is accompanied by a coloured plan (Plate 32), showing the state of the building when the Crown began work. Daru explained that the various galleries were blocked, sometimes up to 4 m high, and that modern walls obstructed the porticoes and prevented access to the arena.[63] The work of the Crown began on 1 June 1811.[64] The motive, of course, was to find works of art. Daru the Elder, Intendant in Paris, was to write to his brother, complaining that the objects found in the first six weeks did not seem to be very valuable and hoping for better results in the excavations in the Domus Aurea.[65] It was in fact on 27 July that the most valuable objects recovered came to light: two silver candelabra of the sixteenth century, weighing 4 pounds. They were found in arcade 29, and given to the Vatican.[66]

On 10 November, Daru returned to survey the work with Canova, Camporese and Giardini. Galleries BCD on the plan (Plate 33) were now clear, and so were corridor F and vault E on the north. The wall closing the porticoes on the external gallery BCD had been demolished, and the debris in the upper interior galleries cleared. The wall H–J was finished. The clearing of the entire northern section was, in fact, complete: 15,401 cu m of earth had been removed, one third to S. Maria Maggiore and the Via Labicana, the other two-thirds being dumped in the Colonna garden; 427 m of wall had been demolished, and 247 m (I–J) constructed. More than one hundred fragments of sculpture, architecture and inscriptions had been found, of which seventy-three had been given to the Vatican Museum, as had nearly 10,000 coins.[67] Galleries which had been so blocked that a man could scarcely pass now allowed passage in a carriage (Plate 34). By December excavations had begun on the arena, and the drainage had been found.[68]

An enormous amount of the work at the Colosseum was carried out by the Accademia di S. Luca, under the terms of the decree of late 1810, by which it was to see to the repair of ancient monuments. These operations were well under way by August 1811, as the lower galleries were cleared by the Crown. The stones found lying on the ground were used to repair the vaults. The wall to hold back the earth around the building had collapsed and had to be reconstructed; this was finished by September. Drains were also built, 114 m long. By the end of the year, the Accademia had spent 6,259 frs. In January 1812, repairs were being carried out to the vaults of the outer *ambulacrum*, towards the Oppian Hill.[69]

On 13 November 1811, Camporese and Valadier for the Embellisements estimated the earth to be removed around the outside of the amphitheatre from the Meta Sudans to the Via dei Mendicanti at 9,416 cu m and from there to the Via Labicana another 31,680 cu m, in all 40,096 cu m which would cost 60,644 frs.[70] On 7 January 1812, the Commission des Embellisements met to estimate the area and value of the land contained in an ellipse around the Colosseum (see Plate 35), and voted that one of the companies at the Basilica of Maxentius should be transferred to remove earth between the amphitheatre and the Meta Sudans. The Commission's work began on 10 January and extended until May, employing for the most part two companies, 200 or more workers. They were transferred in May back to the Basilica of Maxentius.[71]

On the night of 21–22 March 1812, the most severe earthquake known to 'history or tradition', as Tournon described it to Montalivet,[72] struck Rome. The worst-affected building was the Colosseum, part of which collapsed, although all palaces and churches were affected. The already vastly over-extended Accademia was to have even more burdens as a result.

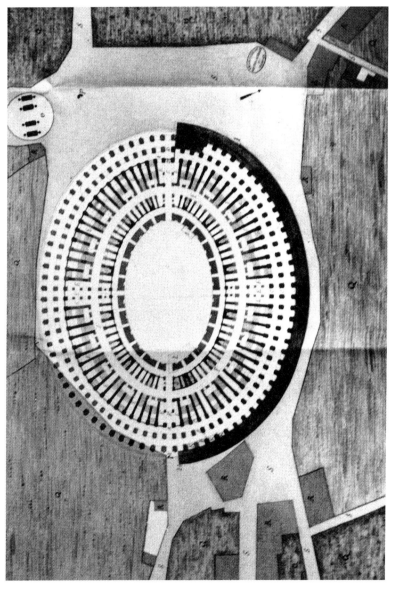

Plate 32 Coloured plan of the Colosseum at the beginning of the Crown's work in May 1811, to accompany Daru's report. The parts of the building surviving are shown in dark wash; in lighter wash, the parts of which little is left. The two main entrances are on the right and left. All galleries were blocked, the outermost 1 m high, the second to between 1 and 4 m, the third (F), 4 m. In addition, modern walls blocked the porticoes and access to the centre. Two pits are shown in the arena, evidence of an attempt to find the ancient level.

Plate 33 The Colosseum on 10 November 1811, Daru's report. Galleries BCD, corridor F and vault E on the north were now cleared. The wall closing the porticoes of external gallery BCD was demolished. Debris in the upper internal galleries had been removed. The entire northern section was, in fact, now cleared, in all of 15,400 cum of earth. The parts excavated are shown in light blue (i.e. the lower half in the drawing, which is the northern side).

Plate 34 *Escavations du Collisée*, artist unknown. The convicts are hard at work, guarded by French soldiers. Note the clearing of the drains.

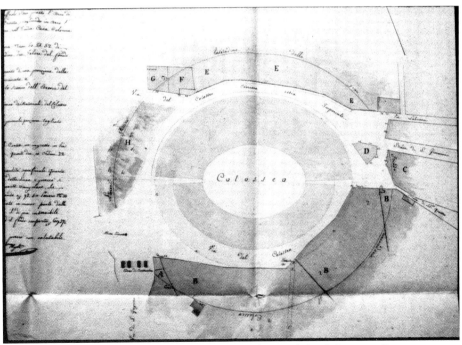

Plate 35 Giuseppe Valadier, plan of the road around the Colosseum, January 1812. This may be understood by comparing it with the sketch in the Archives Nationales (Fig. 2).

On 28 April, the Commission des Embellisements approved the idea of a circular space around the amphitheatre.[73] The list of acquisitions for demolition naturally grew (Fig. 2). By June or July these buildings included: the garden of Nicola Giorgioli, 2,140 frs; the garden of Francesco Corvini, 2,491 frs; the garden of the Cortesi brothers, 1,872 frs; the barn of Domenico Diotallevi, 4,280 frs; the garden and house of Principe Colonna, 3,639 frs; the garden and house of Raffaele Stern (one of the leading architects and author of the buttress!), 4,365 frs; the garden of Achille Brandi, 3,745 frs. These came to a total of 22,532 frs. It is recorded that everyone had signed the agreement to sell, save Diotallevi, who, it will be remembered, had purchased from the previous owners precisely on this condition. What is interesting in the list of proposed demolitions is the nature of the private property around the Colosseum: little presence of the aristocracy, and the revelation as one of the owners of Raffaele Stern. The problem of these obstructions must have been one of the reasons for slackening of work by the Embellisements in May, whatever the need for more labourers in the nearby Basilica.

The Accademia di S. Luca realised that security at the amphitheatre was important, with the vast internal clearings. At its meeting on 12 July, it was agreed to establish a guard and to close the entrances. Carlo Lucangeli was appointed on 30 August, with a salary of 12 scudi per month. From this he had to pay an assistant, who was the real guard and to be present day and night.[74] These precautions were soon shown to be needed. In September, the Accademia deputed Camporese to make arrangements for the storage of the famous cross while excavations were carried out in the arena.[75]

On 22 September, the Commission des Embellisements agreed to proceed with the great elliptical road around the Colosseum. In December, the Mayor's assistant, Principe Gabrielli, was empowered to negotiate to buy the Colonna garden, Stern's garden, and the Diotallevi barn.[76]

Despite all its precautions, the Accademia was fated to be the victim of disaster – and of the wrath of its governmental supervisor, Daru. Valadier and Camporese reported to Canova on 19 November that a pilaster on the northern side, which supported a travertine arch and one of the *vomitoria* and which had been damaged in the earthquake so that repairs were planned, had fallen during the night. It could, however, easily be replaced, since all the pieces were preserved. Many pilasters had, in fact, been damaged by the earthquake. Daru's reaction was terrible. He not only wrote to the Accademia[77] but also to Camporese, describing his excuse for the accident as 'pitiful'. He seems to have been absent from Rome without permission. Daru claimed that the architect had been warned just a few days before of the imminent collapse of the arch, but that it was not even closed off. Early in December, two pylons were provisionally buttressed and an arch was walled in on the side towards the Meta Sudans.[78]

The accounts of the Embellisements show that work resumed in January

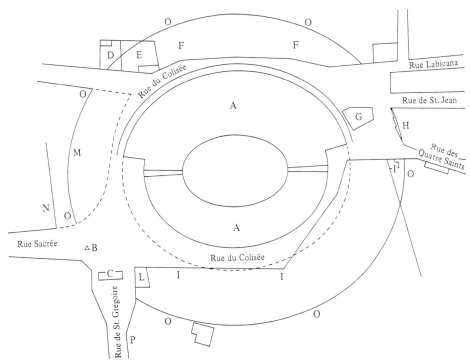

Figure 2 Proposed acquisitions and demolitions at the Colosseum (F 13 1646A).
A Colosseum; B Meta Sudans; C Arch of Constantine; D garden of Nicola
Giorgioli; E garden and stores of Francesco Corvini; F garden of Cortesi
brothers; G hay-store of Domenico Diotallevi; H garden of Collegio Greco;
I garden and house of Principe Colonna; L garden and house of Raffaele Stern;
M public land; N vineyard and garden of S. Francesca Romana; O road border-
ing the Colosseum, to be planted with trees; P garden of Achille Brandi.

1813, with at first two companies, then three or four (four to five hundred
workers) until May, making this site the major undertaking. Then from
June to October, the workers were reduced to two companies, as labour
concentrated on the 'Garden of the Forum'. By winter, however, the number
of companies had again risen to three or four. And the year began with
significant success in the acquisitions: by 31 March, all buildings had been
acquired (save Diotallevi's), although none had yet been demolished.[79]

The visit of Gisors and Berthault did not, fortunately, have anything to
do with the work at the Colosseum. The internal clearing was obviously
necessary. Daru did, however, write to Gisors, setting out the costs of his
undertaking, and justifying them. The average cost per cubic metre was
1.55 frs, which Daru admitted was higher than at his other sites, the Domus
Aurea and the Forum of Trajan, but that was because the work in the arena
was more difficult and transport of the debris had to be by barrow rather
than cart, and that was more expensive.[80] As the clearing of the arena pro-

gressed, the question of drainage also became pressing. Daru claimed to understand how water in antiquity was introduced into the arena and drained away. If those drains could not be cleared now, the arena might have to be refilled with earth.[81] This turned out to be a prophetic statement.

On 13 June the inscription of Lampadius (*CIL* 6.1763) was found in the great middle portico beside a chapel.[82] On 23 August appeared the inscription of Decius Venantius Basilius (*CIL* 6.1716), which had originally been on the northern podium towards the Temple of Venus and Rome, whence it had fallen into the arena.[83] A copy, it should be noted, had already been known to Pighe and Ligorio in the sixteenth century. The two inscriptions mentioned the arena and the podium, and began an unholy war among antiquarians (see Chapter 4).

Repairs to the amphitheatre were obviously the largest undertaking of the Accademia di S. Luca at this time. The architects met at Canova's house to discuss them. In July, Camporese and Valadier reported to Canova that many repairs were finished to the walls and vaults, but excavations on the east near the buttress had found one of the pylons and internal arches in urgent need of intervention, because they had been damaged by fire. They noted that a general report had long ago been sent to Daru. If these repairs were not carried out, the architects disclaimed responsibility. At the end of the same month, they announced that repairs to four arches damaged by fire were beginning; they were to be built up in brick.[84]

The situation of the drainage was by now critical (see Plate 36). Daru ordered Valadier, Giardini and Bianchi to meet him at the Colosseum at midday on 10 September. Water was discovered 10 m deep and the pumps were unable to cope. The ancient drains had to be found. The funds of the Accademia were insufficient, so Bianchi, Inspector for the Embellise-ments, was to have his organisation clear the drains of both the Colosseum and the Forum Boarium. The repairs required of the Accademia were also listed: lining with travertine the arcade of the main entrance on the east, repairing with brick the imperial loggia, the two great pillars supporting the huge vault at the main entrance on the west, and one of the subterranean vaults.[85]

Although pits were dug around the Arch of Constantine and a drain found towards the Circus Maximus which, it was thought, possibly joined the Cloaca Maxima and drained the amphitheatre, by the end of October Daru told Tournon that the drains could not be traced, and that the city's fire-pumps would have to be used to keep the water down until the end of the bad weather.[86]

The condition of the fabric never ceased to cause alarm. Valadier had fears for the 'safety of some parts of this marvellous building'. He now took the extraordinary step of appealing to Daru against the Accademia of which he was a leading member, complaining that he had made many requests

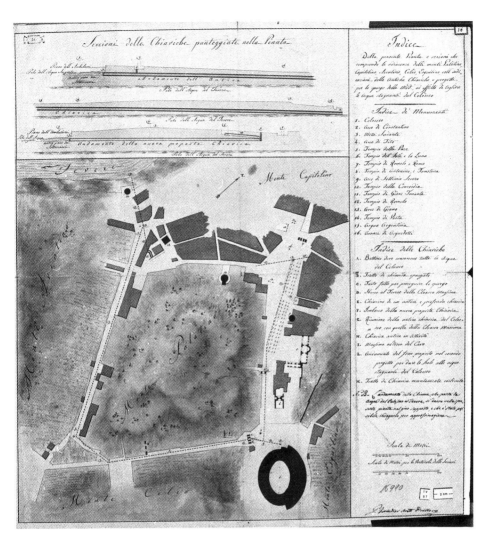

Plate 36 Giuseppe Valadier, plan of the supposed course of the drains from the Colosseum to the Tiber. The drains are marked by broken lines. The plan is undated.

for repairs. The Intendant told him to take whatever steps he thought necessary: the public was more concerned about this building than any other, he reassured him. The architect reported to Canova on repairs to the main entrance, where 'fire, the collapse of infinite masses from above and barbarism had attempted total destruction'. The workers had been insufferably slow. One of the underarches had been restored, and the stone cutter was sawing masses of travertine to replace missing stone in the external pillars. Valadier described the condition of this section of the building as 'terrifying'. Small precautions such as ties or bolts would not suffice.[87]

And if all this were not enough, the night guard was attacked on 29 October. About 10 p.m. Antonio Bonetti heard hammer blows, and went with his son to investigate. They found men who wounded Bonetti in the chest with a shot gun before running off. Fortunately he was not seriously wounded.[88]

The most urgent repairs were to the two entrances and a large section of the vault in the third *ambulacrum*. Daru admitted that the Accademia had done some work. Four brick arches at the southern entrance were complete, but the pylons still needed iron ties to hold the splitting travertine, the internal arches all needed brick underarches, and the external arches were missing a lot of travertine. Valadier estimated all these repairs at 80,000 frs. (One may note that this was more than the entire sum at the disposal of the Accademia for repairs for one year.) Canova was ordered by Daru to occupy himself 'seriously' with the Colosseum. Valadier had given a timely warning. If some disaster occurred, who would be to blame, Daru asked sinisterly?[89]

The last act under the French was the approval given by Montalivet on 4 January 1814 for the purchase of Stern's garden, with half the price to be paid within six months, and an indemnity of six months' rent.[90] On 23 January, as if nothing had happened, Camporese and Valadier urged repairs to the vaults and pylons on the south side, to be carried out by the Accademia.

Accounts show that, first for the Embellisements, work concentrated in 1812 in the first five months, employing generally two companies and expending by the end of the year more than 22,000 frs. Already nearly 13,000 cu m of earth had been removed. In 1813, with first two companies employed (January–February), then three or four (March–May), with a drop to two before a return to three or four (November–December), daily costs oscillated between 300 and 600 frs.

The work for the Crown appears in Daru's accounts between July and October 1811, throughout 1812, and from April to November 1813. It was thus the most intensive of the three monuments, along with the Domus Aurea and Forum of Trajan, where the Crown carried out excavations for works of art. Daru was using about 100 workers, with some reduction in the hottest summer months. He reported as well to Gisors, in April 1813, that he had so far spent 45,272 man-working days here, and cleared 35,239 cu m of earth, at a cost of 80,810 frs![91]

Camille de Tournon summed up the French work as

> (i) clearing the northern side of the Colosseum and building a retaining wall for the Naples road,
> (ii) clearing the porticoes,
> (iii) excavating the arena, finding the complex of elliptical and concentric supporting walls,

(iv) repairing the vaults and walls and clearing the vegetation.[92]

In short, we may recognise this as the greatest undertaking in modern times to free the Colosseum of the debris of centuries.

There were, of course, numerous articles in the newspapers.[93] On 15 November 1813 it was proudly asserted that one could now walk inside the amphitheatre on the ancient stones and that soon a double row of trees outside 'would offer a pleasing shade to the spectator without hiding the building'. The administration, readers were assured, thus not only excavated but also preserved the monuments of classical Rome.

It is of some interest to follow the records of the Commission des Embellisements under first the Neapolitan and then the restored papal governments. In May 1814 it was reported that the clearing of the external arcades could be completed within three to four months, at a cost of about 450 scudi per month. In August, Camporese and Valadier again listed necessary repairs. The Commission ordered that 'for now' temporary pinnings should be continued, but that the architects could make small repairs in the walls where most needed. In November, discussion centred on the problem of the difference in level between the amphitheatre and the surrounding roads and buildings. A retaining wall had been constructed on the north; to continue it around to the main entrance would be both costly and obstructing to the view. Monsignor Rivarola, president of the Commission, proposed a slope with trees on top, to unite the Colosseum with a 'pleasant walk'. Wooden gates should close the arcades, of pleasing design and painted to resemble bronze. Finally, the question of the arena, the greatest undertaking of the French. To leave it open for 'public admiration' seemed proper, but the Dean of Cardinals wanted it reburied. The main concern was the chapels.

The fate of the arena is told by Angelo Uggeri, with characteristic wit.[94] On the return of the Pope, work continued on the Colosseum, reaching the base of the walls in the arena. The Commissario delle Antichità (Fea) was 'burning with desire and impatience' to reach the foundations (doubtless to find proof for his impossible interpretation of the arena). Water, however, filled the deep excavations, and a great debate ensued about how to pump it out. Fea, according to Uggeri, became a 'spectacle', inducing the government to spend vast sums on his chimera. When other experts were consulted, however, they declared that these schemes were too costly and the stagnant water too dangerous. The arena was thus refilled – but the French had anticipated that. Fea denounced the recommenders of this solution as vandals.

The garden, however, became established (Plate 37): 'French taste has formed a little public garden at the very base of the Colosseum, so woefully misplaced, that even I, notwithstanding my natural passion for flowers, longed to grub them all up by the roots, to carry off every vestige of the trim paling, and bring destruction upon all the smooth gravel walks.'[95] It

Plate 37 Angelo Uggeri, *Vues des édifces de Rome antique déblayés et reparés*, 1816. The garden around the Colosseum which so annoyed Charlotte Eaton is shown here, with men and women in French-style dress taking a stroll, complete with parasol and dog.

seems that, in the eyes of the English who had experienced the Napoleonic wars, the French could never be given credit for anything. Now, at nearly two centuries' remove, we can surely be more just.

THE COLUMN OF MARCUS AURELIUS

This is not customarily accounted one of the monuments to which the French paid any attention, but some care was given to it during their administration, if not at the instigation of their conservation of monuments scheme. In the Roman archives may be found a note that Carlo Fea used the antiquities tax in 1810 to clear the column of plants and grasses.[96] In his report on the antiquities service to Tournon on 18 March 1811, Fea specified that this work had cost 60 bajocchi.[97] The problem was a continuing one. At its meeting on 14 June 1812, the Accademia di S. Luca, which had been entrusted at the end of 1810 with the care of the classical monuments, voted to clear the column of plants.[98]

THE COLUMN OF PHOCAS

Few monuments of the Roman Forum had a more bizarre struggle to recover their true identity than the last of all in chronological order. The column was thought to be part of the Temple of Jupiter Custos, of the Graecostasis, or of the Portico of Caligula from the Palatine to the Capitol. When the French arrived, it was hidden among houses.

It is hidden in another sense, since it appears very rarely in the Roman or Paris archives. In the general statement of expenses for the Embellisements from 28 September 1811 until 31 March 1813, it is revealed that clearing around the column took 101 man-working days, and cost 136 frs; 128 cu m of earth were removed, costing another 128 frs. These are, in fact, the figures for March 1813.[99] In April some further work was carried out, costing 27 frs for excavations and 13 frs for transport (so another 13 cu m of earth was removed).[100]

The most important discovery was the inscription on the column, which finally gave it secure identification (Plate 38). If we exclude the Temple of Venus and Rome as being outside the Forum, the column, the latest monument in the area, was the first among the many not clearly identified by long-known inscriptions to have its identity re-established.

The announcement was made by the antiquarian Filippo Aurelio Visconti to the Accademia di Archeologia, and reported in the *Giornale politico* on 9 June 1813. Visconti relied on plans drawn up by the architect, Pietro Bianchi. The inscription was slightly damaged. Most importantly, the emperor's name, as a tyrant, had been erased, but could easily be restored from that

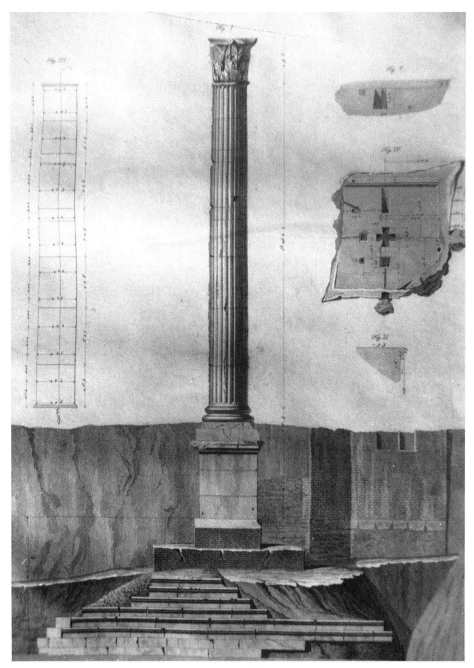

Plate 38 Giuseppe Valadier, *Raccolta delle più insigni fabbriche di Roma antica*, part 5, 1818, pl. 2, the Column of Phocas. It was somewhat extravagant of Valadier to include the miserable column in his grand collection of the most outstanding buildings of ancient Rome. This is explained, however, by the great excitement caused by the finding of the inscription. The plate in fact shows the further work undertaken in 1817 by the Duchess of Devonshire.

of the dedicator, the exarch Smaragdus. Visconti – or the report – carelessly gave no date for the discovery. And thereby hangs a tale.

Another publication of Visconti in the same year was his *Lettera sopra la colonna dell'imperatore Foca*, to Martial Daru, in which he especially praised the intelligence and energy with which Daru had seen to the carrying out of Napoleon's wishes concerning the monuments.

The precise date of the discovery of the inscription is given by Carlo Fea in his *Iscrizioni di monumenti pubblici*: 23 March. In this discussion he was, as usual, mostly taken up with defence of his own supplements in the inscription.[101] In agreement with him is Giuseppe Guattani, *Memorie enciclopediche* (1817).[102] As time went on, however, the date fluctuated, often becoming 13 March.[103] Fea himself went on to offer a third date: 23 February.[104] This confirms the day as the 23rd since everyone else agrees that the month was March. Further confirmation comes in a letter of Tournon to Montalivet, announcing the discovery: the letter is dated 5 April, and the Prefect was more likely to have delayed two weeks rather than one month in announcing the exciting find.[105] It must have been in the face of all the above uncertainties, easily solved, that Bormann and Henzen, editors of *CIL* 6 (1200), dated the finding of the inscription only 'mense Martio anni 1813'.[106]

Who was responsible for the work on the column at the time? The expenses for the clearing, as we have seen, are given in the accounts of the Commission des Embellisements. The discovery was first announced by Visconti, who mentioned Bianchi and Daru. The last named may be discussed first. His function was to carry out excavations in order to find works of art. He was thus occupied in the Colosseum, Domus Aurea and Forum of Trajan. He was also to oversee the work of the Accademia di S. Luca in the maintenance of the monuments. There was no prospect of finding masterpieces of ancient art around the column, however, and the Accademia is not known to have restored the column. Second, Pietro Bianchi happens to have left an account of himself; for he wrote just after this, in June, to Daru, seeking work, and stating that he had been occupied for the last three years drawing all the most celebrated monuments.[107] And so we see him employed by Visconti.

Filippo Aurelio Visconti would seem to be either advising the Commission on the excavations or chosen by it to make the most prestigious announcement of the discovery to the Accademia di Archeologia, which the French had re-established. He was, in fact, chosen by the Vatican librarians to make the announcement of the finding of the inscription; Daru had left the nomination to them. Although not in the same class as his brilliant and infamous brother, Ennio Quirinio (1751–1818), who was so pro-French that he had to live in exile in France from 1799, and who would have been a worthy antagonist for Fea as the leading antiquarian, Filippo Aurelio (1754–1831) was Commissario delle Antichità, 1784–1800, and Secretary of the Accademia di Archeologia. With Guattani he produced *Il Museo Chiaramonti* (3 vols.), 1808–43 and wrote the (mostly fatuous) notes for Valadier's *Raccolta delle più insigni fabbriche di Roma antica*, 1810–26.[108]

THE DOMUS AUREA

The history of this ill-fated and complex monument is fascinating. Its old name was the Baths of Titus, until the French excavations turned up brick-stamps of Trajan. The Baths of Titus were, in fact, between the Colosseum and S. Pietro in Vincoli.

The earliest modern knowledge of the subterranean rooms goes back to the late fifteenth century. Nibby recorded that the earliest signature he had seen there was from 1493. Weege dates the earliest excavation to 1488. The most spectacular find was the Laocoön in 1506, although controversy surrounds the baths and the Sette Sale.[109] Vasari in his life of Giovanni da Udine tells the famous story of the descent of the young man with his master, Raphael, into the underground rooms to admire the arabesque frescoes and stucco reliefs; this was obviously after 1509 when Raphael came to Rome and before he decorated the Vatican Loggie (finished 1519). In 1547, twenty-five statues were found, and in 1594 cornices were extracted for the chapel of the church of the Gesù.[110] Palladio made a plan of the baths.[111] It henceforth never lacked for publication[112] until sixteen rooms were uncovered by Ludovico Mirri in 1774 (see Plate 39), who had the paintings copied and published with Giuseppe Carletti, *Le pitture delle terme di Tito*, 1776.[113]

The French administration marked a turning-point, as with so many other classical monuments:

Die erste systematische Ausgrabung und den ersten brauchbaren Plan machte der römische Architekt de Romanis, der in den Jahren 1811–1814 einen Teil der untererdischen Räume bis zum Fussboden freilegte (1–48 in meinem Plane). Das Resultat dieser Ausgrabung, die ausser Decken-und Wandmalereien ein paar Restchen von Mosaikfussboden, sonst keine Funde von Bedeutung brachte, hat er in seinem gründlichen und vorzüglichen Buche, Le antiche camere esquiline, Rom 1822, niedergelegt.[114]

The real story is told, as usual, in the archives, both of the state in Rome and Paris, and in those of the Accademia di S. Luca.

In March 1810, the ex-Commissario delle Antichità, Filippo Aurelio Visconti, compiled a report on the site. He admitted that to comment on everything which deserved it would be too lengthy a task; he limited himself, therefore, to a description of the paintings near the door. The first three rooms, commonly called Rossa, Gialla and Nera and which still showed the vaguest plastering, deserved to be cleared and protected from water. Valadier was nominated to estimate the cost and choose a place for the earth to be dumped.[115] One can only agree that this was a most vague report,

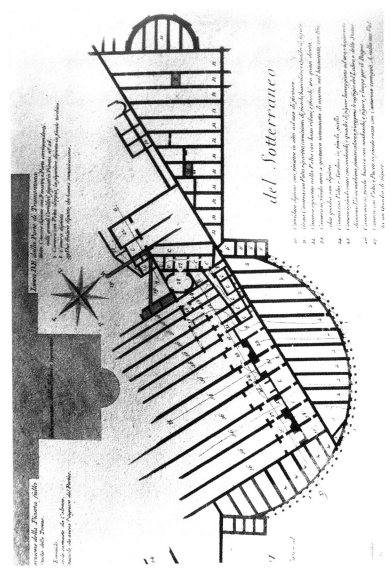

Plate 39 Giuseppe Carletti, *Le antiche camere delle terme di Tito*, 1776. The plan shows the rooms 'rediscovered' by Ludovico Mirri in 1774, some sixteen in all, grouped into three: 23–6: paintings of Bacchus, a bath scene, Mercury with three women and children, Romulus and Remus, two warriors, and two women and a horse; 9–18, 21: the 'second journey' of Mirri (15 is the 'room of the philosophers'); 27, A, 28, 29: the third 'route' of Mirri, with the superb painting of Pirithous and Hippodamia in 27.

enough to prove that Visconti had little interest in, or knowledge of, the site. With his usual indefatigability, however, within four days Valadier suggested the use of convicts to clear the rooms and that the earth should be taken to surrounding gardens and S. Pietro in Vincoli. There was no estimate of costs.

On 21 April, a Saturday, General Miollis and the Commission of Antiquities together with Valadier visited the Domus Aurea. It was agreed that the most energetic measures were necessary to protect the paintings, and that gates should be erected. The work of the convicts began to appear in the accounts in May, and the Consulta authorised the payment of 803 frs to the Director-General of Police to pay for their labour here and at the Temple of Vesta.[116]

By the end of June enough had been done to justify another report by Valadier. No plan had ever before been made for future work, because it was not known how deep or how difficult the work might prove. It was simply to be suspended when it was thought sufficient. Valadier went on to point out that the paintings were being stolen and the rooms needed clearing. The Consulta had appointed Valadier and Fea to supervise the excavation. Three rooms had already been freed, and the paintings were being secured by a band of lime where parts were missing. A wooden door with a good lock had been erected. Work was now progressing in two other rooms, and the cost would amount to 915 frs. Perhaps an opening in the roof for light might be provided. Further work should cost 1,880 frs, making a total of 2,795.[117] Valadier's vision of the project was obviously a very modest one. By 24 July, costs amounted to 1,602 frs, and on the same day Valadier wrote to de Gérando stating that the work was really finished because access had been provided to the paintings.[118]

By August something more was in the air. The French artist, Pierre Paris, had been consulted about excavations. By 1 September, after some illness, he finally visited the baths, accompanied by Guillaume Lethière, Director of the Académie de France at Rome. His report was damning. There was nothing new to be discovered. All the drawings had already been published by Mirri, Cameron and Uggeri. What remained was 'barely recognisable' or very degraded, not worth the money which could be better spent elsewhere. The rooms, moreover, had been filled by a contractor with powder and saltpetre, an action more worthy of the barbarians than a Roman. When he had to clear them, Paris recommended, he should be made to do it carefully. In this way the subterranean structures could be opened without expense to the government. The only thing to be done at present was to close the area to prevent further damage. When there were fewer more urgent tasks, the convicts could be employed again.

The effect of Paris' report was instantaneous. On 3 September, de Gérando ordered an immediate suspension of work. The same day he also wrote to Valadier, saying that this was so and seeking his advice on how to protect the paintings. Two months later de Gérando reported to the Consulta. Work had been undertaken to discover rooms unknown for artists and the public. Five rooms had been cleared, and although the work should have been continued, funds were insufficient. The building had been closed to protect the paintings. The Commission should draw up a plan for the future.[119]

Valadier's and Fea's work for the Commission des Monuments in 1810 was thus short lived. All was not lost. Martial Daru, Intendant de la Couronne, took up the challenge.

The Archives Nationales possess his report of 16 June 1811 when the excavations carried out by the Crown commenced.[120] The building was visited by Camporese, Bernasconi, Canova and Daru, as at the Colosseum on 31 March of the same year.

Another report was made on 1 October, on progress since the work began in June.[121] The total earth removed was 8,740 cu m, of which one quarter was taken to the Via Labicana, the rest to S. Maria Maggiore. A coloured plan again shows the work in detail. By December work was beginning on the first floor, not previously entered. A statue of the god Pluto had been found, but subsequent reports declared it to be 'second class'.[122]

For 1812 there are few sources, save the accounts. Camporese was specified as the architect in charge of works, Giardini as the Controller.[123] It is obvious that on average fifty workers were employed until August, when work was scaled down, but by November the average was eighty a day. In the first few months of the year, the workers were receiving less than 1 fr for each cubic metre of earth dug out, perhaps because they did not have to move it at all, since, as Daru explained, an opening had been made for carts to be brought inside. The carters were paid little more than 1 fr per cubic metre; the earth was being taken to the Via Labicana and S. Pietro in Vincoli, to the east and north of the site.

On 9 March 1812 was found an inscription recording a dedication to Gordian (*CIL* 6.1091), and on 1 October a series of brick-stamps (*CIL* 15.52–5). The problem of preserving the paintings was obviously paramount, and it was natural that the Accademia di S. Luca should be called in. Valadier described to Canova the use of hooks (*rampini*) and lime to shore them up. Then a secret method of restoring and fixing them was communicated to the same body by Daru, but the artists rejected it after tests in November, because it was found to damage the colours; modern retouching had also been detected. The Accademia might also help in recording the paintings. Bartolomeo(?) Pinelli was engaged in making copies in November, but was considered slow. Camporese was putting pressure on him; if Pinelli was 'insolent', another artist would be found. This turned out to be unnecessary, it seems, for early in 1813 he was at work together with Mazzoli. The latter was drawing the architectural details, Pinelli the figures.[124]

The visit of the Parisian agents of the Ministry of the Interior in 1813 saw Daru reporting to Gisors on his work, which had cost by then 75,203 frs.[125] The undertaking continued through most of 1813, centring on room 26, and then moving to gallery 97.

When the French left, the restored government's Commission des Embellisements reported in May 1814 that there was work here still for many years, and that it would cost about the same as the Colosseum, 450 scudi per month. A guard had to be established night and day, apparently because the site was regarded as 'dangerous' (nothing about 'precious'), until a wall was suggested instead. This was favoured by Canova, but the cost (263 scudi) was thought too great, and brambles or a hedge were to be used, costing 25–30 scudi.[126]

The *Giornale del Campidoglio* paid little attention to the excavations at the Domus Aurea, and equally little is to be found in the *Giornale politico*.[127] Tournon, however, though he may have left the monument almost to the last of the French achievements, accorded it high mention. The excavations added seven or eight new galleries to the seven already known. Their walls and vaults were covered with perfect stuccoes and paintings: 'à voir leurs caissons, leurs arabesques, leures dorures fraîches et éclatantes, on dirait que la veille, pour la première fois, le maître du monde vint les visiter'. Clearing had, it is admitted, been carried out before, but without order, and the debris was moved from one room to another as curiosity compelled. The old investigations had uncovered the Laocoön; the French could not claim results as brilliant, but at least this 'admirable musée souterrain' had been permanently revealed.[128]

The main published account of the French work was by Antonio de Romanis, *Le antiche camere esquiline*, 1822 (see Plate 40). His plan and legend are the best summary of the condition of the Domus Aurea after the French excavations. He noted that the identity of the building was still controversial: the Baths of Titus, the House of Maecenas, or the Domus Aurea. The first regular clearing had been undertaken then and had reached the ancient paving. This was of porphyry, serpentine and giallo. The walls were found covered with marble, or painted. It was, of course, the paintings which called forth de Romanis' praise for their delicacy, perspective and imagination.

The antiquarians were understandably enthusiastic. Giuseppe Guattani noted the discovery of the main western corridor in 1813 and was particularly pleased with an inscription: 'duodecim deos et Dianam et Iovem optimum maximum habeat iratos quisquis hic minxerit aut cacarit' (*CIL* 6.29,848b). He concluded with a characteristic complaint, best appreciated in the original, with its light evocations:

Egli è un vero piacere de poter percorrere queste spaziose camere e gallerie, ove l'uomo istruito trova in mille modi da pascere il suo spirito; solo rincresce che ora l'altezza delle volte in cui sono le principali pitture è tal che fa duopo vederle in gran distanza dall'occhio, al debole chiarore di piccole candele racomandate a lunghe canne unite insieme, che oscillando nella mano del custode fanno temula luce, illanguidita e velata dall'aria umida e crassa che regna in quei sotterranei.[129]

THE FORUM BOARIUM

The rectangular temple in the Forum Boarium is traditionally known as that of Fortuna Virilis. More correctly perhaps it belonged to the harbour god Portunus. The *Giornale del Campidoglio* mentions the temple on 12 January 1811, stating that, whereas its most beautiful parts had previously been buried, it had now been restored and the substructures could be seen (Plate 41). Immense labour had been expended to excavate and remove the earth. On 9 March it was further announced that almost all the earth between this temple and that of 'Vesta' had been cleared. Tournon, in his *Etudes statistiques* noted merely that the French had cleared the temple to its stylobate.[130]

Following the tremendous crisis over the restoration of the neighbouring 'Temple of Vesta',[131] the main French work in the Forum Boarium was this simple clearing of the other temple and the levelling of the ground between them to approximately the ancient level. The story can once again be pieced together from the archives, this time mainly in Rome.

On 28 December 1810 the Director of the Imperial Domains directed that the house of the Orientalist monks against the Temple of Fortune should be demolished.[132] Work was under way clearing the temple by January 1811. Tournon corresponded with Collicola, Inspector of Works, regarding the use of baskets by the workers to carry away the soil. This was, he declared, a waste of time. Until carts could be employed, the workers were to be transferred to the Temple of Saturn in the Forum.[133] And on 11 January the Consulta passed a decree on the work of the 'Commission for the Re-establishment of the Forum': the space between the two temples in the Forum Boarium was to be lowered to the level of the stylobate of the Temple of Fortune.[134] The earth excavated was dumped outside the Porta Portese, a little way down the river, using two ships. By the end of March, the cost was 840 scudi, and the work was little more than half completed, since another 648 scudi would be needed.[135]

The work ran into the usual trouble. In March and April 1811 there were claims by Conte Bolognetti for damage to his gardens caused by the interruption of his water-supply. Camporese was asked by Tournon to make a report. The outcome is unknown. Perhaps about the same time (for it is undated), the brothers Andosilla, owners of a hay-loft in the Bocca della Verità, claimed they were suffering considerable damage from the dumping of earth and stone, although the loft had been burned down some years before![136]

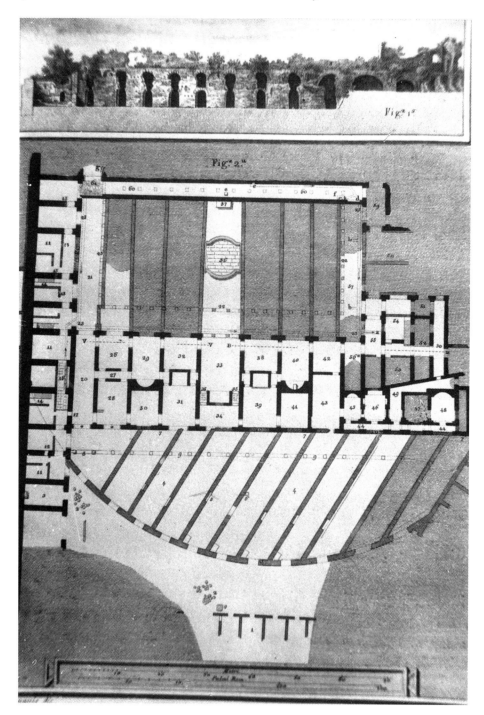

Plate 40 Antonio de Romanis, *Le antiche camere esquiline*, 1822, pl. 2: 4 substructures of the buildings above; 7 front wall of the original building; 8 bases

By October, Camporese and Valadier began to provide valuations of the properties to be acquired and demolished: they were mostly houses in the Via Ponte Rotto and the Via Porta Leone, some of which belonged to the Borghese, as well as the hay-loft and garden of Marchese Bovio. In a report to the Consulta on 28 December, Tournon asked again for the house of the Orientalist monks against the temple, although no estimate was given.[137]

The general statement of work for 28 September until 31 December 1811 gives the total man-working days in the Forum as 3,640, cubic metres of earth removed as 1,186, and the cost as 4,250 frs.[138]

The properties to be acquired are given in a fuller list by June–July 1812, showing again the predominance of gardens and hay-stores of the aristocracy in yet another classical centre of Rome (Fig. 3):[139]

hay-store of Conte Capizucchi	2,953 frs
garden of S. Rita	241
hay-store of Conte Carpigna	3,210
hay-store of Principe Gabrielli[140]	7,500
hay-store of the Propaganda Fide	1,316
hay-store of the Marchese Vincentini	4,280
hay-store of the church of S. Eligio de' Ferrari	1,271

of the portico columns; 11 side rooms; 13 windows onto the communication corridor; 14 stairs to the second storey; 16 corridor where the vase of coins was discovered; 20 the great corridor, once finely decorated; 22 foundations of the portico; 26 finely decorated room, festoons of myrtle and figures on a blue background; 29 room with a semicircular niche for a statue, colours blue and rose, walls decorated with little shrines; 31 winter triclinium (?), in the eighteenth century containing the celebrated picture of the centaurs; 32 once beautifully decorated; 33 great hall giving onto the cortile: summer dining-room (?), wall covered with marble, then a terracotta frieze in various colours, a cornice of dark blue with little figures in relief in gilded stucco; the imaginative ceiling now all lost; 36 fountain; 38 room decorated with little porticoes in perspective, now almost all lost, but the vault shows pavilions, pergolas with birds, and a flying putto in the centre; 39 room with a beautiful frieze with volutes of foliage, a rose fascia with white meanders, candelabra with columns, festoons, landscapes, masks, etc.; the upper section had little porticoes with roses, festoons, shields, and figures in relief – now almost completely covered with saltpetre; 40 the room where, popularly, it was believed that the Laocoön was found: the decoration wonderful – a double order of porticoes, Bacchantes and pavilions, which have now mostly disappeared; 41 room decorated with shrines, festoons of myrtle on a dark blue ground, now destroyed by nitrous earth; 42 the room of the famous painting of Hektor and Andromache, drawn by Annibale Carracci; 43, 44, 49–50 corridors, the last with the Rhea Silvia vault; 52 corridor filled with earth, where Mirri saw figures of philosophers; with festoons and hanging lamps above, and Bacchus and Apollo in the vault; 53 room with Bacchus between two nymphs on the vault; 55 long corridor to the cortile; 56 corridor decorated with gymnastic exercises; 58 originally the largest room of the complex; 60 corridor discovered in 1813.

Plate 41 Giambattista Piranesi, *Vedute di Roma*, the 'Temple of Fortune'. Piranesi's engraving before the French work shows the late Republican temple, rather of Portunus than of Fortune, converted into the church of S. Maria Egiziana, built around on two sides, and now in a well owing to the rise in the ground level.

Figure 3 The Forum Boarium in 1811 (F 13 1568A). A the Arch of Janus; B the Temple of Fortuna Virilis; C the Temple of Vesta; D hay-stores belonging to Conte Capizucchi; E garden of the church of S. Rita and S. Francesca; F hay-stores of Conte Carpigna; G hut belonging to the municipality; H hay-stores of Principe Gabrielli; I hay-stores of the Propaganda; L hay-stores of Marchese Vincentini; M hay-stores of the church of S. Eligio de' Ferrari; N houses of the hospice of S. Maria Egiziana of the Armenians; P garden, storeroom and hay-stores of Marchese Silvestri Bovio; QR gardens of Conte Cenci Bolognetti; S garden of Principe Borghese and the Albertazzi brothers.

house of the hospice of S. Maria Egiziana	3,389
garden of the Marchese Silvestri	12,405
garden of the Conte Bolognetti	7,133
garden of Principe Borghese	2,835
	46,539 frs

Attached is a portfolio of agreements between the owners and the Mayor. The state of demolitions on 31 March 1813 shows that all these properties were bought, but that none had been demolished. We are reminded of the identical situation on the Palatine.

Plate 42 One of a set of twenty watercolours of Roman monuments in 1811 (artist unknown). The temple is described as 'newly excavated and restored to its ancient form'. In fact, little has changed since Piranesi's engraving: the surrounding buildings still crowd the temple as they were to do until the 1920s, but the ground level has been lowered on the other two sides, leaving the entrance in mid-air, and the area has been generally cleaned. The ancient paving (?) is visible.

Valadier declared that 'with these clearances one will have on the left bank of the Tiber a most beautiful spot adorned with two precious remains of antiquity'.[141] Angelo Uggeri adopted his usual critical approach. He could not complain about the work carried out, since the Temple of Fortune had only been cleared to its base (Plate 42). Rather he criticised the 'nonchalance' of 'the person supposed to look after these things': soon the temple would be re-covered by earth brought by water and by the continued dumping of building refuse.[142] We may suspect a reference to none other than the Commissario delle Antichità: Fea.

It was, in fact, only under the Fascist government between 1921 and 1924 that the Temple of Fortune was completely isolated.[143]

THE FORUM DOMITIANI

There is no mention of this famous monument of Domitian, now known as the Forum of Nerva, in the archives alongside the other archaeological undertakings of 1809–14. Only Stendhal in his *Promenades dans Rome*, under 30 May 1828, states that it was covered under debris 12–15 feet deep. In the civil list of 1814, Napoleon ordered operations here similar to those in the Forum of Trajan. The French were thus about to begin work which may have precluded the famous clearing by Corrado Ricci this century.

THE FORUM HOLITORIUM

It is to be noted that, by some inexplicable paradox, although Valadier had begun excavations in the three temples around S. Nicola in Carcere in 1808, the French did not continue the work. The architect resumed and completed the excavation in 1816.[144]

THE FORUM ROMANUM

The modern, 'scientific' excavation of the centre of classical Rome, the focus of its political and commercial life, the Forum, began in 1788 with Baron Fredenheim's investigation of the Basilica Julia.[145] When the French arrived, however, little had changed. As an example of what the Forum looked like at the beginning of the nineteenth century, we may quote one of the best-known English travellers of the time, John Eustace, who visited Rome in 1802. The only way down from the Capitol to the Forum was a 'steep and irregular descent'. In the latter were to be seen only

a few shattered porticoes and here and there an isolated column standing in the midst of broken shafts, vast fragments of marble capitals and cornices heaped together in masses . . . A herdsman seated on a pedestal while his oxen were drinking at a fountain, and a few passengers moving at a distance in different directions, were the only living beings that disturbed the silence and solitude which reigned around.[146]

It was, however, only natural that French attention should be concentrated here, where the most evocative and spectacular temples, basilicas and triumphal arches still showed their remains (Plate 43). Camille de Tournon described the early nineteenth-century ground level as 4 m above the ancient, caused in part by using the Forum as a rubbish dump. At the foot of the Capitol, however, it was 10 m deep, and there was an artificial hill on which a senator had constructed stables! Where excavations had been undertaken, the earth was simply thrown back when they were finished. As well, much of the space was covered with houses and store-rooms. Tournon was to sum up the French achievement, apart from work on individual monuments, as the removal of the convent and stores around S. Francesca Romana (the church itself escaped demolition only because of local veneration for it), and the building of drains to carry water to the ancient outlets. The French had hoped to excavate the whole Forum down to the ancient level; this was realised only in the later part of the century.[147]

Progress on this most ambitious undertaking was noted in the *Giornale*

Plate 43 Francesco Morelli, *Veduta generale del Foro Romano*, c. 1810. The artist combines the folkloristic and the antiquarian in the fashion of the time. Romans in local dress watch as musicians accompany two dancers. Below, a group crosses the Forum with donkeys. The spatial relations of the temples to the Arch of Severus are incorrect, but we can see the large block of houses against the Column of Phocas, and others in and against the Temple of Saturn. The famous avenue of trees is clear.

del Campidoglio. On 9 January 1811 it was announced that two houses in the middle of the Forum had been removed, allowing a clear view of the whole from the Capitol to the Arch of Titus. Three days later came the publication of the grand plan to convert the whole area into a public garden (Il Giardino del Campidoglio, or Le Jardin du Capitole). On 9 March the opening was announced of the new road to the Capitol, passing the Temple of Saturn, and the planting of a row of laurels to give shade. Exotic trees were being planted for the public garden. The long-dreamed-of proposal to clear the whole area to the ancient level soon proved, however, to be too ambitious. The *Giornale* announced on 20 April that parts of the Via Sacra had been found, but at a depth of thirty palms (6.6 m), too deep to be completely cleared. And the great cattle fountain in the middle had been uncovered. After a strange gap of eighteen months, when news resumed beautification schemes dominated: 'immensi scavi ci fanno godere quel colpo d'occhio veramente unico nel mondo, e che verrà ancora abellito dalle piantaggioni che si preparano' (*Giornale politico*, 15 November 1813).

In the archival sources which follow, only the work on the Forum as a whole will be described. The excavation and restoration of individual monuments can be found under each separately in their alphabetical order.

Tournon sent de Gérando the 'Plan général d'embellisements pour la Ville de Rome' on 24 October 1810.[148] The only ancient monuments included were the Forum and the Portico of Octavia. The former was described as encumbered with houses and markets. The best solution was therefore to convert the whole area into a public garden from the Capitol to the Arch of Constantine. The convent of the Olivetani had to be acquired. The ancient levels were to be sought, and plantations used to 'frame' the ancient remains. Here, then, was the genesis of the Jardin du Capitole.

Tournon wrote again to de Gérando on 17 November, enclosing a detailed plan:[149]

1. All buildings against the Tabularium were to be demolished and the slope terraced with a moderate glacis from the Temple of Vespasian to the Arch of Severus.

2. The Temple of Saturn was to be cleared and the ground levelled.

3. There was to be a stair from S. Giuseppe to the Arch of Severus, and an easy ramp on the other side of the arch. The entrance for pedestrians to the Forum was to be under the arch.

4. The three houses below the Temple of Saturn were to be demolished.

5. The bases of the columns of the Temple of Antoninus and Faustina were to be excavated, as the sides of the temple.

6. The avenue was to be continued to S. Adriano and the Basilica of Maxentius, to uncover their foundations.

7. The space between S. Francesca Romana and the Basilica was to be

bought and the buildings demolished, and the same between the Arch of Titus and the convent of the Olivetani.

8. The area between the Colosseum and the Olivetani was to be purchased by the Crown.

9. The Basilica and the Temple of Venus and Rome were to be cleared and united to the Colosseum.

10. The whole area was to be planted with trees to frame the monuments, and with lawns where suitable.

11. The earth excavated was to be placed behind the Basilica and between the temples of the Dioscuroi and of Saturn and the Arch of Janus (i.e. on the Velabrum). The earth was to be kept as hills, indeed sown and planted as vantage points.

12. There was need for a monumental entrance on the south. Tournon proposed to realign the road past the Colosseum to the Meta Sudans and the Arch of Titus. From here there were two possibilities: in the first, the road could follow the foot of the Palatine to the foot of the Capitol. This would leave the Forum free and make the road from Naples pass at the foot of 'the most magnificent monuments of ancient and modern Rome'. The disadvantage was that it would require the demolition of twenty houses between the Consolazione and the foot of the Capitol.

The second possibility was to take the road via the Arch of Severus, the Mamertine, the Via di Marforio and the Ripresa dei Barberi. This would cut the Forum in half, but Tournon thought it preferable, without saying why.

13. The road between the Caelian and Palatine, and the Via Appia were to be planted.

The Forum would thus be a promenade for pedestrians, and carriages could circle the Palatine.

Tournon finally suggested that the work should be divided over three years, as follows:

1. Lowering the level at the Arch of Severus and at the temples of Antoninus and Faustina and of Saturn; beginning at the Colosseum and on planting of the gardens.

2. Demolition of the convent of S. Francesca Romana, clearing the Temple of Venus and Rome, the Basilica of Maxentius, planting, building the road from the Colosseum to the Arch of Titus, clearing of houses between the Arch of Severus and the Ripresa dei Barberi.

3. Completion of the road and garden.

Calculating 300 workers for the five winter months each year, the cost would be 50,000 frs per year, not counting acquisitions and restoration.

The obvious question which we must at least attempt to answer is, who was responsible for the conception of this grandiose plan? Tournon's love of the monuments is well attested, but the burdens of his office hardly allowed him to carry out the professional surveying and detailed antiquarian and town-planning manifested here. There were, however, two men above all others who were to be instrumental in the supervision of the 'embellisements'. They were the architects Giuseppe Camporese and Giuseppe Valadier. These two we may assume with all certainty had devised the above plans.[150]

De Gérando replied on 19 November, thanking Tournon for all the work and offering some observations. First, the excavations would lower the Forum to the same level as the Tiber. What about the drainage? Second, the English garden concept was described as rather 'tortuous' and 'affected', ill-adapted to the august and grandiose view. Third, the Colosseum must be included: it was 'the most beautiful restoration which could be attempted in Europe'. Fourth, the Domus Aurea could also be included. And, finally, the road through the Forum must reach the Tarpeian Rock.[151] Meanwhile, a meeting of the Commission for the Preservation of Monuments considered the plans for the 'pubblica passeggiata', and the architect Francesco Ferrari reported to Principe Gabrielli, assistant to the Mayor, on the houses below the Capitol near the Arch of Severus. There were granaries, houses belonging to the monastery of S. Chiara di Gallese, the house of Sig. Ciogni, and that of Duca Mattei. In total they were valued at 20,865 frs or 3,900 scudi. Tournon told Mayor Braschi to go ahead and agree on a price with the owners, given the modesty of the valuations.[152] A more detailed description of the Mattei house appears in the valuation by the architect G. B. Monati. It consisted of two rooms on the upper floor and an *osteria* on the ground level, with annexed large shed and nearby hay-lofts, valued in all at 1,331 scudi (5,123 frs).[153] Who could now imagine such a complex in the very middle of the Forum? This turned out to be a celebrated and drawn-out acquisition. By December there was consideration by the Commission of Monuments of demolishing a house with foundry belonging to a man called Blasi, or at least the tower, which impeded the view of the Capitol.

The list of demolitions was growing (Fig. 4). On 8 December, Valadier wrote to the Inspector of Works, Collicola, listing the garden and barn at the Arch of Titus belonging to S. Francesca*, the small house and yard at the Basilica of Maxentius belonging to the Conservatorio dei Mendicanti, the little barns at the Basilica belonging to the priests of SS. Cosma e Damiano*, the house of Rinaldi at the Basilica, a house near the Temple of Antoninus and Faustina belonging to the University, a house near S. Luca belonging to the Università de' Falegnami, a nearby house of the Accademia di S. Luca, a house near the Temple of Saturn belonging to the Municipality, the house of the nuns of S. Cecilia*, houses belonging to the monastery of S. Chiara di Gallese*, a house belonging to the priests of S. Agostino*, the house of Sig. Ciogni, the house and barn of Duca Mattei, and the cortile of the church of S. Maria Liberatrice.[154] The properties asterisked already belonged to the state. Here is invaluable and fascinating evidence for the condition of the Forum in the early nineteenth century: a mass of properties belonging for the most part to various churches, but also some privately owned dwellings, in one case of an aristocrat. Before the year had ended, Mattei signified his willingness to settle for 1,000 scudi, considerably below the lowest valuation.

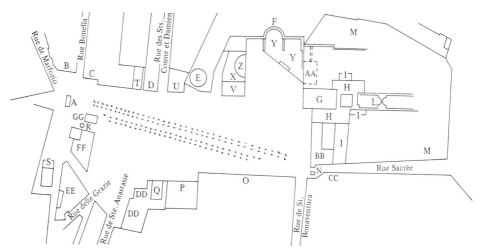

Figure 4 The Forum Romanum before French work, *c.* 1810 (F 13 1568A). A Arch of Severus; B church of S. Luca; C church of S. Adriano; D Temple of Antoninus and Faustina (S. Lorenzo in Miranda); E Temple of 'Romulus and Remus' (SS. Cosma e Damiano); F Basilica of Maxentius; G church of S. Francesca Romana; H convent of S. Francesca Romana, to be retained; I idem, to be demolished; L Temple of Venus and Rome; M vineyard of S. Francesca Romana; N Arch of Titus; O Farnese Gardens; P property of Giovanni Vidali; Q church of S. Maria Liberatrice; R Column of Phocas; S Temple of Saturn; T house belonging to S. Lorenzo in Miranda; U house of convent of SS. Cosma e Damiano, already demolished; V house and grain-store belonging to Signori Rinaldi and Leonardi; Z grain-stores of same; Y court and house of Conservatorio dei Mendicanti; AA factories of Marco Airoldi; BB grain-stores of Francesco Pereyra and Marchese Pianetti; CC vineyard and garden of Principe Barberini; DD grain-stores of Antonio Zani, Principe Borghese, hay-stores of Marchese de Cavalieri; EE houses of the Ospedale della Consolazione, houses of S. Eligio de' Ferrari (the French form of the name is given: S. Elige des Forgerons; the church of S. Eligio de' Ferrari was on the other side of the Palatine, near S. Omobono) grain-stores of Sig. Ciogni; FF houses of Sig. Ciogni, grain-stores of Domenico Blasi (the small square at the top of the block belonged to S. Chiara di Gallese); GG house of Cardinale [sic] Mattei.

The accounts for Forum work from 12 November 1810 within a month amounted to 3,015 scudi (16,000 frs).[155] When Tournon asked the Consulta for the monastery and garden of S. Francesca and the house which had once belonged to S. Chiara, he was told that they were on long lease and that compensation would have to be paid.[156]

Work began on the supporting wall for the road to the Capitol and for the drain under the latter in January 1811.[157] In the same month, the Consulta decreed that the ground at the foot of the Capitol should be terraced or sloped according to the substructures found. The construction of the road naturally required the demolition of the house by the Temple of Saturn.[158]

Problems of payment for the workers arose by February. Tournon informed the Directeur Général de la Comptabilité des Communes that 25,000 frs had already been spent and asked for another 25,000 which had been allotted. The Prefect stated that he would not put off any of the four or five hundred poor who were employed here.[159] Not only pay for workers caused worries. Braschi and Tournon corresponded throughout April over 3,000 frs owed to the contractor, Andrea Lezzani.

By April, the valuations of the various properties were ready:[160]

the barn of the Augustinian monks	1,540 frs
the house, barns and storeroom of Sig. Ciogni	22,534
the indemnity to Sig. Blasi who leased the above and established a foundry	4,442
the house of the nuns of S. Cecilia	2,439
the house of the nuns of S. Chiara di Gallese	2,568
the house of Duca Mattei	2,804
the house of the Consolazione	3,364
the house of the 'Confraternité des Serruriers'	3,929
the granaries of the Domaine against the Basilica of Maxentius and the house alongside the Temple of Antoninus	14,894
the house of Sig. Rinaldi	4,173
the house and granaries of the Olivetani monks	10,272
land belonging to the hospital of the Fratelli di Dio	252
six barns belonging to Sig. Diotallevi	2,140
	75,355 frs

This list is again instructive for the nature of private property. Now we have not only the properties and their owners but also their respective values, showing the two major proprietors to be Sig. Ciogni and the Olivetani monks. The sum was not small when one considers that it was almost the entire annual budget of the Jardin du Capitole as established by imperial decree in July of the same year.

It was that decree which totally changed the administration of the archaeological and town-planning works and which established the Jardin du Capitole as one of the main projects within the entire Embellisements programme.

By October, masons were busy with demolitions, and the vines and trees in the garden of S. Francesca were to be cleared.[161] Another example of negotiations with the aristocracy was provided by the granary in the courtyard of the monastery of S. Francesca, which belonged to Marchese Agostino Pianetti and was rented for 28 scudi per annum. Camporese and Valadier valued it at 336 scudi (1,797 frs); the owner testified that he had paid 2,000.[162]

In November, work began on the demolition of the convent of S. Francesca. Two houses belonging to the Domaine had been taken down. Much of the 1811 funds were to be spent on resumptions, but all monies in 1812 were to be spent on works. At the end of the month, the Commission des Embellisements decreed that the mass of earth placed in the Forum the year before was to be taken away in twenty carts to behind S. Maria in Cosmedin. Camporese and Valadier submitted the valuation of another house, that of Pietro Leonardi, worth 1,300 scudi (6,955 frs).[163]

A summary of the work to the end of the year revealed that demolition of houses had occupied 1,998 man-working days and cost 2,635 frs, while that of the convent of S. Francesca had occupied 669 man-working days and cost 844 frs. The 'petite montagne', the earth dumped in the Forum which the Commission had ordered removed, had comprised 1,046 cu m and been removed at a cost of 1,307 frs.[164]

It was somewhere in the middle of the Forum in 1811 (neither place nor date is more clearly specified) that a fragment of the list of the Roman augurs was discovered, naming these priests from Sulla (88 BC) to Caecilius Creticus (AD 7) (*CIL* 6.1976). The contemporary witness, Fea, says only that it was turned up while digging a drain from the Temple of Antoninus and Faustina to that of the Dioscuroi and then to the Column of Phocas.[165]

By February 1812 the garden was being laid out from the Forum to the Colosseum and the plantations commenced, and by the beginning of March the garden between the Basilica of Maxentius and the Colosseum was finished. All the trees that could be obtained had been planted. One hundred workers were making avenues and planting trees in S. Francesca.[166]

On 21 March, Tournon estimated that the Jardin du Capitole, which had already cost 134,520 frs (and for which 100,000 had been allotted each year), would cost another 200,000 in 1812. Its total area, however, was 25 ha and included the most important monuments in Rome.

A major new development was revealed in the meeting of the Commission on 28 April 1812. The architects Valadier and Camporese were asked to present a 'projet raisonné' for the clearing of the Forum to the ancient level.[167] As for the demolitions, some houses had already been removed around the Temple of Saturn and the Tabularium. Still to be demolished were the Casa Mattei, most of the next block (FF on Fig. 4), and all of the next (EE). On the Palatine side, all the granaries and storerooms (Q, P, DD) still had to be taken down. Towards S. Francesca Romana granary BB had to be demolished to link up with what had already been cleared. Near the Basilica of Maxentius, finally, although some houses and storerooms had already gone, more had to be demolished up to the church of S. Adriano (especially V, X, Z).[168] The Commission listed properties to be acquired in July, mostly grain- and hay-stores, totalling 91,891 frs.[169]

Camporese and Valadier submitted the report requested of them on 28 April on 28 September, exactly five months later (see Plate 44).[170] Either they were fully occupied with all their other tasks or the survey was enormously demanding. To restore the Forum to its 'ancient splendour', all earth was to be removed down to the ancient level. This was to begin at the Arch of Severus and work would move gradually to the temples of Antoninus and Faustina and the Dioscuroi. The ancient roads and buildings which formed the perimeter of the Forum were to be traced, up to the Basilica of Maxentius, the Palatine, the Arch of Titus and the Temple of Venus and Rome. The monuments and antiquarian debate would establish clear proof of what existed here and would make the Forum much more worthy than at present. It was admitted, of course, that the work would be long and costly, but it was not to be impeded by modern buildings or roads. The whole project could not be realised in less than four to six years. The architects then quaintly noted that the debris would be enough for a new monument in itself, a new Testaccio! The best place for the dump would be between S. Giovanni in Laterano and S. Croce. The other main problem was admitted to be the modern roads which entered the Forum. The architects proposed that they should be elevated on ramps, lowered, or abolished. (It was only in 1982 that the last modern road dividing the Forum Romanum, the road across the foot of the Capitol, was removed.)

By December, the total earth removed since September 1811 was 15,109 cu m, and the work had cost 18,887 frs. The work of planting had cost 6,873 frs.

Early in 1813 negotiations continued for the purchase of private properties. Principe Gabrielli was trying to buy the barn between S. Francesca and the Arch of Titus, the houses alongside the Basilica of Maxentius, and the houses and barns between the Consolazione and the Arch of Severus. It was hoped that these might be vacated by 1 February. Payments made on 23 January included: the barn of Pereyra, 2,000 frs; that of Pianetti, 1,000 frs; the foundry and house of Blasi, 2,000 frs; and the house of Mattei, 3,921 frs.[171]

The year 1813 was also that of the visit. Louis Berthault came to check on the Jardin du Capitole. He admitted to Tournon that it was more difficult than the Jardin du Grand César. The Forum was the very centre of the Embellisements, linked to both the Capitol and the Colosseum. The gardener was rather defensive about his first trip to Rome: he had not been here before, but he had studied the city from his youth! He promised not to present 'ideal projects which were impossible to carry out' and assured the

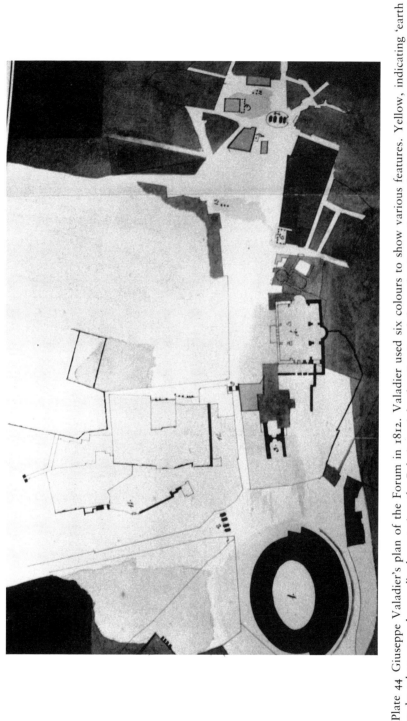

Plate 44 Giuseppe Valadier's plan of the Forum in 1812. Valadier used six colours to show various features. Yellow, indicating 'earth to be taken up or lowered', characterises the Palatine; pink, showing 'earth heaped up', are the two darker patches on the Caelian and Palatine; light blue indicated earth already removed, and is used for the main monuments from the Colosseum to the Capitol; light green is used for the houses already demolished (against the Tabularium, the two blocks near the Column of Phocas, and next to the Arch of Titus); and grey is used for the areas which are not to change (the bottom and right-hand side of the plan).

Prefect that he was in Rome to obtain the advice of the 'fortunate artists' born there. His first impression of the plans, however, was critical: there did not seem to be an overall concept, but rather 'un cadre pour chaque tableau'. The Forum was, he admitted, difficult with its very different levels and the monuments which one 'dared approach only with awe'. It was, in all, 'a Gordian knot, easy to cut but hard to untie'.[172]

Gisors provided information about the progress of demolitions to the Parisian bureaucracy. Already pulled down were the Conservatorio dei Mendicanti (2,675 frs), the house of Airoldi (1,000 frs), the barns of Pereyra (2,945 frs) and Pianetti (1,872 frs), and the house of Mattei (3,921 frs). One third of S. Francesca Romana also had been demolished. The houses of Rinaldi and Leonardi, however, had not been paid for, so the corner of the Basilica of Maxentius could not yet be cleared; they were valued at 12,840 frs.[173]

It seems to have been Berthault who drew up the lists of the different levels in the Forum.[174] They give telling evidence of the difficulties of the plans to unify the monuments. Only a selection is offered here: the Arch of Severus was lower than the Temple of Saturn by 17 feet 7 inches; than the Capitol by 71 feet 5 inches; than the Temple of the Diocuroi by 11 feet 3 inches; than the Column of Phocas by 5 feet 7 inches, than the Basilica of Maxentius by 34 feet 4 inches; than the Temple of Antoninus and Faustina by 8 feet 10 inches. (Only by clearing everywhere to the ancient level could these problems be solved, because in antiquity they were all linked conveniently.)

Berthault's report on the Jardin du Capitole is dated 25 March.[175] The imperial decrees had implied, he asserted, three separate sections: the Forum, the Palatine and the Colosseum. He suggested uniting the first two and extending the promenade around the three other sides of the Palatine. It would, he admitted, be very interesting to discover the ancient level of the Forum, but too inconvenient, especially because of drainage problems. So each monument was to be exploited individually and to be accessible by a promenade shaded by trees. The Via Sacra was to be cleared from the Arch of Severus to the Basilica of Maxentius, giving a slope of 11 m in 321 m. The houses on the north side of the Forum were to be demolished from S. Adriano to the Basilica. This would create the need for a retaining wall and trees to mask the remaining buildings. The slope of the Capitol was to be terraced. There were to be ramps to descend to the base of the columns of the Temple of Antoninus. It was, Berthault asserted, unfortunate that only two-thirds of S. Francesca Romana could be demolished; for it hid the Temple of Venus and Rome and the Colosseum. The last was to be cleared, the surrounding ground levelled, and the wall around the Arch of Constantine removed.[176]

The Commission adopted Berthault's proposals on the same day. Further arguments were offered against any attempt to reveal the ancient level of the Forum. The Capitol would be inaccessible, modern levels on the north would be left suspended, and roads from that side would no longer work. (Interesting to see here already the modern obsession with roads and traffic.) The great project of Camporese and Valadier of September 1812 was thus abandoned, but it was readopted in 1827.

Tournon apparently approved of Berthault's ideas. The plan as submitted to the Commission would cost 2,151,866 frs on top of the 370,985 frs already spent! The enormity of this, the Prefect admitted, might appear terrifying if one overlooked that the design was 'to preserve and make visible the most beautiful monuments of antiquity'. He thus suggested that the plan be carried out in stages, spending 300,000 frs each year. He did not seem to realise that this meant seven years' further work.[177]

Time was, of course, running out. In the middle of the year, 400 workers were lowering the ground between the Forum and the Colosseum, in accordance with Berthault's plan.[178] By September, attention was focussing on the Palatine, where immense substructures had been found. No light could be thrown on them except that they were to support the artificial level of the hill. They were being retained until further excavations indicated whether they should be removed or not. A great head of Medusa had been discovered. By December, the lowering of levels towards the Arch of Titus and S. Francesca Romana was complete, and the great 'substructures' between the Colosseum and the Arch of Constantine had been cleared.[179]

Charlotte Eaton, dominated by her anti-French prejudice, jeered at their talk of excavating to the ancient level of the Forum during the fourteen (sic) years they possessed Rome. This was simply another proof that they talked more than they acted. She forgot what she had written earlier: 'What was then my astonishment – instead of the vacant space I expected to find with no trace remaining of its ancient splendour – to behold Corinthian columns, ruined temples, triumphal arches, and mouldering walls, not less affecting from their decay.'[180] French efforts had obviously not been in vain (Plate 45).

It is not without interest to conclude the story with the restored Papal government. In May 1814, 405 men, fifty women and fifty boys were still employed in the Forum and Colosseum. This could not continue for long. By the middle of the year it was decided for public safety to wall in the excavations around the Temple of Antoninus and Faustina and the Column of Phocas, to check the stability of the Temple of the Dioscuroi and then fill in around it – and to abandon all other work. The excavation of the Forum resumed in 1827.[181]

Embezzlement in the Forum

As with the Basilica of Maxtentius, where we extracted one episode of great human interest, so with the Forum. In the sixth register of the Abbellimenti

Plate 45 Luigi Rossini, *Cinquanta principali vedute*, pl. 31, general view of the Forum Romanum, 1817. It is important to note the artist's licence, since he is so often credited with exactness. The three buildings in the foreground are quite wrong, and there should be a considerable drop down to the Forum. The modern buildings have been removed by the French. The pit around the Column of Phocas is clear; less so that around the portico of the Temple of Antoninus and Faustina.

di Roma in the Archivio dello Stato is preserved a collection of letters from the heads of the companies working in about April 1812.

The first is a very strange account by Matteo Torelli, head of the second company. The letter is obviously very excited and very defensive, with many underlinings, and hard at first to understand. It begins with a history of the second company from October 1811 to March 1812, claiming that it consisted during this time mostly of invalids so that its performance as a working team was very poor. At the end of March, the Inspector Camporese noticed this state of affairs (a leisurely observation, some might think) and substituted more able-bodied men. Then the company was plagued by absenteeism, up to thirteen men out of seventy-five on 7 April. The day before, however, was 'un giorno rimarchevole': only one man was absent and the workers were all present until the midday *zuppa*, when they took a rest. The letter next mentions a roll-call by none other than Principe Gabrielli, assistant to the Mayor. Torelli is here very excited in his account, asserting that Gabrielli discovered only what Torelli himself would have done and what he would have announced without fail. He admits that it is strange that so many workers could be missing in such a short time, but cannot deny that it was so. He goes on to protest that he has always kept his records accurately and has always shown absences. His past conduct, he asserts, demonstrates his honesty, and he finally offers proof that the number of absentees could not be higher than his records, in that his company worked in the very centre of the Forum, under the eyes of all. (It was, in fact, in the Basilica of Maxentius.)

What does this highly defensive letter mean? The many missing elements begin to appear in succeeding documents. The next is an unsigned report by someone delegated by Gabrielli to carry out an investigation. The heads of companies, we discover, were naturally required to take a second roll-call in the afternoon, after the resumption of work following the *zuppa* and rest. The investigator declares that Torelli's afternoon roll did not show absences, and that on the very day he claimed to be so extraordinary for attendance (6 April), twenty-seven out of seventy-four were absent. It is suggested that, contrary to Torelli's assurances, similar absences must have occurred on other days, that abuses in this company must have been frequent, and that the number of workers shown in the records was 'ideal rather than real'.

The following reports are from the other company heads. Francesco Grassetti of the fifth (also working in the Basilica) asserts that his company has always been at full strength, as the pay sheets and the work completed attest. Giuseppe Danieli of the third (working in the Colosseum) provides more details to understand the crisis. Gabrielli came indeed to the Forum on 6 April and took a roll-call 'in un ora che attesa la stravagante giornata sicuro doveva essere di trovare delle mancanze, come tale è accaduto'. What time was it? Why was the day 'strange'? Danieli also protests that absences in his company would have been reported but that Gabrielli took his roll-call before he could furnish his report! A new element is added: Gabrielli ordered the suspension of Danieli and the Inspector. These were not the only dismissals, as we shall see. Danieli gives details on the absences after lunch on 6 April: in the first squad, two men were not seen again and another two were sick (it is remarkable how many of these afflictions awaited the midday rations). In the second squad, one man was 'per la sua professione accommodato', one 'accommodato per cambio di fornaio', one who had gone off on his own business later returned to work, and a fourth went away and was not seen again. In the third squad, one was sick with 'pains', one not seen again. In the fifth, one was absent for his own reasons, but returned the next day, and one replaced in the morning did not return.

There is a second document from Danieli asking how it would be possible to falsify work-sheets when the Inspector 'almost daily' (an interesting admission) passed through the corridors counting heads at rest time, especially the Jews, who did not take the *zuppa* (presumably it was not kosher). There follows the inevitable appeal for re-employment, stressing his honour and interests, after some seventeen months' faithful service. Danieli concluded by noting the regulations regarding sick workers. If one became sick well into the morning, he was credited with half a day's work, if at 'an advanced hour' the whole day.

Although the work on the Jardin du Grand César at the Piazza del Popolo does not usually concern us, the reports of the heads of companies there show a much worse situation and clarify some details of the scandal. Paolo Ravaglia of the eleventh company explained that the work sheets were being left blank and filled in by the Vice-Inspector, Corvi, with inflated numbers, whose pay, of course, was still being collected. Here we have at last the fundamental reason for the investigation. Corvi was also using skilled craftsmen after the great earthquake to repair his own house, instead of employing them in the public works. He was accustomed to fill in the attendance sheets even before the lunch-break and force the company heads to countersign them. Corvi's crimes were attested also by Giovanni Burri, head of the twelfth company, and Gregorio Castellani of the tenth. The latter tried to circumvent Corvi, but Giulio Camporese, the Inspector, told him to conform to practices in the Piazza del Popolo (he had been transferred from the Forum.) There are also fascinating affidavits by some of Castellani's workers. On 7 April, after *zuppa*, three men were 'struck by fever' (they sign with varying degrees of difficulty), another three went off after lunch and came back so late they decided it was not worth returning (these three were illiterate, and signed with a cross), and one went home for private reasons.

The summaries of absences on 6 April were as follows: second company, twenty-seven men; third, twelve; fifth, fourteen: total, fifty-three.

The end of the story can be seen in two ways. A list of the company heads dated 1 May 1812 shows no trace of any of the above men. They were all dismissed, as was Corvi, replaced by Filippo di Medelburg as Vice-Inspector. More far-reaching were the new regulations drawn up by Clemente Giardini on 24 April. The most remarkable was that all employees must be 'active', that is, alive! The lists for the week were to be drawn up on Monday mornings. The hours of work were to be publicly displayed. Lateness of up to one hour meant loss of a quarter of a day's pay for workers, a third for corporals and heads. After one hour, latecomers were excluded.

The situation in 1812 was obviously scandalous. Supervisors were not keeping accurate attendance (and therefore pay) sheets. Especially after the midday break, workers absented themselves, and the foremen fraudulently showed them as present. There was undoubtedly a high level of absenteeism, but it seems that many workers were old or ill or lacked motivation because of the heavy labour and low pay. Among the absentees, certainly, there is strong evidence for illiteracy, but that may not be representative, given what was sometimes said about the professional people who turned to work for the Embellisements.

The real dishonesty, however, was to be found in the higher ranks: those who controlled, collected and distributed the pay, and who simply pocketed what they had collected for absent workers.

The most important result of the whole affair is revealed elsewhere. In the register of the meetings of the Commission des Embellisements, the roll-call scandal was discussed. On 14 April the resignation was accepted of Giulio Camporese, who was replaced as Inspector by Clemente Giardini. Camporese, probably the son of one of the two Architect Directors of the works of the Commission des Embellisements, had been Inspector of Works since September 1811, the beginning of the Commission's work.

Nothing shows more clearly the problems of the organisation and execution of these mighty undertakings than this scandal, yet it has been quite overlooked by previous accounts of them.

THE FORUM OF TRAJAN

Antonio Nibby described the Forum of Trajan at the beginning of the nineteenth century as exhibiting the famous column in a kind of well, surrounded by a wall built by Sixtus V (1585–90). Around it was a little piazza surrounded by houses, convents and the two churches of S. Maria di Loreto and the Nome di Maria (Plate 46).[182]

In truth, Paul III (1534–49) had cleared away medieval constructions near and against the column, demolishing the parochial church of S. Nicola de Columna and some private houses. One belonged to Vincenzo della Vetera, who in compensation was made guardian of the column with a salary of

Plate 46 Giuseppe Vasi, *Magnificenze di Roma*, 1747–61, pl. 38, Trajan's Column. This shows the piazza as it had been left following the systematisation by Sixtus V. The convent of S. Eufemia is the building on the extreme left. The church on the right is S. Maria di Loreto. Out of sight on the right is the Nome di Maria.

48 ducats in 1546. In 1558, the Commune decided to carry out Michelangelo's plan for the beautification of the piazza by constructing a wall to keep away earth and water. All neighbours contributed to the cost. Sixtus V spent 10,000 scudi on the piazza and 2,837 on repairs to the column in 1589.[183]

The area, like so many other pagan centres, had been a favourite one for churches. The earliest were S. Maria di Campo Carleo, demolished in 1861, and the little church and monastery of S. Nicola, using Trajan's column as its campanile, demolished in 1535. In the fifteenth century were added the church and monastery of S. Spirito and S. Eufemia, both demolished in 1812, in the sixteenth century S. Maria di Loreto, designed by Sangallo, and in 1738 the Nome di Maria, designed by Antonio Desiret (see Plate 47).[184]

A more vivid impression of the state of the monument before French work than given by the antiquarian Nibby is offered by the English visitor, Joseph Forsyth: 'The objects which detain you longest, such as Trajan's Column and the Fountain of Trevi, etc. are inaccessible for ordure.'[185]

This was to be one of the greatest undertakings of the French, a clearing on a grand scale and extensive excavations, with enormous problems of town-planning. The whole project made an appropriate entrance in the decree of Napoleon signed at St Cloud on 27 July 1811, which established the Commission des Embellisements. The enterprises listed for attention included the piazze of the Pantheon and Trajan. And a start was to be made immediately: 'En attendant que les projets pour la place Trajana aient reçus notre approbation, il sera procédé à la démolition des convens du St Esprit et de Ste Euphémie.'

On 1 October 1811, the Commission asked Camporese and Valadier to prepare valuations of the houses, and specified that the fittings of S. Eufemia were to be moved to S. Urbano (in the Via Alessandrina). The demolitions were to be let by tender.[186] It is presumably at this point that Gertrude Rizzoli, Prefetta di S. Eufemia, sent a letter to the Commission, stating that, although the superiors had decided to transfer the convent to S. Urbano, the Conservatorio itself, which ran a school, considered that S. Caterina di Siena would be more suitable. The decision was not changed.

The valuations started to come in in November, made out by Valadier: the house of Michele Cesanelli, 5,778 frs, although the owner claimed to have paid 8,703 frs in May, and Vincenzo Grazioli's fine house and macaroni factory, with a shop and six rooms on the ground floor, seven rooms on the first floor, and five on the second, which was valued at only 4,000 frs, with 1,740 frs removal costs for his machinery.[187] The Commission laid down on the 26th that the demolitions were to start immediately, and that when the ground was clear, Martial Daru was to excavate for the Emperor.[188] There were, however, no tenders for the demolition of the two convents. It was therefore decided that the work should be undertaken by the labour-

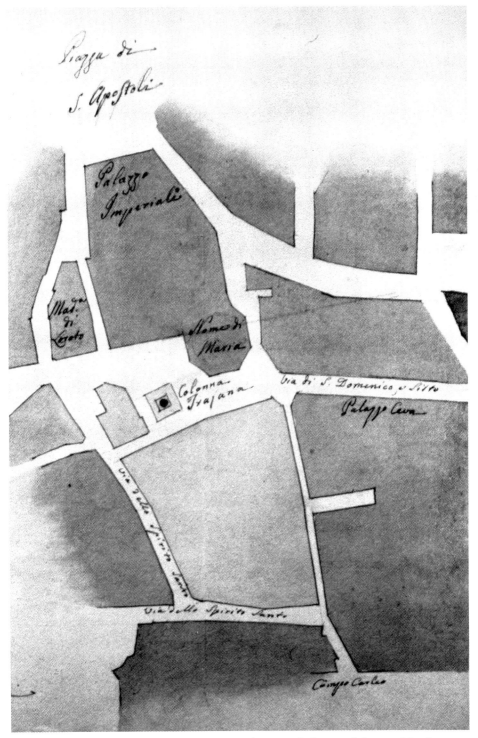

Plate 47 Valadier's plan of the Forum of Trajan, before work began, March
1812. The Column is shown hemmed in by the two churches of Nome di
Maria on the right and S. Maria di Loreto on the left, and the Palazzo Imperiale.
The Convent of S. Spirito occupies much of the Trajanic Basilica. The drawing
is coloured most attractively in pink and brown.

ers, supervised by the architects. The demolition of S. Spirito began on 9 December 1811, and by the end of the month 1,778 man-working days had already been spent at a cost of 2,203 frs.[189]

The planning of the new square began in January 1812. The Commission examined various projects presented by Valadier and Camporese and chose the one it considered most economical and easiest to execute.[190] The new public space was to be elliptical in shape, with entrances on the long sides (see Plate 48).

By the end of the month barrows were no longer being used to transport the debris away, only carts, and many workers were moved to the demolition of the convent of S. Francesca Romana in the Forum.

The Minister of the Interior in Paris, Montalivet, was kept informed about the work by Tournon. The Prefect sent plans, drawings, projects and estimates. He declared the project the most difficult in Rome because the ancient level was 5.25 m lower than the modern. The variations in the Forum Romanum were much greater, but the space was vast, whereas the two churches were only 21 m and 35 m away from the column. Tournon declared that they were not of great merit, but that it was too expensive to demolish them, and demolition would leave a gap which would be very costly to fill! The square was therefore to be on two levels, one 4 m lower than the other and joined by steps. The elliptical plan would solve the problem of the proximity of the two churches, and a fountain at the other end would balance the column. Tournon concluded with hopefulness: antiquarians considered this area to be the richest in Rome for the possible remains of monuments and works of art, because it had not been excavated. The work was therefore awaited with impatience.[191] There was also an interesting note in May. Half a day was spent removing the archive of S. Eufemia to the Capitol.[192]

As with all other major projects of the Embellisements, initial estimates for the Forum of Trajan proved to be inadequate. On 21 May, Tournon informed Montalivet that, although 50,000 frs had been allotted, the piazza would cost another 125,000; the other 75,000 frs would have to come from the 1812 budget. And only a few days later Camporese estimated that the surrounding wall alone would cost 67,492 frs.[193]

Alongside the work of the Embellisements, Daru began excavations for the Crown in the Forum on 23 March. The architect was Giuseppe Camporese, and the Inspector was Clemente Giardini. These excavations demolished the sixteenth-century wall around the column and uncovered the surrounding Basilica. Within two months, they had begun to bring to light stumps of columns of blue granite and cippolino only a few feet below the modern level.[194]

We have, on the other hand, rare details on the workers for the Embellisements at this site in the middle of the year (Plate 49). The fourth and seventh

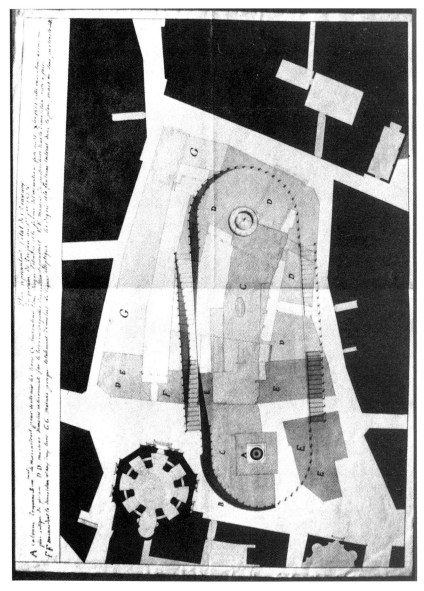

Plate 48 *Plan représentant l'état des travaux du Forum de Trajan au 1er janvier 1813.* Here is the original plan for the extensive lateral stairways and the fountain opposite the Column.

companies were operating. The former consisted of thirty-two men, ranging in age from sixteen to seventy-three (average forty-one), four women between twenty-two and fifty years of age (average forty-one again), and three boys ten to thirteen. The seventh company was thirty-two men, eighteen to eighty years, four women between twenty-two and fifty-three years, and two boys (fourteen and fifteen years old).[195] Daru's excavations were creating a 'circus' around the column. The demolition of S. Spirito would be completed within the month it was hoped, but that of S. Eufemia would take much longer. Then the surrounding wall had to be constructed and the area paved. At the end of July the Commission decided to begin the wall immediately, to prevent collapse of the earth.[196]

As in the Forum Romanum, the list of properties for acquisition and demolition was considerable. In July the Commission listed them as follows (Fig. 5):

house of Michele Cesanelli	5,350 frs
houses of Vincenzo Grazioli	11,770
house of Francesco Lucernari	19,726
house of Conte Camillo Mariscotti	4,544
house of Tiberio Piccolomini	2,140
house of Tiberio Placidi	2,003
house of Mario Farsarelli	1,926
house of Nicola Rutiloni	2,652
hut of S. Loreto	1,605
granary and house of S. Eufemia	30,816
	82,532 frs[197]

According to his accounts, Daru's work in 1812 stopped in August or September. In his customary monthly report to Montalivet, in the latter month Tournon noted that demolition of S. Spirito was complete, that of S. Eufemia was still in progress, that the elliptical wall was under construction, and that 100 workers were employed.[198] The demolitions had progressed far – perhaps too far. Valadier and Camporese reported that the convent of S. Spirito had supported two houses, those of Signori Cesanelli and Grazioli. Now that the convent had been demolished, they threatened ruin and had to be demolished immediately. The Commission approved the payment of 6,000 frs to the owners, with the outstanding 11,120 to be paid when the Minister of the Interior approved, which he fortunately did![199]

In December an ominous new note was sounded. The Commission asked the two architects to report on the conservation or demolition of the church of the Nome di Maria.[200]

The new year, 1813, opened with Tournon writing to Montalivet to tell

Plate 49 Angelo Uggeri, *Vues pittoresques*, demolition and clearing in 1813.
The location is clearly the Forum of Trajan.

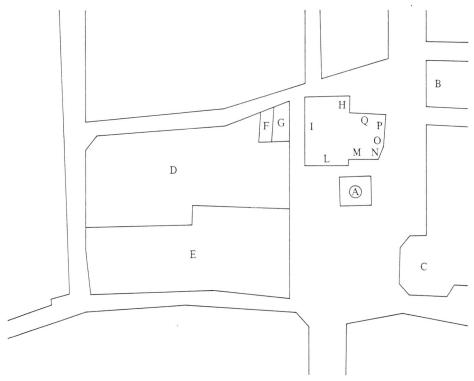

Figure 5 Plan of the Forum of Trajan before the French work, *c.* 1811 (F
13 1568A). A Trajan's Column; B church of S. Maria di Loreto; C church
of Il Nome di Maria; D convent of S. Spirito; E convent of S. Eufemia; F
house of Michelangelo Cesanelli; G house and shop of Vincenzo Grazioli;
H house of the Ospedale di S. Maria di Loreto; I house of Cavaliere Lucernari;
L house of the Delfini heirs; M house of Tiberio Piccolomini; N house of
Cavaliere Placidi di Siena; O house of Mario Farsarelli; P house of Michelangelo Fantera; Q huts of the church of S. Maria di Loreto.

him that 79,199 frs had already been spent on the Forum of Trajan, and
that another 125,337 would be needed.[201] The total cost was now going to
be 200,000 frs, instead of the 125,000 announced in the previous May. Not
unexpectedly, the two visitors from Paris then appeared.

Guy Gisors presented his report to the Commission on 23 February. He
set his sights on the church of the Nome di Maria. It 'blocked the view'
and left only 4 m for the public way. The architect opined that its destruction
would cause 'no regret to friends of the arts'. He also proposed abolishing
the lateral ramps which descended to the Forum. There was need for only
one entrance at the end opposite the column and within the enclosure, so
that the public way could be at least 10 m wide here, instead of the 6 m
with the lateral ramps; it was, he declared, 'much frequented by carriages'.
The remains found by Daru, finally, were to be investigated to see if there

was any way to adapt the enclosure to them. The Commission, needless to say, adopted all these recommendations without quibble (see Plate 50).[202]

Few demolitions apart from the two convents had yet been completed: only the houses of Cesanelli and Grazioli. That of S. Spirito had cost 32,164 frs, but material recovered was worth 33,052 frs.[203] Operations of the Embellisements which returned a profit were few and far between. By April, however, all houses in the projected square had been pulled down, except for a small block·near the column. One hundred and twenty workers were still employed.[204] Without the demolition of these houses, however, nothing further could be done. Accounts of Daru show the work of the Crown resumed from April to September.

Although the Commission had accepted Gisors' proposal to demolish the Nome di Maria, it transpires that there had been vigorous protests from the Austrians, who had built the church to commemorate the deliverance of Vienna by Jan Sobieski. They intervened with the Minister of Foreign Affairs in Paris, and saved the church.[205]

In July, Tournon wrote impatiently to Montalivet seeking funds promised last December for the vital demolitions.[206] And the suggestion of Gisors was taken up. The Accademia di S. Luca visited the excavations on 13 July and was of the opinion that they should continue in order to find the limits of the ancient Forum and that new walls should not be constructed until that had been done. Canova wrote in these terms to Tournon.[207] There may also have been some problems with the work which caused delay. Contracts for the removal of debris had to be readvertised. Giardini, the Inspector, issued strict instructions: carts were to follow the Via Porta di S. Paolo to the 'magazzini de Polvere ossia marmorate'. They were not to leave this road or fraudulently dump material elsewhere, under penalty of a fine of 50 frs for each cart. And payment was not to be by the load, but for each 1,000 cu m, two-thirds paid by the Commission, one-third by the Municipality.[208]

The bureaucracy in Paris meanwhile ground on. The projected expenses before Gisors' visit had been another 125,000 frs to complete the job. Gisors' plan would cost 67,972 frs for the wall, and 6,512 for demolitions, recouping 6,178 frs from the materials of the Nome di Maria. This gave a total of 67,326 frs. It was suggested that Montalivet approve this plan.[209] One can only be thankful the bureaucracy was so slow, but Austrian protests to another quarter were, as we have seen, more effective.

The block of houses near the column was demolished by September and the ancient drains were discovered and cleared. Found 6 m below the modern level, they were of 'solid and admirable construction'. The ancient paving was still being uncovered, showing column foundations. The foot of a colossal statue was discovered. The clearing had advanced from the column 35 m towards the Quirinal.[210] Again, accounts of Daru show his work in progress from April to September 1813.

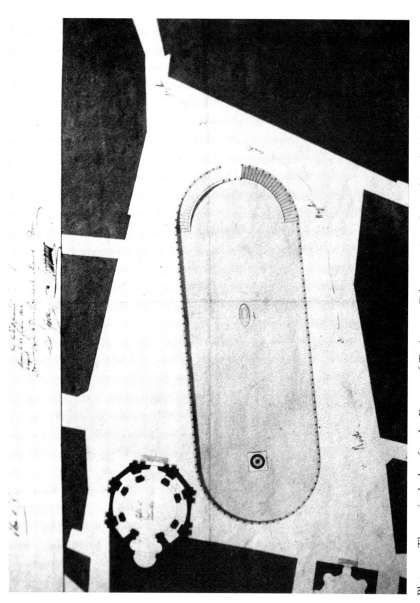

Plate 50 The revised plan for the Forum of Trajan, 23 February 1813. Gisors has abolished the lateral ramps and substituted descents at the end opposite the Column. There is no fountain. The revised plans are signed by Tournon, Braschi, Daru, Gisors and Berthault.

How to terminate the excavation, which looked like being endless, became the main problem. Valadier offered a solution in October. The most important thing, he declared, was to clear a space around the column. It had been planned to clear down to the ancient level, making a hippodrome, with hemicycles at each end and two ramps to allow easy descent. Gisors had approved this, only replacing the ramps with steps. Then with the discovery of the precious remains of the Basilica in every direction (column stumps, pavement in precious stone, fragments of cornice and sculpture), work had to be suspended on the retaining wall. At this point, Valadier stressed three considerations: that the discoveries were of great interest for art and antiquity, that 'professors and dilettanti' wanted to see the excavations extended, and that the remains should be maintained for posterity, so that future generations would not have to complain of these undertakings as Valadier and his contempories did of the barbarians who destroyed precious buildings in the past. As far as allowed by modern buildings, the excavations, he recommended, should continue. Weather, however, would destroy everything. There was, furthermore, no point in re-erecting a column base here and there. His solution, therefore, was to keep the retaining wall as in the original plan, with access only near the column. The uncovered area should be paved over, after making an exact scale model (1:10) of the ancient remains which had been uncovered, which was to be placed in a museum. The excavations could then be carried on under cover with the modern street level supported on vaults and pilasters. In this way the remains would be preserved forever, but the modern piazza would not be seriously disrupted.[211] It is difficult not to be reminded of the assertion of the Fascist town-planners more than a century later that the Via dei Fori Imperiali preserved the ancient remains, which could be re-excavated at any later date. The remains of the great Basilica thus still lie under modern roads.

Early in November, Bianchi reported that the demolition of the *cantine* was complete, as was the semicircular wall around the column, so that the retaining wall could now proceed. The clearing of the lower part of the square towards the Forum Romanum had also been finished, and the drains unblocked for 110 m.[212]

The demolitions and clearing by the Embellisements had begun in December 1811 and averaged nearly 6,000 frs per month in costs through 1812. The demolitions began with S. Spirito and generally occupied one company. By the end of the first year, more than 40,000 man-working days had been spent, nearly 20,000 cu m of earth removed, at a total cost of 73,000 frs. Throughout 1813 one company was similarly always at work, while between five and seven were occupied in the Forum. By the time the French left in January 1814, the Embellisements had spent 182,883 frs on the Forum of Trajan in little more than two years. The budget laid down in the imperial decree of July 1811, it will be remembered, was 50,000 frs per annum.

On the other hand, the excavations of the Crown supervised by Daru show his workers in action from March to August 1812 and from April to September 1813. In 1812 he was employing an average of twenty workers a day. By April 1813 these works totalled 8,866 man-working days, 10,497 cu m of earth excavated, and an expenditure of 10,888 frs for digging and 14,430 for transport, making 25,318 frs in all.[213] In 1813, his workers varied more widely, but usually between thirty and forty-five.

The architects for the Embellisements were both Camporese and Valadier, as shown by the projects submitted and the valuations.[214] Camporese, on the other hand, was as usual the architect for Daru and the excavations by the Crown.[215]

Tournon was justly proud of the French achievement in the Forum of Trajan. When the new administration took over, the column, famous as it was, was almost hidden among a mass of modern buildings, and rose out of a pit so narrow that it could scarcely be seen. The most natural solution would have been to create a large square, but this was rendered impossible by the presence nearby of the two 'remarkable' churches.[216] The solution adopted was the elliptical square, after the two convents and some houses were demolished. The foundations of the Basilica Ulpia then came to light and were methodically exposed.[217] In his short paper to the Bordeaux Academy, Tournon specified the dimensions of the excavations: 300 feet long by 180 feet wide, and 13 feet below the modern level.[218]

The undertakings here gained the special attention of a contemporary, Stendhal, who indulged in extravagant praise of Daru's excavations: 'Rome doit la plupart de ses embellisements sous Napoléon à M. Martial Daru, Intendant de la Couronne, amateur fort éclairé et ami intime de Canova; et entre autres les travaux de ce Colonne Trajane.' The works here, he declared, 'marqueront plus dans la posterité que les travaux de dix pontificats des plus actifs'.[219] The solution is all too simple: Daru was Stendhal's cousin.

With modern hindsight, we now understand more of what the French had found (Plate 51). They had uncovered part of the library portico, the central section of the Basilica, and part of the northern side of Trajan's Forum. Of the Basilica, some twenty columns had come to light, together with the precious pavement and the entrance on the Forum side.[220]

The rest of the story may be quickly told, for it was the completion of the project much as the French had planned it. The wall on the north was completed by the end of January, the very month the French left. By May, work was continuing, but at a much slower rate, 700 scudi per month, to avoid burdening the treasury. The last estimate for the square was 91,538 frs (17,109 scudi); 4,117 scudi had been spent, leaving 12,992 still to be found. Early in August, Camporese was busy clearing the drains. The wall was

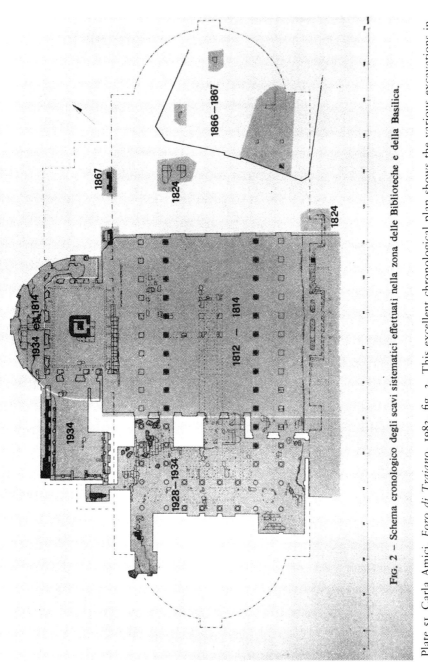

FIG. 2 – Schema cronologico degli scavi sistematici effettuati nella zona delle Biblioteche e della Basilica.

Plate 51 Carla Amici, *Foro di Traiano*, 1982, fig. 2. This excellent chronological plan shows the various excavations in the Forum, with the French work concentrated in the central area.

now the main project, and the contractor is revealed as the ubiquitous Lezzani, who was to be fined if he did not complete it on time. By February 1815 the steps and paving were under way. The costs of the brick-layer and stone-cutter had exceeded the estimated 9,151 scudi by 4,380! (It was not only the French who underestimated.) The Accademia di S. Luca in August was advising on the erection of fragments and remains of columns.[221] Thus the Forum took the form we see in Fea's drawing, just as the French had planned it – only now plaques were set up celebrating the work as that of Pius VII (Plates 52 and 53).

The account of the Forum of Trajan cannot conclude without a summary of the contributions to epigraphy from the excavations. In 1812 (the date is not given more precisely) was found Hadrian's remission of debts (*CIL* 6.976).[222] On 23 April 1813 was found an inscription thought to be from a statue of Trajan near the main entrance (*CIL* 6.959). And on 30 April appeared the inscription of Merobaudes (*CIL* 6.1724), to be the source of great argument.[223]

Another inscription, without date of discovery, mentioned 'Valer. Vict. leg. xv. Apol.' (6.32902). In polemical mood, Fea[224] explained that this referred to two legions, xx Valeria Victrix and xv Apollinaris, because someone 'who did not understand Latin, and had information only from elementary books for children' (a typical way of referring to his rivals) wanted to read it as 'Valerianorum Victrix legio xv Apoll.', as if the Fifteenth were being commemorated for defeating the Valeriani. The guilty party turned out to be his old foe, Giuseppe Guattani, who still made the same claim in his *Memorie enciclopediche* 1817.[225] Fea, to the contrary, suggested that Trajan in his Forum wanted to commemorate the legions which had conquered Dacia, but the fact that the letters were not in gilded bronze made him suspect that this inscription was not at the very front of the Forum. There was therefore a 'more imposing' building in advance of where this inscription had been found. Another of Fea's old rivals, Angelo Uggeri, suggested that the two legions were named because they contributed to the cost of the building, and had the wickedness to direct readers in general to Masdeu's 'interesting' letters![226]

The inscription as now published in *CIL* also includes fragments referring to legio x and legio xi Claudia, so obviously listed a number of legions. Some have thought that it recorded all those which had fought in the Dacian wars, set up here on the Basilica Ulpia. The main objection to this is the strange order.[227] Fea was thus right and his rivals wrong: 'Valeria Victrix' was legio xx, and there was more than one legion mentioned.

THE MAUSOLEUM OF AUGUSTUS

One of the shortest and most bizarre stories of the French clearing and restoration programme concerns one of the most important and evocative monu-

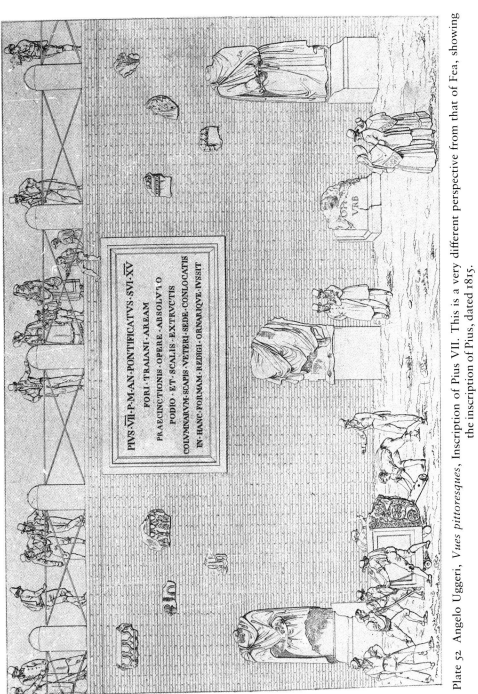

PIVS·VII·P·M·AN·PONTIFICATVS·SVI·XV
FORI·TRAIANI·AREAM
PRAECINCTIONIS·OPERE·ABSOLVTO
PODIO·ET·SCALIS·EXTRVCTIS
COLVMNARVM·SCAPIS·VETERI·SEDE·CONLOCATIS
IN·HANC·FORMAM·REDIGI·ORNARIQVE·IVSSIT

Plate 52 Angelo Uggeri, *Vues pittoresques*, Inscription of Pius VII. This is a very different perspective from that of Fea, showing the inscription of Pius, dated 1815.

Plate 53 Carlo Fea, *Nuova descrizione di Roma*, 1.406. A general view of the Forum of Trajan as it was completed, according to the French plans, under the restored government of Pius VII. The modest steps descending to the ancient level can be seen at each end.

ments, the tomb of the first emperor. Surely this was an obvious object of French veneration while Napoleon ruled France!

The vicissitudes of the mausoleum are barely credible. It had been a fortress in medieval times, belonging to families such as the Colonna and Soderini, who turned it into a 'hanging garden'.[228] In 1780 it became a bull-ring (Plate 54), air-balloon flights were launched from its roof, and Goethe observed bear-fighting there, to his disgust.[229] In our century it was to become a concert hall until the Fascist clearances.

Under the French it appears in the archives twice. The Consulta on 24 November 1809 paid 8,667 scudi to Domenico Schiavoni, master mason, for 'restorations and additions'.[230]

More famous is the correspondence of 1811.[231] Principe Gabrielli, assistant to the Mayor, wrote on 26 August to Martin Gaudin, Duc de Gaète, Minister of Finances in Paris, asking for the cession of the monument to the city of Rome. It was described as 'antico monumento, ora ridotto in Anfiteatro, e destinato per le Feste pubbliche, già appartenente al Passato Governo'. The petition mentioned that Napoleon's birthday had been celebrated there on 15 August. Emphatic reference was made to the Emperor's interest in the conservation of ancient monuments and in increasing the number of public buildings. Gabrielli was anxious to prevent the building being given

Plate 54   Bartolomeo Pinelli, bull fighting in the Mausoleum of Augustus, 1810.

to a private purchaser: rather it should be given to the city, to preserve 'a celebrated monument of the happy century of art' and to provide citizens with a 'decorous amphitheatre' for public festivals.

The Minister of Finances on 20 September passed this petition on to Montalivet, the Minister of the Interior, on the grounds that, as it was an ancient monument, it fell under his control. Montalivet obviously sent the whole matter back to Tournon, for we have his reply of 19 October: '[Il] n'est autre chose qu'un amphithéâtre récemment construit sur les ruines du tombeau de la famille d'Auguste, dont il ne reste que quelques souterrains.' There were, indeed, only some inner parts, as the present century was to find, but the fact that it was the tomb of the whole imperial family, as Tournon realised, makes his off-hand reply amazing.

The building was apparently ceded to the Municipality.

THE PALATINE

The hill of the palaces of imperial Rome was included by the French in the great plans for the Jardin du Capitole. Attitudes at the time were summarised perfectly by Camille de Tournon: 'Le Palatin devait devenir un immense jardin qui aurait eu pour fabriques le palais des Césars, les bains de Livie, les aqueducs de Claude, pour cadre le Forum, le Vélabre et le Grand Cirque, et d'où la vue aurait atteint les six montaignes et la vallée entière du Tibre, des Thermes d'Antonin au tombeau d'Adrien.'[232] It was simply a sylvan glade or an exquisite garden, redolent with classical ruins and atmosphere, itself framed by other parts of the ancient city with more accessible monuments or providing from its vantage-point a view of 'the whole Tiber valley'. At the same time, demolitions planned, as we shall see, were very extensive.

One ruin mentioned by the Prefect early claimed attention. Filippo Aurelio Visconti in 1809 reported on the so-called 'Baths of Livia'.[233] They consisted of two rooms, to which one descended by a stair choked with rubbish. The vaults of these rooms were still gilded. Roundels showed Bacchants on a gold ground and some paintings were of the 'highest elegance', and had been engraved. Market gardeners, however, had controlled the area for generations, and long tracts of ruins became accessible when the earth collapsed. Visconti proposed that the rooms be cleared and the paintings copied and preserved. He nominated Valadier because of his special experience with ancient monuments.

Major changes were foreshadowed for the Palatine by 1811. In August, Tournon, who was in Paris, had his plans approved by Montalivet and decreed the demolition of the convent of S. Bonaventura.[234] By March 1812, 200 workers were occupied on various demolitions, and the archives speak at length henceforth of the laying out of gardens. The work proceeded, however, at a very slow pace. The costs for September to November were only 1,896 frs.[235] By comparison with other undertakings, this sum was paltry. Other appropriations began to be considered by December, and the Commission des Embellisements deputed Principe Gabrielli to negotiate for the gardens of Zanetti and Massimi.

February 1813 saw the appearance of the French emissaries, Gisors and Berthault. The latter was a garden expert, so the Palatine came under his scrutiny. In his report on the Jardin du Capitole, on 25 March, he proposed that the hill should be all plantations, avenues, fountains and picturesque views. Part of the Villa Magnani with paintings by Raphael was to be preserved, but the rest demolished, as with the Farnese pavilion. The convent of S. Bonaventura had, of course, gone, but the church was to be preserved as an orangerie. The total area of the garden would be 473,908 sq m.[236] On 6 April, the Commission accepted Berthault's plans.

The next day, Gisors wrote to Montalivet offering further comments. The principal entry to the Palatine was to be by the Vignolle gate, opposite the Basilica of Maxentius. The hill on the Forum side was to be terraced, with trees in groups of five. From the Farnese aviary to Raphael's casino would be a huge plateau, as wide as the Basilica was long (note the attention to symmetry). An avenue from the Arch of Titus would allow access for carriages, which could leave by the Avenue de Constantin (Via S. Gregorio).

The ruins of the imperial palaces were to be arranged in picturesque gardens. To the south and west of the plateau was to be a botanical garden. In short, no ancient monument would be hidden; instead, all would be accessible, part of a 'delightful promenade', or a kind of 'earthly paradise', instead of their present disordered state. The account finishes with some (unwittingly) amusing remarks. The expenses, Gisors informed Montalivet, would be enormous, because of the incapacity and inexperience of the workers. These Romans did one third of what a Frenchman could manage! What an advantage it would be to have three or four experienced and intelligent Frenchmen to conduct the work – but then, they would have to know Italian, so perhaps it was impossible after all.[237]

A list of the proposed acquisitions and demolitions is preserved in the Paris archives, with valuations (see Fig. 6):

gardens of Gregorio Filippini	10,700 frs
garden of Conte Colocci	15,886
garden of Commissione degli Stabilmenti Esteri and Conte Castelli	3,210
garden of the Commissione and Paolo Biondi	17,510
garden of Marchese Massimi	4,205
garden of S. Anastasia	1,257
garden of the Zanetti brothers	16,050
garden of the Ospedale Sancta Sanctorum	642
garden of the Collegio Romano	1,332
storerooms of Paolo Biondi	5,392
garden of Principe Barberini	14,134
house and garden of same	2,354
garden of the Ospedale dei Benfratelli	6,149
garden of Giuseppe Piastrini	3,798
garden of Signor Sampieri	535
garden of S. Anastasia	535
hay- and oil-stores of same	6,634
storerooms of S. Anima	1,984
storerooms of Bern. Olivieri	4,750
hay-store of Conte Bolognetti	3,076
garden of Commissione degli Stabilmenti Esteri	1,222
	121,355 frs

The list is a portfolio of contracts. Only Bolognetti had refused to sell.[238]

These property lists are, as always, invaluable evidence for the condition of some of the most sacred archaeological areas in Rome as recently as the beginning of the nineteenth century. There is the usual concentration of religious and aristocratic properties covering the imperial remains of the

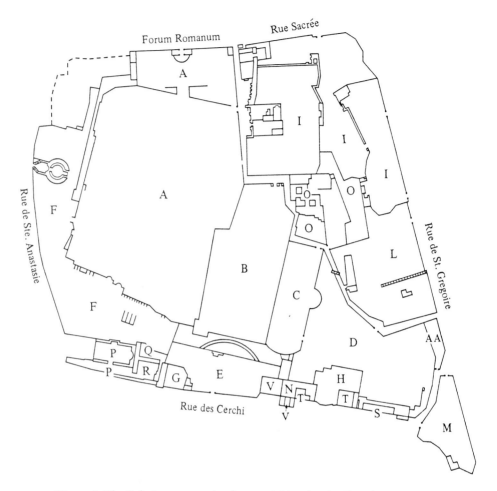

Figure 6 The Palatine: properties for acquisition by the French government
(F 13 1568A). A The Farnese Gardens of which Gregorio Filippini had usufruct;
B Colocci garden; C garden of Commissione degli Stabilmenti Esteri and Conte
Castelli; D garden of the Commissione with Paolo Biondi; E garden of Marchese Massimi; F garden and vineyard of S. Anastasia and the Zanettis; G
garden of the Collegio Romano and Ospedale Sancta Sanctorum; H hay-stores
of Paolo Biondi; I vineyards and garden of Principe Barberini; L garden of
Ospedale dei Benfratelli; M garden and tavern of Sig. Piastrini; N garden
of Signori Maccarani and Sampieri; O church of S. Bonaventura; P church
of S. Anastasia; Q garden of S. Anastasia; R hay and oil-stores of S. Anastasia;
S joined to D; T hay-store of Sig. Olivieri and church of S. Anima; V joined
to N; U hay-stores of Conte Bolognetti; AA garden of Commissione degli
Stabilmenti Esteri.

Palatine. Less than a year before the French left, by 31 March 1813, all properties had been purchased, but none had been demolished. This great work
of clearance had thus passed the major hurdle, in contrast to the grave problems of acquisition in the Roman Forum and around the Pantheon. Nothing

could be done, however, on the Palatine, for there were too many other enormous projects, notably in the Forum below and in Trajan's Forum.

The earlier history of this magnificent temple has been told under the work of Pius VII.[239] The work of the French under the Embellisements was, strictly, for the most part just that: more town-planning than archaeological activity. Given the importance of the building, however, the great plans for giving the temple a worthy setting cannnot be passed by in silence.

The defilement of the Pantheon in the early nineteenth century sprang from many abuses. One of the most infamous was the fish market in the piazza. The Consulta ordered its removal in one of its first decrees, on 19 July 1810. As usual, nothing was done to comply with this order. The architect Raffaele Stern turned to Tournon for help in October. He listed the various appeals he had previously made, and now called on the Prefect to remove this blot 'on the view of the most beautiful temple, the most perfect building of Antiquity'. 'Se sono troppo insistente per tutto ciò che riguarda il bello di Roma lo attribuisca a quelli sentimenti che nutre ogni Artista Italiano e che Vostra Eccelenza stessa mi ha virtuosamente inspirato ogni volta che abbiamo tenuto proposito delle Belle Arti.'[240] The Commission des Monuments took up the question the very next day, 30 October, and directed that negotiations be undertaken again to remove the market. Principe Giustiniani offered his stores to relocate the market. These shops were to be equipped with everything the fishmongers could want, including water. The Commission offered compensation to the Capitolo della Rotonda (the priests of the Pantheon) for the 500 scudi realised from the market rents. It then transpired that the Prince was not acting out of kindness, but on condition that he be allowed some monopoly. Tournon informed him that this was against the law.[241]

Another pressing question was the physical state of the temple, and the need for repairs and maintenance. By the imperial decree of 6 November 1810, this came under the aegis of the Accademia di S. Luca, yet another call on the 75,000 frs each year to care for all classical monuments in Rome. The Accademia was left in no doubt about its duties in this case: Daru, Intendant de la Couronne, under whose surveillance the Accademia fulfilled this task, wrote to Canova in July 1811, informing him that the repairs to the Pantheon were at the expense of the Accademia.[242] Valadier had already been commissioned to carry out one of his never-ending reports, which he sent to Tournon in May. Water damage to the pronaos vault was considerable, caused by years of abandon and the growth of a veritable thicket (*boschetto*) of vegetation. The water had damaged the roof-beams and walls also, since it could not run off. The lead covering of the roof needed repairing.

Valadier was horrified: this monument 'che per ogni titolo dovrebbe essere il più conservato, il più vigilato, il più custodito di qualunque altro – ed è purtroppo più trascurato e negletto'. He thus proposed clearing all growth on the external walls and roofs, and repairing the roofs of the pronaos and cupola. He estimated the costs at a modest 1,577 frs.[243]

Camporese was told to devote himself with the 'greatest attention' to the roof repairs. By September, the main roof was cleaned, and repairs could start. The drains especially needed attention. Next month, the roof of the pronaos was cleared. Plans for repairs could be submitted. Only provisional remedies could be effected, however, before work was suspended for the season in December.[244]

We will not be surprised that at its meeting on 21 January 1812, the Commission des Embellisements ordered a plan to be prepared immediately for the removal of the fish market. Much grander, however, was the call for valuations of the houses around the Pantheon, with a view to demolitions (Plate 55).[245] The famous imperial decree of July 1811 had included the Pantheon along with the Forum of Trajan as one of the major sites for town-planning. And as early as April, Tournon was able to send the plans to Montalivet. All buildings up against the Pantheon were naturally to be cleared. The piazza was to be enlarged on the left side as it was on the right, and to be extended for a 'suitable' distance. Resumption of the houses was admitted to be expensive, because the area was very populous. On the left of the portico, for example, was the Palazzo Giustiniani, which was too expensive to buy; it would have to project out into the new square. Tournon naturally sought general approval before going ahead with the toil of estimates, but admitted that he was desperate to employ 1,300 workers.[246] Montalivet replied on 21 May that the plans were 'assez convenable' – a phrase capable of much misunderstanding – but that he needed to know the costs.

Valadier submitted a more detailed report in July (Plate 56). The Pantheon was to be freed of all the houses which covered it on both sides and at the back. The piazza was to be enlarged symmetrically, by demolishing the houses on the east from the Via de' Pastini to the Via del Seminario (nos. 96–137). On the north, the movable booths in the piazza were to be demolished, as well as the houses from the Via degli Orfanelli to the Via della Rotonda (nos. 65–88). On the west to be removed were the houses from the piazza to the Via de' Crescenzi (nos. 9–54) and from the latter to the Via della Palombella (nos. 3–6). In this way, there would be created a piazza 83 m wide and 65 m deep in front of the Pantheon.[247] The area was, however, as Tournon had warned, very populous, and the owners highly placed: for example, Marchese Melchiorre, Duca Bonelli Crescenzi and Marchese Androsilla.

One of these, the Duca Bonelli, cleverly took his case direct to the Minister of the Interior, stating that his palazzo was 8 m from the Pantheon and

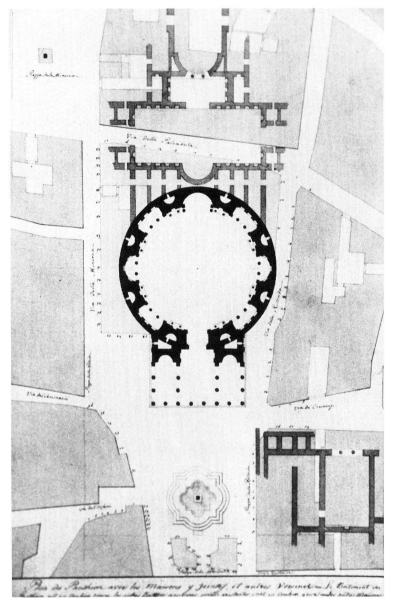

Plate 55 'Plan du Panthéon avec les maisons y jointes, et autres voisines. Le bâtiment du Panthéon est en couleur noir, les autres Batisses (?) anciennes, partes existentes, sont en couleur grise. Les autres maisons de particuliers en couleur plus claire. Le [sic] bâtiments qui devraient s'abattre pour dégager la Place et le Panthéon sont en couleur rouge.' The black of the Pantheon, the grey of the Baths of Agrippa, and the lighter colour of surrounding private buildings are perfectly identifiable in the reproduction. Only the red, which is very faint even in the original, needs to be identified: it is the buildings around the Pantheon on the left and at the rear, and the two small blocks behind the fountain. This was the most conservative proposal for demolitions. It is not signed or dated.

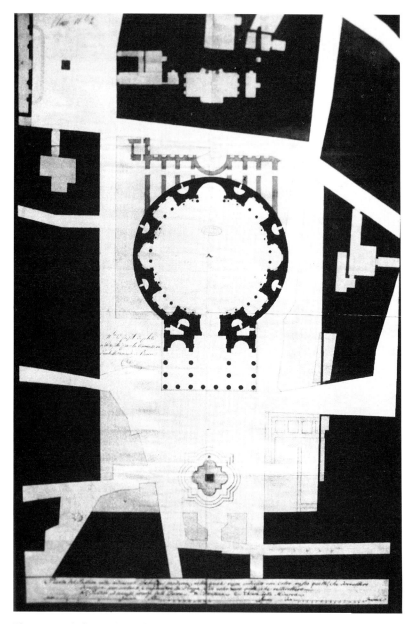

Plate 56 Valadier's plan of the Pantheon. 'Pianta del Pantheon colle adiacenti Fabriche moderne nella quale viene indicato con color rosso quelle che dovrebbero demolirsi per isolarlo e ingrandire la Piazza e in color nero quelle che resterebbero.' *A* Pantheon; *B* Fontana; *C* Chiesa della Minerva. Note (by left portico): 'Ce projet de place a été rejeté par la Commission d'Embellisements de Rome.' Again the plan can easily be made out in the reproduction: all the buildings in light outline (red in the original) were to be demolished. The latter were more extensive than in the S. Luca proposal, with the aim of making a more symmetrical and spacious piazza.

that it had recently been redecorated. The Commission des Embellisements told the duke that demolition of at least part of his house was indispensable for the beautification of the piazza. For his part, Tournon was trying to placate Montalivet over the provision of estimates. The plans for the piazza had been approved in principle in April, but preparing long lists of property values was complicated work.[248]

Meanwhile, the Accademia di S. Luca continued its task. It became involved in attempts to free the monument of modern defacement, clearing the portico of vendors in July.[249] By September, it was the season for repairs, which concentrated on the lead roofing.[250]

In February 1813 Gisors arrived to check all the plans of the Embellisements. His attention was directed not least to the project for the Pantheon piazza.[251] Montalivet had approved the demolitions in principle in May of the previous year, but had asked for detailed estimates. These had so far not been provided. The main problem, as Gisors saw it, was that according to the law, owners whose buildings were required in part by the government could demand compensation for the whole! The expenses for the enlargement of the piazza would thus be far greater than estimated – double or three times the value of the land for the piazza itself. (It is extraordinary that this is the first time this incredible legal problem had been raised, as far as the archives preserve the story. Were people like Camporese and Valadier unaware of such a law?) Even allowing this enormous expense, Gisors pointed out that the piazza would be too shallow to see the attic and cupola. It was, in short, impossible to give the space the depth it required. His proposals were therefore more modest: to demolish all modern constructions against the building, to retain the streets on the two sides for the present, to buy and demolish only the properties between the Piazza della Maddalena and the Piazza del Pantheon, and to adjust the houses bordering the new square only as they were repaired or rebuilt (Plate 57). The Commission, as we have come to expect, accepted these new plans on the same day, 23 February,[252] and the Conseil des Bâtiments in Paris approved them on 1 July. Valadier estimated that the costs would be: demolitions, 32,777 frs, but with 25,147 recouped from the sale of materials; terracing and paving: 21,614 frs; acquisitions: 282,845 frs; in all: 312,089 frs.[253]

The Accademia di S. Luca's work on the roof was finished on 7 September. In November, Canova wrote to Daru to inform him that the Accademia was bankrupt and could not pay any workers. This matter was especially urgent for all those who had worked on the Pantheon. Such were the Accademia's activities and anguish, revealed by the archives. The public saw only the commemorative plaques to be set up to the organisation and to Napoleon.[254]

The last act known to us is significant. Montalivet was consulting Tournon at the end of the year over Bonelli's complaints, namely, as we have seen,

Plate 57 Plan of the piazza around the Pantheon, 23 February 1813 (Projet de place à former au devant du Panthéon de Rome adopté par la Commission d'Embellissements de cette ville dans la séance du 23 février 1813. (Light grey): à démolir par mesure de voierie; (yellow): à acheter et démolir sans delai). The plan is signed by Tournon, Braschi, Gisors and Berthault, and on the bottom left by Valadier as both its artist and attesting it as a copy conforming to the original. This is Gisors' revised plan. The colours of the original can easily be distinguished in the reproduction: the yellow, for immediate demolition, are the buildings to the left and rear of the Pantheon and those immediately in front, behind the fountain. The grey is darker, denoting those buildings to be demolished to make the piazza more symmetrical.

that he had recently redecorated his palazzo at vast expense. Appeals at the highest level were obviously proving most effective in halting the work, even though Gisors' modified plans had long been approved.[255]

Thus it is that Tournon's account of the French achievements presents a very restrained account of the Pantheon. He was able to say only that the lead roof had been repaired, that it had been planned to demolish the campaniles and to create a piazza in front.[256]

The main clearances as planned by the French were in fact carried out by Pius IX: in 1854, houses on the east side were demolished, and in 1876 parts of the palazzi Crescenzi and Aldobrandini. The detested campaniles were finally removed in 1881–2.[257]

THE PORTICO OF OCTAVIA

The famous complex built by Augustus in the name of his sister contained libraries and art collections. Piranesi's *Vedute* give us two views of the sorry remains in the eighteenth century, one outside and one inside. The main archways had been blocked, and inside was a busy fish market. It formed at this time part of the Ghetto.

Tournon listed the portico as one of the projects, along with the Forum of Nerva, the Theatre of Marcellus, and the Antonine Basilica (i.e. the Hadrianum), intended for attention by the French.[258] That the restoration of the portico was seriously suggested is proved by the announcement in the *Giornale del Campidoglio* on 2 May 1810 (very early, one might note). A survey had already been carried out after repairs by the department of drainage.[259] Unfortunately undated is a report by the antiquarian Filippo Aurelio Visconti, who had visited the ruins. Fea had rightly suggested that the building could be much improved at small cost. Visconti as always nominated his favourite valuer, Valadier, to estimate the worth of the house to be demolished, the cost of the demolition, the value of materials which could be recovered, the cost of restoring what remained, and the cost of replacing two missing columns.[260]

Obviously in accordance with this, on 9 February 1810 de Gérando wrote to Valadier asking him for a 'piano dimostrativo' with the costs of the proposed restoration.[261] Within less than three weeks, Valadier submitted his report.

The house of Sig. Ambrogi was up against the front of the portico. It was valued at 600 scudi, and would need twelve convicts to demolish it, costing another 45, but materials recovered would be worth 60. Repairs to the portico to ensure its stability would cost another 198 scudi. Two columns had to be replaced in travertine: 2,056 scudi, of which 624 for the stone, 823 for the working, and 609 for the erection. The total was therefore 2,840 scudi or 15,194 frs.[262]

This report requires comment for its general interest, and in so far as it illustrates Valadier's methods. The indications of relative cost are valuable: apart from acquisition of houses, which could be very expensive, demolition was cheap, using convicts or later the poor. The major costs came in reconstruction of any part of an ancient building. The columns were nearly 9 m high. As for Valadier, it is important to note that already here, in early 1810, he was proposing restoration in materials other than the original, presumably for reasons of economy.

In October, Tournon wrote to de Gérando stressing the need to devote attention to the portico and the Theatre of Marcellus. The houses between them needed to be demolished to give an open space in this 'excessively dirty quarter' of the city.[263]

It was precisely Tournon who did not forget the portico. In a report on the budget for 1812, he again singled out the same two monuments as the most important not yet given attention. Of the portico, he admitted that only 'a few columns of rare beauty' survived. He proposed to remove the fish market, to demolish the chapel and houses within the columns, and to create a small square to allow the monument to be enjoyed.[264]

These calm plans were overturned by the disastrous earthquake of 21–22 March 1812. Camporese and Valadier, architects to the Accademia di S. Luca, which bore responsibility for repair of ancient monuments, reported on the damage, as also did the municipal architect, Fabio di Marchis. There was damage on the side of the portico towards S. Angelo in Pescheria, but that was not caused by the earthquake. There was old damage also on the arch towards the Ghetto. The pillars holding up the arches were worn, and the walls were partly missing. The damage on the side of the oratory was much greater than on the side of the church.[265]

That is all. In 1817 Luigi Rossini drew the monument for his fifty views of Rome. The fish market was still in place.[266] It was transferred by Pius VII. The masking houses were demolished only in 1878.[267] The remains are still some of the sorriest in Rome. It was not for lack of interest that the French did so little. The vast projects of the Embellisements required all their energies elsewhere.

THE TABULARIUM

The sub-structures of the Capitol facing the Forum are formed by the Tabularium, or archive of ancient Rome. Piranesi's engraving in his *Vedute* shows three rows of windows of the Palazzo del Senatore, and just the top of the classical arches and their flanking columns, but there was still a considerable drop from this to the level below, which was masked by modern constructions. This level was made by Piranesi to be almost that of the capitals of the Temple of Vespasian. Unlike so many other classical monuments, we may note that the Tabularium had not lost its correct name.

Tournon, paradoxically, does not mention the building in his account of French achievements. The *Giornale del Campidoglio*, on the other hand, announced its proposed restoration on 2 May 1810 and listed it on 7 November as one of the locations for the work of the poor. Merely a week later, it was stated firmly that work would be completed during the winter, and the revelation of the Doric order was triumphantly announced by the end of the month. Luigi Rossini's views show the substructures completely cleared.[268]

The archives, however, reveal that the main work was in 1812, in association with the restoration of the Temple of Vespasian. The accounts of the Commission des Embellisements record that the clearing began in the week of 17–22 August. By October, the substructures were being revealed, in *peperino*. Tournon was hoping that a monument of the regal period might be revealed.[269] Next month the foundations were discovered to be on the same level as those of the Temple of Vespasian.

The Commission met on 13 November and specified that it must be discovered what substructures existed right along the foot of the Capitol. Only then could all the earth be removed between the Tabularium and the temples of Vespasian and Saturn. The progress of the work in the last months of 1812 may be seen in the accounts:[270]

	excavation of the foundations	clearing of the inside chambers
August	141 frs	
September	1,468	733
October	1,390	204
November	1,302	288
December	1,201	322

A general totalling of expenses until 31 December gives the total of earth removed as 6,376 cu m at a cost of 7,317 frs.[271]

In 1813 the search continued for substructures, and the earth between the Tabularium and the Temple of Vespasian was still to be removed. The visitor Louis Berthault wanted to take a hand in the work, anxious to investigate also the foundations of the Temple of Saturn, the Column of Phocas and the Temple of the Dioscuroi.[272]

No figures are given for work in January or February, but 579 frs were spent in March and 671 frs in April.[273] Nothing more seems to appear in the archives.

The French thus cleared to the outside foundations the remains of one of the most impressive Republican monuments of the Forum, and also removed the accumulated debris from the inner chambers. The work was not very expensive, but is a telling example of the respect shown for even the plainest monuments. It was just one part of the enormous programme of work under the Capitol.[274] The days when the Tabularium was used as a salt-store were finally over.

THE TEMPLE OF ANTONINUS AND FAUSTINA

Another of the few monuments of the Forum which had not lost its name was the temple of the deified couple Antoninus Pius and Faustina. In the seventh or eighth century, however, it had been converted into the church of S. Lorenzo in Miranda. By the end of the eighteenth century the ground-level had reached the base of the columns, obliterating the great flight of steps, and the columns had been walled in. A baroque façade towered, as indeed it still does, above the portico.

The history of this temple during the French years is rather complicated and certainly sad, with too many institutions and individuals involved with it.

The Académie de France in Rome had been given permission to survey the temple in May 1807 under the architect J. F. Menager. This was extended to permission to excavate in February 1809, and the work was carried out between April and June under Giambattista Ottaviani, an architect engineer, with Giuseppe Orlandi as contractor. The bases of the columns were discovered. The new French administration inherited the work, including an open trench on the south-east.[275] Plans were called for the continuation of the work.

Ottaviani made a submission in July 1809. The excavations already made by the Académie's scholars were 32 palms (7 m) long, 24 palms (5.2 m) wide and 37 palms (8 m) deep and had reached the Via Sacra. The Director, Guillaume Lethière, proposed forming a permanent excavation, 'to perpetuate the enterprise of uncovering such a monument', useful for both studies and the beautification of the city. The plan now proposed was for an excavation 120 palms (26 m) long, 40 palms (9 m) wide, and as before 37 palms (8 m) deep. This would require a strong wall to support the modern level, with a bridge crossing the great pit to give access to the temple. Steps would allow one to descend to the lower level (see Plate 58). The total cost was estimated at 3,090 scudi.[276]

Meanwhile, on 9 June, Valadier had visited the site with Canova, to see if the excavation could be left open. The two agreed that a general clearing to reveal the steps, although they were stripped of marble, would be a 'glorious work'. It would also be very extensive and expensive, and take up a lot of the modern road in front of the temple from the Arch of Titus to S. Adriano. On the other hand, a circular wall could support the modern level and leave the steps and the Via Sacra visible. The estimated cost of the wall was 1,300 scudi.[277]

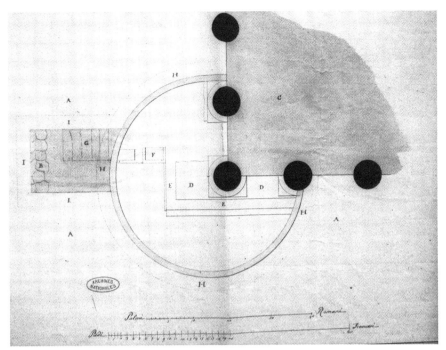

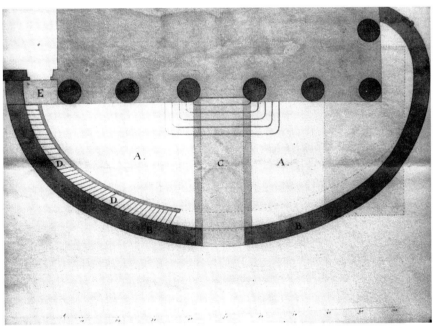

Plate 58 Contrasting plans for the systematisation of the excavation of the portico of the Temple of Antoninus and Faustina. Above is Valadier's proposal for a limited exposure of only the right-hand corner, surrounded by a circular retaining wall. Below is Ottaviani's proposal for a much more extensive clearing of the whole front and steps down to the ancient level, with a ramp across to the portico on the same level as the modern one, and curving steps for those who wished to descend to the Via Sacra.

A much more ambitious plan evolved by November. Filippo Aurelio Visconti assured everyone that it was unanimously desired to uncover the whole façade, to take away the intercolumniations and to clear down to the Via Sacra. This would require leaving a space of 40 palms (9 m) surrounded by a solid wall. This was strangely estimated at 3,090 scudi, precisely Ottaviani's quote for a different operation.[278] And on the same day, the painter Vincenzo Camuccini assured Visconti that the plan had his total support. He was not the only one. None other than Canova came to Visconti's house, but not finding hiffh home, he also wrote expressing whole-hearted support for the new, grander plans.

Then things began to go wrong. On 21 November, de Gérando wrote to the 'Commission administrative de Rome' talking of 'more accidents'. It would be best to complete the excavation, he admitted, but there was no money. Public safety had to be protected. The waters banked up had to be released. A barrier had to be erected.[279] Here, as so often in correspondence, we gain glimpses of a total situation, and one of some seriousness. The saga of the temple was just beginning.

The names of Visconti and Luigi Martorelli appear on a report dated 30 November.[280] A man had fallen into the mud and stagnant water in the excavation. The Tribunal of Roads had been appealed to, and Conte Camillo Mariscotti had ordered the contractor, Orlandi, to prevent any repetition of such an accident by covering the hole with beams and planks and then stones and earth and surrounding the area with a fence. The Académie de France had thoughtfully handed over all expenses from August to the government and sent to the Commission for the Preservation of Monuments all Orlandi's expenses after that date. In the same file is found the contractor's claims. The Académie had paid him until 3 August. Since then, apart from the expense of complying with Conte Mariscotti's orders, he had spent 74 scudi for surveillance, including 48 scudi for a guard night and day to ensure that the wood was not stolen and nearly 5 scudi for a lantern for ninety-seven nights.

Hopes for a restoration of the temple were still being cherished by some. Valadier prepared estimates, totalling 19,589 frs. De Gérando replied in April 1810 that it was far too costly.[281]

The long agony of the poor contractor, Orlandi, continued. De Gérando requested payment of long-standing accounts from the Académie de France, and was finally informed four months later in August that they had long ago been settled. Then the Commission was asked to pay its share. By September, Orlandi's expenses for the guard on the still-open excavations totalled 133 scudi. Tournon sent the bill to de Gérando, who sent it back to the Prefect. De Gérando also promised to write to the police to ask them to send a guard, but we have in fact the very sympathetic letter of Tournon to the Director of Police, requesting them to take over.[282]

The report of a commissioner to the Director General of Police fills in some of the details of the story not previously mentioned.[283] Orlandi had carried out excavations for the Académie de France from April to August 1809. The hole was then to be filled in and the road replaced. Fea, Visconti and Canova, however, told him to leave it open, since they had decided to extend the excavation. Nothing had happened since, and Orlandi had had to set a guard. De Gérando had written to Tournon telling him to settle the affair and that it could not continue through the winter. Nobody, we may be sure, was more anxious about that than Orlandi! Now the police assured Tournon that their nearest post would protect passers-by from danger.[284]

In November, Tournon told Braschi to pay Orlandi, but he obviously did not receive the money. His undated petition may be quoted: 'Con le lagrime agli occhi unitamente alla sua infelice famiglia, supplichevole ricorre al magnanimo cuore della prelodata Eccelenza ... Il povero Orlandi spera con la sua numerosa famiglia in ricorrenza della prossima festa Natalizia stare consolato.'[285] Christmas 1810 was approaching, obviously, when that was written, but on 29 December, de Gérando told Tournon that the payment to Orlandi supported by the Prefect was entirely unauthorised by the Consulta. Perhaps Tournon could pay from the funds at his disposal![286] This dossier contains nothing more, but as late as April 1813 Mayor Braschi was writing to Tournon pleading for payment to Orlandi of 313 scudi, which included 73 for the wood to shore up the excavation. Orlandi stated that he would be glad to receive only that smaller sum for the moment, to feed his 'poor and numerous' family.[287]

Plans to keep the excavation open with a wall to hold back the surrounding earth were again sent to Tournon by Collicola in January 1811.[288] The estimates were by Camporese and Valadier. The cost was small, 408 scudi (2,182 frs) because it was to be built by the Beneficenza with materials found in the Forum excavations. Its height was to be 20 feet, including foundations, and the length 349 feet.

More important was the decree of the Consulta on 11 January, setting out the programme for the year.[289] The excavation was to extend to the level of the bottom step. A wall was to be built to the right to support the house against the temple. On the other sides, access would be provided to the base of the portico. The underground drain to take away water to the Cloaca Maxima was to be completed.

The poor Accademia di S. Luca was, of course, not to escape involvement. Daru wrote to Canova in September, telling him to see to the building of a wall around the excavations and to restore the road alongside the temple.[290]

The clearing of the portico did, in fact, take place, although we have few details of the work. By the end of 1811, a total of 4,267 man-working days had been spent and the cost was 5,263 frs.[291] In January 1812 the clearing

Plate 59 *Tempio di Antonino e Faustina nuovamente scavato, e reso nella antica sua forma*, c. 1811 (artist unknown). The view, despite its simplicity, seems not very accurate, since the columns are clearly excavated, but the steps are nowhere shown, and the Académie de France at Rome had already made a considerable excavation which had been left open. Note the dump to the left.

was complete and the plinths and bases of the columns were exposed (Plates 59 and 60).[292] There were short notices in the newspapers: the restoration was announced in the *Giornale del Campidoglio* on 2 May 1810, but 'rapid progress' was publicised only on 14 and 28 November. The portico was declared clear on 9 January 1811, and down to the Via Sacra in the *Giornale politico* on 2 January 1812.

There are, paradoxically, few eye-witness recollections of these momentous years. The uncovering of the Via Sacra of the temple, however, was not only seen but also recorded by none other than Tournon:

J'étais, je m'en souviens, au milieu des ouvriers, avec le savant abbé Fea et l'indéfatigable orientaliste Akerblad, enlevé trop jeune aux lettres, lorsque le pavé de cette voie apparut à la lumière après tant de siècles. Comment dirai–je les transports de ces doctes antiquaires, leur empressement de se précipiter dans la profonde excavation, à toucher les premiers, à presser de leurs lèvres ces pierres où ils croyaient voir empreints encore les pieds d'Horace et de Virgile?[293]

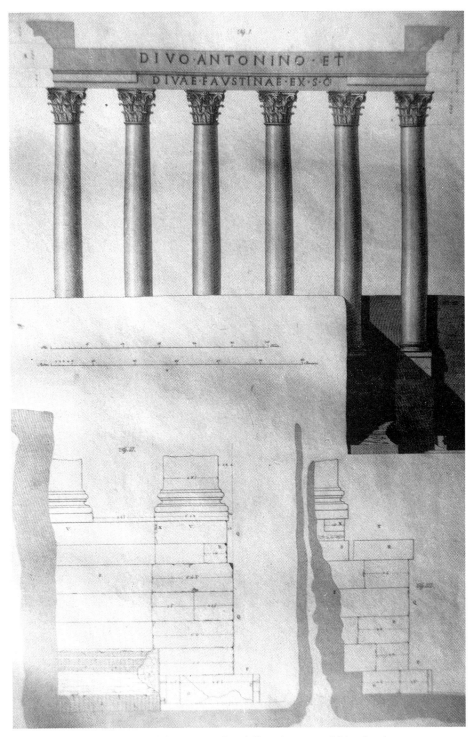

Plate 60 Giuseppe Valadier, *Raccolta delle più insigni fabbriche di Roma antica*, fasc. 1, 1810, pl. 2, the Temple of Antoninus and Faustina. He gives a view of the hexastyle portico and an illustration of the foundations of the columns.

THE TEMPLE OF CASTOR AND POLLUX

Tournon laconically stated in his *Etudes statistiques* that the columns of this temple (known then as that of Jupitor Stator) had been deeply buried when the French arrived, but that under his administration they had been cleared down to the paving.[294] The *Giornale del Campidoglio* mentioned on 2 May 1810 that the work was proposed, and on 28 November its completion. This was, indeed, one of the smaller undertakings of these years, and the archives preserve little documentation, but enough to ascertain the main lines.

As early as April 1810, Valadier made a report.[295] The columns, he noted, were not deeply buried, but what lay beneath the bases had never been verified. The clearing would not be difficult, especially because there was enough space around so as not to impede the public. (We are constantly being reminded, as with the Temple of Antoninus and Faustina, that the Forum was still a major public thoroughfare at this time.) The Commission of Antiquities had asked him three questions. An excavation to the base of the columns would require the removal of 4,500 cu feet of earth, or 562 cart-loads. At 5 bajocchi for the excavation and another 5 for the transport of each load, the cost would be 56.25 scudi (299 frs). Second, to prevent damage to the columns from carriages some 'small pieces of travertine' could be erected. Third, a sounding to examine what lay beneath the columns would cost another 176 scudi (941 frs). One week later, de Gérando told Valadier to go ahead with his proposed 'piccolo scavo', using convicts.[296]

Grander plans appeared in December. De Gérando asked Tournon's authorisation in order to excavate the foundations, to see if the temple had a stylobate, and to discover the whole plan. This would now be easy, he noted, since the column bases were free. These hopes of the cultural member of the Consulta seem to have been approved, although not immediately. It is, in fact, in February 1813 that we hear of excavations in progress to find the temple's foundations, which seem to have been undertaken between January and April.[297]

The Accademia di S. Luca also played a part. When the bases of the columns were exposed, they were found, as with the Temple of Vespasian, to be insecure. The gaps were filled with travertine and clamped with leaded iron. Valadier and Camporese reported that this was finished by the end of May. In July, however, Daru wrote to Canova stating that the foundations were not secure and that the columns would collapse. He demanded that the Accademia examine the bases to see what repairs were needed. If 'neither art nor learning' found the work necessary, then the Accademia was ordered at least to put back the earth from the recent excavations.[298]

The accounts for the operations show until 31 March 1813, 261 man-working days, 248 cu m of earth removed, and the cost 360 frs.[299] This

Plate 61 *Avanzi del Tempio di Giove Statore, di nuovo scavato e reso nella antica sua forma* (artist unknown), 1813 (?). The anonymous watercolour shows the three columns in very unsophisticated form, cleared to their bases and held together by iron, as confirmed by other views.

was little more than Valadier estimated for the excavation to the base of the columns. The work to find the substructures in 1813 cost at least 463 frs from January to April (Plates 61 and 62).[300]

The French here carried out the same basic work as with the Temple of Vespasian, although under much less spectacular conditions. The columns were freed, the foundations excavated, and consolidation undertaken. As for the long-standing problem of the plan of the temple, and the question which went back to the Renaissance of how many columns were on the sides, they were solved by further work in 1816–18, when the temple's outline was fully revealed for the first time and its true identity established.[301] It was in the light of this further work that Valadier included the temple in his *Raccolta delle più insigni fabbriche*, fascicule 4, 1818 (Plates 63 and 64).

THE TEMPLE OF SATURN

Until its true identification by Luigi Canina in 1834, the surviving eight columns of this enormous building under the Capitol were known as the Temple of Concord. It was in 1817 that the true position of the latter was uncovered. In his *Vedute di Roma*, Piranesi gave two views of the Temple

Plate 62 Angelo Uggeri, *Vues des édifces de Rome antique*, pl. 25. Uggeri shows the famous cattle fountain by the remains of the Temple of Castor and Pollux.

Plate 63 Giuseppe Valadier, *Raccolta delle più insigni fabbriche di Roma antica*, fasc. 4, 1818, pl. 1, the Temple of Castor and Pollux. Valadier's fine drawing shows the capital of the corner column and the entablature.

Plate 64 Giuseppe Valadier, *Raccotta delle più insigni fabbriche di Roma antica*, fasc. 4, 1818, pl. 4. This plate shows the three columns of the temple, together with the foundations as revealed by the excavations of 1816.

of Saturn, from the front and from the rear. In the first (Plate 65), looking towards the Velabrum and the Ospedale della Conciliazione, the temple portico was shown as rising above the pastoral slope of the Capitol, with houses and other buildings between its columns (even washing hung between two of them), on the left-hand side and stretching down the street beside it. The second view, from behind, showed a row of mean stables occupying the temple platform.

The transformations of the French here were remarkable. Tournon noted simply that the temple was cleared of the structures built up against its columns, so that the portico could be isolated and a road constructed to the Capitol.[302] The *Giornale del Campidoglio* announced the proposed work on 2 May 1810 and on 14 November stated that it would be completed by winter. The isolation was declared completed on 9 January 1811, and the foundations were being excavated by 9 March. The whole task was accomplished by 2 January 1812, according to the *Giornale politico*.

The work was, as in few other French undertakings, straightforward and not very costly. The archives preserve little detail. In November 1810 Tournon ordered the demolition of the abutting houses. The costs were still to be fixed, but the plans had been drawn up by the architect Toniazzi.[303] By December excavations had begun[304] but as late as April 1813 the demolition of the tower (*tourelle*) at the foot of the temple was still in progress.[305] The total costs were 75 frs for excavation and 78 frs for transport of 78 cu m of earth. The work took fifty-five days.[306]

The effort and cost were obviously small, yet the splendid results are recorded in various illustrations. Luigi Rossini drew the temple in 1817 (Plate 66), showing it cleared to the base of the foundations, with the road to the Capitol, as Tournon planned, running behind it.[307] This excellent work is ignored by contemporary sources, all caught up in the controversy about its identification.[308] Uggeri made his characteristically wicked complaints, this time about the loss of the 'rather picturesque little house' which used to fill the portico![309]

THE TEMPLE OF VENUS AND ROME

This, the largest temple in Rome, was designed by the emperor Hadrian, although we are unsure when exactly it was completed (perhaps under Antoninus Pius). The entire platform measures 100 x 150 m and the double-cellared temple itself is decastyle at both ends, with twenty columns along each side. Perhaps it was most damaged by an earthquake in the time of Leo IV (847–55), who built in the ruins the church of S. Maria Nova, which was rebuilt in 1612 as S. Francesca Romana.

The archives contain virtually nothing concerning work by the French on this temple. The architect Pietro Bianchi reported on what had been

Plate 65 Giambattista Piranesi, *Vedute di Roma*, 1748–78, the Temple of Saturn. The eighteenth-century engraving shows the debris on the slope of the Capitol and a variety of modern buildings engulfing the temple: even houses built into the portico, with washing hung out.

Plate 66 Luigi Rossini, *Cinquanta principali vedute*, pl. 26, the Temple of Saturn. The engraving is dated 1817, and shows the temple now completely cleared, with the new French road to the Capitol running behind it, and the Clivus Capitolinus on the right-hand side (revealed in the same year as the artist made this drawing).

done until 30 September 1813.[310] One of the cellae, that of Rome towards the Capitol, had been cleared, showing its marble paving and the remains of the great altar in the apse. The other, of Venus facing the Colosseum, was well advanced, but many drains which had been found impeded the work.

The most complete description of the undertaking is provided by the French artist, Augustin Caristie.[311] He dated the work between 1813 and early 1814.[312] The excavations showed the 'disposition of the masonry', the shattered tufa, peperino and lava. The floor level had been found. The pronaos was almost 1 m lower, down four steps, together with the surrounding porticoes floored with white marble. A further flight of seven steps led to the ground level at the western end. Since the temple had long been used as a quarry, only the foundations of the columns were recovered, along with some fragments of the columns themselves and of the entablature. Since the temple was 50 m wide and the columns were shown to be 1.88 m in diameter, Caristie declared that this proved the temple was decastyle with twenty columns on each side, just as it was shown on the coins of Hadrian and Antoninus. The cella walls when laid bare still revealed traces of the decoration in the niches.

Angelo Uggeri also gave an account of the temple as left by the French (Plate 67).[313] It had been completely cleared on the southern (Via Sacra) side of earth and buildings. Its plan and substructures were clear, the latter thought to belong to the Palace of Nero stretching from the Palatine to the Esquiline. Three sides of the area around the double cellae were also clear. The decoration of the apses was preserved, the vaults lined with rhomboidal caissons. Two large columns on the sides of the niches supported a projecting entablature. Here and there were fragments of granite columns similar to those in the Basilica of Trajan.

Tournon himself made only brief allusion to the excavations to the foundations, and grouped the temple with the nearby Basilica of Maxentius and the Arch of Titus in his discussion of the buying and demolition of modern structures.[314]

We may note the finding of one inscription, on 15 January 1813: a dedication to Hadrian by a freedman, Amaracus (*CIL* 6.978).[315]

A complete clearing of the temple was undertaken within a few years by Antonio Nibby, 1827–9, which finally confirmed its Hadrianic date from brick-stamps. It was then neglected for a century until the remains were 'systematised' in 1934 and 1935 and the almost completely vanished plan of the temple on the platform was recreated in shrubs and flowers.[316]

THE TEMPLE OF VESPASIAN

Tournon rightly called the clearing and restoration of the three remaining columns of the Temple of the Deified Vespasian on the slopes of the Capitol

Plate 67 Luigi Rossini, *Cinquanta principali vedute*, pl. 25, the Temple of Venus and Rome. The engraving is dated 1817 and shows the basic French clearing, which was not very extensive, exposing only the eastern cella. The major excavation came under Nibby, 1827–9.

'peut-être l'opération la plus hardie qui ait été entreprise sur les monuments usés par vingt siècles d'abandon'.[317] As if to underline that, alone of the operations of these years special drawings were made of it, before, during and after, by one of the leading artists of the day; they were published in Tournon's book.

As the Prefect explained, the ground-level here was 10 m higher than in antiquity, because of all the debris which had been tipped down from the Capitol and piled up against the slope. A senator had actually built stables here. The three columns were buried up to their capitals, and it was to be revealed that they were half a column's diameter out of line, and in reality supported only by the accumulated earth (Plates 68 and 69).

The story begins in the archives with accounts of December 1810, which include payments for the construction of wooden scaffolding.[318] With the columns now supported, excavation could begin.[319] The accounts for January 1811 include special payments for securing and chaining the columns, with chains weighing up to 1,410 pounds.[320]

The full account is preserved in the archives of the Accademia di S. Luca, which was responsible for the work under the imperial decree of 6 November 1810 making it the body to see to the maintenance and repair of classical monuments. In July 1811, Daru, as supervisor of the Accademia in this capacity, warned Canova, its president, to make sure that the columns did not fall during the work, 'un accident non seulement préjudiciable en lui-même, mais qui produirait encore une très mauvaise impression dans le public'.[321] Four days later, he informed his brother, Daru the Elder, Intendant de la Couronne in Paris, that the excavations had revealed that the bases were missing for two of the columns. He included the report of the architect Camporese, which was to be shown to Napoleon.[322]

Such a report, undated, exists in the Paris archives.[323] Camporese stressed the difficulty of the work. The architrave, frieze and cornice (i.e. the entire entablature) were fragmented but at the same time so beautifully decorated, and the ground was so 'fragile' because it was simply made up of waste ('di semplice scarico'). Camporese had made drawings which were shown to a commission composed of Canova, Paris, Camuccini and Stern. Scaffolding had been constructed (Plate 70) and, in the presence of Daru and other authorities, the entablature had been raised, without reducing it to a 'mass of fragments'. The excavation of the three columns could thus begin. They had been found, however, to be very damaged, resting on single pieces of travertine which supported only one third of their circumference. At some time, then, almost all the stone of the foundations had been plundered. Camporese had called in Canova and Paris to observe the operations to secure the columns. The report ends with his expression of frustration over all the unforeseen difficulties.[324]

A commission of the Accademia, made up of Andrea Vici, Tommaso

Plate 68 Giambattista Piranesi, *Vedute di Roma*, 1748–78, the Temple of Vespasian. One of the artist's most striking perspectives, with the enormous capitals and entablature alone unburied and towering over the bizarre and intriguing human figures, with the Tabularium on the right. The general impression is, however, confirmed by contemporaries such as Vasi.

Plate 69 Bartolomeo Pinelli, the temple before excavation and restoration
(Tournon, *Etudes statistiques*, 1831, pl. 18).

Plate 70 Bartolomeo Pinelli, the restoration of the columns in progress, a view paradoxically not included by Tournon in his *Etudes statistiques*. This is one of the most exciting illustrations of all the French undertakings. The entablature is being removed by the mighty arrangement of scaffolding and windlasses. In the left foreground may well be important people. The windows of the Tabularium are occupied by spectators. A tricolour justifiably flies proudly from the scaffolding.

Zappati and Pasquale Belli, also compiled a report on 19 July.[325] The temple was coming apart ('scatenato'), very cracked, leaning, about to fall. To right it and stabilise it would, in short, be a very hard job. Camporese had been given the task of lifting the entablature and supporting the columns with scaffolding. The foundations, however, had been found in such a state that the three above-named architects had been asked to give their opinion about what should be done. (The seriousness of the problems is amply demonstrated by the Accademia's assembling all available expertise.) It was, they suggested, the corner column of the three which was in danger of bringing down the other two. It and the rear one had now been excavated to their foundations, which had been found to be almost non-existent. The cost of rebuilding them could not be estimated.

Three days later Camporese and Valadier[326] stated to Canova that work had to continue to support the plinths and that the workers had to be paid. They disclaimed any responsibility if their advice was not followed.[327] It is obvious that uncertainty had arisen over what course to take and the problems of payment endemic in the period were already arising. By this time, accounts for the work totalled 4,500 frs, and that sum was advanced to the Accademia by Daru on 26 August.[328]

During August and September, the foundations of the corner and rear columns were rebuilt, stone by stone (Plate 71).[329] The third column could then be excavated. The extremely narrow shaft dug around it reached as deep as 10 m. Supports were needed for the scaffolding and the surrounding earth.[330] By the end of October it was clear that the third column was as precarious as the other two. Steps between the front and corner columns had been found.[331] Work on the foundations continued to the end of the year, but by December preparations were under way to reconstruct the columns.[332] The total cost of the Accademia's work by the end of 1811 was 6,724 frs.[333]

On 27 February 1812, the three Academicians who had reported in July of the previous year made a second report.[334] Vici, Belli and Zappati stated that all three columns were now cleared and righted. This had been a most difficult and delicate operation. The foundations and intercolumniations at the base were now built up in travertine and there had been a 'praiseworthy excavation' on the two sides to find the ancient foundations.

Daru was, as always, ready to believe the worst of the Accademia. In March he wrote to Canova saying that he had heard that the travertine for the repairs was being taken from the Colosseum, and protesting that it was a very bad principle to rob one monument to repair another and that this abuse must stop.[335]

These hearsay complaints may be put aside, in order to appreciate the triumphant finale, as recorded in a precious letter by the directing architect, Camporese, to Tournon, dated 31 March 1812:

Plate 71 Giuseppe Valadier, plan of the restored foundations of the three columns. The attention to detail is noteworthy in this illustration of how the missing foundations for the columns were reconstructed.

Mi affretto di participare all'E.V. la notizia che in questo momento è stato collocato al suo posto il grande sasso di Marmo, che forma l'architrave, e Fregio del Magnifico Tempio di Giove Tonante, questa importante operazione è riuscita con il miglior successo, ed a giorni continuerò a collocare gli altri due massi che compongono la cornice superiore, in tal guisa spero di avere adempito a quanto promisi all'E.V. che del mese di aprile tutto sarebbe compito.[336]

The work may have taken a little longer than Camporese anticipated. Suffice to say that the accounts of the Accademia show a total expenditure between August 1811 and July 1812 of 15,695 frs, with expenses at their highest between November and April, attaining even 4,526 frs in February.

The most important document of this undertaking has already been mentioned: the views published by Tournon. By August, the Prefect sent these to Montalivet, to illustrate the state of the monument before work began and its present appearance.[337] The authorship of these drawings is not commonly given, but is known from the archives. In the same month, payment is recorded of 187 frs to the engraver Pinelli 'pour avoir enluminé dix planches représentant le temple de Jupiter Tonans', as well as 30 frs for 243 sheets of paper to print sixty plates, 94 frs to buy four copper plates for the engravings, and 214 frs to Pinelli for the actual engraving.[338]

With the columns restored, the work of the Embellisements could begin, clearing the slope of the hill overlooking the Forum and back to the Tabularium. Accounts show this work in progress from April to August 1812. The total expenses to December were 25,203 frs, and 23,078 cu m of earth were removed.[339] In his general report to Montalivet on 6 January 1813 Tournon informed his Minister that the clearing of earth around the columns was now complete. That earth had been 30 feet high, 60 wide, and 30 deep.[340]

In his *Etudes statistiques*, Tournon was justly proud of the achievement: 'Les colonnes du temple s'élancèrent isolées dans leur noble élégance, et on s'étonna de voir briller dans les airs l'admirable frise sculptée que naguère souillait le pied des curieux.'[341] Strangely he went on to specify that the work was carried out by both Valadier and Camporese. It was the achievement of the latter, working for the Accademia di S. Luca.[342] What Tournon must mean here is that Valadier had been 'at Camporese's side during the whole of the restoration'.[343]

Despite the greatness of this achievement, which saved the last three columns from imminent collapse, and the enormous care and expense which the Accademia and the architect devoted to the work, contemporary antiquarians give what can only be described as an astonishingly restrained account. These sources are often more interested in the fact that the temple was proved to be hexastyle and that the steps up to it were, unusually, between the columns because there was no space to have them extending in front of the building.[344] Modern accounts, with one exception, show

virtually no interest in what is obviously one of the proudest French achievements.[345]

THE 'TEMPLE OF VESTA'

One of the earliest monuments to which the French turned their attention
was the little round temple in the Forum Boarium by the Tiber (Plate 72).
It had first been identified as the Temple of Vesta by Flavio Biondo in the
sixteenth century, and was still in the French period known as such, although,
shortly after, Carlo Fea suggested that it was rather a temple of Hercules,
because of inscriptions found nearby.[346] In about the twelfth century the
temple became the church of S. Stefano, which was changed in 1560 to S.
Maria del Sole.

In the retrospective account of his administration in Rome, Tournon
explained the high hopes which had been held for the operations in the
'cattle market' of ancient Rome. The two temples here had been given the
highest priority after the monuments of the Roman Forum. The result was
that the houses around the Temple of Vesta had been demolished, and
excavations had revealed the temple's circular form and beautiful proportions. 'Ce charmant édifice parut dans toute sa gracieuse élégance.'[347]

For the inhabitants of Rome at the time, the main source of information,
apart from their own eyes, was the *Giornale del Campidoglio*. On 2 May
1810 it was announced that work was beginning on the restoration of the
temple. It was noted that Fea had attempted during the time of Pius VII
to have the modern additions which defaced the temple removed, but in
vain. The French intended to demolish such additions, replace the missing
column, and protect the restored temple by the installation of iron gates
between the columns. The beginning of work was again announced on 28
November. By 12 January 1811 a modern house had been removed. Another
year elapsed, however, before the *Giornale politico* could record that the
modern closing of the intercolumniations had been demolished and the steps
of the temple revealed.[348]

These official announcements conceal, in fact, one of the most dramatic
stories of the French archaeological campaign. The story can be disinterred
only in the archives of Paris and Rome.[349]

French attention had been directed to the Temple of Vesta by Fea. His
report (undated) showed its parlous state. It was used as a hay-store by
its priest, and the columns were therefore in danger of collapse. Although
the Papal government had approved repairs in 1804, work had soon been
suspended for 'economic reasons'. Fea appealed to de Gérando, as the member
of the Consulta responsible for monuments, to resume the work.

Dated securely to 27 August 1809, however, is the proposal of Fea to
de Gérando[350] which mentions a plan by Valadier of 2 May: the temple
was to be freed of the house and wall against it; the whole area was to

Plate 72 Giuseppe Vasi, *Magnificenze di Roma*, 1747–61, pl. 94, the Forum Boarium. The temple appears as it was before the French work: the columns walled in, no sign of foundations, and buildings up against it, with even a bell-tower! Opposite is the 'Temple of Fortune', equally buried and encroached upon.

be cleared of rubble, an area of 45 × 9 canne (155 × 27 m), which needed clearing to a depth of 10 palms (2.2 m). Fea calculated the astonishing total of 13,360 cart-loads to take it all away, and the debris was to be dumped along the Tiber near the Ripa Grande, to build up the banks against floods and help in dragging ships up the river. If these excavations were carried out by convicts, paid 8 bajocchi per load, the cost would be 1,068 scudi. Repairs to nearby houses and the two temples would by Fea's calculations cost a further 2,800 scudi, making a total of 3,868 scudi.

Such excavations concerned not only antiquarians and architects. On 6 February 1810 de Gérando wrote to Principe Giustiniani, patron of the church of S. Maria del Sole, after receiving the reports of the Commission for Monuments and Fea.[351] He noted that the temple was very ruined on the Tiber side with the modern walls which had been built between the columns threatening to pull them down. The portico was being used as a wood-store, which put enormous pressure on the walls. De Gérando promised to demolish the wall in the intercolumniations and replace it with metal grilles. The prince obviously approved the plans, for shortly after de Gérando wrote to thank him.

Powerful support came from Fea's predecessor as Commissario delle Antichità, Filippo Aurelio Visconti. His undated report[352] approved of the continued use of convicts, as employed at the Colosseum and Ostia, but they must, he stated, be directed by an antiquarian, and the excavation must be planned by an architect. He suggested as economical and able candidates Andrea Vici, Giuseppe Valadier, Raffaele Stern or Girolamo Masi. As overseer he nominated Carlo Lucangeli, who had carried out much work at the Colosseum.

Another undated report by Visconti urged that there was 'no site in Rome which can at a glance present so many worthy antiquities' as the Forum Boarium. He suggested that the work be directed by de Gérando with no outside interference. Valadier had by now apparently been chosen as the architect, for he was to draw up a plan and estimate. As a small bonus, Visconti suggested, the material removed could be used to fill the holes made earlier in a private garden near the Circus Maximus, for which the Papal government had been paying annual damages of 50 scudi.

A third report of Visconti is dated 12 February 1810. In this he set out a programme of work: to find the steps of the temple, to remove the house built up against it, to demolish the walls between the columns, to replace the missing column, to close the intercolumniations with gratings, and to separate the temple from the buildings on the right. By the end of February, de Gérando sent Valadier Fea's report on the dangerous state of the temple, and that of the Commission of Antiquities (obviously Visconti's) on the work to be done. He asked Valadier to estimate the costs. Here began one of the most unpleasant episodes in the architect's life.

As prompt as always, Valadier's estimate is dated 26 February. He stated that the tools would cost 93 scudi, and materials another 286. He did not include the cost of demolishing the adjoining house, of the iron gratings, or of the transport of earth to the Circus Maximus. The report may have been in two parts; at least it is now, in the Paris Archives. The second part suggested that it would be easy to find the ancient level in the Forum Boarium, about 7 feet below the modern one. The missing costs can be found here:

employment of 50 convicts	216 scudi
demolition of the house	216
demolition of the wall between the 19 columns	127
(the work to support them and the roof was described as delicate) cleaning of the cella, remodelling the door and windows	140
replacement of the missing column	50
grilles between the nine columns facing the piazza	260
demolition of the shed against the west side, belonging to the Marchese Bovio di Bologna	150
cupboard for the sacristy	25
	1,184 scudi

This was converted by Valadier as 5,210 frs, from which could be deducted the income from the sale of material from the demolitions, 668 frs, making a total cost of 4,542 frs.[353]

The municipal administration had to be involved. Senator Giuseppe Origo had agreed with Valadier and Fea on the excavations, and had ordered twenty carts not being used at the Colosseum to be brought to the temple to begin work on 15 March 1810; others were to be constructed. Then some delay occurred. Valadier reported to de Gérando that it was not his fault: he had been waiting five days for the necessary tools. Lucangeli was to be his assistant.

As we learn from later reports, work began on 17 March. Progress soon occupied Valadier. He wrote to de Gérando on 3 April concerning arrangements if the work were to proceed with speed. A stable work-force of fifty convicts was needed, without any who were weak or convalescent. De Gérando wrote across this: 'Have Olivetti [Director of Police] issue a decree. Let Valadier and Fea choose the convicts for themselves.'

Following the advice of the Governor, General Miollis, the Commission of Antiquities visited the temple on Saturday 21 April. It reported to de Gérando that everything seemed to be progressing well, but that work should begin as soon as possible on the demolition of the walls between the columns, and of the adjoining house. It was suggested that Valadier find a mason to direct the workers occupied in these tasks. In less than one month the ancient form of the temple would thus be recovered.

In retrospect a dramatic turn can be detected at the end of May. Tournon wrote to Valadier asking for an estimate for the raising of the temple roof, apparently in response to the architect's proposal. He replied that each capital would need a pilaster 60 cm high. The walls of the cella would also have to be raised. In all, he estimated the cost at 1,872 frs. On the back of this estimate, Tournon commented that this would complete the restoration of the temple and that the work would be a precious way of recording for all educated people the stay of de Gérando in Rome. This seems typical of Tournon's consideration for others. When de Gérando saw the proposal, however, he asked that Dagincourt and Paris[354] be consulted. Here was the beginning of a fatal clash of vision, the cause of much anguish for Valadier.

The first problem arose on 2 June. De Gérando wrote to General Miollis, announcing that work at the temple had been suspended because there were not enough soldiers to guard the convicts. Miollis was asked to see to the removal of this 'inconvenience'. What of the new restoration proposals? Tournon appended a note to de Gérando's letter of 6 June, asking for his reaction to the notion of raising the roof, because Valadier was awaiting this with the 'greatest impatience'. Two days later, Valadier himself wrote to de Gérando with a third project, going far beyond adjustments to the height of the roof.

The more that was uncovered, Valadier noted, the more everyone wanted to see the temple restored. The only condition was that the restoration must enhance the ancient remains. Valadier's new proposal was nothing less than the reconstruction of the whole entablature, in accordance with the Vitruvian canons which he thought governed the whole structure. This had been confirmed by the few remains of the entablature found in the excavations. The reconstruction was to be, in fact, in marble (a departure from the usual methods, we may note). First, the cella wall was to be raised 4 m, with modern arches to support the roof. Second, the missing column had to be replaced. Third, the cornice would then be reconstructed, reinforced with iron chains, but stuccoed to imitate the damaged state of the cella and columns. Fourth, the roof would then be built over the portico in 'cassettone style', to accord with the fragments found, and the ceiling of the cella replaced. The steps, finally, could be rebuilt, in travertine rather than in marble. Valadier estimated the total cost at 20,447 frs. It was thus nearly five times his estimate in February for the simple isolation and cleaning of the temple.

By 17 June he was again writing to de Gérando. Work had ceased because the labourers could not be paid. If some disaster befell the roof or columns left without proper support, Valadier declined responsibility. This letter shows how grim the situation was becoming. A dream was turning sour. Tournon loyally reiterated Valadier's arguments, but the Baron's reply was abusive. He told Tournon that all requests for payment for work on the temple were being sent back because they were not in order. He told the Prefect to consult the Mayor's assistant for information on this branch of the administration, since it had nothing to do with him, de Gérando. To Valadier he replied a day later, 22 June. He expressed surprise at the suspension of the work: he knew nothing about it, nor had it been approved by the Prefect. Convicts could always be employed, he informed Valadier. As for their pay, all documents were in the hands of Tournon. There is obviously a deceitful contradiction between these two letters, separated by only a day. The expenses so far, we can discover, had been paltry: the total for both the temple and the Domus Aurea for the month of May totalled only 162 scudi, and the total for the temple until 17 June stood at 3,163 frs. On 25 June, Valadier wrote to Tournon, asking how the work was to be completed, whether according to the original estimate of 5,210 frs, or the restoration proposed on 8 June, increasing the cost to 25,658 frs.

An undated report of the architect must have been compiled about this date, in the wake of the crisis. Valadier listed the work already carried out by himself, assisted by Fea, with the convicts overseen by Lucangeli. Two-thirds of the soil had been removed to the ancient level; the walls between the columns had been demolished; ten columns had been realigned and repaired; repairs had also been undertaken on the roof and cella. Debris had been used to resurface the road to S. Saba on the Aventine and also placed behind the Bocca della Verità. All this had cost 3,163 frs. Measures required to complete the work were: completion of clearing down to the ancient level; restoration of the steps; closing off the temple from the neighbouring garden; paving of the cella; closing of the columns with grilles (from the Fabbrica di S. Pietro); resetting another seven columns; restoration of the cella's windows and door; raising of the roof 65 cm above the capitals; replacement of the missing column; and the construction of a branch drain to the Tiber. These works would cost 9,031 frs. It may be noted that these proposals included at least the raising of the roof, as first suggested by Valadier in May.

An alternative, also undated, but obviously a variant of the above, set out the cost of restoring the temple to its ancient appearance. In addition to the 3,163 frs already spent, it would cost another 20,447 frs, as reported on 8 June, plus another 3,043 frs, making a grand total of 26,654 frs!

Valadier wrote again to de Gérando on 4 July, asking which of the two recently presented projects should be followed. The more economical was admitted to be the clearing down to the ancient level, with the temple surrounded by a retaining wall, the raising of the roof, the roofing of the cella, the construction of a replica for the missing column, and finally the placing of the grilles to close off the building. The other project was, of course, the rebuilding of the entablature. De Gérando replied the same day. He had submitted the plan to raise the roof to the Commission of Antiquities, which judged it too costly. As for the restoration of the entablature, that would leave the temple too long without a roof. Valadier was ordered to continue the work as originally approved. And de Gérando was as good as his word. The next day he wrote to St Peter's, asking that some 23 m of iron grating in the Fabbrica be given to the architect to close the temple. Valadier was furthermore ordered by the bureaucrat to be at the temple at 6 a.m. to be cross-examined. We know this from the letter he sent stating that he had received this order only at 9 a.m; he offered to be present the next day. It is obvious that Valadier realised that his dream of the restored temple would not be realised: he talked of stopping 'useless' work and devoting himself to the grilles.

The whole question was re-opened by Tournon on 10 July. He wrote to de Gérando asking if the temple was to be completed with only indispensable work for 9,031 frs or restored for 23,491 frs. Activity was suspended until the Baron's reply should be received. It was dated 14 July. Ever the bureaucrat, de Gérando lectured Tournon, stating that the most essential principle in public works is not to allow any unauthorised activity. It was well known, he claimed, that architects become involved in enterprises by submitting modest estimates and are then caught by rising costs. He called Valadier's estimate 'scandalous'. The original had been 4,542 frs. Now, after only two months, there were two new ones, for 12,414 and 26,654 frs. The architect was roundly abused for claiming that the expenses had not been foreseen. This was indeed 'grande imprévoyance' if he could not anticipate two-thirds of the work! Would he treble the cost again in two or three months, de Gérando asked viciously? And three-quarters of the project had not been carried out, although 3,163 of the 4,542 frs had been spent. Either the architect had made serious miscalculations, or he had carried out unauthorised work. He was to be removed from the direction of the operation, and all accounts were to be checked. The best man for that, he asserted, would be Paris.

Tournon's reply is one of the few occasions on which he can be detected in a bad light. On 15 July he replied to de Gérando that he had become involved in the undertaking long after its commencement: he had never seen the estimates. He therefore abstained from any judgement on Valadier. The architect had been ordered to stop all work, save that with convicts. Tournon had asked Paris to review the estimates, but the latter had, to his credit expressed 'extreme repugnance'. Tournon therefore suggested a jury of three architects to investigate the whole affair, with Valadier remaining in charge until they delivered their verdict. (At least Tournon believed a man was innocent until found guilty, but his abandonment of the plans which he seems to have so warmly supported is hard to explain.)

The cost of work on the temple hardly rose: by 17 July expenses totalled

4,131 frs. On 24 July Valadier sent a report to de Gérando, explaining the whole story. On 24 February he had been asked to compile an estimate, which he had done by the 26th. Work had begun on 17 March but there had been many hidden costs (here de Gérando angrily scribbled in the margin, as he read, that Valadier had no right to undertake work not on the original estimates). Valadier's defensive mood is obvious as he asserted that de Gérando, Miollis and Tournon knew all this: they visited the work almost every morning – a telling comment on the great interest in, and control over, such operations by the most important administrators. So far, 4,131 frs had been spent, and the essential works still needed were: the roof, 125 frs; the drain to the Tiber, 430; work by stone-cutters, 180; fitting of the gates, 430; levelling of the ground, 580; the cost of the grilles, 1,240; and the demolition of half the building against the temple, 300, a total of 3,285 frs (a modest sum). If these works were not authorised, Valadier noted, activity would have to be entirely suspended. At the end, de Gérando again wrote a comment: his overriding intention was to consult Paris and Ottaviani.[355]

The French archives do, in fact, contain two anonymous, undated reports, one in Italian and one in French. Their authors, then, are not difficult to divine. The Italian was a fierce detractor of Valadier, and very scathing of the increased costs which he proposed. Much was made here of confusion in the estimates, where the same item was included, it was asserted, more than once. It was admitted, however, that the resetting of the columns had added enormously to the costs. In sum, Valadier was made out to be very unstable and imprecise. His reports were said to omit details, and the statements of amounts paid were claimed not to tally.

The Frenchman was much more restrained (and we have seen Paris' reluctance to stand in judgement). The costs for the work from March to June were, it was admitted, not exorbitant, and work could hardly stop where it was. It might cost as much as another 9,000 frs, but grilles could soon be installed and then the work could be completed when the money was available. Everything done so far was in accordance with the estimates which had been approved (a remarkable vindication of Valadier). Across the front, however, de Gérando, prone to writing himself notes, had scrawled, 'Consult Paris. I am inclined to give him direction of everything.' This would indicate that Paris could not be the author of this report. In that case, there is only one other name we have seen mentioned in this connection, and it is another Frenchman, Dagincourt.

The next month, de Gérando turned on Valadier's associate, Carlo Fea. He has rarely been mentioned so far. De Gérando wrote abusively on 14 August to say that since work began, he had not received the slightest report. What he had been able to find out had been only with his own eyes. De Gérando was so beside himself that words are omitted in this letter. Fea replied the next day, asserting that he had made regular reports on the work and on any important objects found. His function, obviously, in this essentially architectural project was very much on the sidelines, as the antiquarian consultant.

Valadier, however, began to crack under the strain. On 17 August he wrote a rather pathetic defence. If he had pushed to have the various artists working on the project paid (not many will consider this to be a crime!), that was because Miollis was pressuring him to finish it. He had sought nothing for himself, he asserted, and had been at the site almost every day.

Se con tutte queste cautele, con tutta questa assiduità, senza il minimo utile ma anzi con qualche remissione non sia riuscito a soddisfare le intenzioni dell'Ecc. Vostra, l'attribuirò a mia disgrazia, poiche l'impegno, l'onoratezza, e la volontà è tutta dedicata alli commandi de' miei superiori, ed al buon fine dell'opera, di cui ho la compiacenza, che tutti mi fanno giustizia.

While the bureaucrat vented his wrath on the architect and antiquarian, however, he neglected much humbler people. On 30 August the convicts sent him a petition. This revealed the incredible fact that only on 25 August had they been paid for work since 9 July, but that they had received from Lucangeli not the miserable 5 bajocchi agreed upon, but between 2 and 4, on the grounds that they had been incompetent with their wheelbarrows. This was their pay for ten hours' work a day. The petition of the workers was supported by a letter from the lawyer Meloni.

By September, even Tournon was anxious about accounts, presumably under pressure from de Gérando, with whom he was corresponding. He had asked Andrea Vici[356] to check those for the Temple of Vesta, but was told that it was extremely difficult owing to the nature of the work. The Prefect had therefore asked Valadier for more details. So far, to the end of August, 5,690 frs had been spent, and 3,467 frs were outstanding to workers on this temple and the Domus Aurea together. Again Tournon asserted that he had not been responsible for this project until the beginning of May, and that even after that de Gérando had continued to give orders. It was a classic case of conflicting direction.

The end of the story can be found in the Roman archives. The records of the Consulta contain a report by de Gérando of 2 November, asserting that the temple could be restored economically.[357] He again summarised the various plans proposed by Valadier, indicating that it was Tournon's idea that the roof be raised to see the capitals of the columns. It was revealed also that, until 19 September, 6,866 frs had been spent and that work was progressing, albeit slowly. Accounts in December record payments to the stone-cutters, Francesco Antonini and Giuseppe Colli, and then all is silent.[358]

Attention turned now to attempts to free the neighbouring 'Temple of Fortune' from the buildings which invested it, a work achieved only in the

1920s, and the clearing of the Forum Boarium from the amazing accumulation of buildings which, like the Forum Romanum, crowded upon it.

In July 1812 Valadier reported simply that the beautiful temple, which had been hidden by various buildings and even used as a hay-store, was now cleared (Plate 73). He suggested that some further work was needed to expose it and unite it with the neighbouring temple.[359]

Of contemporary reactions, the most outspoken was, as usual, Angelo Uggeri in his *Journées pittoresques*. The aims of the work had been to strengthen the building, to benefit architecture, and to give greater pictures-que effect. None of these, he roundly asserted, had been achieved. The capitals were ruined, and the 'miserable roof' would probably be damaged in the next earthquake. No addition had been made to architectural knowledge. And in his opinion, the little house and the wall between the columns had added to the effect. He had to admit, however, that everyone else was satisfied. Fea himself, who had played some part, was the author of a guidebook to Rome. His only admission of any French work during these years in the whole book is in connection with this temple, although he is hardly generous in details: 'fu poi ridotto allo stato presente nel 1810'! Stendhal described the building, on the other hand, as 'si bien mis en évidence par l'administration de Napoléon (1810)', but went on to echo Uggeri, urging that 'someone rich' replace the horrible mushroom-shaped roof. Apart from this, the temple was described as lacking only one column and its entablature. Of Romans, Antonio Nibby could later be more expansive: 'informi muri ne coprivano le colonne, e meschine fabbriche erano state fatte entro il portico: queste deformità disparvero nell'anno 1810, allorchè la parte antica del tempio rimase intieramente scoperta'.[360] More recent specialist works on archaeology or on the Napoleonic period hardly mention the temple.[361]

Let Valadier have the last word. In the same year as he had devised such grand plans for the temple, he initiated one of his most ambitious projects, not this time on the ground, but on paper, a collection of lavish monographs on the most important classical buildings in Rome. Only seven folio fascicules appeared, but the third was the Temple of Vesta, 1813. This building, he asserted, 'would always be regarded with pleasure by the Arts and Learning as that lucky ruin which began in Rome the revival of its antiquities, which had come forth from the earth into the light thanks to the beneficent care of the government' (the French were, of course, still ruling Rome in 1813). He told in his own words of the state of the temple before his intervention: only the foundations of the steps remained, nineteen out of twenty columns survived, but they were damaged by fire and many had lost part of their capitals, the cella survived to only half its height, there was no trace of the cornice, lacuna and roof, and the columns were covered by modern walls and threatening to collapse. Appointed by the Consulta to direct operations, Valadier listed his achievements as the righting of the columns, the

Plate 73 Luigi Rossini, *Cinquanta principali vedute*, 1817, p. 14, the 'Temple of Vesta'. This plate shows the temple as left by Valadier, and essentially as it remains today, cleared to its steps, with the walls between the columns removed, and with a modern roof.

removal of the wall blocking the intercolumniations, the uncovering of the
steps, and the draining of the water. That is all.

His work was vindicated in a remarkable irony. When the Accademia
di Archeologia was refounded in 1810 by the French, at de Gérando's instigation, the monument chosen for the Accademia's symbol was precisely the
Temple of Vesta, because it was the first ancient monument to be cleared.
The motto added was 'in apricum proferret' (may it bring forth into the
light), a reference to the Accademia's purpose of making new discoveries.

The project for the temple is important under many aspects. It throws
much light on the restoration principles of Valadier at such an early date,
more than a decade before his other two much more famous undertakings
on the Colosseum and the Arch of Titus. It also gives some idea of the
confidence possessed by architects of this time concerning their ability to
carry out such thorough-going interventions, albeit based on the considerable
fragments of the entablature which had been found. For the historian of
the Napoleonic period in Rome, however, the whole sorry story throws
into very sharp relief the impossible conflicts within the administration
between men of such strong character as Tournon and de Gérando.

THE THEATRE OF MARCELLUS

It was only on 5 December 1811 that Tournon mentioned the theatre along
with the Portico of Octavia as an overlooked monument for French attention.[362] The 'Maison Orsini' was described as a 'barbarous construction'
which had almost destroyed the theatre. If prompt remedies were not carried
out, 'the last vestiges would disappear'.

Just how seriously the theatre had been ruined was discovered when its
restoration was finally carried out in the 1920s.[363]

4

The great Colosseum debate

One of the most important undertakings of the French work was not only the clearing and restoration of the Colosseum from the neglect and even the attack of centuries, but also the excavation of the arena (Plate 74). This had not been completed when, on 17 December 1812, a paper was read to the Accademia di Archeologia by the architect Pietro Bianchi. This paper was the work of both Bianchi and the professor of archaeology at Rome University, Lorenzo Re. The central question addressed by the paper was the nature and level of the floor of the arena. The evidence provided by the two experts was a combination of the results of the latest excavations and the various epigraphic and literary sources, notably the inscription of Basilius recently found, together with some commonsense and architectural observations. The literary sources were the main area of uncertainty, comprising not only historians such as Herodian and Dio, but also biographers such as Suetonius, and even poets and novelists. The evidence of all these combined, however, proved according to the two scholars that the arena was set up high, on the substructural walls which had been discovered.

Within little more than a month, Carlo Fea replied with a combination of abuse and patronage. In flat contradiction of the above view, Fea claimed that the substructures were medieval and that the arena had been at ground level. To prove this, he abused every drawing of the architect as wildly inaccurate, and relied primarily on Dio's assertion that the Colosseum had opened with a mock naval battle: how could the arena have been flooded had it been elevated? All the literary sources had, of course, to be reinterpreted to show that the animals appeared horizontally to the arena rather than coming up from below.

The view of Bianchi and Re was soon uncompromisingly supported by the antiquarian Luigi Martorelli, who, perhaps in fear of Fea, published his *Logica nel Colosseo* anonymously.

The debate had so far been conducted among Romans. It was then that a Spanish abbot and antiquarian, Juan Masdeu, attempted the fanciful ploy of 'conciliating' the antagonists with his 'pacific reflections', which in fact

Plate 74 Pietro Parboni, *Veduta dell'interno dell'Anfiteatro Flavio detto il Col-osseo e dei scavi che vi furono fatti nel* 1813. A particularly fine and detailed view of the French excavations in the arena.

amounted to a very particular solution of his own. Masdeu claimed that the raised arena had been constructed only at the end of the third century!

Fea replied to his various critics at the end of 1813 in his *Admonitions*, in which he subjected especially Masdeu to ridicule. The latter, who had in the meantime been addressing endless letters to Fea about his misunderstanding of various Latin inscriptions, now added eight letters to the collection, supposedly on the Colosseum debate, but in reality an attack on Fea's whole career and standing.

These are the main lines of a controversy which lasted from December 1812 until March 1814, all excited by the excavation and interpretation of the Colosseum arena. The 'arguments' may now be examined in more detail before revealing the verdict of modern archaeologists and historians of architecture – a verdict whose brevity is the very antithesis of the early nineteenth-century debate.

The paper of Bianchi and Re as published[1] is illustrated by plans, perhaps used to illustrate the lecture and certainly essential to follow the text. The paper had two major theses.

(i) The arena was supported on a complex of underground walls and corridors.

(ii) The podium (the balcony near the arena) does not exist now, but on the face of what others call the podium are traces of its supporting vault. Within it was an *ambulacrum* (corridor).

The defence of these two propositions required Bianchi and Re to enter the Colosseum as 'gladiators', fighting 'reason in hand'. They had, they announced, 'one thousand reasons' for their views, which they proudly stated were based on mature examination, a daily inspection of the excavations, and a consultation of all ancient sources.

Their basic argument was simply that the 'substructures' are of the same date as the building itself; only the sections in brick are later restorations (Plate 75). That they are an integral part of the building is shown by their centrality and orientation. Their structure accords perfectly ('goccia a goccia') with the porticoes and arches. The authors foresaw sophistic attacks, and they countered them: the claim that the blocks were cut early but here reused. Are we to suppose that blocks could be transported from another building and still fit this one so perfectly?

The restoration, on the other hand, replaced fallen stone with brick, and this work is very bad. What date was the restoration? The time of the Frangipani, when the Colosseum was a fortress belonging to this family in the twelfth century, is impossible. How could this family have repaired so faithfully a building already buried? The repairs belong obviously to the time when the Colosseum was still in use. We know of repairs in the second (Scriptores Historiae Augustae, *Antoninus Pius* 8) and third centuries (*Elagabalus* 17, *Alexander Severus* 24, *Maximus and Balbinus* 1).

The inscription of Basilius found in the Colosseum itself provides the answer. Here the authors cited their principal rival. Carlo Fea had declared that it was necessary to see whether the excavations would confirm the effects of the earthquake and restoration mentioned in this inscription.[2] That answer had now been given, Bianchi and Re asserted. The arena, supported on substructures, would easily have been destroyed. The building and the inscription are in perfect accord. Basilius could not in his time restore the building perfectly according to Flavian standards: he did not even have a piece of new marble for his inscription, but had to reuse an Antonine statue base.

The second argument was a very interesting one. The first rule of any architect building an arena is to provide proper lines of vision (Plate 76). With the raised arena (a–b), almost all of it was visible to the spectators. If, however, the arena were at level g–h, then i–b would be invisible to the nearer spectators.

The third category of proof was the literary sources. Bianchi and Re,

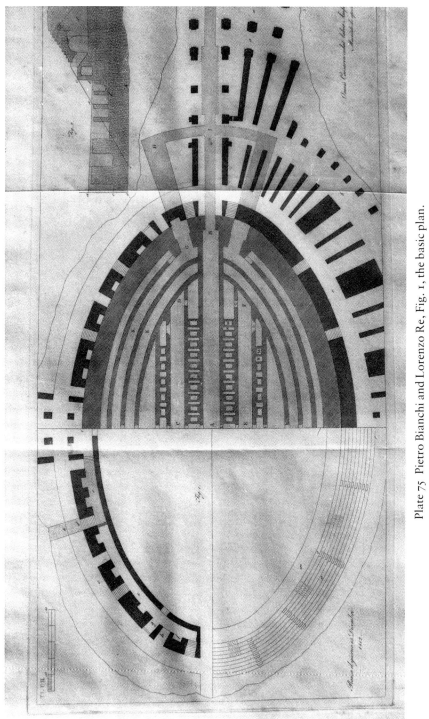

Plate 75 Pietro Bianchi and Lorenzo Re, Fig. 1, the basic plan.

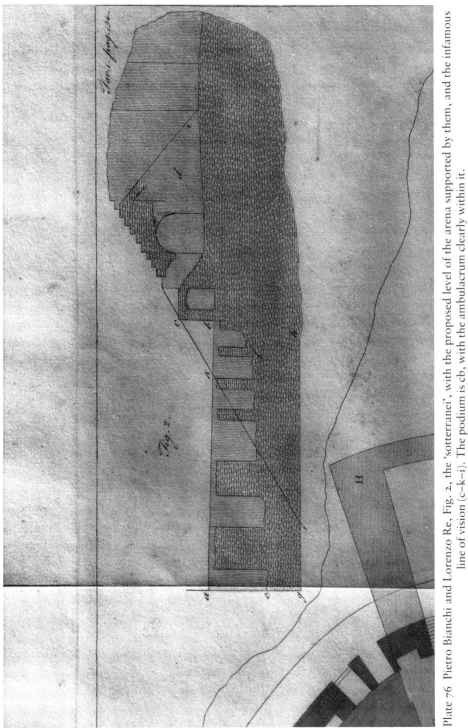

Plate 76 Pietro Bianchi and Lorenzo Re, Fig. 2, the 'sotterranei', with the proposed level of the arena supported by them, and the infamous line of vision (c–k–i). The podium is cb, with the ambulacrum clearly within it.

indefatigable gladiators, put down the arms so far employed and took up new ones, no less sound. Herodian (1.15.6) refers to beasts coming *ex hypogaion*. Calpurnius (*Eclogues* 7.70) has beasts emerging 'ruptaque voragine terrae' ('when the abyss of earth is broken').[3] And Petronius (*Satyricon* 9.8) mentions a gladiator 'quem de ruina arena dimisit', that is, he was granted mercy after he fell into one of the trap-doors, which opened by chance.

Here, declared the two authors, they could rest, except that a mighty roar had shaken Rome (no need to guess at the identity of the objector), on the grounds that all this disregarded the authority of Dio, who says that at the opening of the Colosseum, Titus gave a naval show (66.25). This would seem to be a vital proof that the arena was 20 feet lower. The answer of Bianchi and Re was that the amphitheatre was not built for this kind of show. Dio calls it *theatron kynegetikon*, for beast hunts. If Titus held a *naumachia* (mock naval battle), this was completely irregular. The usual separation of the location of these two kinds of games is shown by the fact that the first stone theatre was constructed at Rome by Statilius Taurus in the time of Augustus (Dio 51.23), while the emperor built a special place for the naval battles (*Res Gestae* 23). Dio was therefore to be rejected, because he is contradicted by Suetonius (*Titus* 7), who states that the naval battle was held in the Augustan basin. The only reliable mention of naval games in the Colosseum is under Domitian (Suetonius, *Domitian* 4), which would be typical of that extravagant and bizarre man. How would they have been possible? Only by sealing all the doors and trapdoors and by bringing water by temporary conduits from the Esquiline or Caelian. The podium was about 10 French feet high: 3 to 4 feet would have sufficed for the ships. After this rash assertion, Bianchi and Re turned to the podium. 'The battle is now over, we can approach the podium in peace.'

The podium, according to the two authors, no longer existed. It was the seat of the magistrates and priestesses (Plate 77: Fig. 3). The usual identification of it with wall B was improper. That space could not support the thrust of the first zone of seats or serve as adequate seating for the dignitaries. The vital clue was the series of steps leading up within this wall. Where did they lead? To the podium is the obvious answer. Within the podium was an *ambulacrum*, lit by twelve light-wells and equipped with two dozen niches, for the convenience of the workers below (Plate 77: Figs. 4–6).

The architect and archaeologist now playfully urged their audience in imagination to step up on to the podium. Some may have been afraid, considering 10 feet too little protection against the beasts. They were reassured: Calpurnius mentions a marble wall, with cylinders revolving on top of it to thrust back any animal which tried to climb up, and with nets hanging on tusks to entangle them (cf. Pliny, *Natural History* 37.3).

The attention of the audience was finally drawn to the secret passage (Plate 77: Fig. 1, kde), built later, certainly by the time of Commodus

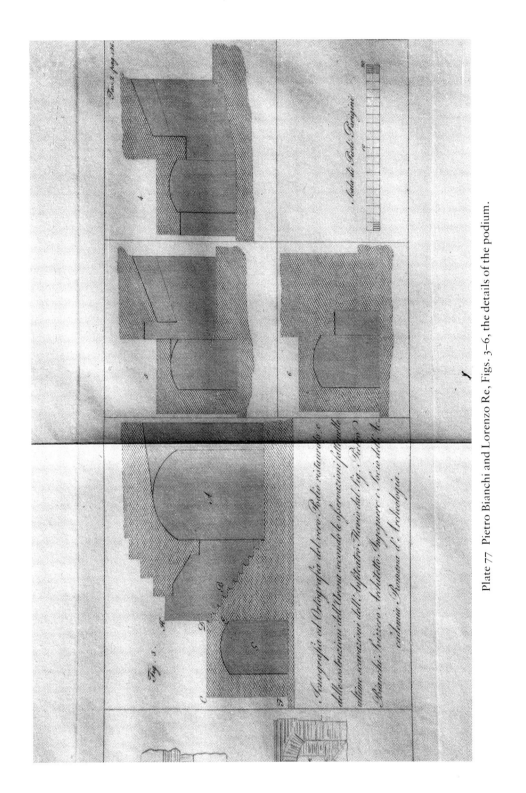

Plate 77 Pietro Bianchi and Lorenzo Re, Figs. 3–6, the details of the podium.

(Her. 1.8.6?). That it was for the emperor is shown by the rich stucco and mosaic decoration. Its deviser was perhaps Domitian.

Their task complete, Bianchi and Re promised not to take up arms again in the arena unless provoked. In fewer than thirty pages they had given a radically new interpretation of the Colosseum in the light of the latest excavations. They had also roused a formidable adversary, one who was the last person ever to leave a critic unanswered.

On 18 January Martial Daru wrote to his elder brother, Intendant Général in Paris, noting that all antiquarians and even the public were talking about the discoveries in the arena. He enclosed a copy of the dissertation of Bianchi and Re, and revealed that he knew that others did not agree and were preparing replies. Daru the Elder replied that the row brewing was all to the good; for it would maintain interest in art and learning, and thus fulfil one of the principal objects in undertaking the excavations![4]

On 25 January and 18 February 1813 appeared Carlo Fea's *Osservazioni sull'arena e sul podio dell'Anfiteatro Flavio*, totalling more than one hundred pages. The wiliest of gladiators had entered the Colosseum. When his antiquarian views and his standing as an oracle were under attack, brevity was a crime.

The first part (thirty-nine pages) answered Bianchi's architectural arguments, the second (sixty-three pages) countered Re's handling of classical texts. The prelude reveals Fea's customary homilies and patronising approach to those who dared cross him. Such hasty publication 'irrevocably closes the ways that the favour of time may open', he lectured. (His rivals might reply that his idea of the favours of time was a little extreme: he so often promised fuller treatment of his own summary expositions which never eventuated.) Fea announced characteristically that only his own work had, in fact, made that of his rivals possible and that he had been engaged in this kind of study for many years before them. He offered a short list of his achievements to illustrate this: the solving of the date of the Pantheon, the attribution of the Temple of Vesta in the Forum Boarium to Hercules Victor, a paper on the Basilica of Maxentius; and he promised further contributions on the Domus Aurea, the Temple of Vespasian, the Forum Trajanum, and the three temples in the Forum Holitorium.[5] Fea finally roundly asserted his pre-eminence as an antiquarian in the twenty-eight years since his essay on the ruins of Rome in the Italian edition of Winckelmann's *History of Art*. As a final proof for the wavering, he stressed that it was under his direction and at his instigation that in 1802 there was carried out what Carlo Fontana had asked in vain of so many popes, namely the removal of the stores of potassium nitrate in the porticoes of the Colosseum, the expulsion of the stone-carters, the erection of the buttress, and the cleaning of the whole structure.

After this autobiographical introduction, Fea then made an unfortunate allusion. Martial (5.58) advised a father that if his son were slow-witted, he should become a crier or an architect. Fea was later to claim that all this was misunderstood in the opposite sense to that which he had intended and that he had the greatest respect for architects, but he went on to say that antiquarians and scholars had written more sense than architects about the Colosseum. He then turned to attack Bianchi's plan of the building.

How did the inclined planes work to bring up animals from the 'sotterranei'? The *ambulacra*, Fea claimed, did not connect with the other passages (Fig. 1, k). The spaces (*vani*) for the animal cages (m) were then analysed, with endless philological probing (even of the verb 'to contain'). How did the animals get there, and from there how did they reach the arena? A more devastating point was that Fea had measured some of these spaces and found them 6 × 4 palms (1.3 m × 0.9 m). These, he declared, were large enough only for rabbits, hares, sheep, deer or dogs. They were, moreover, of modern construction. The adjoining spaces for manoeuvring the animals (n) measured 9 × 2 palms (2 m × 0.45 m). Fea ridiculed the whole notion of safe operations in such a space and drew a lively picture of attempts to open the cages and goad the animals out.

The newly discovered podium was dismissed. The stairs within it (d) led perhaps merely to terraces from which to view the spectacles. The niches (f) in the *ambulacrum* below the podium are stuccoed and painted: Fea ridiculed the idea that such a 'noble coffee-house' ('caffeaus a quella nobilità') could be for the workers or gladiators. The so-called light-wells in the *ambulacrum* were again another place for spectators, half way up the real podium.

As for the secret entrance to the imperial tribunal (k), this was rather the grandest entrance from the imperial palace to the box. The subterranean entrance was not of later date, but an integral part of the first construction.

Bianchi and Re had claimed that the animals were introduced into the arena through the main doors (LL), but only one opposite the Meta Sudans had so far been found, and it did not continue straight through; the two lateral passages (H) were much wider. Fea confidently claimed that 'within a few days' a great access to his lower arena would be found.

Turning to Fig. 2, Fea denounced the claim that the tops of the substructures (a–b) constituted a horizontal line, and began his repeated fascination with the problem of where the water, blood, urine and faeces were drained away from the arena if it were elevated as his rivals claimed. The tops of some of the underneath walls were higher, and some lower, than the line. Was the arena concave or convex, he asked facetiously. By Bianchi's plan, similarly, the distance from the arena to the floor of the underground chambers (a–g) measured 25 feet, 'an abyss', in contrast to Fea's arena of about 25 palms (5.5 m). The vital question of the line of vision, one notes, was postponed by Fea for some reason until the end of his discussion of the literary sources.

The existence of the new *ambulacrum* and the new podium hinged on the remains of its vaulting (Fig. 3). For Fea, this was simply a small piece of cornice to cover the precinct wall of the podium. The front wall of the podium (FC), Fea asserted, could not be found, and it had been deduced from fragments of travertine which could never have belonged to it. What architect could imagine a wall of travertine all around the arena just to hold a few people on portable chairs? The width of the new podium was 9 feet, which according to Fea was room for only one row of chairs, not for two or a passageway behind. And the height of the new podium was only 10 feet, hardly enough to protect important spectators from the wild beasts or the ships in combat. In the midst of all this, Fea inserted a discussion to determine which was the largest animal; on the authority of Bomare's *Dictionnaire d'histoire naturelle* (1764), he decided on the elephant! Behind the podium was a precinct only 5 feet high (DH), quite inadequate to separate the plebeians from the 'gran signori' on the podium. And how high was the door in this wall giving access to the podium?

The smaller illustrations were also criticised. The twenty-four niches in the *ambulacrum* under the new podium (Fig. 6) were not 3 feet deep, but 3½ palms (75 cm), according to Fea. He reserved his chief ridicule, however, for Figs. 8–10, the crucial substructures of the arena. The artist employed by Bianchi, he asserted, was a 'skilful drawer', who knew how to improve. Even an ignorant observer would exclaim, 'What poor stuff! [robaccia] Badly built walls of barbarian times!'

The last question addressed to Bianchi concerned the floor of the arena. The subterranean walls shown on the plan were 3 feet thick, but in fact, claimed Fea, they were 2–2½ palms (44–55 cm). If they were 25 feet high, how could they bear the floor? The *ambulacra* were shown as 13–15 palms (2.9–3.3 m) wide: how could they be covered with slabs of travertine? Would they have been waterproof? Could they have supported the weight of elephants? Once again the problem of water, blood and urine was raised, and a vivid picture painted of the sealed-off underground, lit only by torches, occupied by men and beasts, reeking with 'mephitic vapours of every kind'. The problem of the *naumachia*, however, was enough to overthrow the whole reconstruction attempted by Bianchi and Re. It was to the relevant literary sources that Fea turned next.

The second part of Fea's attack, addressed to the archaeologist and the literary sources, was half as long again as the first part, although much was occupied by the 'line of vision' argument. Fea began characteristically with an ironic compliment to Re: he was so delighted that they agreed that the only way to reach a definitive solution to the problems raised by the ancient monuments, to publish them with good illustrations, and to make them worthy of admiration, was to 'clean them, uncover them, and restore them to their original state at public expense, as far as possible'. This meant

drawing up new plans, making engravings, writing books, establishing academies and chairs, and taking casts to publicise their beauty to the furthest
countries and to awaken the curiosity of those who have never shown any
interest in antiquity.

Fea turned at last to the assertions of his adversary: that there were no
naumachiai in the Colosseum; that the ancient writers knew of the substructures and the elevated arena; that the inscription of Basilius refers to their
restoration; and that the line of vision necessitates an elevated arena.

Fea was horrified that the invaluable Dio was declared wrong in mentioning
a *naumachia* at the dedication of the Colosseum in 80 BC. His reply was
categorical: the Greek historian is too particular and too detailed to be
rejected, and, moreover, he is supported by Suetonius, among others. Fea
had to admit that the biographer states that the naval show was held in
the 'old' (i.e. Augustan) basin, but on this vital matter Suetonius was writing
only a 'compendium'; he was not to be preferred to Dio, author of 'minute
annals'. (It is obvious that Fea wanted to accept only as much of Suetonius
as suited him.) Bianchi and Re had not, on the other hand, rejected the
statement that Domitian gave naval games here (Suetonius, *Domitian* 4).
For these they suggested that temporary conduits brought water from the
neighbouring hills and that 3–4 feet would have sufficed. Martial tells us
that the conduits were large enough to fill the arena quickly (Tertullian,
de spectaculis 24.3f). Fea's triumphant objection, however, was to the absurd
idea that such shallow water would have sufficed for ships such as biremes,
triremes and quadremes used in these games (Suetonius, *Caesar* 39, *Domitian*
4). The Euripus in the Circus Maximus was, by contrast, 10 feet deep (Diony-
sios Halikarnassos 3.68).

On the second matter, the subterranean structures, Fea contested the meaning of Herodian's *hypogea* from which the beasts emerged (1.15.6), claiming
that the context excluded their emergence from below. He asserted that
no author mentioned such a novelty in any theatre.[6] And in a practical sense,
the 'sotterranei' would only have been an 'incalculable complication', in terms
of expense, difficulty of operation, and the darkness. He illustrated this by
endless silly questions about what happened to the dead animals which piled
up in front of the trap-doors, as if they were despatched the moment they
reached the arena, or if one jumped backwards, and how one released
hundred of lions simultaneously, failing to see that much the same questions
could be asked of the system of doorways as he imagined them. Even the
meaning of *hypogeum* was contested, by reference to Vitruvius (6.11); they
were not perpendicular, as Bianchi and Re thought, but underground rooms
or passages entered by doors and stairs. The interpretation of Calpurnius
offered by his antagonists was declared by Fea to be a violation of grammar.
The arena did not open into an abyss, the passage had nothing to do with
trap-doors, and the idea of *vorago* is something which opens to devour,

not to send something up. Fea's view of the passage was that a floor of
wood had been suddenly removed, allowing the animals to leap out of their
dens. (How this did less violence grammatically to 'ruptaque voragine terrae',
the reader may decide.) For such artificial devices, Fea cited Strabo 6.2.6,
Apuleius, *Metamorphoses* 10.34, Seneca, *Epistles* 88.22, Dio 76/77.1. The
last literary source was Petronius: 'gladiator . . . quem de ruina arena dimisit'
meant not that he fell down below the arena, but that he was let down
among the beasts from a machine. The crucial objection was, in fact, seen
by Fea: Petronius can have no reference to the Colosseum, since he wrote
under Nero. In any case, anyone who fell 25 feet, as Bianchi's plan required,
would be more likely killed than saved! There was, moreover, no evidence
that such an accident would have meant the granting of his life to the gladiator. Fea's own interpretation of the passage may not be cogent, but no
one could fail to see the practical difficulties with the alternative offered![7]

It was time to turn to the inscription of Basilius, discovered in 1810. Fea
hastened to assure his readers that he, in fact, had been the first to announce
the find to the Accademia di Archeologia, and he had been the person who
ensured that it was set up in the external portico near where it was found.
The antiquarian thus virtually appropriated as his personal property his opponents' key witness. What was to be made of the vital text, then, mentioning
arena and podium? Fea simply dismissed Bianchi and Re as offering 'many
gratuitous assertions, many other suppositions, but proof – nothing'. The
excavations were only half finished, Fea warned. For his part, he would
await their completion. He then expected to find all elements of the arena
where he said they would be: rooms for gladiators, stairs, animal enclosures,
even a travertine floor, and drains.

As for the restorations in the substructures claimed to be by Basilius, they
are in brick, but peperino and tufa were never lacking. Why could he not
have restored the stone thrown down in the earthquake to its proper place?
Did the porticoes not suffer as well in the disaster? On the other hand,
if the podium were as well constructed in travertine as Bianchi and Re supposed, could it have been as entirely and suddenly overthrown? Not one
trace of that travertine had been found – because it never existed, Fea asserted.
He claimed that the restorations in the 'sotterranei' were of three different
materials, but there were no traces of such restoration in the podium. What,
then, did Basilius mean? Fea's unsatisfactory answer was simply that he
was not to be taken literally, and he unfortunately compared Dio's exaggeration over the fire in the Colosseum in 217 (78.25). (That historian, claimed
to be such a careful source for the Colosseum under the Flavians, is now
accused of exaggeration about it in his own time!) As for Basilius' date,
as so often his wont, Fea promised to deal with this problem at another
time.

And so finally to the vital question of the line of vision. Fea simply refused to accept that everyone had to be able to see everything. Some spectators could see less than three-quarters of the arena on the major axis. Besides, he asserted mysteriously, everything contributed to focus attention on the centre of the arena: the day light, the awnings, and the funnel (*imbuto*).

To conclude, Fea offered a long discussion of other theatres, the height of their podia, and the date of the introduction of animals to the Roman circus. As for Bianchi and Re, they were told to await new discoveries – and to reflect further.

Between the date of Fea's response and 19 May, when a review appeared in the *Giornale politico*, an anonymous booklet was published in Rome by Luigi Salvioni, in fourteen pages: *La logica nel Colosseo*.[8] This purported to be an answer to someone who had asked for clarification of the present 'combat' by the 'noble gladiators of a new kind in the arena'! The author replied by stating that, instead of resorting to dusty tomes, obscure monuments, ancient texts, and even more obscure modern commentators, he would introduce into the arena a strange combatant, one rarely seen, save in the company of Bayle, Leibniz and Newton, not a robust competitor armed with hundreds of folio volumes and hands full of ancient stones and ruins, but a simple girl, almost unarmed. Her name was Logic.

The first rule for an architect is line of vision – unless the arena were made so that spectators could not see the spectacle for which it was built. The author of a certain 112 pages was blamed for not providing any illustration of his interpretations (incredible but true). The anonymous critic then exposed some of Fea's wilder sophistries: the claim that visibility was satisfactory because the games were held in daylight (you cannot see Monte Mario at any time if the view is blocked by St Peter's!) and because there were awnings. Talk of 'difficulty' in seeing is nonsense: either one can see or one cannot. Irrelevancies were also dismissed: circuses have nothing to do with amphitheatres. In the former, spectators at one end could not see the other, and some could not see for the *spina*. Parallels with modern theatres were also ridiculed: they are designed so that one can see from all sides as well as from the front, sound is considered along with sight, and the action on a fixed central place is visible to all. So much for 'line of sight'.

The author then turned to ancient sources. Dio called it a 'hunting theatre' but that does not mean it was only for hunts. It also became a church, although the builder never intended it. The question of the naval battles was admitted to be difficult, but the writer declared that the Colosseum was no more for naval games than the Piazza Colonna for balls, although they had once been held there. The height of the water would, paradoxically, allow everyone to see, but the rest of the games in Fea's arena would have been in an abyss. Fea's vaunted knowledge of animals was also demolished. Dio does not mention hippopotami, but only bulls and horses; they can swim, but cannot fight in water.

Suetonius is precise: the naval games were held, but in the old basin. Dio was exalted by Fea simply because he says what he wanted him to say, but he spent most of his life abroad and lived in the third century. Suetonius lived in Rome fifty years later than the events under Titus and was a member of the court. Logic must have died laughing when Suetonius' statement was declared by Fea 'an argument from silence', as if he said nothing.

As for Herodian's *hypogea*, Fea could not deny that they were 'sotterranei' but he claimed that they were not perpendicular. Where were they then? When Vitruvius refers to perpendiculars, Fea claimed he spoke of no such thing. When Calpurnius says animals burst forth from the earth, Fea asserted that they came from above, not below. The critic turned finally to the decisive source, Basilius' inscription: if the arena was 'thrown down', previously it must have been held up.

Nothing was left of Fea's arguments. His standing of logic on its head at every turn was held up to relentless ridicule. His discussion was described as 'a congeries of absurdities delivered in a magisterial tone'. Age increases obstinacy. Fea was advised to hide himself for shame, in the country or in the drains of the Colosseum!

As we know from Daru's comments early in the year, the feud was public knowledge and attracted great attention even in circles normally unaffected by antiquarian argument (Plate 78). On 3 May a report of the Bianchi and Re lecture appeared in the *Giornale politico*. Again the report was anonymous, signed only 'B'. Whoever the author, he was an enemy of Fea and an unrepentant supporter of his antagonists. The mask, we can only note, seems to have been impenetrable, since Fea in reply calls him only 'B'. Had he been able to discover the real authors of the *Logica* or the article, his triumph would have known no bounds. The first article (for there was to be a series) summarised the lecture of Bianchi and Re, in total agreement with it. The second article (5 May) discussed Fea's rejoinder, characterising his style as prolix and obscure, emphasising his self-praise, and criticising his lack of diagrams. The reviewer denounced the attack on architects drawn from Martial. Fea's claim that the *ambulacra* did not connect with the other passages was ridiculed: they were used together during the excavations. For the rest, his arguments were quoted with obvious disapproval. The third article (10 May) entered into the argument more fully over the literary sources. One of Fea's more pedantic footnotes went into the etymology of podium, derived from the Greek *pos*, foot. The reviewer held this up as an egregious error for *pus*. Fea's defence of Dio was characterised as beginning with a 'tender peroration' and ending with a 'confused narrative'. The treatment of Suetonius was called a 'forced interpretation contrary to the first rules of grammar'. There was a long attack on Fea's selective evidence for marine animals in the arena in support of his claim that it was intended for aquatic

Plate 78 *Fiorentissimo combattimento fra gli antiquari di Roma nell'anno* 1813.
Dedicato al sig. Barone (artist unknown). The anonymous satirist depicts Basilius holding his inscription, Lorenzo Re with the plan he has drawn of the arena, and Pietro Bianchi with his architect's equipment standing on the sotterranei confronting Fea, dressed as an abbot, who holds aloft the various literary sources on which he relies, as well as some works of his own (*Orazio nuovo, 'Pompeio decapitato'*) and some of his rivals (*Lettera di Bajocco*). Behind, two men with pumps vainly try to stop the excavated arena filling with water.

games. On the *hypogea* Fea was happy to use Vitruvius, forgetting that he was an architect. All this was inexcusable for someone like Fea who held lectures every day in this 'abyss'. Attention to the poor workmanship of Basilius' inscription had been simply to undermine what it says about the repairs. 'Risum teneatis amici' (Restrain your laughter, friends).

The editors of the *Giornale* were obviously no friends of Fea. Little more than a week later (19 May) appeared a summary of the *Logica nel Colosseo*. To the modern reader all this publicity for an antiquarians' debate in a political journal must seem strange. The paper had regularly reported the progress of the various excavations, but nothing else of this archaeological kind or extent. Those conversant with Fea's character could be sure that these pamphlets and articles would not pass unchallenged.

The discovery of the inscription of Lampadius on 13 June gave him a first chance to restate his views in his *Notizie degli scavi nell'Anfiteatro Flavio*, dated 20 June and 11 August 1813, extending to forty-four pages. He dealt in turn with the four elements mentioned in Lampadius' restorations: the arena, podium, doors and seating. The discussion of the second was the most complicated, indeed incomprehensible. Fea admitted that it was impossible to understand for anyone who had not been in the Colosseum or without illustrations – so as before, he did not give any! They were to be provided as soon as possible. (We remember that Bianchi and Re had been roundly abused for rushing into print.) As for the arena, Fea simply reasserted that a supported construction would have been an 'unpardonable and impractical extravagance'. He concluded with his usual resort to hopes that soon there would be 'more complete and final proof' of his theories.

There is yet another (the last) contributor to the Colosseum debate. This was a Spanish abbot, who was to become notorious for endless controversies with Fea.[9] In 1813 appeared Juan Masdeu's *Riflessioni pacifiche dirette a conciliare le contrarie opinioni de' chiarissimi antiquarii Lorenzo Re e Carlo Fea intorno all'arena del Colosseo*, published by de Romanis. There is no precise date for the treatise, but it must have appeared after the two sides clashed, after February, and before Fea's reply in November.

Masdeu admitted that it was very difficult to act as a pacifier, especially when one side is armed with breast-plate and lance, with logic and reason, and the other relies on 'intrepid bravura and courage of spirit' (a fascinating description of the antagonists). If the combatants would not listen, however, Masdeu hoped that those who were merely spectators would do so.

His theory was simple but bold: an attempt to distinguish two kinds of machine, the 'above-ground' ('sopraposti') used in all theatres and amphitheatres, and the 'underground', used only in the Colosseum, and there only after AD 282. For the former he offered a vast array of sources, which need not detain us here, an extraordinary collection of information on every aspect of such devices in Roman theatres.

For the vital assertion that underground machinery was used only in the Colosseum and that only after 282, Masdeu offered two sources: the inscription of Basilius, and Calpurnius, *Eclogues* 7. The inscription states that the arena was in ruins, which was possible (as had been pointed out in the *Logica*) only if it were previously above ground-level. Fea had already taken pages to 'reply' to Lorenzo Re, Masdeu bravely asserted, without a single word which weakened the argument, let alone *overthrew* it. Calpurnius, a writer he dated to Diocletian's time, implies 'sotterranei' so they existed by the late third century.

Three sources were claimed to mention such underground devices before this date, but they had been misunderstood. Petronius referred only to the practice of putting criminals on 'machines' and dropping them among the beasts. (He here agreed with Fea, and with Lips and Scioppio's edition of Petronius, 1709.) Apuleius' disappearing wooden mountain required only a temporary device. Herodian's mention of the animals emerging from *hypogea* was admitted to be more difficult! The word should mean underground areas, but a Latin translation is *cavea*, often used by good Latin writers for animal cages. And so Masdeu took it here in Herodian.

Why did he then date the underground structures to 282? The *Historia Augusta* (Carinus 19) talks of 'new' games. Masdeu admitted that he was not sure what this meant, but that it was 'probably' the substructures recently discovered. And that, in his view, was confirmed by the contemporary Calpurnius' mention of devices to fend off beasts from the spectators, devices required by raising the level of the arena. The great advantage of Masdeu's theory, as he stressed, and hence the pacifying intention of his observations, was that it allowed for naval games to be held in the Colosseum before the late third century in the ground-level arena.

The Spanish abbot's solution was bold, but fatally disregarded the archaeological evidence that the 'sotterranei' were an integral and original part of the amphitheatre. They were ascribed to Carinus (283-5) by misdating Calpurnius, a fantastic interpretation of the *Historia Augusta*,[10] and a desperate reading of Herodian.

All this was too much for Fea. He took the opportunity to reply to both his recent antagonist and critic and the would-be pacifier in his *Ammonizioni critico-antiquarie ... a varii scrittori del giorno*, dated 15 October and 13 November 1813. The first section (pp. 12–26) replied, unexpectedly, not to the author of the *Logica nel Colosseo* but to its anonymous summariser in the *Giornale politico*. The author's anonymity rightly annoyed Fea. The critic had attempted to overcome the problem of the small spaces in the underground for the animal cages by claiming they measured 5 feet on the diagonal. Fea's ridicule was unlimited: 'Euclid, Archimedes, Galileo, Newton, where are you? Come and learn!' A square cage which could not fit in a square space could fit on the diagonal! The author had not in fact mentioned cages, but animals. Fea asked whether the panthers, tigers and lions were pulled in by the neck. He then attempted to clear himself of the attack on architects, a weak and vague defence, even though Martial may have been attacking only charlatans. In defence of Dio, Fea again stressed his detail and asserted that he was a frequent attender at the games in the Colosseum and so could not have mentioned naval games in AD 80 had the building not been able to hold them. The long-standing exchange of abuse about expertise regarding aquatic animals led Fea to indulge in one of his most childish assertions: he could say 'without vanity' that he knew more about natural history than Re or the 'sheriff of logic', because he was the author of thirty volumes! He then reaffirmed his claim that the literary sources describing animals coming into the arena were referring to horizontal entrances. This was interlarded with abuse of Re for his ignorance of texts: to be really learned, one has to know them in the original and not just copy extracts from others and twist them for one's own purposes. To conclude, Fea made an emotional defence of his etymology of podium. It was all to show that with Bianchi and Re's arena one would, in fact, go up to it, rather than descend to it, since it would have been higher than the outside road. And *pos* was simply the Aeolic form of the word!

The second and longer part of the *Ammonizioni* (pp. 27–80) was reserved for the unfortunate Masdeu. The position of mediator is always dangerous (Masdeu had admitted as much): he runs the risk of offending both parties, and if he falls down a precipice, no one will mourn. There were few people treated more harshly among Fea's critics than the Spanish abbot. Fea accused him flatly of knowing nothing and proving nothing. He was informed that he had no idea of technical terms, could assert only on his own authority, and had produced an absurd chimera ('irococervo') because he had stepped outside his own field of competence. Fea talked of his 'infinite mistakes of sense and his unconsidered expressions'. His whole system was supported only by air.

Masdeu, he asserted, had not the faintest glimmer of understanding about architecture or masonry. The 'sotterranei' could not have been built in a few months. Nor can he claim to agree with Bianchi and Re, since he did not accept their podium. He had, moreover, confused Carinus (cos. 284) with his father Carus (cos. 282). The *Historia Augusta* speaks of games in the theatre and circus, not the Colosseum. Calpurnius is not a third-century author. If both sources talk of novelties, it is in the kind of games, not the building. Fea's abuse was boundless: the underground machines emerged for the first time at the end of the third century from Masdeu's brain, like the goddess of Wisdom from that of Jupiter.

The last word, it seems, fell to Masdeu. In his *Lettere sette al Fea sulle antiche iscrizioni romane ne' recenti scavi rinvenute*, July 1813, he had argued bitterly with Fea over various inscriptions, and another six letters were added to the original seven in October. The inscriptions were forgotten in December when, by way of reply to Fea over the Colosseum, a further eight letters were published. The reader must be warned that in these letters the last concern was any discussion of evidence. There was obviously nothing more to be said on that head. The letters instead indulged in an attack on Fea's whole career, and stung him deeply. They need not be recounted in turn; rather, an indication of the main themes will suffice.

The last eight letters were dated between 1 December 1813 and 15 March 1814, and bore titles such as 'The sphinx', 'The missed target', 'Happy New Year', 'Fea the mason', and 'Fea the page/train-bearer'. Masdeu began by threatening to publish a weighty volume entitled *Storia veridica della vita litteraria di Dom Carlo Fea*, a chronology of his 'literary tricks' over thirty years from Bajocco to Cefalo. There was henceforth merciless allusion to the various opponents of Fea over the years since the famous letter of Bajocco (Onofrio Boni), over Fea's edition of Winckelmann's *History of Art*, to the more recent attack by Cefalo.[11] Masdeu descended, on the other hand, to a general defence of himself, as the author of a history of Spain which was civil, political, ecclesiastical, military, commercial, artistic and literary in its compass. At the same time, he asserted that he was an acknowledged antiquarian, having had his works published by the Accademia Italiana di Scienze, Lettere ed Arti.

Fea's titles, of which he seems to have been inordinately proud, were again witheringly attacked. Now he was 'Ammonitore' (warner), from the title of his *Ammonizioni*, but Masdeu preferred 'Monitore' (prompter) because he simply intoned others' ideas. The abbreviation 'Avv.', meant as 'Avvocato' (lawyer), from Fea's legal degree, Masdeu suggested meant 'Avvilupatore' (entangler, or cheat), because he falsified the dates of his writings to cover his copying from others.

Masdeu then turned to Fea's methods of argument, or logic. He was accused of offering not one iota of evidence for his views about the Colosseum, but indulging in a number of deceits. He accused others of a lack of logic, but he had been guilty of this himself for thirty years, trained by the second-hand dealers of the Piazza Navona. There was no system in his ideas: they hopped like idle little birds from one branch to another; he thought with his feet. He accused others of having no learning, just like every source with which he disagreed. He accused others of copying his ideas. He did not have to offer any proof for his assertions: he was an infallible oracle, the Despot of Truth and Falsehood, the Grand Turk of judges and judgement. When others told him anything, he claimed he knew it all along. Trying to teach him, indeed, was like trying to whitewash an Ethiopian. He claimed to be expert in everything, the 'artigianello caro' (dear little craftsman), but showed 'complete ignorance of every art and insufferable vanity in wanting to speak of it without the least practice or knowledge': in the Colosseum debate, the architect Bianchi was the expert.

Fea's style had long been held up to ridicule by Masdeu. His diction was as complicated as an Egyptian labyrinth. He really enjoyed the anonymity of his rivals, because it made him seem like 'a ravenous literary wolf of whom all little lambs had to be afraid'. As for his pitiful attempts to escape his ill-fated reference to Martial and architects, Masdeu suggested that Fea bury it in one of his two celebrated 'ditches': his Pantheon excavation or his Colosseum arena. There were finally Fea's masks to be stripped away: the orator, in his attacks on antiquarians and architects, and the etymologist, who explained the derivation of podium and claimed that it could not be found in any book, when it existed in every lexicon.

By 1 January 1814 ('Happy New Year'), the attack had widened, if that were possible. Masdeu listed Fea's four vices as falsehood, trickery, lack of thought and logic, and lack of respect for honour. At the end of the letter of 1 March he claimed that he had not yet said much. It was time to lift the veil for the world of letters. The last epistle, dated 15 March, is hard to parallel in the annals of feuds. The promised literary life of Fea was finally offered in synopsis. It would be divided into five parts:

1. Fea as writer of Greek, Latin and Italian. Here would be treated the mistranslated and misunderstood Greek, and the unknown dialects of it (Masdeu in fact referred to jokes at Fea's expense by none other than the Portuguese ambassador, the comte de Funchal); in Latin, his senseless prose, diabolical verses, barbarous doggerel; in Italian, his disgusting maltreatment of the language in orthography, construction, conjugation, gender, articles and meaning, not to mention his notorious 'French infection'. In sum, a plaque was to be affixed to Fea's door to commemorate the 'Fea epoch' in language.

2. Fea as historian of Fine Arts. Here he was represented by the mole, because he was blind. He never said a word about sculpture or art that did not excite pity, asserted Masdeu, who referred to many old feuds now hard to understand, except such matters as the 'infernal abyss' of Fea's arena.

3. Fea as antiquarian. Here, Masdeu claimed, were a series of misunderstood inscriptions and excavations which ended in satire or hisses. If Fea found the bones of a poor Roman, he would claim them to be Brutus or Hannibal. He was a peacock: his tail had one thousand eyes, but they were all blind.

4. Fea's works. Where they were his own 'husk', they were mostly clumsy errors; where they were a 'second sifting', the flour mixed with Fea's stones and grit was provided by Visconti, Marini or Dagincourt.

5. Fea's literary tricks. Here finally was a summary of much already adumbrated: claiming to know what he did not, pretending not to know books from which he copied, claiming old ideas as his inventions, answering only one of a hundred objections and pretending the others did not exist, resorting to calumnies, giving false dates to his works, and inventing evidence.

All the above was Masdeu's response to Fea's ridicule of his attempt to act as 'pacifier' in the great Colosseum debate. The evidence in question was finally thrown aside completely, and both parties attempted to destroy the other's reputation entirely. It recalls the deadly feuds of the earlier Humanists, although one cannot help feeling that Masdeu and Fea would have recognised the invective of a Housman. Within four years Masdeu was dead, but Fea remained a dominant figure in Rome for almost another quarter of a century. The Spanish abbot is now forgotten while even Fea is known only to those who have an antiquarian interest in the early nineteenth century.

As for the Colosseum, the paradox could not be more striking. For the first time since late Antiquity, the inside of the amphitheatre was cleared.

One might have thought that at last clear answers would have been provided to the interesting questions of how the spectacles were staged. Contrary to all expectation, the excavations produced only the most bitter feuds and violent enmities.

There is another paradox, admittedly more modest. What is the answer to the great questions debated in 1813? Where was the arena? Where was the podium? Could naval battles be held in the Colosseum? The answer to the first question is that which can most easily be found, and Fea is now acknowledged to have been completely wrong: 'The floor of the arena, which must have been of wood, rested on lofty substructures ... In the substructures are traces of dens for wild beasts, elevators and mechanical appliances of various sorts.'[12] Others speak of 'the network of service corridors and chambers below the arena' and lifts with an ingenious system of counter-weights for hoisting scenery or wild beasts to the floor above'.[13] Perhaps most direct of all, 'Immaginare infatti un edificio anfiteatrale senza gl'ipogei dell'arena sarebbe lo stesso che immaginare un corpo animato senza gli organi interni. La vita, dirò così, dell'anfiteatro si svolgeva negl'ipogei, e si manifes-tava sull'arena.'[14] Of all these authorities, only one mentions the podium and states that it was about 4 m above the arena.[15] Most modern authorities avoid the question of the *naumachiai*, which is a much more serious matter, since we have Dio's assertion that Domitian staged them. Only one recent writer ventures the view that his implication that the arena was flooded is a confusion.[16]

Conclusion

THE AFTERMATH

The registers of the Commission des Embellisements contain the records of the Neapolitan government which succeeded the French in 1814.[1] On 1 March a report was presented on what had been finished and what work was still in progress. The four major French undertakings singled out were the Jardin du Grand César, the Forum of Trajan, the Forum Romanum, and the Tiber works. The expenses so far totalled 1,299,241 frs. The sums needed to complete them were as follows: the Forum of Trajan: 91,538; the Jardin du Grand César: 998,278; the Tiber: 1,097,000; and the Forum Romanum: 1,556,664. The first three, in that order, were to be given priority, together with the building of cemeteries.

In May, Clemente Giardini made another report. The plans for the Pincian hill (the Jardin du Grand César) could, he suggested, be modified. The Forum of Trajan's completion was urgent and necessary, but could be carried out by monthly instalments. The plans for the Forum Romanum were subject to infinite modifications, in accordance with the condition of the monuments and the need to provide work. The expenses for the first three projects, presumably those mentioned, were calculated as 181 scudi a day (pay for 630 men, 100 women and 80 boys) plus 551 scudi per month for staff. This list of employees, it may be noted, included Giuseppe Camporese, Giuseppe Valadier and Pietro Bianchi.

The major reorganisation came on 3 July. The staff were reduced to nineteen. The architects' monthly salaries were reduced from 37.38 to 25 scudi, and Bianchi's from 37 to 18 scudi! Giardini was now director with 35 scudi. And by August, the dismissal of workers had begun. All able-bodied young men were to be dismissed with one week's pay, while the boys were to be given to institutions to be taught a trade. The pay-rate of 23 bajocchi a day (1.25 frs, the French rate) was declared too high.

Work had continued. The monthly expenses for 1814 were as follows: January: 38,451 frs; February: 36,496; March: 42,015; April: 45,656; May:

9,438 scudi; June: 6,816; July: 7,419; August: 8,595. In contrast to an average of nearly 50,000 frs per month for the Embellisements in the last six months of 1813 under the French, this represents little reduction, if the exchange rate for the franc held at 5.35 to the scudo.

We have noted the presence under the new government of names long familiar to us during the account of the French undertakings. What were the vicissitudes suffered by the architects, engineers and antiquarians in Rome who had not only lived under but also worked for the early pontificate of Pius VII, the French occupation, and then the Papal restoration? The matter is inexplicably neglected by almost every account of the period. Some clues may be gleaned about Giuseppe Valadier. In his *Opere di architettura e di ornamento*, 1833, he gives a brief autobiography, including the following:

Nel meglio per di un tal cammino, sorsero le politiche turbolenze che guastavano molto miei avvenimenti, onde dovetti riordinare le vie per porre in attività con onore e con arte la mia prima distinzione, contrastando alle avversità di fortuna e di rovinose imprese; ma collo scudo di rettitudine e della fatica mi sono acquistato sempre appoggi, protettori, ed amici, ai quali intendo di donare e dedicare la presente raccolta . . .[2]

The only disappointment is that the work, in fact, has no dedication: Valadier's benefactors remain anonymous!

One historian talks of the 'citizens of those days' begging forgiveness of the Pope for having served his enemies, and Pius made 'un gran' crocione' and took them all back into service. Given what we know of Pius VII, the story is credible. Valadier in particular is mentioned as asking pardon. To show their devotion to the old regime and as a protest against the Jacobins and the Napoleonic system, such people powdered their hair, grew the queue and readopted short trousers.[3] They had, after all, we must admit, for the most part only followed their profession in order to continue to earn their living.

ARCHAEOLOGICAL WORK DURING THE REST OF THE NINETEENTH CENTURY

The main excavations after the French and until the age of Giacomo Boni may be listed as follows, after Lanciani's account in his *Ruins and excavations*:

1817: Temple of Concord discovered[4]
1818–19, 1828: Nibby excavates the Basilica of Maxentius[5]
1827–9: Nibby excavates the Temple of Venus and Rome[6]
1820: discovery of the *statio* of Cohort v of the Vigiles on the Caelian[7]
1838: Grifi clears the tomb of Eurysaces, following the project of Valadier[8]

1842: excavation of the Temple of Mars Ultor[9]

1848: Canina excavates and identifies the Basilica Julia[10]

1860–7: Guidi excavates under the Baths of Caracalla[11]

1861–70: excavations for Napoleon III in the Palace of Domitian[12]

1868–70: Visconti excavates the Marmorata[13]

1867: Rosa discovers the Temple of Jupiter on the Palatine[14]

1869: Rosa discovers the 'House of Livia' on the Palatine[15]

1868–93: excavation of the Stadium on the Palatine[16]

1870–2: Rosa completes the clearing of the Basilica Julia[17]

1872–8: the Horti Maecenatis[18]

1881–2: demolitions to restore the view of the Pantheon; excavation of the Baths of Agrippa[19]

1882: clearing of the whole of the Via Sacra[20]

1883: Lanciani excavates the House of the Vestals[21]

1886, 1889: identification of the Regia and excavations by Jordan and Hülsen[22]

1888: Lanciani excavates the southern hemicycle of the Forum of Augustus[23]

1892: Chedanne discovers the real date of the Pantheon[24]

1893: discovery of the *statio annonae* under S. Maria in Cosmedin[25]

Boni's new era began with his excavation of the Regia, 1898–9. One of the leading young archaeologists of the time, and a participant in these discoveries, was Christian Hülsen. In his *Forum Romanum*, 1904, he suggested that these works, at least in the Forum, should be divided into periods. Some work was carried out after the return of Pius VII in 1814, but then there was a pause. A new era began in 1827 under Leo XII, when the large-scale clearing of the Forum was approved, which led to new work by Antonio Nibby, revealed especially in Ernst Platner and Karl Bunsen, *Beschreibung der Stadt Rom* (3 vols.) 1830–7, and Luigi Canina's *Esposizione storica e topografica del Foro Romano*, 1834. Another burst of activity came with the Roman Republic, 1848–9, and lasted until 1853. This was dominated by Canina, who died in 1856. From 1853 until 1870 there was another long break. With the Unification, archaeological excavations were confided to Pietro Rosa, who cleared most of the central Forum. Apart from his own *Relazione sulle scoperte archeologiche della città e provincia di Roma negli anni 1871–1872*, 1873, a testimony to this activity may be found in F. Dutert's *Le Forum romain*, 1876. Rosa's successor was Giuseppe Fiorelli of Pompeian fame, now Director General of Antichità e Belle Arti 1875–96, who concentrated on the eastern end of the Forum (the Temple of Antoninus and Faustina to that of Venus and Rome). In 1882 the two roads which cut the Forum, the Via Bonella and the Via S. Lorenzo/S. Maria Liberatrice, were removed, reuniting the area: Lanciani excavated the House of the Vestals, Jordan and Hülsen the Regia. There was another thirteen years' pause, 1885–98, before the twentieth century was ushered in by Giacomo Boni.[26]

To be kept in a separate category from the above excavations, and marking a stronger link with the French period, are two famous restorations.

The first is that of the Arch of Titus, which the French had cleared and left paradoxically in a weakened state. Guy Gisors, it will be remembered, had proposed that it be dismantled and rebuilt in 1813. Nothing was done until 1818, when there were two proposals: that of Scaccia and Martinelli, to pull the arch back into shape by force and to bind it with iron, or to dismantle it and rebuild it.[27] Raffaele Stern played a leading role in plans for the second approach, but died in 1820, when the work was continued by Valadier.[28] Of the latter's work, we have only his report of the work in progress, read to the Accademia di Archeologia on 20 December 1821, with the published version dated 8 February 1822. By this time, the scaffolding was erected, the unsafe pieces had been dismantled, and the bearing of the arches had been reconstructed. The task of rebuilding the new sides and the attic lay ahead. It should be stressed that Valadier gave Stern full credit for the idea of rebuilding the missing sections in travertine. The work was finished by 1824, and the commemorative inscription of Pius VII gives his twenty-fourth year (14 March 1823 to 1824).[29]

The arch thus stands solid and secure, with the missing sections painstakingly reconstructed on the sure information provided by what remained. By the use of travertine, these can be instantly distinguished from the marble of the original. Had it not been restored when it was, it would simply have collapsed, and one of the most familiar monuments not only of the Forum but also of Rome would no longer exist.[30]

The other great restoration was also the work of Valadier, the second Colosseum buttress. It makes the strongest contrast with the earlier work of Stern on the same building.[31] Stern used a massive sloping pylon of brick to hold back the masses of stone as they collapsed. Valadier adopted the same slope, and also used brick for the most part, but with travertine as well. The crucial distinction is that the younger architect attempted to make his buttress as unobtrusive as possible, reproducing the arches of the three storeys.

The exact story of the undertaking is provided by Luigi Canina: the scaffolding was erected in July 1822, work began in August 1824, and was completed in July 1826.[32] Thus, again, the commemorative inscription of Leo XII is dated to his third year (September 1825 to 1826).[33]

It is in connection with this work that a fascinating insight is given. Pius VII, visiting the Colosseum, remarked that if each Pope had added one arch, the building could have been completely restored. Some 'Eminentissimo' had replied that it could be done still within a century.[34] Such words would not have been necessary to fire Valadier's enthusiasm, but imminent collapse required his intervention in the 1820s. Valadier died in 1839, sadly not to see the seven arches rebuilt by Gregory XVI in 1845.

THE FRENCH CONTRIBUTION

With this brief sketch of the archaeological work of the rest of the nineteenth century to complete our perspective, we may finally attempt to assess the French contribution in a brief six years, remembering that their efforts were, in fact, concentrated in the last four, from 1810.

No one was more qualified than Camille de Tournon to state what his administration had tried to achieve, and how far it had been successful. In his Mémoire to the Bordeaux Academy in 1821, he set out the intentions:

L'administration française se propose de réaliser la grande pensée de Raphael; elle voulut en même temps donner aux restes des monumens toute la stabilité qui pouvait leur être rendue, et par les plantations bien combinées autour de ces belles ruines ouvrir aux Romains de nouvelles sources de jouissance, et offrir aux étrangers de nouveaux motifs d'admiration.[35]

He admitted that not every plan had been realised. The French had not attained their goal in regard to the Pantheon, the Theatre of Marcellus, the porticoes of Octavia and Nerva, and the Temple of Mars Ultor. He took his leave again of Rome, addressing her directly, seven years after that emotional day in January 1814 when he had been forced to depart: 'Des rives de la France, appelé, bien jeune encore, à devenir témoin de tes malheurs, peut-être de diminuer leur poids, j'ai vu ta noble infortune, j'ai vu les ruines de tous tes âges et ma faible main a tenté d'arrêter la main puissante du temps . . . O Rome! reçois mes vœux! . . . sois heureuse!'[36]

A decade later, he published his authoritative *Etudes statistiques*, the basic published source for every later history of the French administration. The last chapter is devoted to the restoration and preservation of the monuments. Each is described in turn, both before and after the French work. Of general remarks, he offered little, but they are telling: 'L'honneur d'avoir éloigné l'époque où tant de précieux débris ne seront qu'un souvenir est assez grand pour que je veuille fournir la preuve que mon pays peut aussi prétendre à cette palme pacifique.'[37] The meaning of this will be clear in the light of our first chapter. Tournon admitted the 'flagrant injustice' of the occupation, but asserted that France had been more attentive to Rome as a conquered city than to her own.

In more precise detail, he acknowledged that French attention had perforce been concentrated on the heart of the ancient city. He listed the main difficulties: buying and demolishing many houses, removing vast quantities of earth, carting it away where it would not harm other and later work, repairing monuments in danger, and seeing to the enormous problem of drainage for the new levels.[38]

Given the scant attention shown to the French undertakings in histories of archaeology, as we have demonstrated in the prologue, it is difficult to find assessments of their contribution. The greatest historian of excavations in Rome, Rodolfo Lanciani, summed up the French work in one of his lesser known books: 'furono gettate le basi, e studiati a fondo i criteri di quelle opere pubbliche che, pur rispettando l'antico, dovean provvedere alla necessità della vita moderna.'[39] The French showed that art and science do not preclude the improvement of a city, that monuments are assisted by being brought into prominence, even isolated, instead of being hidden by slums. These last words of Lanciani, written long before the 1920s and 1930s, have taken on since then an unfortunate meaning, but his general verdict is a high compliment to the principles followed by the French.

A Frenchman, on the other hand, Ferdinand Boyer, suggested that it was a shame from the archaeological point-of-view that the Jardin du Capitole was not completed at the time. We should have known the Forum seventy-five years earlier, he lamented.[40] With all respect, one may question this claim. The French used unskilled labour to clear great monuments from the accumulated debris of centuries, and under the direction of the best architects and antiquarians of the day they were able to carry out some brilliant restorations. Had they progressed further, to the classical levels of the Forum which were reached only at the end of the century, what would they have made of the poor ruins of buildings such as the Regia? What were to become for the archaeologists of the later century, of the generation of Boni (and W. M. F. Petrie in Egyptology), the most precious clues for the reconstruction of the palimpsest of the past might have been swept away as unimportant, unilluminating. Archaeology was to be radically transformed in the nineteenth century, and to have come upon the oldest layers of the Forum before techniques and understanding were ready to cope with them would probably have been an irreplaceable loss. We know enough, to our anguish, of the destruction of such precious ruins through ignorance even in the last third of the century, not to mention our own.[41]

Most recently, an Italian historian briefly stressed the innovations of the French period. Winckelmann had begun to introduce 'a new aesthetic tendency and a new historical awareness'. The Napoleonic regime introduced new techniques of excavation, and of restoration and preservation of monuments. There was a new concept, most importantly, of the public patrimony.[42] To be fair, we have seen the beginning of a new attitude to the monuments of classical Rome in the first years of Pius VII.

The French achievement may best be seen by a brief recapitulation of the monuments on which they worked.

Clearing

The Arch of Janus was cleared of earth banked up 2 or 3 m deep.

The Arch of Titus was freed of surrounding – and supporting! – buildings.

The Basilica of Maxentius, degraded and buried to an enormous depth, was cleared to its pavement and the portico uncovered. A total of 60,000 cu m of earth were removed.

The entire slope of the Capitol was cleared after restoration of the Temple of Vespasian: 23,000 cu m of earth.

The Colosseum was cleared by both the Embellisements and the Crown: all galleries and the arena, and a space to the north with a retaining wall for the skirting roadway.

The Domus Aurea saw the first regular clearing, in contrast to the erratic digging, plundering and general use of the rooms to store saltpetre. The Crown by early 1813 had already spent 75,000 frs.

The Temple of Fortune in the Forum Boarium was cleared to its foundations, and the ground-level was lowered between it and the Temple of Vesta.

In the Forum, where the rubbish level was in general 4 m high, it was hoped to clear the whole area, but the task was too great. The houses in the middle were bought and demolished, as also the convent of S. Francesca Romana; old dumps were carted away.

In the Forum of Trajan, where the difference between the ancient and modern levels was more than 5 m, the large block of houses beside the column and the two large convents in front of it were demolished. The central section of the Basilica Ulpia, part of the Forum and of the library portico were then able to be uncovered. The cost was 180,000 frs for the Embellisements and more than 25,000 frs for the Crown.

The Pantheon project, to create an ample square around the building, was too costly (more than 300,000 frs) and did not proceed beyond the planning stage.

The Tabularium was cleared to its foundations, despite the plainness of the monument.

The portico and steps of the Temple of Antoninus and Faustina were cleared down to the Via Sacra at a cost of 5,000 frs, but the building had to be left in a deep excavation, since the Forum around could not be lowered to the ancient level.

The Temple of Castor and Pollux was first cleared to its platform; later the foundations were exposed.

The Temple of Saturn was cleared of modern buildings and the portico fully exposed.

The three remaining columns of the Temple of Vespasian, buried in debris to their capitals, were completely cleared.

Repairs and restoration (by the Accademia di S. Luca)

The Basilica of Maxentius: the western vault and the portico.

Enormously extensive and expensive repairs were made in the Colosseum, the largest classical monument and the one most in danger of collapse: brick supports such as under-arches, replacement of travertine, and special attention to the southern side.

The Pantheon required costly and extensive repairs, notably to the entire lead roofing.

The Portico of Octavia was intended to be the object of basic restoration, but despite Valadier's recommendations in February 1810 nothing was done.

The columns of the Temple of Castor and Pollux were reinforced.

The foundations of the columns of the Temple of Vespasian were virtually rebuilt, the columns realigned, and the entablature reset at a cost of 15,000 frs.

The Temple of Vesta in the Forum Boarium was cleared to its foundations, the walls blocking the intercolumniations were removed, and the many out-of-line columns were righted. The cost was about 7,000 frs.

In sum, for the first time since the main classical buildings of Rome had performed their intended function and then had been subject to centuries of depredation or been slowly buried under metres of debris, they were again brought to light. Almost every major monument known to us was carefully cleared and restored. One remains astounded at the vastness of some of these undertakings, such as the Basilica of Maxentius and the Colosseum and the Forum of Trajan. In other cases we must be amazed at the technical bravura which alone preserved beloved monuments to our own day, such as the complete rebuilding of the remaining columns of the Temple of Vespasian.

These projects were greatly influenced by conceptions of Napoleonic grandeur and town-planning, and were largely designed to give employment to the poor, so cruelly deprived of their sustenance by Napoleon's religious bigotry. In the last analysis, however, if these had been the only guiding principles, then nothing need have been done about Rome's classical past. All attention could have been focussed on projects such as Tiber navigation, roads, cemeteries and markets.

There is no doubt that it is to a trio of men that this unparalleled archaeological programme was due: one Frenchman, the best loved of the occupiers, and two Italians. They were Camille de Tournon, Giuseppe Camporese and Giuseppe Valadier. These three were ably seconded by the assembled talents of the Accademia di S. Luca under Antonio Canova. In his Memoirs, Tournon wrote: 'J'aime à me flatter que lorsque mes enfants iront visiter Rome, ils trouveront encore quelques traces de mon passage, et qu'il y restera de moi un souvenir dont ils n'auront pas à rougir.'[43] His shade has nothing to regret. His wish has been granted. The impress of this man above all others in the French archaeological programme is outstanding. The concept of the Embellisements and their execution were due especially to him. At the same time, alongside the Prefect, the architects and antiquarians, we must not forget the thousands of Romans who laboured with their hands to realise the grand projects, and perhaps in so doing for the first time came to feel some pride and involvement in Rome's classical past, began to have a sense of their common cultural patrimony.

Although it has never been recognised so far, it is time to realise that the French administration saw both the beginnings of Roman archaeology and a campaign unequalled in effort and expense before or since.

Appendix 1. Chronological Table

1808

2 February: Miollis and the French occupy Rome.

                                    March: France invades Spain; Joseph Bonaparte king.

1809

April–July: Académie de France at Rome excavates the front of the Temple of Antoninus and Faustina.

17 May: Napoleon decrees the Papal States incorporated in France (carried out in Rome on 10 June).

10 June: creation of the Consulta Straordinaria (Miollis, de Gérando, Janet, del Pozzo, Balbo).

21 June: the Consulta establishes the Commissione per l'Inspezione e Conservazione de' Monumenti Antichi e Moderni (Luigi Martorelli, Antonio Canova, Vincenzo Camuccini, Gaetano Marini).

                                    5–6 July: Battle of Wagram: defeat of Austria.

6 July: arrest of Pius VII (aged 67) and deportation to France.

21 July: Consulta establishes a commission to oversee work between the Ponte Milvio and Piazza del Popolo: Principe Ludovisi, Palombi, d'Orimond, Stern and Valadier (Ludovisi Commission).

2 August: Papal States divided into Tiber and Trasimene.

6 September: Camille de Tournon appointed Prefect of Rome.

5 November: arrival of Tournon.

20 December: regulations of the Consulta for excavations and export of antiquities.

1810

17 February: division of the Papal States renamed Rome and Trasimene.

27 February:	Valadier proposes the restoration of the Portico of Octavia.
17 March:	Valadier begins the restoration of the Temple of Vesta.
6 April:	Valadier proposes to clear the platform of the Temple of Castor and Pollux.
17 April:	imperial decrees dissolve religious corporations.
May–September:	clearing of the Domus Aurea (Valadier and Fea).
3 June:	appointment of Fouché as Governor-General; rescinded 1 July, and no successor appointed: Miollis as effective governor.
9 July:	Consulta replaces Commission of June 1809 by Commission des Monuments Antiques et des Bâtiments Civils (Commissione per i Monumenti Pubblici e le Fabbriche Civili): Tournon, Braschi, Gabrielli, Albani, Vici, Lethière, Canova, Laboureur, Stern, Camuccini, Landi, Visconti, Fea, Guattani, Ottaviani (see p. 286).
4 October:	de Gérando re-establishes the Accademia Romana di Archeologia.
4 November:	offer of work to the poor by the Commissione della Beneficenza.
6 November:	an imperial decree assigns 200,000 frs for excavations in Rome on behalf of the Crown.
6 November:	imperial decree assigns 100,000 frs to the Accademia di S. Luca, of which 75,000 for repairs to the ancient monuments.
12 November:	work of the Commission begins in the Forum.
December:	erection of scaffolding to begin clearing the Temple of Vespasian by Camporese.

1811

11 January:	the Consulta lays down a programme for clearing around and inside the Colosseum (to continue through to 1814).
January:	clearing around the 'Temple of Fortune' in the Forum Boarium.
17 February:	Miollis is confirmed as Lieutenant Governor. A 'second Consulta' henceforth rules Rome: Miollis, Tournon, Norvins, Janet, Daru.
March:	arrival of Martial Daru, Intendant des Biens de la Couronne.
25 March:	Birth of the King of Rome.
May:	Valadier reports on repairs to the Pantheon.
1 June:	the Crown begins clearing the Colosseum galleries and arena; the Accademia di S. Luca carries out repairs.
6 June:	the Crown resumes work at the Domus Aurea (until late 1813).
June:	formation of the endowment of the Accademia di S. Luca.
June (end)–September (end):	Tournon absent from Rome for his wedding.
27 July:	Napoleon's decree assigns 1 million frs for works in Rome: excavations, Tiber navigation, bridges, squares around the

	Pantheon, the Forum of Trajan, abattoirs, public gardens. Establishment of the Commission des Embellisements: Tournon, Braschi, Daru.
26 August:	the Municipality asks the Minister of Finances for the Mausoleum of Augustus.
17 September:	first meeting of the new Commission.
28 September:	the Commission's work begins: the Arch of Janus and the 'Temple of Fortune', in the Forum Boarium.
30 September:	the Basilica of Maxentius (the major site during the next year).
30 September–3, 13–15 October:	visit to Rome by Henri Beyle (Stendhal).
c. October:	visit to Rome by Alphonse Lamartine.
November (late):	demolition begins in the Forum of Trajan of the convents and houses (completed late 1813).

1812

21 January:	the Commission plans demolitions around the Pantheon.
January:	clearing completed of the portico of the Temple of Antoninus and Faustina.
21–22 March:	severe earthquake in Rome, damaging many monuments.
23 March:	the Crown begins excavations in the Forum of Trajan (to August/September).
31 March:	Camporese announces the successful restoration of the Temple of Vespasian.
March (?):	demolitions begin on the Palatine (S. Bonaventura).
April:	scandal over workers' absences in the Forum: many company chiefs dismissed; Giulio Camporese, the Inspector of Works, resigns.
April–August:	clearing of the slope of the Capitol.
4 May:	exile and confiscation of property for all officials who refuse the oath of allegiance to the regime.
	May–December: the Russian campaign.
20 July:	Valadier's general scheme for the Embellisements (Palatine, Forum, Forum Boarium).
August:	clearing begins of the Tabularium.
28 September:	Camporese and Valadier recommend clearing the Forum to its ancient level.
17 December:	Pietro Bianchi's and Lorenzo Re's paper on the Colosseum is read to the Accademia di Archeologia.
	26 December: the 29th Bulletin announces disaster in Russia.

1813

25 January:	Concordat of Fontainebleau: the Pope to reside at Avignon, amnesty to the Papal States.

25 January,
18 February: Carlo Fea's *Osservazioni sull'arena e sul podio dell'Anfiteatro Flavio*.
5 February: Louis Berthault arrives in Rome.
14 February: Guy Gisors arrives.
23 February: Gisors' report on the Forum of Trajan and piazza of the Pantheon plans.
23 March: discovery of the inscription on the Column of Phocas.
25 March: Berthault's report on the Jardin du Capitole, abandoning the attempt to clear the whole Forum to the ancient level.
April–December: visit of Mme Récamier.
April–September: the Crown excavates in the Forum of Trajan.
10 May: Gisors leaves Rome.
c. 20 May: Berthault leaves Rome.
                                        June: France abandons most of Spain.
1 July: Juan Masdeu begins publishing his letters against Fea.
                                        9 September: alliance of Russia, Prussia and Austria.
                                        5/6 October: the English raid and burn Anzio.
                                        18 October: defeat of Napoleon at Leipzig: Italy, Germany and Netherlands lost.

1814

                                        January: the allies invade France.
19 January: Neapolitan troops seize Rome. Miollis retreats to Castel Sant'Angelo.
20 January: Tournon leaves Rome for France with his family.
10 March: Miollis capitulates with full honours.
                                        31 March: allies enter Paris.
                                        11 April: Napoleon abdicates.
24 May: return of Pius VII to Rome.

Appendix 2. Biographies

GIUSEPPE CAMPORESE (1763–1822)

Student of his father, Pietro Camporese the Elder, and Pasquale Belli.

Worked with his elder brother Giulio (1754–1840) on S. Andrea at Subiaco, S. Tommaso at Genzano, the chapel in S. Stefano Rotondo on the Caelian.

Collaborated with Michele Simonetti on the Museo Pio Clementino, 1771–.

Pontifical Architect, 1786, worked on the Sala della Biga.

Under the French Republic (1798–9), one of the aediles, decorated the Altare della Patria, planned naval museum, baths, a monument to peace, etc. (plans in S. Luca).

Cleared the Arch of Severus, with Tommaso Zappati, 1802–3.

Devised the buttress for the Colosseum, with Giuseppe Palazzi and Raffaele Stern, 1805.

Restored the tempietto of Bramante, 1806.

During the French occupation (1809–14):

> Architect Director for the Commission des Monuments, 1810, with Valadier.
>
> With Valadier, one of the two main architects for the Commission des Embellisements, 1811.
>
> Architect for Martial Daru in the excavations of the Crown, 1811–.
>
> Opened the Ghetto, 1810.
>
> Restored the temple of Vespasian, 1811–12.
>
> Remodelled the main room of the Palazzo del Senatore, 1811.
>
> Modified the Palazzo della Cancelleria into the Palazzo della Giustizia, 1812.

F. Gasparoni, *Biografia di Giuseppe Camporese*.

M. Fischer, *DBI*, Vol. 17, pp. 587–9.

ANTONIO CANOVA (1757–1822)

Born near Treviso.

Studied in Venice, Rome.

Commissioned to sculpt the monuments to Clement XIV in SS. Apostoli, 1783; to Clement XIII in St Peter's, 1787.

Visited Vienna, Prague, Dresden, Berlin, Munich, 1798; returned to Rome 1799, where he lived henceforth, save short absences.

Member of the Accademia di S. Luca, 1800.

In Paris, where he sculpted a portrait of Napoleon, September–November 1802.

Inspector-General of Fine Arts at Rome, 1802, and Superintendant of the Vatican and Capitoline Museums.

Finished his portrait of Pauline Bonaparte, 1808.

Director of Museums in Rome, 1811.

Principe of the Accademia di S. Luca, September 1810–February 1814.

President of the Accademia di Archeologia, 1812.

Principe perpetuo onorario of the Accademia di S. Luca, 1814.

Superintended in 1815 the recovery of Italian art works ceded to France in 1797.

Visited London to see the Elgin marbles.

Named by Pius VII Marchese d'Ischia, 1816 (he gave the income to the Academies and artists).

Pavan, *DBI*, Vol. 18, pp. 197–219, with a wealth of bibliography.

MARTIAL DARU (1774–1827)

Under-Inspector of Reviews, 1800; took part in the Italian campaign.

Inspector of Cavalry and Artillery, 1805.

Intendant at Brunswick, 1806.

Inspector of Reviews, 1808; took part in the Spanish campaign.

Intendant at Vienna, 1809.

Intendant des Biens de la Couronne at Rome, 1811–14.

Baron of the Empire, 1813.

Intendant Militaire, 1820, retired 1822.

Cousin of Stendhal; translator of Sheridan; author of *Jeunes gens* (comedy), *Théorie de l'art dramatique, Histoire de Rome pendant l'occupation française* (all unpublished).

Of his character, his cousin Stendhal said that he 'n'avait ni tête ni ésprit, mais un bon cœur, il lui était impossible de faire du mal à quelqu'un' (*Œuvres*, Vol. 35, p. 184); he further claimed that he died from overdoses of aphrodisiacs (Vol. 36, p. 27)!

Madelin (*La Rome de Napoléon*, pp. 409ff.) notes that he was disliked by Tournon as 'violent, presumptuous and puffed up by the credit and merit of his brother'.

Hamon, *DBF*, Vol. 10, p. 228.

CARLO FEA (1753–1836)

Born in Liguria, studied in Nice and Rome, taking a degree in civil and canon law.

An enemy of the French Republic (1798–9): three times imprisoned and deported, then arrested as a Jacobin.

Commissario delle Antichità, 1801–36.

Prefect of the Biblioteca Chigiana, 1801.

Excavated around the Pantheon with Valadier, 1804.

Under the French (1809–14), superintendent of works for the Commission des Monuments: associated with Valadier in clearing the Domus Aurea and the Temple of Vesta in the Forum Boarium.

Excavated the Temple of Castor and Pollux, 1816, for the Duc de Blacas.

Excavated the Temple of Concord, 1817, for the Conde do Funchal.

Member of many institutions: Accademia Romana di Archeologia, Accademia dei Lincei.

Author of many works, and promised many more never written.

Involved in endless feuds with other antiquarians.

Buried in S. Lorenzo in Lucina.

P. Visconti, *Biografia dell'abate D. Carlo Fea*, Rome, 1836 (originally published in *Album*).

d'Angelis d'Ossat, 'Carlo Fea e lo studio dei monumenti romani'.

E. Re, 'Brumaio dell'abate Fea', *Nuova Antologia*, 16 Sept. 1928, 216–31.

Notizie della vita e delle opere degli scrittori romani 1, 1880, 115–24 (bibliography).

R. Ridley, 'Carlo Fea', *DBI*.

JOSEPH-MARIE DE GÉRANDO (1772–1842)

Participated in the rebellion of Lyons, 1793: condemned to death, but escaped to Switzerland, returning to France under the amnesty of 1796.

Accompanied his friend Jordan into exile in Germany on the *coup d'état*, 1797.

Appointed consultant on arts and commerce in Ministry of the Interior by Lucien Bonaparte.

Taught moral philosophy at the Lycée de Paris.

Member of the Académie des Inscriptions et Belles-Lettres, 1804.

Secretary-General to the Minister of the Interior, 1804: accompanied Napoleon to Milan for the coronation.

Member of the Consulta for Tuscany, 1808.

Maître des Requêtes to the Conseil d'Etat, 1810.

Member of the Consulta Straordinaria for the organisation of the Papal States, 1809: especially concerned with arts and antiquities; re-established the Accademia di Archeologia.

Baron, 1811.

Intendant for Upper Catalonia, 1812.

Member of the Commission to liquidate the Public Debt, 1815.

Professor in the Faculty of Law in Paris, 1819.

One of the founders of the Ecole des Chartes, 1821.

Member of the Académie des Sciences Morales et Politiques, 1832.

Pair de France, 1837.

Author of *Des signes et de l'art de penser*, 1800; *De la génération des connaissances humaines*, 1802; *Histoire comparée des systèmes de philosophie*, 1804; *De l'éducation des sourds-muets de naissance*, 1827; *Du perfectionnement moral*, 1824; *Institutes de droit administratif français*, 1829–36.

J. B. Bayle-Mouillard, *Eloge de J.-M. Baron de Gérando*, Paris, 1846.

G. Berlia, *Gérando, sa vie, son œuvre*.

Trenard, *DBF*, Vol. 15, pp. 1197–9.

SEXTIUS-ALEXANDRE-FRANÇOIS MIOLLIS (GENERAL) (1759–1828)

Wounded at the siege of Yorktown, 1781.

A supporter of the Revolution, elected lieutenant-colonel, defeated the Piedmontese at Villefranche, 1792.

Brigadier-General, 1794, defeated a vastly superior Austrian force at Mantua where he was appointed governor, 1797: laid out the Piazza di Vergilio.

General, 1799; governor of Genoa, 1800.

Voted against Napoleon's consulate for life, 1802, retired.

Governor of Mantua again, 1805: transferred the ashes of Ariosto to the University of Ferrara; restored the amphitheatre at Verona.

Commander of all French troops in Italy, 1805.

Governor of Livorno, 1807.

Count, 1808.

Occupied Rome, 1808; head of provisional government, 1809–10; lieutenant governor 1811–14.

Commander of the division at Marseilles, tried to stop Napoleon's landing, 1815.

Governor of Metz during the Hundred Days.

Retired, September 1815.

He was 'upright, courteous, moderate and loyal'. His wound at Yorktown scarred his face and left a speech impediment, but he spoke Italian well. Extremely brave (he defeated 26,000 Austrians with 3,000 men), he was not at Austerlitz or Jena, and was never made a Marshal. He was devoted to Virgil and Ariosto. In Rome he was very courteous to priests (his brother was a bishop), on good terms with artists and academies, devoted to women of the nobility. He was considered mean, but paid for any art he liked. His main fault was his refusal to act unless instructed from Paris (Madelin, *La Rome de Napoléon*, pp. 209ff.).

A high tribute was paid by Cardinal Consalvi to Miollis' virtues: 'désintéressement, la modestie, l'énergie, la modération, l'absence la plus complète de toute vanité et de tout orgueil, et une justice incorruptible' (*Mémoires*, Vol. 2, p. 155).

Six, *Dictionnaire biographique des généraux et amiraux de la Révolution et de l'Empire*, Vol. 2, p. 203.

H. Aureas, *Un général de Napoléon, Miollis*.

JEAN PIERRE BACHASSON, comte de MONTALIVET (1766–1823)

Member of an ancient and noble family.

Entered the Nassau Hussars at the age of 13.

Lieutenant in La Rochefoucauld's Dragoons.

Studied law, entered Grenoble parliament, Conseiller 1785.

Espoused the principles of the Revolution, but a constitutionalist.

Volunteered in the army, served in Italy.

Mayor of Valence, 1795.

Prefect of La Manche, 1801.

Prefect of Seine-et-Oise, 1804.

Director-General of Ponts et Chaussées, 1806.

Minister of the Interior, 1809–14 during the French occupation of Rome; carried
out an enormous programme of public works in Paris.

Intendant-Général de la Couronne, 1815, during the Hundred Days.

Pair de France, 1815.

Famous for his integrity, competence and judgement; one of the most devoted sup-
porters of Napoleon.

M. Daru, 'Eloge du comte de Montalivet', *Le Moniteur*, 1823.

NBG, Vol. 36, pp. 94–7.

CAMILLE DE TOURNON (1778–1833)

Intendant at Beirut, November 1806 (he spoke German): captured by the Austrians,
June 1809 (freed in August).

Prefect of Rome, September 1809–January 1814. He did more than any other French
official to win over the Italians.

He had close relations with the Minister of the Interior, Montalivet.

Many stories are told of his humanity: notably the help to the bishops in signing
the oath of loyalty, which almost cost him his post (Moulard, *Le comte de
Tournon*, Vol. 2, pp. 62ff.). He was also opposed to the suppression of monasteries and convents, which he rightly declared to be politically stupid (he managed
to preserve the four largest convents and two monasteries for sick men (*Lettres
inédites*, Vol. 1, pp. 38, 57).

He was an opponent of the death penalty for political crimes: although his arguments
may have been practical, the results were humane (ibid., Vol. 1, p. 198).

From February 1810, he occupied the Quirinal, where he held receptions each Monday and dinners each Wednesday. His work-load was punishing, and his relaxa-
tion little (ibid., Vol. 1, p. 48). At the end of 1811, he moved to the Palazzo
Mattei, and finally in autumn 1813 to Montecitorio.

He was not on speaking terms with Janet of the Consulta; was not fond of Daru,
Intendant de la Couronne; but friendly with Olivetti, Director of Police, another
moderate.

He was famous for his love of the Roman campagna and the antiquities of Rome
(Camillo Capitolino).

On 29 August 1811, he married Adèle de Pancement. It is amusing to read Tournon's
account of the negotiations. Friends were sent to France on his behalf to interview
the girl and report back. Tournon declared them the worst negotiators ever:
one was a 'metaphysician', the other 'celtique'. They did not even say if she
was thin or fat, blond or brunette, and had omitted the essential detail: her
teeth (ibid., Vol. 1, pp. 41, 134). The marriage turned out to be a perfect match!

Appointed Prefect of Finistère and Hérault during the Hundred Days, he declined.

Prefect of Gironde, July 1815.

Maître des Requêtes Extraordinaires, 1818.

Prefect of the Rhône, January 1822–3.

Pair de France, Conseiller d'Etat, 1823.

President of the Conseil des Bâtiments Civils.

C. de Tournon, *Etudes statistiques sur Rome*.
    Lettres inédites, ed. J. Moulard.

J. Moulard, *Le comte Camille de Tournon.*
L. Madelin, *La Rome de Napoléon.*

GIUSEPPE VALADIER (1762–1839)

His grandfather migrated from France to Italy in 1714. His father, Luigi (d. 1785)
    was a famous founder in the Via del Babuino, and trained his son.
Architetto dei Sacri Palazzi, 1781.
His earliest works include:

> restoration of the cupola of the cathedral at Rimini, 1786
> the orphanage at Gubbio
> the façade of the Palazzo Valloni at Rimini, 1788
> repair to the church at Urbino, 1789
> rebuilding of the cathedral at Spoleto, 1792
> design of the Palazzo Ugolini at Macerata, 1793
> restoration of the cathedral at Orvieto, 1798.

Married Laura Campana (d. 1811), 1790: five children.
Architetto Camerale, 1786.
Architetto Coadiutore at Vatican, 1790.
Member of the Accademia di S. Luca, 1798.
After the treaty of Tolentino, 1797, commissioned to pack the art treasures to be
    transported to Paris.
Under Pius VII responsible for:

> the Zagnoni theatre at Bologna, 1800
> restoration of the Ponte Milvio, 1805
> façade of S. Pantaleo, 1806.

During the French occupation, Architetto Direttore for the Commission des Monu-
    ments, 1810, and for the Commission des Embellisements, 1811. Most connected
    with:

> le Jardin du Grand César, Forum of Trajan.

On the return of Pius, reinstated:

> completed Pincian Hill project
> restored Teatro Valle, 1821 (one of the arches later fell, but he was exonerated)
> designed awnings for Anfiteatro Correa, 1822 (they fell in 1826, he was fined
>   1,000 scudi, but Pius cancelled the fine)
> appointed director of the rebuilding of S. Paolo, 1823, but resigned
> restored S. Lorenzo in Damaso
> restored the 'sotterranei' in S. Francesco at Assisi
> baptistry in the chapel of Paul V in S. Maria Maggiore
> restored tempietto of Bramante
> restored the portico of the Palazzo Quirinale
> façade of S. Rocco, 1834
> Palazzo Lucernari on Via del Babuino.

Remarried: Margherita Spagna, 1817.

Rebuilt the Arch of Titus after the death of Stern, 1820–4.

Architetto del Camerlengato, 1824.

Buttressed the Colosseum on the Forum side, 1822–6.

Valadier died of dropsy, and is buried in S. Luigi dei Francesi.

He is said to have borne such a striking resemblance to Louis XVI that female relatives of the executed king wept when they saw him. He is even said to have posed for historical portraits of Louis.

His eldest son, Luigi (1791–?) married Camporese's daughter, Maria.

I. Ciampi, *Vita di Giuseppe Valadier*.

P. Marconi, *Giuseppe Valadier*.

Elisa Debenedetti, *Valadier, segno e architettura*.

Appendix 3. The accounts of the Commission des Embellisements and of the Crown

NOTE ON MONEY

1. Papal currency: 100 bajocchi = 1 scudo
2. French currency: 100 centimes = 1 franc
3. Conversion: 1 scudo = 5.35 frs

ACCOUNTS OF THE COMMISSION DES EMBELLISEMENTS

1811: Monthly totals

(Comm. Emb. register 5)

	October	November	December
Basilica of Maxentius	6,943 frs[1]	12,839	14,842
	2,319		733
Forum Boarium	1,879	1,459	
	910		
Arch of Janus	2,299	2,959	2,122
	790		
Forum Romanum[2]	2,722	2,942	1,307[3]
			844
Forum of Trajan			2,203[4]

1812
Extracts from the daily work reports for the first working day of the month (Comm. Emb. registers 6–7)[5]

	Companies	Men	Women	Children	Cubic m	Cost
2 *January*						
Basilica of Maxentius	7	519[6]	75	70	283	887 frs
S. Francesca (Forum)		57	14	6		97
Convent of S. Spirito						
(Forum of Trajan)		152	24	10		249
On 10 January, work						
began at the Colosseum	1	75	10	10	72	120[7]

	Companies	Men	Women	Children	Cubic m	Cost
1 *February*						
Colosseum	2	139	25	10	140	233
Basilica of Maxentius	6	433	65	57	221	727
S. Francesca	1	57	14	6		100
S. Spirito	1	75	10	10		124

(Weekly reports also show that 4,418 cu m of earth, at a cost of 6,321 frs, were removed in levelling the Forum.)

	Companies	Men	Women	Children	Cubic m	Cost
2 *March*						
Colosseum	2.5	191	32	15	109	189
Basilica of Maxentius	4	298	43	39	106	291
S. Francesca	2	148	26	16		249
S. Spirito	1	75	10	10		124

(Further levelling in the Forum removed another 3,414 cu m and cost 4,258 frs.) On 27 March, work started demolishing S. Eufemia:

	Companies	Men	Women	Children	Cubic m	Cost
	0.5	30	4	4		49

	Companies	Men	Women	Children	Cubic m	Cost
1 *April*						
Colosseum	2	149	21	20	150	149
Basilica of Maxentius	4	299	42	39	192	500
Jardin du Capitole	1	75	14	6		125
S. Spirito	1	75	10	10		124

(Weekly statements also show work at S. Eufemia from 13 April, levelling in the Forum, 1–4 April, and enormous work removing earth from the Clivus Capitolinus: at least 1,454 cu m near the Temple of Vespasian.)

	Companies	Men	Women	Children	Cubic m	Cost
1 *May*						
Colosseum	1	61	10	10	68	106
Basilica of Maxentius	3	198	30	30	67	337
S. Eufemia	1	60	8	8		100
S. Spirito	1	69	10	10		104

(Work ceased at the Colosseum allowing one company to transfer to the Basilica. Weekly records show 4,952 cu m of earth removed from the Clivus Capitolinus, costing 5,776 frs.)

	Companies	Men	Women	Children	Cubic m	Cost
1 *June*						
Basilica of Maxentius	4	85[8]	31	28	79	182
S. Spirito	1	30	4	2		50

(Again, weekly records show removal of earth near the Temple of Vespasian: 6,092 cu m, costing 6,245 frs, and the transport of debris from the Forum of Trajan from 22 June: 489 cu m at a cost of 584 frs.)

	Companies	Men	Women	Children	Cubic m	Cost
1 *July*						
Basilica of Maxentius	4	280	40	40	217	483
S. Spirito	1	91	12	10		150

(Weekly totals show the other two main tasks in July were removal of earth around the Temple of Vespasian: 6,146 cu m, costing 6,313 frs; and transport of debris from S. Spirito: 1,996 cu m, costing 2,385 frs.)

	Companies	Men	Women	Children	Cubic m	Cost
1 *August*						
Basilica of Maxentius	3	193	26	29	288	326
S. Spirito	1	87	11	10		148

(The uncovering of the Tabularium began in the week 17–22 August. Removal of earth from Temple of Vespasian: 2,877 cu m, costing 2,948 frs. Transport of debris from the Forum of Trajan: 1,857 cu m, costing 2,220 frs.)

	Companies	Men	Women	Children	Cubic m	Cost
1 *September*						
Basilica of Maxentius	3	160	29	28	112	281
S. Spirito	1	74	10	10		126

(Weekly totals show uncovering the Tabularium and clearing inside rooms: 2,086 cu m, costing 2,452 frs. Transport of debris from Forum of Trajan: 1,582 cu m, costing 1,827 frs. Breaking up fallen masonry in the Basilica of Maxentius began on the 12th.)

	Companies	Men	Women	Children	Cubic m	Cost
1 *October*						
Basilica of Maxentius	4	203	40	40	145	383
Clearing debris in same	1	58	9	10		100
Forum of Trajan	1	74	10	10		124

(Clearing of the Tabularium: 1,672 cu m, costing 1,677 frs. Transport of debris from the Forum of Trajan: 1,631 cu m, costing 1,948 frs.)

	Companies	Men	Women	Children	Cubic m	Cost
2 *November*						
Basilica of Maxentius	4	219	40	38	142	394
Clearing debris in same	1	59	10	10		103
Demolition in Forum of Trajan	1	74	10	10		124

(Clearing Tabularium: 1,414 cu m, costing 1,588 frs. Transport of debris from Forum of Trajan: 1,465 cu m, costing 1,750 frs.)

	Companies	Men	Women	Children	Cubic m	Cost
1 *December*						
Basilica of Maxentius	3	178	30	29	94	314
Clearing debris in same	1	74	10	10		124
Garden of S. Francesca	1	60	10	9	31	105
Forum of Trajan	1	74	10	10		124

(Clearing the Tabularium: 1,337 cu m, costing 1,533 frs. Transport of debris from the Forum of Trajan: 1,297 cu m, costing 1,551 frs. On 3 December, work resumed on the Colosseum:

Companies	Men	Women	Children	Cubic m	Cost
3	277	30	29	204	349

reducing the Basilica of Maxentius companies to one for clearing and one for breaking.)

Total monthly expenses 1812
(Comm. Emb. register 5)

	Basilica[9]	Forum Romanum[10]	Forum of Trajan[11]	Jardin du Capitole[12]	Colosseum
Jan.	14,672 frs	6,419	6,010		2,342
	2,383	2,847			
Feb.	11,393	6,772			
		5,340	5,149	3,146	5,993
Mar.	10,054	4,255			
		4,566	5,978	1,926	4,966
Apr.	9,226		7,629	1,712	3,869
May	8,895	1,038	8,133	2,394	211
June	7,413	725	5,533	838	
July	11,621	822	6,460		
August	7,858	664	6,008		
Sept.	7,479		5,348		
	1,654	658	908		
Oct.	9,871		5,840		
	2,663	751			
Nov.	8,438	794	4,843		
	2,172		1,693		
Dec.	5,626	1,841	4,863		
	1,618		2,518		

Grand total expenses 28 September 1811 to 31 December 1812
(Comm. Emb. register 7)

	Foremen	Corporals	Men	Women	Boys	Cu m	Cost
Arch of Janus	72	438	4,828	685	673	5,143	8,131
Basilica of Maxentius							
i) clearing	1,444	8,040	93,075	14,614	13,897	55,701	153,607
ii) breaking, transport	80	427	4,738	802	787		8,108
Forum Boarium	38	322	2,566	373	340	1,186	4,250
Colosseum	196	1,011	14,835	2,233	1,478	12,727	22,480

	Fore-men	Cor-porals	Men	Women	Boys	Cu m	Cost
Forum road	44	180	2,395	403	333	1,661	3,883
Ground levelling in Forum						15,109	18,887
Temple of Vespasian						23,078	25,203
Tabularium						6,378	7,317
Demolition of 2 houses in Forum	29	144	1,589	140	96	1,998	2,636
Temple of Antoninus and Faustina	44	223	3,168	452	380		5,263
Demolition of convent of S. Francesca	122	612	8,893	1,749	991		13,895
Jardin du Capitole	52	272	3,911	668	489	3,329	6,171
Masons in Forum and on Palatine	181	196	2,320		215		3,988
sculptors			75				191
materials							2,221
plantations							702
Demolitions in Forum of Trajan	584	2,234	30,103	4,298	3,294		48,803
transport						19,882	24,770
new wall							5,119
sculptors			202				442

Note: The figures for the various ranks of workers are total working days.

1813

Extracts from the daily work reports for the first working day of the month (Comm. Emb. register 8)

	Companies	Men	Women	Children	Cost
2 January					
Colosseum	2	169	29	19	271 frs
Jardin du Capitole	1	62	10	9	108
Basilica of Maxentius	1	78	10	10	129
S. Francesca Romana (demolition)	1	89	10	8	144
Forum of Trajan (demolition)	1	94	10	10	152

(On 28 January, 19 men were also employed at the Temple of the Dioscuroi.)

	Companies	Men	Women	Children	Cost
1 February					
Colosseum	2	188	20	20	309
Jardin du Capitole	1	94	10	10	153
Basilica of Maxentius	1	56	10	10	99
Temple of the Dioscuroi		19			27

	Companies	Men	Women	Children	Cost
Forum of Trajan (demolition)	1	94	10	10	152
S. Francesca Romana (demolition)	1	77	7	10	127
Forum Romanum (demolition)		19			27

1 *March*

	Companies	Men	Women	Children	Cost
Colosseum	3	282	30	30	465
S. Francesca Romana (demolition)	2	206	20	21	331
Forum of Trajan (demolition)	1	94	10	10	152

(In the week beginning 22 March, also 10 men at the Temple of Saturn, and 10 at the Temple of Vespasian.)

1 *April*

	Companies	Men	Women	Children	Cost
Colosseum	4	368	40	40	609
S. Francesca Romana (demolition)	2	202	20	21	325
Forum of Trajan (demolition)	1	90	10	10	147

May (for the rest of the year there are only weekly statements; a daily average has been calculated from the first week)

	Companies	Men	Women	Children	Cost
Colosseum	4	352	40	40	575
Forum of Trajan (demolition)	1	86	10	10	142
(transport)					94
Jardin du Capitole (daily average 17–22 May)	3	272	22	29	438

June

	Companies	Men	Women	Children	Cost
Jardin du Capitole	5	385	53	50	506
Colosseum	2	150	20	20	256
Forum of Trajan	1	78	10	10	148

(14–19 June: cleaning of drains in the Forum of Trajan; 20–30 June: work resumes in the Basilica of Maxentius.)

July

	Companies	Men	Women	Children	Cost
Jardin du Capitole	4	209	39	36	373
Colosseum	2	123	22	22	213
Basilica of Maxentius	1	55	10	9	95
Forum of Trajan	1	67	10	10	120

(19–24 July: demolitions near the Arch of Severus.)

	Companies	Men	Women	Children	Cost
August					
Jardin du Capitole	4	221	38	21	385
Colosseum	2	133	20	19	225
Forum of Trajan	1	75	10	10	84
Forum Romanum	1	73	10	10	131
Temple of the Dioscuroi (23–31 Aug.)		10	1		16
September					
Jardin du Capitole	5	318	48	46	551
Colosseum	2	123	19	19	220
Forum of Trajan	1	60	10	10	108
October					
Jardin du Capitole	5	323	46	46	563
Colosseum	2	130	20	20	230
Forum of Trajan	1	62	10	10	112
November					
Colosseum	3	192	29	29	271
Jardin du Capitole	3	202	28	28	288
Forum of Trajan	1	50	9	8	75
Forum Romanum		8	1	1	16
Arch of Constantine (drains)		11			14
December					
Colosseum	4	284	38	40	448
Forum Romanum	2	148	28	22	248
Forum of Trajan	1	54	7	7	74
(drains)		13			23

General statements

Totals from September 1811 to 31 January 1814 (attached to a copy of Napoleon's decree of July 1811)

Jardin du Capitole	570,687 frs
Jardin du Grand César	306,280
Forum of Trajan	182,883
Markets	15,147
Tiber navigation	100,000
Administration	107,810

Grand total of expenditure on the Embellisements until 2 February, 1814: 1,279,022 frs.

ACCOUNTS OF THE CROWN

The Colosseum

Extracts are given from the first working period of each month (weeks where available, otherwise fortnights), to show the extent and rhythm of the excavations.

	Man-working days	Earth cleared	Cost
1811 (O 2 1080)			
1–13 July	876	1,127 cu m	1,142 frs
(transport to S. Maria Maggiore)		659	785
1–17 August	823	1,182	1,094
		506	602
2–7 September			
(clearing ambulacra)			
(transport to via Labicana)		305	362
1–5 October			
(clearing F, K, and internal	629	574	809
galleries)		389	463
1812 (O 2 1078)			
2–4 January	312	208	365
1–8 February	834	347	858
March	715	349	864
1–4 April	471	216	541
1–2 May	195	95	240
1–6 June	587	286	722
1–4 July	322	179	400
		179 (32 carts)	173
10–16 August	333	222	419
		222 (60 carts)	234
7–12 October	600	705	1,001
		731 (122 carts)	870
2–9 November	407	371	461
		462 (70 carts)	349
1813 (O 2 1079)			
12–17 April	715	544	848
		544 (104 carts)	544
4–8 May	528	454	618
		454 (90 carts)	454
1–5 June	599	454	687
		454 (90 carts)	454
1–10 July	626	451	789
		451 (88 carts)	464

	Man-working days	Earth cleared	Cost
2–7 August (main galleries, drain)	488	376	612
		376 (74 carts)	376
1–4 September (arena and drains)	211	115	281
		115 (23 carts)	115
1–9 October (arena)	611	330	769
		360 (64 carts)	330
2–6 November	300	185	254
		185 (36 carts)	185

The Domus Aurea

Extracts are given from the first working period of each month (weeks where available, otherwise fortnights), to show the extent and rhythm of the excavations.

	Man-working days	Earth removed	Cost
1811 (O 2 1080)			
1–13 July	727	1,300 cu m	1,006 frs
		709	829
1–17 August	522	788	683
		1,844	2,261
2–7 September		531 (110 carts)	640
1–5 October		219 (43 carts)	256
1812 (O 2 1078–1079)			
2–4 January	180	180	233
(galleries 6–8)		464	467
1–8 February	411	508	440
(galleries 8, 25, 37)		956 (162 carts)	1,070
March (first week)	346	507	424
(galleries 25, 70, 76)		722 (109 carts)	807
1–4 April	223	256	268
(galleries 26, 67, 76)		251 (45 carts)	281
1–2 May	114	133	139
(rooms 27, 28, 47, 64)		173 (31 carts)	194
1–6 June	341	350	417
(gallery 2, room 26)		457 (117 carts)	512
1–4 July	213	217	262
(room 26)		347 (112 carts)	389
10–16 August	214	313	267
(the rooms around 26)		313 (99 carts)	?
7–12 October		346 (62 carts)	404
(garden in front of the baths)			

	Man-working days	Earth cleared	Cost
2–9 November	555	1,204	602
(galleries 3–5, rooms 27, 64)		819 (123 carts)	936
1813 (O 2 1079)			
12–17 April	192	201	231
(room 26)		201 (42 carts)	225
4–8 May	159	232	199
(room 26)		232 (50 carts)	260
1–5 June	153	167	193
(room 26)		167 (35 carts)	187
1–10 July	263	324	333
(room 26)		324 (69 carts)	363
2–7 August	126	140	158
(rooms around 25)		140 (31 carts)	157
1–4 September	180	180	227
(gallery 97)		180 (38 carts)	202
1–9 October	337	291	478
(gallery 97)		291 (64 carts)	326
2–6 November	187	98	161
		98 (21 carts)	110

The Forum of Trajan

Extracts are given from the first working period of each month (a week).

	Man-working days	Earth cleared	Cost
1812 (O 2 1074)			
1–4 April	80	105 cu m	96 frs
		104 (16 carts)	156
1–2 May	80	110	99
		165 (42 carts)	139
1–6 June	240	302	297
		302 (108 carts)	436
1–4 July	160	208	198
		208 (75 carts)	281
10–16 August	140	167	177
		167 (55 carts)	227
1813 (O 2 1079)			
12–17 April	282	295	?
		295 (72 carts)	398
4–8 May	160	213	201
		213 (55 carts)	287
1–5 June	80	37	105
		37 (10 carts)	50

	Man-working days	Earth cleared	Cost
1–10 July	277	165	348
2–7 August	95	84	125
1–4 September	150	131	164

Notes on the tables of expenses and accounts

1. The upper figure is the cost of clearing the earth, the lower its carting away.
2. Where no more precise monument is mentioned.
3. The upper figure is the removal of earth, the lower is for the demolition of the convent of S. Francesca.
4. Demolition of the convent of S. Spirito.
5. The first working day of each month serves as a sample of ateliers, distribution of workers, results and costs.
6. Excluding foremen and corporals: five for each company.
7. These were winter months. What happened when the weather made work impossible? 31 January: Giulio Camporese wrote across the blank columns: 'A motivo del tempo piovoso è stata accordata la zuppa soltanto a tutti i lavoranti.'
8. The month of the grasshopper plague!
9. The upper figure is the cost of clearing of earth; the lower its carting away.
10. Where no more precise monument is mentioned. The upper figure is clearing of earth; the lower is demolition of the convent of S. Francesca.
11. Demolition of the convent of S. Spirito; where two figures are given, the lower is the new wall around the elliptical clearing.
12. Construction of a road and garden in the Forum.

Notes

PROLOGUE

1 See chapter 1, pp. 9ff.
2 See below, p. 89.
3 Stendhal, *Oeuvres*, vol. 56, p. 328.
4 Boyer, 'Stendhal, Martial Daru et les fouilles à Rome en 1811', pp. 145–56.
5 *Journal*, 17 March 1811 (*Oeuvres*, vol. 74, p. 75).
6 *Mémoires inédits de Lamartine*, 1790–1815, p. 133. He was staying in the Via Condotti: where was the 'temple contigu'?
7 Lenormant, *Mme Récamier, les amis de sa jeunesse et sa correspondance*, pp. 141ff.; Récamier, *Souvenirs et correspondance*, pp. 218ff., 143ff.
8 Mme de Staël, *Correspondance générale*, ed. Jasinski, vol. 5, 1985.
9 *Corinne*, book 4, chapters 2ff.
10 There is, as far as I know, nothing about the classical remains, but we must await the publication of the full edition of her letters.
11 *Mémoires d'outre tombe*, book 31, chapter 12.
12 Forsyth, *Remarks on antiquities, arts and letters, being an excursion to Italy in the years 1802 and 1803*.
13 Eustace, *Classical tour*, vol. 4, p. 424.
14 See below, pp. 217ff.
15 Mayne, *The journal of John Mayne during a tour on the Continent upon its reopening after the fall of Napoleon, 1814*, edited by his grandson, pp. 168, 169, 177, 180, 184, 192–3, 213, 217, 241.
16 Douglas, *The diaries of Sylvester Douglas*, ed. F. Bickley, vol. 2, pp. 144ff. The editor could easily have identified Fea from the note about his edition of Winckelmann. Venuti was Commissario *before* Winckelmann.
17 Byron, *Letters and journals*, ed. L. Marchand, vol. 5, p. 221 (letter to John Murray). The editor makes no attempt to identify the guidebook. The first Murray's guide to central Italy was published in 1843. Mayne and his companions (see above) went to Mr Vasi's and purchased his, 'which is considered the best of its kind' (Mayne, *Journal*, p. 164). An English version was published in 1818: *A new picture of Rome and its environs*.
18 Eaton, *Rome in the nineteenth century*, vol. 1, p. 132 (Colosseum), p. 284

(Forum), p. 326 (Forum of Trajan), p. 366 (Vesta), vol. 2, p. 71 (Colosseum), p. 97 (Domus Aurea). See under these monuments in chapter 3 for Mrs Eaton's comments.

19 Burton, *Description*, p. 44 (Vesta), p. 185 (Dioscuroi), p. 186 (Antoninus and Faustina), p. 187 (Phocas), p. 189 (Vespasian), pp. 190ff. (Saturn), p. 193 (Basilica of Maxentius), p. 200 (Janus), p. 268 (Domus Aurea), p. 351 (Colosseum).

20 Madelin, *La Rome de Napoléon*, pp. 535–41.

21 Driault, vol. 4, *Le grand empire*, chapter 7.

22 See below, pp. 71ff.

23 Bartoccini, *Roma nell'Ottocento*, pp. 102–4.

24 *Atti della Pontificia Accademia Romana di Archeologia*, vol. 1, 1821 (1823), pp. 127–56. See below, chapter 4.

25 Bunsen, 'Scavi Romani: escavazioni del Foro Romano e delle sue adjacenze', *Bull. Ist. Arch.* 1, 1829, 26–37, especially p. 28, with the only name mentioned being Fea's.

26 Petit-Radel, *Voyage historique*, vol. 2, pp. 287, 346, 371. Petit-Radel (1756–1836) was Canon at Couserans and then (1819) an administrator of the Bibliothèque Mazarine, and was an expert on Pelasgian and Cyclopean art.

27 Nibby, *Del Foro Romano*, for example p. 143 (the Temple of Vespasian), p. 236 (arena of the Colosseum).

28 Lanciani, *Ruins and excavations*, pp. 165, 204, 218, 249, 260, 272, 290, 313–14, 362, 372, 377, 387, 421, 516.

29 Lanciani, *Ancient Rome in the light of recent discoveries*, pp. xx–xxi. Since this and the previous work were both published out of Italy and in English, and within ten years of each other, the dramatically different approach is hard to account for.

30 Hülsen, *Das Forum Romanum*, p. 40.

31 Marucchi, *The Roman Forum and Palatine*, p. 16.

32 E. de Ruggiero, *Il Foro Romano*, pp. 153, 188, 201 (the most generous allusion: the dismantling and reconstruction of the Temple of Vespasian, but without mentioning the architect!), pp. 208, 425, 460, 496.

33 Thedenat, *Le forum romain*, pp. 36ff.

34 Ladolini, 'Scavi nel Foro Romano dal 1800 al 1836', pp. 138–55.

35 *La cura dei monumenti*.

INTRODUCTION

1 Highet, *The classical tradition*, pp. 390ff.

2 Parker, *The cult of antiquity and the French revolutionaries*.

3 Hautecœur, *Histoire de l'architecture classique en France*, vol. 5, p. 150 (henceforth, *Architecture*).

4 Hautecœur, *Rome et la renaissance de l'antiquité à la fin du XVIII siècle*, pp. 134ff. (henceforth, *Antiquité*).

5 Hautecœur, *Architecture*, vol. 5, p. 283.

6 Ibid., pp. 139, 192; *Antiquité*, p. 266.

7 Hautecœur, *Architecture*, vol. 5, p. 197.

8 Ibid., p. 140.

9 Ibid., p. 121.

10 French architects of the late eighteenth century visited Rome to renew their inspiration: Wailly for the Odéon, Gondouin for the School of Medicine, Antoine for the Mint, Rondelet for Ste Géneviève etc.: Hautecœur, *Antiquité*, pp. 112ff.

11 Ibid., p. 158.

12 G. Stenger, *Société française pendant le Consulat*, 6 vols., Paris 1903–8, vol. 4, pp. 288ff.

13 F. Boucher, *20,000 years of fashion*, New York n.d., p. 346.

14 Hautecœur, *Antiquité*, p. v.

15 Ibid., pp. 79ff.

16 Ozzola, *Gian Paolo Panini, pittore*.

17 Burda, *Die Ruinen in den Bildern Hubert Roberts*.

18 Hautecœur, *Antiquité*, pp. 44ff.

19 Vien was Director of the Académie in Rome 1775–81, and leading students were Jean-François Peyron and David.

20 Highet, pp. 261ff.

21 The art works left Rome on 9 April. It should be noted that many of the most prominent French artists signed a protest against this plunder: Hautecœur, *Antiquité*, pp. 261ff.

22 Pius VII went to Paris to crown Napoleon, the first papal crowning of a European monarch since Charles V in 1530.

23 On this remarkable man, lay cardinal and Secretary of State 1800–6, 1815–23, see his *Mémoires* and J. Robinson, *Cardinal Consalvi*.

24 The population, in fact, oscillated wildly: 166,000 in 1797, 147,000 in 1799, 135,000 in 1805, 129,000 in 1810, 118,000 in 1812, 135,000 in 1820, 147,000 in 1830, 154,000 in 1850, 184,000 in 1860 and 226,000 in 1870: Bartoccini, *Roma nell'Ottocento*, p. 264. These fluctuations in the Revolutionary and Napoleonic periods were caused by foreign occupations, exile, food shortages, disease.

   How many were state employees? Madelin estimated 30,000, but Bartoccini thinks this too high. In the 1840s she accepts 5–6%, but including the *families* of these employees, one quarter of the population was dependent on the state. The rates were high because state employment was a means of 'assistance' and of control.

25 During the reign of Clement XIII (1758–69), for example, there were 10,000 murders in Rome (Madelin, *La Rome de Napoléon*, p. 66).

26 Brigandage remained a major curse during the French period. It increased vastly after 1810, swollen by those whose lives had become impossible, not least the conscripts for the army. The administration was powerless; for even after mounting large-scale military operations, any captured and executed were commonly regarded by the Romans as martyrs.

27 He advised the bishops to sign the oath, then add any qualifications they might

have under that. These additions he then cut off when he received the papers, before sending them on. The ruse was later revealed, to Tournon's peril, and to save him, the bishops then signed without qualification. See Moulard, vol. 2, pp. 62ff.

28 Bartoccini, p. 22. Yet the French regime undermined the aristocracy: their centralised administration was retained by the restored papal government, but in the hands of clergy instead of prefects and mayors: ibid., p. 276.

29 Madelin, pp. 484ff., Bartoccini, pp. 225, 239ff.

30 Madelin, pp. 550-1. It must be stressed that the system of public works initiated by the French to assist the poor was retained by the papal government, 'a justified form of indirect assistance behind the shield of public utility'. The work was mostly simple clearances, in the Forum, at Ostia and in the swamps. One of the most important innovations of the French was the programme for cemeteries outside the city walls. The dead had previously been buried in churches, making them charnel-houses, and exposing the population to endemic disease.

31 Bartoccini, pp. 342–3. Not least striking among French 'modernisations': the introduction of secular time, with the day divided into twenty-four hours, whereas previously the divisions had been ecclesiastical, marked by the ringing of church bells: ibid., p. 23.

I THE PROTECTION AND DESTRUCTION OF CLASSICAL ROME BEFORE 1809

1 Fea, 'Dissertazione sulle rovine di Roma', in J. Winckelmann, *Storia dell'arte di disegno*, vol. 3, pp. 267–416 (henceforth *Dissertation*).

2 Ibid., pp. 267ff., Lanciani, *Destruction of ancient Rome* (henceforth *Destruction*), pp. 56ff., 75ff.

It is commonly thought that Fea was the first to contest the medieval and Renaissance view that Rome's destruction was owed to the barbarians (E. de Ruggiero, *Il Foro Romano*, p. 95). This is far from true. The idea of exculpating the barbarians goes back at least to 1587: Pietro Angelino (Bargaeus), *de privatorum publicorumque aedificiorum urbis Romae eversoribus epistola*. Fea in fact began by citing this work. Using, of course, the same sources as Fea, Angelino showed that the Goths and Vandals were interested in booty, not destruction. Natural disasters, civil disturbances and later wars (Henry IV, Robert Guiscard) took their toll, but the destruction of the public buildings of paganism is credited to the Popes, anxious to destroy monuments redolent of paganism, for which Angelino gave them fulsome praise. Muratori, *Dissertazioni sopra le antichità italiane*, diss. 23–4 also discounted the barbarians. Edward Gibbon, *Decline and fall*, vol. 6, 1788, chapter 71, regarded civil war as the main culprit, citing Petrarch, *Carmina latina*, book 2, no. 12.

For Gregorovius, the ninth century was the turning-point: 'Ecclesiastical Rome was restored in the Carolingian time – its second monumental period, if the age of Constantine be regarded as its first. And since the Popes of these times built so largely, they must necessarily be regarded as the chief destroyers of the ancient city', Gregorovius, *Rome in the middle ages*, vol. 3, p. 25 (cf. vol. 1, pp. 158ff., 214ff.).

3 Fea, *Dissertation*, pp. 291ff.
4 *CT* 15.1.11, 19, 25; 16.10.3, 4, 8, 15 (cf. 16), 18, 19. Gregorovius, vol. 1, pp. 62ff.
5 Gregorovius, vol. 1, p. 225.
6 In Cassiodorus, see also 1.21 (general), 2.7 (walls), 3.29 (all ruined buildings to be repaired), 3.30, 31 (public buildings being plundered, including ruined temples), 51 (circus), 5.42 (Colosseum). On Theodoric, see further Gregorovius vol. 1, pp. 290ff., on Totila pp. 439ff., on the Goths in general pp. 470ff.
7 *Liber pontificalis*; Fea, *Dissertation*, p. 284, Lanciani, *Destruction*, pp. 110ff. 'The finest architectural monument of ancient Rome has to thank the Church, which hallowed it for Christian uses, for its preservation from the spoiler. Had this transformation not taken place, the splendid building would undoubtedly have been converted into the fortress of some noble in the Middle Ages, and, after having undergone assaults innumerable, would have survived, like the tomb of Hadrian, only in ruinous and mutilated guise' (Gregorovius, vol. 2, p. 112). As Gregorovius pointed out, the principle goes back to the edict of Theodosius and Valentinian in 435 (*CT* 16.10.25): 'We command that all their fanes, temples and shrines, if even now any remain entire, shall be destroyed by command of the magistrates and shall be purified by the erection of the sign of the venerable Christian religion.' By 'destroyed' was obviously meant only for pagan purposes, otherwise they could not have been purified by the cross.

In the Forum alone, we may list the conversion of classical buildings to churches as follows (see de Ruggiero, pp. 98ff.):

526:	SS. Cosma e Damiano in the Templum Urbis and Temple of Romulus (*Liber pontificalis*, vol. 1, p. 979)
c. 630:	S. Adriano in the Curia (vol. 1, p. 324)
?	S. Martina in the Secretarium Senatus
760s:	SS. Pietro e Paolo in the Basilica of Maxentius (*Vita Paolo I*)
seventh or eighth century?:	S. Lorenzo in Miranda in the Temple of Antoninus and Faustina
eighth century:	S. Giovanni in the Basilica Aemilia
	SS. Sergio e Bacco near the Temple of Concord under the Capitol (*Liber pontificalis*, vol. 1, p. 512)
eighth or ninth century:	S. Maria in Cannapara in the Basilica Julia; renamed S. Maria delle Grazie in the fifteenth century
	S. Maria Antica, later S. Maria Liberatrice near the Fountain of Juturna (*Liber pontificalis*, vol. 1, p. 385)
840s:	S. Maria Nova, later S. Francesca Romana, in the Temple of Venus and Rome (vol. 2, p. 140).

In the same connection, we may note that the two great commemorative columns were also assigned to churches: that of Aurelius to the convent of S. Silvestro in Capite in 955 by Agapitus II, and that of Trajan before 1162 to S. Nicolai ad Columpnam Trajanam and thence to the convent of S. Ciriaco in 1162 by the senate (Gregorovius, vol. 3, pp. 547ff., vol. 4, p. 686), thus preserving them! And in 1199 the church of SS. Sergio e Bacco was given possession of half (!) of the Arch of Severus (ibid., vol. 4, p. 683).

8 *Liber pontificalis*; unmentioned by Fea, *Dissertation*; Lanciani, *Destruction*, p. 122.

9 Paul the Deacon, *History of the Langobards*, vol. 5, p. 11; Fea, *Dissertation*, p. 311.

10 Lanciani analysed in detail the first of the eleven itineraries. The *Itinerary* (*c.* 800) in its various rambles indicates many monuments, which may perhaps best be grouped according to type, asterisked where inscriptions were also copied (for which see *CIL* 6.ix–xv).

The temples of Saturn*, Vespasian* and Concord*, the Pantheon;
The theatres of Pompey*, and Marcellus*, the Colosseum, the Circus Maximus, the amphiteatrum Castrense, the circus Flaminius (i.e. circus of Domitian);
The arches of Arcadius, Honorius and Theodosius*, of Gratian, Valentinian and Theodosius*, of Titus in the Circus Maximus*, of Severus*, of Constantine*, of Titus in the Forum*, of Drusus (?);
The baths of Diocletian*, of the Julii*, of Caracalla, of Commodus (i.e. Agrippa behind the Pantheon), of Constantine, of Trajan, of Sallust;
The column* and forum of Trajan, the column of Aurelius, the Forum Palatini*, the equestrian statue of 'Constantine'*, the Septizonium*, the Meta Sudans, the macellum of Livia*, the aqua Claudia*, the obelisk of the Campus Martius, the Vatican obelisk*, the mausoleum of Hadrian and various other tombs, the Sessorium, the 'palace of Nero' (Basilica of Maxentius?).

See Fea, *Dissertation*, p. 326, Lanciani, *Destruction*, pp. 142ff.

11 Fea, pp. 330ff. See further Gregorovius, vol. 5, pp. 661ff.

12 Fea, pp. 337ff, Lanciani, p. 166. Gregorovius (vol. 4, pp. 251ff.) agrees with Fea: 'Within the city the Palatine and Capitol had been laid waste, and the fate of the Septizonium, at that time the finest portion of the imperial palaces, must have been shared by other fortified buildings ... The Field of Mars, possibly as far as the Bridge of Hadrian, was destroyed by fire; the remains of the porticoes in this neighbourhood and several other monuments perished; the Mausoleum of Augustus escaped owing to the mode of its construction, and the Column of Marcus Aurelius owing to its isolated position on an entirely open piazza ... the Colosseum, the Triumphal Arches, the remains of the Circus Maximus can hardly have escaped.'

13 Fea, *Dissertation*, pp. 351ff., Lanciani, *Destruction*, pp. 174ff.; on both sources, Gregorovius, vol. 4, pp. 653ff.

The *Mirabilia* knew little more than names. When history was attempted, the results were ludicrous: the incredible explanation of the equestrian statue of Aurelius (part 2, chap. 3), the claim that the Pantheon was built after Agrippa's conquest of the Persians (part 2, chap. 4), the idea that Caesar was buried in the ball of the Vatican obelisk (part 3, chap. 1); on the other hand, the author knew that Nerva was buried in the Mausoleum of Hadrian. The monuments of the Forum are sufficient to show how little was known of classical Rome:

the temples of Saturn and Concord were given correctly (part 3, chap. 9, although in part 3, chap. 8 they were said to be on the *clivus argentarii*, mindlessly following *Notitia*), but the Basilica Julia is the temple of Ceres and Tellus (part 3, chap. 10), the Temple of the Dioscuroi apparently was thought to be the palace of Catiline, the Regia was the Temple of Pallas, the Temple of Antoninus and Faustina – despite its inscription – was the Temple of Minerva, the Basilica of Maxentius the Temple of Romulus, the Arch of Titus – again despite a simple inscription – was simply the Arch of the Seven Lamps (from its decoration admittedly), and the Arch of Severus – a third neglected inscription, or rather a misreading of it – was the Arch of Caesar and the senators (part 1, chap. 4).

The Ordo of Benedict may be found in Mabillon, *Museum italicum*, vol. 2, pp. 118ff. or Urlichs, *Codex topographicus*, pp. 79ff.

14 Fea, *Dissertation*, p. 355.

15 Mabillon, vol. 2, p. 143.

16 Gregorovius, vol. 4, p. 466.

17 *Monumenta Germaniae Historica* vol. 20, p. 407, vol. 19, p. 242, and the bull of Anacletus. See in general Rodocanachi, *Le Capitole romain*, pp. 60ff., 73.

18 Petrarch states: 'Cecidit edificiorum veterum neglecta civibus stupenda peregrinis moles; turris illa toto orbe unica quae Comitis dicebatur, ingentibus rimis laxata dissiluit et nunc velut trunca caput, superbi verticis honorem, solo effusum despicit; denique ut ire celestis argumenta non desint, multorum species templorum, atque in primis Paulo Apostolo dicate edis bona pars humi collapsa et Lateranensis ecclesie deiectus apex . . . cum Petro mitius est actum.'

To the above list of churches, Lanciani adds the outer shell of the Colosseum, and the nave and right aisle of the Basilica of Maxentius (*The golden days of the Renaissance in Rome*, p. 8).

19 Stella Casiello, 'Aspetti della tutela dei beni culturali nell'Ottocento'.

20 Of 1820: Mariotti, *La legislazione delle Belle Arti*, p. 235.

21 Fea, *Relazione di un viaggio ad Ostia*, p. 82 (henceforth *Relazione*). For Pius II's treatment of the monuments, see below, p. 18. The bull is mentioned by Pastor, without understanding its historical significance. Pius II was mostly involved, Humanist though he was, with the Turkish threat and his own insolvency, until the discovery of the alum mines at Tolfa. He was the author of an epigram on Rome's ruins:

Oblectat me, Roma, tuas spectare ruinas,
    Ex cuius lapsu gloria prisca patet.
Sed tuus hic populus muris defossa vetustis,
    Calcis in obsequium marmora dura coquit.
Impia ter centum si sic gens egeris annos,
    Nullum hinc indicium nobilitatis erit.
                                        (Mabillon, vol. 1, p. 97)

('O Rome, thy very ruins are a joy, fallen is thy pomp, but it was peerless once! The noble blocks wrenched from thy ancient walls are burned for lime by greedy slaves of gain. Villains! If such as you may have their way three ages more, Rome's glory will be gone.')

Ludwig Pastor, *History of the Popes*, vol. 3, p. 304. Although a monumental work, based on enormous labour in archives all over Europe, it is too often guilty of unashamed apologetics. It covers papal history from 1305 to 1800.

22 Fea, *Relazione*, p. 91. This has often been misinterpreted to say that Raphael was an early Commissario delle Antichità: even by Lanciani, *Renaissance*, p. 246.

23 Fea, *Relazione*, p. 94.

24 On Manetti, see L. Dorez, *La cour du Pape Paul III*, 1932, vol. 1, pp. 115–41. On the fasti and triumphal lists, see below, p. 21.

25 Fea, *Relazione*, p. 96.

26 Ibid., pp. 99ff.

27 Ibid., p. 103. Even Pastor admits the calamitous situation under Clement VIII (1592–1605): 'The use of ancient materials for new buildings continued . . . Permission from the government, however, was required, both for excavations and for the exportation of works of art. In spite of this prohibition so many antiquities were sent abroad, especially to the courts of Florence and Mantua, that the representatives of the city as well as the Pope himself complained that Rome was being robbed of its treasures' (vol. 24, p. 505).

28 Yet the edict of 1624 was always cited in later edicts as the first precedent.

29 For all these, Mariotti, pp. 208ff.

30 Ibid., p. 214. Pastor notes that the papal archives reveal that the inspirer of this edict was Francesco Bartoli, Commissario delle Antichità (vol. 33, p. 509).

31 Mariotti, p. 217.

32 Ibid., p. 218.

33 Ibid., p. 220.

34 Ibid., p. 226. For an interesting setting of the document in the artistic sacking of Rome, but unfortunately only from the point of view of painting and not antiquities, see Orietta Pinelli, 'Carlo Fea e il chirografo del 1802'.

35 Fea, *Dissertation*, p. 316, Lanciani, *Destruction*, p. 191.

36 Archives quoted by Müntz, *Les arts à la cour des Papes*, vol. 1, p. 48, Flavio Biondo *Roma instaurata*, book 3, chap. 64–6.

37 Müntz, vol. 1, p. 105. His evidence convinced both Pastor, vol. 2, p. 180, and Gregorovius, vol. 7, pp. 585ff. For the archives quoted, see Müntz, *Rev. Arch.*, 2(32), 1876, 170ff.

38 Poggio Bracciolini, *de varietate fortunae*, first publ. 1723, p. 5; Biondo *Roma instaurata*, book 1, chap. 104.

39 Müntz, vol. 1, pp. 266–7; vol. 2, p. 7.

40 Ibid., vol. 2, pp. 7, 92. Vasari, *Life of Giuliano Majano*. For the archives see Müntz, *Rev. Arch.*, 2(32), 1876, 162, 163, 165.

41 Müntz, vol. 3, pp. 14–15.

42 Ibid., vol. 3, pp. 174, 176, 177. On the destruction of the temple of Hercules, see Leto, *de antiquitatibus urbis Romae*, p. 24; Fauno, *de antiquitatibus urbis Romae*, p. 72.

43 Fea, *Dissertation*, p. 373.

44 Rodocanachi, *Le Capitole romain*, pp. 191ff; Pastor, vol. 4, p. 459.

45 Lanciani, *Destruction*, pp. 207–10. Even Pastor admitted the ruthless destruction of ancient monuments by Alexander VI (vol. 6, p. 167). For the archival documents on stone-workers in the Forum and Colosseum, see Müntz, *Rev. Arch.*, 2(32), 1876, 174.

46 The only comment known to me on this mysterious church is in the index to Valentini and Zuchetti, *Codice topografico di Roma*, vol. 4, p. 571: = S. Salvatore di Statera?

47 Fea, *Relazione*, p. 86. A contemporary does name monuments he had seen destroyed. Albertini, *Opusculum*, 1509, cites the arches of Theodosius and Gratian, of Valentinian, of Aemilius Paullus, and of Fabius (cited by Müntz, *Rev. Arch.*, 3(3), 1884, 306).

48 Fea, *Relazione*, p. 88.

49 The monuments destroyed were the Vatican pyramid and the 'Arco di Portogallo'. Della Rovere was presumably the brother of Julius II, and bishop of Ferrara. Leo X, epitome of Renaissance Popes, did nothing for the monuments. Excavations produced, most notably, from the Temple of Isis near S. Stefano, the statues of the rivers Nile and Tiber. This was also the time of Francesco Albertini's *de mirabilibus novae et veteris urbis Romae*, 1510; of the first published collection of Latin inscriptions, Jacopo Mazochi's *Epigrammata antiquae urbis*, 1521; and of Andrea Fulvio's *de urbis antiquitatibus*, 1527. Not to be overlooked is the work of Fabio Calvo (who helped Raphael to read Vitruvius), *Antiquae urbis cum regionibus simulachrum*, 1527, the map of classical Rome. See Pastor, vol. 8, pp. 132, 242ff., 374.

50 Hülsen, *Das Forum Romanum*, pp. 33–4.

51 Lanciani, *Destruction*, pp. 217ff.; also Gregorovius, vol. 8, pp. 580ff.

52 See above, p. 13.

53 Rabelais, *Lettre* 8: 'Et a l'on faict par le commandement du Pape ung chemin nouveau par lequel il doibt entrer, scavoir est de la Porte Sainct Sebastien, tirant au Camp Doly [Campidoglio], Templum Pacis [Basilica of Maxentius], et l'Amphiteatre, et le faict passer soubs les antiques arcs triumphaulx de Constantin, de Vespasien et Titus, de Numetianus [Severus] et aultres, puys a couste du palays Sainct Marc et de là par Camp de Flour et davant le palays Farnese, ou souloyt demourer le Pape, puys par les banques et dessoubs le chasteau Sainct Ange; pour lequel chemin droisser et equaler on a demolly et abastu plus de deux cent maisons et trouys ou quatre eglises ras terre, ce que plusieurs interpretent en maulvays presage.' Fea, *Dissertation*, pp. 375ff.; Lanciani, *Destruction*, p. 228.

54 The bull was published by Müntz, *Rev. Arch.*, 3(3), 1884, 308ff. It cancelled all previous permissions to excavate stone and marble, gave the prefects of St Peter's permission to excavate material for the new basilica anywhere in Rome and outside the city, and forced people holding stone which they wished to sell to give first option to the prefects at a valuation set by them.

55 Lanciani, *Renaissance*, p. 123.

56 Hülsen, pp. 34–5.

57 Lanciani, *Renaissance*, pp. 130ff., for both the Fasti and the Marble Plan.

58 This adaptation was made the centre-piece of a fascinating interpretation by M. Gloton, 'Transformation et réemploi des monuments du passé dans la Rome du XVI siècle'. He begins with Baldassarre Peruzzi's attempts to combine archaeology and architecture with the construction of the Savelli palace in the Theatre of Marcellus, *c.* 1520, showing great respect for the ruins. The only correspondence between the ancient and the modern, however, was the outer curve of the building, and there was no attempt made to coordinate ancient and modern sections. Two other projects, not realised, were the Orsini palace in the Baths of Agrippa, and the convent of S. Maria Liberatrice. In *c.* 1549, the shell of the Mausoleum of Augustus was converted into the Soderini Gardens, and in 1554 Cardinal du Bellay inserted his palace and gardens into the Baths of Diocletian. These Mannerist fascinations with the lure of ruins gave way to Michelangelo's transformation of pagan monuments for Christian purposes, at the same time, according to Gloton, rigorously respecting the ruins both internally and externally. The complete abandonment of such fine principles in the next century is shown by S. Lorenzo in Miranda, built by Torriani in 1602, which preserved the ancient porch of the Temple of Antoninus and Faustina, but followed these Corinthian columns with the Ionic pilasters of the façade and then erected a second baroque storey to tower over the classical portico. Even worse was Martino Longhi's rebuilding of S. Adriano with no respect even for the external appearance, epitomised by the portal 3 m above the ancient level.

59 Pastor, vol. 17, pp. 110ff., 407.

60 Ibid., vol. 20, pp. 566, 598.

61 For the multitude of buildings for which the stone was used, see Lanciani, *Ruins and excavations*, p. 183.

62 Boyer, *Le monde des arts*, p. 299 ascribes the work to Pius VII!

63 Fea, *Dissertation*, p. 381.

64 Lanciani, *Destruction*, pp. 235ff. The main source is the autobiography of Cardinal Santori, in *Arch. Rom. Stor. Pat.* 12, 1889, 327–72; 13, 1890, 151–205. See also D. Tempesta, *Vita di Sisto V*, 1596. The obelisks were those of St Peters (1586), S. Maria Maggiore (1587), Lateran (1588) and Piazza del Popolo (1589). See Domenico Fontana, *della trasportazione dell'obelisco Vaticano*, 1590. The motive, however, in the time of the Counter-Reformation, was to Christianise such pagan remains, as noted by V. Bracco, *L'archeologia classica nella cultura occidentale*, pp. 101ff, who compares the placing of the statues of Peter and Paul on the columns of Trajan and Marcus Aurelius.

65 Montaigne, *Journal de voyage*, pp. 211–12.

66 Fea, *Dissertation*, p. 375; Lanciani, *Destruction*, p. 253.

67 The apologists are a disgrace. Fea claimed that the Pope made better use of the bronze. Pastor admitted that 'this use of the only untouched monument of antiquity filled the Romans with bitter grief', but we are reassured: 'the oft-quoted witticism' (coined by the Pope's doctor, Giulio Mancini) 'is quite unfair for no work of art was melted down, but only girders which were not even visible, hence no one could justly complain that the monument had been damaged' (vol. 29, p. 463). On the baldaquin, see below, n. 132. Pastor ascribes

to Urban VIII, however, the destruction of the Temple of the Sun on the Quirinal (p. 510) and credits Bernini with thoughts of demolishing the Tomb of Metella (p. 511).

68 Many interesting documents of Alexander VII can be found in the appendix to Fea's *Diritti del Principato*, 1806, pp. 62ff. The motive for the restoration of the Pyramid is explained. His predecessors had not only conserved churches and holy places, but had also maintained Roman buildings. This was because they warn us by their ruins of 'human fragility' and provide testimony to the writers of antiquity, many of whom confirm the truth of the Christian religion. As for the Pyramid, its destruction would diminish the fame of the old Romans, and mean that fewer 'virtuosi forestieri' came to Rome to study antiquity and to educate themselves. The demolition, on the other hand, of the Arch of Aurelius was justified by the need to widen the Corso and beautify the city! As for the Pantheon, the replaced columns were specified as coming from the Piazza S. Luigi dei Francesi. The pontifical decree allowed the President of Roads and his *maestri* to make any excavations they wished, without obstruction even from cardinals, in order to find 'columns, bases, pedestals, capitals, friezes, marbles and travertine' necessary for the restoration. All previous 'constitutions, orders, laws, statutes, decrees, customs and privileges' were declared inoperative. There was thus another side to the much lauded restoration. Many Peters were robbed to pay Paul.

69 It was transferred to Piazza di Montecitorio by Francesco Fontana in 1705. Its subsequent history is so tortured and difficult to sort out that it is given here. The column and pedestal remained under a wooden roof for 43 years, until Benedict XIV re-erected the base; the column was too damaged in the excavation. The latter was then destroyed by fire. The pedestal was moved to the Vatican by Pius VI in 1789, restored by de Fabris and placed in the Giardino della Pigna in 1846, and transferred to the Cortile in 1885. See C. d'Onofrio, *Gli obelischi*, pp. 238ff.

70 Pastor, vol. 33, p. 512.

71 The restoration was directed by Girolamo Teodoli the architect and Marchese Alessandro Capponi the archaeologist. The statues were restored by Pietro Bracci. G. Gaddi, *Roma nobilitata da Clemente XII*, Rome 1736.

72 Pastor, vol. 34, p. 398; Rodocanachi, pp. 210ff.

73 Pastor, vol. 35, pp. 170ff.

74 Ibid., vol. 36, p. 184. The same Pope began the practice of clothing 'indecent' statues in the Vatican collection (Winckelmann in Justi, vol. 2, p. 15), just as Michelangelo's *Last Judgement* was being transformed by the 'breech-maker', Stefano Pozzi.

75 Pietrangeli, 'I musei vaticani al tempo di Pio VI'. The architects were Michelangelo Simonetti (1771–87) and then Giuseppe Camporese.

76 An interesting archival survey on excavations (Corbo, 'Gli scavi nello stato pontificio nella seconda metà del secolo XVIII') gives a depressing picture, apart from the growth of the museum, of private or illegal excavations and endless exportation abroad.

For examples of Clement's purchases, 'despite the deplorable condition of his finances' (Pastor, vol. 38, pp. 512ff.): the Meleager for 6,000 scudi (Amelung, *Die Sculpturen des Vatikanischen Museums*, vol. 2, pp. 33ff.), the Mattei collection for 4,300 scudi (1770), the togate sacrificer from the Giustiniani collection, the seated Jupiter for 1,500 scudi (ibid., vol. 2, p. 519), and many items from the Barberini collection.

The full story of the sale of the Mattei collection is available, thanks to the researches of Hautecœur ('La vente de la collection Mattei et les origines du Musée Pio-Clementino'). Despite the will of an ancestor forbidding sale of the collection, Giuseppe Mattei, to pay a debt of 800 scudi, obtained Clement's permission to sell by offering him thirty-four of the best pieces for 4,300 scudi. The rest went to private collections, mostly English. So much for the ancestor's wishes, and for papal bans on export of antiquities.

77 Pietrangeli, *Scavi e scoperti*, pp. 4, 5. One cannot forbear mentioning an amazing confirmation of these negative impressions from a most unbiased and authoritative source: the Papal Commissario, Filippo Aurelio Visconti, who in an undated report to the French government on proposed works in the Forum Boarium mentioned regulations for excavations under Pius VII: only royal princes could then undertake a dig, for only they were sure of the sovereign's indulgence! (F le 148.1).

Accounts of the reign of Pius VI have nothing to counter these statements: 'Accesi di nobile emulazione questi tutti, Principi Romani e persone facoltose, si messero a gira a intraprendere in varie parti del suolo Latino dell'escavazioni, da cui dissotterravano di' più rari e pregiabili monumenti per appagare il sublime genio del Sovrano, il quale ne acquistava quelli che reputati venivano i migliori per arrichiare l'illustre collezione ...' (Becattini, *Storia di Pio VI*, vol. 1, p. 104). For a different picture of Pius as vain, spendthrift and with a disaffected population, see Hautecœur, *Rome et la renaissance de l'antiquité*, pp. 64ff.

78 Pietrangeli, 'I musei vaticani', p. 230.

79 Pietrangeli, 'Archaeological excavations in Italy, 1750–1850', p. xlviii.

80 Mirri and Carletti, *Le pitture delle terme di Tito*.

81 Amelung, vol. 2, p. 76.

82 The full details of these discoveries can be found in Lanciani, *Storia degli scavi*, vol. 2, pp. 216ff. The prizes included many items which went to the Pio-Clementino: heads of Caracalla, Pertinax (?), busts of Trajan, Matidia, Antoninus, Verus, Commodus, Severus, a head and torso of Bacchus, a small bust of Sophocles, Diana with a dog, Pallas with shield, Apollo Citharedus, and a gigantic Hercules. The riches are explained by the fact that the area covered the Temple of Peace, an imperial palace, and a sculptor's workshop. See Amelung, vol. 2, pp. 87, 147, 177, 211, 432, 485, 487, 535, 565.

83 C. Buti, *Pitture antiche della Villa Negroni*; Lanciani, *Ruins and excavations*, p. 147. Pastor (vol. 39, p. 70) has the wonderfully tendentious note: 'When in the autumn of 1777, a house of the imperial period with splendidly preserved pictorial decoration was discovered in the Villa Montalto, the Pope immediately thought of making it accessible to the public, which was done by the architect Camillo Buti.'

84 Lanciani, *Ruins and excavations*, p. 462.

85 Amelung, vol. 2, pp. 448ff.

86 The sculptures were acquired by Thomas Jenkins (cf. n. 94): he paid 1,790 scudi for a Cupid, Faun, Muse, Hercules, Bacchus, and a headless male nude (*Cracas* 26 January 1781, quoted by T. Ashby, 'Thomas Jenkins in Rome', p. 496).

87 The main ancient remains in this area are the Saepta Julia along the Via Flaminia down to the piazza, and to the west (under the Palazzo Venezia) the vast ruins of a villa. See Lanciani, *Forma urbis Romae*, plate 21.

88 Now in the Terme Museum: Lanciani, *Ruins and excavations*, p. 407.

89 Erected on the Quirinal by Giovanni Antinori, 1783–6: d'Onofrio, *Gli obelischi di Roma*, pp. 256ff.

90 Bildt, 'Die Ausgrabungen C. F. von Fredenheim auf den Forum Romanum'.

91 Lanciani, *Ruins and excavations*, pp. 160ff.

92 Ibid., pp. 322–3. With this may be compared Pastor's scandalous note (vol. 39, p. 73). Nogara is more honest:

I monumenti dell'antichità classica erano cercati e ammirati per la loro bellezza intrinseca e non per il loro significato storico, e poca importanza o nessuna si dava perciò alla loro giacitura, agli edifici a cui appartenevano e alla loro conformazione: e a questo criterio errato di apprezzamento si deve ascrivere la rovina di monumenti venerandi e preziosissimi per la storia antica. Con Pio VI e con gli archeologi del suo tempo, per questo riguardo, si respira l'aria del Rinascimento, e nonostante gli splendidi tesori accumulati nel Museo Pio Clementino, siamo costretti a lamentare, per esempio, l'irreparabile spogliazione delle tombe degli Scipioni e l'ignoranza in cui stiamo intorno ai corredi che dovevano accompagnarle; e così è che della maggior parte delle suppellettili di quel museo non si conosce esattamente nè come nè dove esse siano state trovate'.

(*Nel primo centenario della morte del Cardinale Ercole Consalvi*, pp. 85-6).

93 *DNB*, vol. 8, pp. 1039–40. See also D. Irwin, 'Gavin Hamilton'.

94 *DNB*, vol. 10, pp. 743–4. See also Michaelis, *Ancient marbles*, pp. 75ff.; Ashby, 'Thomas Jenkins in Rome'; Ford, 'Thomas Jenkins'.

95 For all this, see Michaelis, pp. 66ff. Pastor refused to mourn the loss of the Medici and Farnese collections: 'But what was this loss as against the wealth of antiques proffered by the palaces of the Altieri, Chigi, Colonna and Spada, the villas of the Ludovisi, Borghese, Pamfili, and Albani, and the Capitol? And to all this was added Pius VI's museum in the Vatican' (vol. 39, p. 85).

96 Ashby, 'Thomas Jenkins in Rome', pp. 509, 510. And in the matter of modern art, one cannot omit Gavin Hamilton's getting out of Italy both the Raphael Madonna from Perugia in 1764 and the Leonardo Virgin of the Rocks in 1785 from Milan, both now in the National Gallery, London: Irwin, p. 99. The English got away with most treasures because they could pay the highest prices (Hautecœur, *Rome et la renaissance de l'antiquité*, pp. 60ff).

97 Fea to de Gérando, 18 August 1809: F le 148.

98 Stefano Piale and Giambattista Monti (replaced 1810 by Alessandro Visconti).

99 On 4 January 1810, Fea gave much the same figures to the Consulta (attached to decree no. 1856). Fea had been Commissario since 1801, Chief Keeper of the Capitoline from May 1801, when Agostino Toffanelli was appointed as his assistant. There was also a Controller of Excavations, Giuseppe Radici, appointed in 1780. He was sacked for theft (F le 148).

100 Fea to de Gérando, 27 August: F le 148.

101 See the Temple of Vesta (below, pp. 205ff.).

102 Decree no. 1613.

103 Attached to decree no. 1614.

104 Fea to Tournon, 15 March 1811: BG 3.132.

105 Fea to de Gérando, 11 September 1809: F le 148.

106 Guattani, *Memorie enciclopediche*, vol. 1, p. 3. Nothing of interest is added by the summary notices in Giucci, *Storia della vita e del pontificato di Pio VII* (vol. 1, p. 168, vol. 2, pp. 7, 134, 198ff.), who ignores the French as far as possible.

107 Consalvi, *Mémoires*, vol. 2, p. 256.

108 Often stated to be Lorenzino de' Medici (1514–48): Nibby, *Itinerario di Roma*, vol. 1, p. 232.

109 Nardini, *Roma vetus*, bk. 5, chap. 6. Some work is attributed to Clement XI (1700–21) by Eva Brues, *Raffaele Stern*, p. 132, who claims to be following Pastor – but he says nothing of this.

110 G. Gaddi, *Roma nobilitata da Clemente XII*, Rome 1736.

111 Guattani, *Roma descritta*, vol. 1, p. 40; Uggeri, Supplement to *Journées pittoresques*, p. 48. It is interesting that Gasparoni, *Biografia di Giuseppe Camporese*, p. 11 claims that it was Camporese who excavated and walled the arches of Constantine and Severus!

112 Nibby, *Roma nell'anno 1838*, vol. 1, pp. 443ff.

113 Platner and Ashby, *Topographical dictionary*, p. 44.

114 Nibby, *Roma nell'anno 1838*, vol. 1, p. 484 states that it was excavated and isolated under Leo X (1513–21), Pius IV in 1563, and Gregory XV *c.* 1621.

115 L. Forcella, *Iscrizioni delle chiese ed altri edifici di Roma* (14 vols.), 1869–84, vol. 1, p. 407.

116 Guattani, *Roma descritta*, vol. 1, p. 70; Nibby, *Del Foro Romano*, pp. 118ff. For illustrations of the arch before the isolation, see Vasi, *Magnificenze*, plate 31, and Piranesi, *Vedute*, plate 89. For after Pius' work, see Rossini, *Le antichità romane*, plate 83. The wall was demolished in 1831.

117 Fea, *Indicazione del Foro Romano*.

118 Uggeri, Supplement to *Journées pittoresques*, pp. 45ff.; Gasparoni, *Biografia di Giuseppe Camporese*, p. 11; Nibby, *Roma nell'anno 1838*, vol. 1, pp. 476ff.; Brues, *Raffaele Stern*, p. 132. See ASR Camerlengato II.6. 192 for the archives.

119 For the early history of the Colosseum, see Nibby, *Del Foro Romano*; Colagrossi, *L'Anfiteatro Flavio*; Cerasoli, 'Nuovi documenti sulle vicende del Colosseo dal secolo XIII al XVIII'.

120 Uggeri, *Journées pittoresques*, vol. 1, p. 37. The same man told a wonderful story of how he was assaulted by beggars and thieves when he came to take measurements in the building (ibid., vol. 23, p. 21).

121 Gori, *Le memorie storiche ... dell'Anfiteatro Flavio*, p. 104. Nibby admitted that the first work to preserve the monument was due to Pius VII (*Roma nell'anno 1838*, vol. I, p. 420).

122 Canina, 'Sul ristabilmento e riparazione ...', 169–94.

123 The quotation is preserved by C. du Fresne Ducange, *Glossarium ad scriptores mediae et infimae latinatis* (3 vols.), 1678, s.v. Coliseum. Gibbon (chapter 71) doubted that this was really Bede.

124 Lanciani, 'Notizie inedite sull'Anfiteatro Flavio', 3–8.

125 Fea to de Gérando, 27 August 1809: F le 148.1. The main archive is Camerale II.7. It was estimated that there were 12,000 cart-loads of nitrate stored in the arches. Fea complained that, as well, the carters in winter lit fires against the pilasters, which were thus eaten away.

126 Lanciani, *Storia degli scavi* (MS notes in the Istituto di Archeologica) dates the beginning of the excavations by Lucangeli to find the podium to 14 November 1801. Carlo Lucangeli (1747–1821) is a most remarkable figure, who was prominent also in the French period. He began his career as a papal courier, riding between Rome and Naples, but became famous for his models in wood and cork of classical and modern buildings. That of St Peter's in wood was bought by Catherine of Russia for 1,000 gold sequins; that of the present state of the Colosseum by Napoleon, and another of it restored, completed by his son-in-law, went to London. It was for this last that he conducted excavations, although he was regarded unjustly with scorn by the antiquarians. The most extraordinary episode in his life was when he became involved with a mad balloonist, and was nearly killed when he fell out of the poorly constructed machine, after it had suddenly been released with him in it. See Tipaldo, *Biografia degli italiani illustri*, Rome 1834, vol. 7, pp. 424–6.

127 F le 156.

128 Guattani, *Memorie enciclopediche*, vol. 2, pp. 49–54 (there is no date, but almost the last item in the volume is March 1807).

129 The relazione conclusiva was signed by Stern, so the design may be attributed to him: Camerale II.7; Michele di Macco, *Il Colosseo*; Righini, 'Raffaele Stern', p. 25; Brues, *Raffaele Stern*, pp. 138ff. Needless to say, Gasparoni, *Biografia di Giuseppe Camporese*, p. 5, implies that the subject of his attentions was sole author of the buttress, and he is followed by La Padula, *Roma e la regione nell'epoca napoleonica*, p. 90. Colagrossi, *L'Anfiteatro Flavio*, pp. 215ff. in a footnote, on the other hand, seems to ascribe the buttress to Valadier.

130 Gisors, March 1813: F 13 1646A.

131 Paolo Marconi puts this restoration in a wider context ('Roma 1806–1829: un momento critico per la formazione della metodologia del restauro architettonico', pp. 63ff.): 'rispetto dell'antico, cultura impregnata del filone tardo-manierista romano, predisposizione romantica al rovanismo' are all combined in this work by Stern. He remarks, as anyone must, on the way the falling stones are caught as if by some giant hand when obviously it would have been possible to put them back neatly in place.

132 Lanciani quotes the Papal account-books to show that the bronze was used only for cannon, not for the four columns of the baldaquin, the metal for

which came from Venice (*Ruins and excavations*, p. 483). This was also known to Fea (*L'integrità del Pantheon*, p. 9).

133 Licht, *The Rotonda in Rome*, p. 242, and figs. 230, 234, 242: engraving by Falda and map of Nolli.

134 See especially Nibby, *Itinerario di Roma*, vol. 2, pp. 433ff.; Cerasoli, 'I restauri del Pantheon dal secolo XV al XVIII'; Bartocetti, *S. Maria ad Martyres*.

135 Guattani, *Memorie enciclopediche*, vol. 1, p. 33, Fea, *L'integrità del Pantheon*. Fea's studies have been described as 'marking the beginning of modern research into the Pantheon' (Licht, p. 242). Ciampi, *Vita di Giuseppe Valadier*, p. 26, claims that Valadier published an account of these excavations: *Relazione e osservazioni di V. sulle scoperte fatte negli scavi a lato e alla facciata del Pantheon nel 1804*, Rome, 1804: I can find no trace of this work.

136 Guattani, *Memorie enciclopediche*, vol. 3, p. 139.

137 Fea, *Diritti del Principato*, pp. 22ff., 85ff. Guattani, *Memorie enciclopediche*, vol. 2, pp. 135–42 preserves an impassioned letter from Luigi Ciccognara Ferrarese, dated 1 March 1807, protesting against the bakery built up against the right-hand side of the Pantheon. The story could not be more bizarre. The Crescenzi had built part of their palace against the cella during the Avignon Papacy in the fourteenth century. It passed to Duca Bonelli, who sold part off to the baker. Then a Tiber flood caused the collapse of the oven. Although the law forbade it, the bakery had been rebuilt. Pius VII had allowed this, in fact, but now a tribunal was investigating the matter. The surrounding wall, as well, had been much extended on the plea of protecting the public. If only the Pope had followed Christ's example and driven the profane from the temple!

'Buon per le Arti che l'attual Conservatore del pubblico diritto riguarda con occhio parziale le antiche memorie di Roma, rivendica gli oltragi ad esse portati dal tempo e dall'iniuria, e riconosce con fino discernimento quanto sia maggiore interesse il conservarle ora che per tante e varie cagioni si sono rese più rare, e sente in tutta la sua estensione quanto la moderna Roma sia debitrice della sua grandezza ai sassi preziosi che si rimangono dell'antica.' (p. 144).

This was high praise for Fea, antiquarian and lawyer, engaged in this bitter struggle against such outrages, but he was powerless.

138 Fea, *Diritti del Principato*, pp. 65ff.

139 See below, pp. 182ff.

140 Guattani, *Roma descritta*, vol. 1, p. 94, P. Pinon in *Forma*, p. 25.

141 Fea to de Gérando, undated, but before 24 February 1810: F le 157.

142 MS notes in the Istituto di Archeologia, Rome.

143 Bunsen, 'Scavi Romani', p. 32.

144 Fea, *Varietà de notizie*, p. 98.

145 Mentioned in passing by Guattani, *Memorie enciclopediche*, vol. 3, pp. 129ff., listing work of 1807 (*sic*); in more detail by Canina, 'Sui tre templi antichi esistenti nella chiesa di San Nicola in Carcere'. More recent notes in Lanciani, *Ruins and excavations*, p. 511; Aite, *I tre templi del Foro Olitorio*, p. 12.

2 THE ADMINISTRATION OF ANTIQUITIES UNDER THE FRENCH

1 Consulta decree no. 37.
2 Consulta decree no. 460.
3 Martorelli to the Consulta, 21 July 1809: F le 148.1. For completeness, we should note the setting up, on 21 July also, of the Ludovisi Commission to develop the area from the Milvian Bridge to the Piazza del Popolo. The members were Principe Ludovisi, Gaetano Palombi, d'Orimond, Raffaele Stern and Giuseppe Valadier. This was the forerunner of the Commission des Embellisements.
4 See the Pantheon, p. 173 and Colosseum, p. 109. On the use of convicts, see the report of de Gérando, 2 November 1810 (Consulta decree no. 4472) explaining that the Consulta had from the beginning thought how to use them in public works, to improve their morality and take advantage of their economy. Tournon, in a letter to Angles, Maître des Requêtes (*Lettres inédites*, vol. 1, p. 78), defended their use: they did not take away work from others, because it was the skilled workers who had been employed in the convents who now lacked work. In May 1810, there were fifty-seven convicts at Castel Sant'Angelo, and 172 in the prison at the Colosseum (ibid., vol. 1, p. 40).
5 Moulard, *Tournon*, vol. 2, p. 4; Madelin, *La Rome de Napoléon*, p. 288; and Boyer, *Le monde des arts*, p. 282 all have Tournon *appointed* in November – perhaps because his appointment on 6 September was announced in the *Giornale del Campidoglio* only on 25 November!
6 See above, pp. 32–4.
7 Consulta decree no. 1613.
8 Attached to decree no. 1000.
9 As interesting evidence for relative expenses and wages, Miollis as governor received 15,000 frs per month (Consulta decree no. 2843) and 10,000 frs as president of the Consulta, while the other members received 3,000 frs per month (decree no. 2844). Tournon as Prefect was paid 50,000 frs per annum in 1810. For more ordinary wages, in October 1809 (F le 156): a manual worker was paid 30 bajocchi per day (= 1.6 frs); a master mason, 40 (= 2.1 frs); a master carpenter, 45 (= 2.34 frs); a master sculptor, 50 (= 2.6 frs); while a sculptor like Canova charged 24,000 frs for his works (O 2 1070).
10 Visconti's report, 25 January 1810: F le 148.
11 De Gérando to Olivetti, 21 April, F le 156.
12 Tournon to de Gérando, 22 April, F le 148.1.
13 Consulta decrees no. 2754, 2798.
14 Consulta decree no. 3482.
15 Marita Jonsson, *La cura dei monumenti*, p. 46.
16 Tournon to his mother, 23 August 1810 (*Lettres inédites*, vol. 1, p. 63).
17 The proceedings of this commission are preserved in Rome (BG 3.132, 128). These classifications, unfortunately, have no internal numbering, which means that documents cannot be located more precisely, many are entirely displaced in their folders, and some may even have been removed without trace. Other sources are Paris F le 137, 148.

The most important question is the membership of the Commission, a question which does not interest Madelin, p. 537, or Boyer, p. 282. On 7 August, Tournon had offered a list of nominations to de Gérando (BG 3.132): Visconti, Guattani and Fea (antiquarians), Stern and Camporese (architects), Canova and Laboureur (sculptors) and Camuccini (painter). The minutes of the first meeting (the only complete list of members) show Tournon, Braschi, Gabrielli (Braschi's assistant), Vici, Ottaviani (architects), Camuccini, Landi (painters), Laboureur (sculptor), Fea, Visconti and Guattani (antiquarians). By 23 October there is mention in the minutes of Stern, and by January 1811 of Canova. Included in BG 3.132 is also a roughly scrawled list, undated, but perhaps an *aide-mémoire* for someone sending out notices of meetings: Tournon, Braschi, Gabrielli, Albani, Vici, Lethière, Canova, Laboureur, Stern, Camuccini, Landi, Visconti, Fea, Guattani, Ottaviani. This list is given by La Padula, *Roma e la regione*, p. 91 and Jonsson, p. 222.

The old Papal commission continued to exist, with Fea desperately trying to give precedence to the old one (ASL 85.64). The Municipality kept up the old one, and paid 24,000 frs per annum (BG 3.132, Braschi to Tournon, 28 March 1812), but with the new duties of the Accademia di S. Luca in 1810, their budget was reduced to 12,000 frs and then to 3,000 in 1812 (F 17 1091). See also Tournon to Montalivet, 6 October 1812 (ibid.).

18 For individual monuments see chapter 3. It is sad that La Padula (pp. 92ff), after an excellent and well-documented introduction, allots each only the odd line and confuses many monuments.

19 The Minister of Police, Duc de Rovigo, wrote to the Minister of the Interior, Montalivet on 8 November (F le 1568B) after corresponding with Tournon. With the suppression of 180 convents in April 1810, there was no work for builders and furniture makers. The Consulta had been giving 15,000 frs per month assistance, but this was insufficient. Work would be much better than a dole. Winter was approaching and bread cost 25 centimes a pound. More than 2,000 families were without work. It had been a year of crisis: poor grain harvests, mediocre vintage, and damaging spring floods. It was feared that crime would increase and public safety would be in danger. Action in Rome was fortunately ahead of correspondence in Paris! The idea of using the poor is credited to Tournon by his biographer (Moulard, vol. 2, p. 312).

20 De Gérando to Giacinto Pollani, 30 October: F le 137.

21 Valadier's report, 2 November: F le 137. Defougères, Inspector of Ponts et Chaussées, misunderstood Valadier to want to be the Engineer-in-Chief.

22 The programme of work and the six ateliers were announced in the *Giornale del Campidoglio* on 7 November.

23 De Gérando to Camporese, 6 November: BG 3.128; to Valadier: F le 137. It is time to alert the reader to a strange puzzle. All modern authorities on these archaeological undertakings, and many of his contemporaries, refer to Giuseppe Camporesi (for example, Canova and Fea, Boyer, La Padula and Jonsson). Some contemporaries, however, spell his name with 'e'. The question is easily solved: Camporese's own signature is perfectly clear.

24. Pollani to de Gérando, 6 November: F le 137. It must be in connection with

this appeal that Valadier's biographer, Ciampi, states that Tournon was unable to cope with the flood of applicants for work and that Valadier stepped in and divided hundreds into the work most suited to them and organised them into squads, achieving 'in a morning what had tired the Prefect's thoughts for days' (Ciampi, *Vita de Giuseppe Valadier*, pp. 29–30).

25 De Gérando to Collicola, 9 November: F le 137. Since Collicola only ever signed his surname on documents, his first name is unknown to me, and his short tenure as Inspector leaves him something of a mystery. I have, however, come across a Carlo Collicola, Maestro di Strade in 1805 (Camerale II, 7.208). We may be almost certain that this is the same man.

26 Ciampi gives a lively evocation in a few lines of the scene at midday, as the hour struck, and a boy shouted from a high point, 'canta il merlo', and tools were downed on all sides and a rush made for the point where 'la bobba', as the workers called the soup, was served. He depicts Valadier as tireless in making sure that the workers were adequately fed (Ciampi, p. 30).

27 De Gérando to Tournon, 11 November: F le 137, BG 3.132.

28 Collicola to de Gérando, 11 November: F le 137.

29 Unsigned report, 12 November: F le 137.

30 Meeting of the Commission, 14 November: F le 137. It was stated that 300 men, women and children were employed and 'staccati dall'ozio, e dalla miseria ricevono una porzione di zuppa economica gradita, non meno che sana; la sera sono pagati della loro giornata una porzione della loro lavoro e delle loro forze. Sono prese le misure opportune, onde una porzione del loro salario serva per provvedere di vestimento quelli, che ne abbisognano.'

31 Unsigned, undated report, with Collicola's letter to de Gérando, 23 November: F le 137.

32 Collicola to de Gérando, 26 November: F le 137.

33 Collicola to de Gérando, 29 November: F le 137.

34 Collicola to de Gérando, 4 December: F le 137. Just how far Paris was behind is revealed by a letter of Neuville of the Conseil des Bâtiments Civils to Montalivet, 13 December, saying that he had written to the Prefects on 9 October, asking what work-places for the poor could be set up, but that he had heard nothing (F 13 1568B).

35 Collicola to de Gérando, 18 December; de Gérando to Tournon, 19 December: F le 137.

36 BG 3.132.

37 Report of Camporese and Valadier, 31 December: BG 3.128.

38 Collicola to Tournon, 7 January 1811: ibid.

39 BG 3.132. It was on 9 January that a 'letter from a traveller' appeared in the *Giornale del Campidoglio*, giving a glowing report on the work in progress, and to which some have paid exaggerated attention. The Tabularium was declared cleared of modern buildings. The Temple of Saturn had been isolated. That of Vespasian was virtually excavated. The whole area of the Capitol had been transformed from a rubbish dump into a delightful garden sloping down to the Forum. The two houses there had been removed, providing an uninterrupted view from the Capitol to the Arch of Titus. The Temple of

the Dioscuroi had been cleared as had that of Antoninus and Faustina. Two hundred workers were busy on the Colosseum.

On 12 January, the next instalment declared that the Forum Boarium was clear. Plans for the Jardin du Capitole were under way, with a double row of trees to be planted around all four sides of the Palatine. The Naples road would pass under the Arch of Titus, to the Piazza Venezia via Marforio. The planting of the trees was announced on 9 March.

40 An interesting figure. In a letter to Tournon, 25 November (Comm. Emb. reg. 6), he complained of his losses with 350 inexperienced workers who did as much as only 100 trained ones, and damaged tools into the bargain. He thus proposed some recompense for himself based on the number of workers: 3 bajocchi per head would be reasonable, but he would settle for 2½. On the other hand, the registers show another side: comments of the Commission on 21 January 1812 about his profiteering on the hire of tools; and on 26 November his wall to support the Jardin du Grand César was declared badly built, and he had to pay the cost of two buttresses (Comm. Emb. reg. 1).

41 Braschi to Tournon, 23 April: BG 3.132.

42 Tournon to Montalivet, 10 June: *Lettres inédites*, vol. 1, p. 137.

43 Tournon to Montalivet, 1 May: F 13 1568B.

44 Camporese and Valadier, 29 July: BG 3.132. This publication was the first of the seven destined to appear in Valadier's (no sign of Camporese) *Raccolta delle più insigni fabbriche di Roma antica*.

45 Madelin, p. 545, La Padula, pp. 105ff., and Boyer, p. 306 all say nothing of this. For the Municipality's finances, some idea may be gained from the budget of 1812 (Tournon's report, 5 December 1811: F 20 102):

Total income: 2,950,790 frs (from a population of 135,000)
Expenses:	2,208,438, including administration	67,500
	municipal guard	80,000
	public works	87,000
	'public helps' (hospitals, etc.)	580,000
	education	220,000
	public festivals	70,000
Surplus	743,352 frs	

By way of contrast, the Arc du Carrousel in Paris cost 1 million frs, and Napoleon planned a new palace (Palais du Roi de Rome) costing 30 millions. Hautecœur describes Napoleon's 'fantaisies budgetaires' over the Embellise-ments in Paris (*Histoire de l'architecture classique en France*, vol. 5, pp. 201, 212).

46 Giovannoni and Patrizi, 'Il programma edilizio del prefetto di Roma, conte di Tournon'. The original is in the Paris archives, F 20 102.

47 Moulard, *Tournon*, vol. 2, pp. 113ff.

48 It is interesting to compare the report of the Crown Architect, Raffaele Stern, 3 August 1811 (F 20 102). The language is extremely evocative of the time and its ideals. The works were: to be 'dignes du héros qui les ordonne et propres à marquer d'une manière éclatante cette heureuse époque'; to join 'à

la magnificence qu'éxige la grandiosité de Rome un genre d'utilité et de beauté tout à fait inconnu à cette ville'. He proposed the demolition of the Borgo S. Pietro (that long-standing desire, finally accomplished this century, to the regret of all lovers of old Rome), expansion of the Piazza Trevi (how?) and demolition of part of the Palazzo Venezia (another 'accomplishment' of more recent times). Most important, everything was to be part of an imposing and magnificent general plan. For Stern at the Quirinal, see Madelin, pp. 413ff.

49 Moulard, *Tournon*, vol. 2, p. 324. For the earlier history of the Jardin du Capitole (1810), see below pp. 139ff.
50 Hautecœur, *Histoire de l'architecture*, vol. 5, p. 148.
51 Tournon to Montalivet, 4 August: BG 3.132 and F 13 1568B.
52 No note on the relationship in La Padula, p. 110. This must be Giuseppe's son, rather than his famous brother of the same name, who would not have held such an unimportant post. Compare Valadier's son, Luigi Maria, Vice-Inspector in the Jardin du Capitole and superintendent in the Forum of Trajan.
53 Camporese and Valadier to Gabrielli, 5 October: Comm. Emb. reg. 6.
54 Montalivet to Tournon, 6 October: F 13 1568B.
55 Tournon to Montalivet, 27 October: *Lettres inédites*, vol. 1, p. 159.
56 F 13 1568B.
57 Tournon to Montalivet, 7 January 1812, 1 February: F 13 1568B.
58 Montalivet to Tournon, 8 February: Comm. Emb. reg. 9, F 13 1568B.
59 Comm. Emb. reg. 9.
60 Braschi to Tournon, 6 March: Comm. Emb. reg. 9.
61 See below, p. 82. One may note that during this century there were six other quakes of force 6 or 7: on 18 February 1811 at 3.15 a.m.; 25 June 1848 at 4.40 p.m.; 1 December 1849 at 8, 9.45, and 10.30 a.m.; 6 December at 8.45 p.m.; 1 November 1895 at 4.38; and on 19 July 1899 at 2.19 p.m. See Gelli, *I terremoti di Lazio*.
62 Neuville to Montalivet, 28 March: F 13 1568B; Montalivet to Tournon, 11 April (ibid.).
63 La Padula, who mentions this (p. 110) offers no explanation. For the full story, see below, 'Embezzlement in the Forum Romanum', pp. 148ff.
64 Comm. Emb. reg. 6.
65 Tournon to Montalivet, 13 April: F 13 1568B.
66 Tournon to Montalivet, 14 April: ibid.
67 Montalivet to Tournon, 5 June: BG 3.132.
68 Tournon to Hedouville, 12 May: *Lettres inédites*, vol. 1, p. 187.
69 Comm. Emb. reg. 9.
70 Tournon to Montalivet, 20 July: F 13 1568B. This left 175,000 frs as a 'fonds commun'.
71 Daru to the Commission, 13 August: Comm. Emb. reg. 7.
72 Comm. Emb. reg. 9.
73 Tournon to Montalivet, 24 September: F 13 1568B.
74 Tournon to Montalivet, 24 October: ibid.
75 Montalivet to Tournon, 28 November: F 13 1568A.
76 Comm. Emb. reg. 9. The difference of 4 frs is caused by the odd centimes.

77 An unsigned report (BG 3.132) gives some vital dates in the history of the Commission down to the end of 1812:

27 July 1811:   the imperial decree setting up the Embellisements
27 Sept.:   work begins
23 Feb. 1812:   plans for the Forum of Trajan sent to Paris
2 Apr.:   plans for the Pantheon sent
28 Apr.:   plans for the Jardin du Capitole sent
                 deficit in funds of 270,000 frs
20 July: allocation of a further 1 million frs
19 Aug.:   trouble paying workers
10 Sept.:   100,000 frs received
29 Sept.:   authorisation sought to buy houses near the Colosseum
16 Oct.:   two houses to be demolished in the Forum of Trajan
23 Oct.:   urgent need for new funds
5 Dec.:   work held up for lack of funds: less than 5,000 frs in the treasury.

78 Montalivet to Tournon, 12 December: Comm. Emb. reg. 9.

Marita Jonsson (pp. 67ff.) points out rightly that the French bureaucrats objected ideologically to the plans: they were not *grandiose* enough, not sufficiently geometrical or classical. The implication that economy was the major concern in Paris turned out to be the very opposite of the truth: for example, Berthault's new plan for the Jardin du Capitole (below, pp. 145–8).

Who was to be sent to Rome occasioned some uncertainty. Lebas was suggested with Gisors (a note of 28 November, F 13 1568A), because, although Gisors was always sure to go, when Montalivet suggested Berthault as his companion, the other had suggested 'repugnance' at the idea (for reasons unfortunately unspecified). Suffice to say, Gisors' intuition was to be justified, as the sequel will show. Lebas had planned Parisian cemeteries, and Gisors approved of him. By early December, however, Berthault had been chosen. On 10 December, Baron Costaz, Intendant des Bâtiments de la Couronne, granted him 2½ months' leave, and Montalivet wrote setting out his duties.

A. J. B. Guy Gisors (the Younger) (1762–1835): a classicist who wanted to return architecture to 'Greek simplicity' and 'Roman grandeur', devoted to endless colonnades, niches and statues. He planned the Ecole des Beaux Arts, 1802, Napoléonville, 1811, and St Vincent de Mâcon (one of the few churches of the time). He is not to be confused with Gisors the Elder, responsible for the Hall of the Convention in the Tuileries and the Hall of the 500 in the Palais Bourbon (Chambre des Deputés). See Hautecœur, *Histoire de l'architecture*, vol. 5, pp. 185, 235, 242, 283.

Louis Berthault (d. 1823): responsible for overseeing the plans of Fontaine and Percier at Compiègne; for gardens at Malmaison, Raincy, Armainville, Condé, Basville; and the Salon of Mme Récamier, 1798. Author of *Suite de vingt-quatre vues des jardins anglais*, 1788.

79 Tournon to Montalivet, 31 December: F 13 1568A.
80 Gisors' report: F 13 1646A.
81 Berthault to Montalivet, 25 March: F 13 1568A. See Forum Romanum, p. 147.

82 Gisors to Tournon, 5 April: F 13 1568B.
83 Gisors' report to Montalivet, 8 May: F 13 1568B.
84 Ibid. and BG 3.132.
85 Gisors to Montalivet, 5 June: F 13 1568B.
86 As his expenses claim proves: 105 days in Rome.
87 By a charming oversight and with unconscious irony, Moulard suggests that
    Gisors and Berthault earned their 10,000 frs and 5,000 frs respectively (*Tour-
    non*, vol. 2, p. 335). If only he had known the rest of the story!
88 These dates must be from the time he left Paris until his return there.
89 Tournon to Montalivet, 6 January 1813: F 13 1568B.
90 Comm. Emb. reg. 9.
91 Daru's criticisms, 23 February: BG 3.132.
92 Comm. Emb. reg. 9.
93 Municipal Treasurer to Tournon, 5 June: Comm. Emb. reg. 9.
94 See below, pp. 217ff.
95 Commission meetings 13 July, 24, 28 September: Comm. Emb. reg. 1.
96 Imperial Treasury to Tournon, 8 October: Comm. Emb. reg. 9; Montalivet
    to Tournon, 4 November: BG 3.132.
97 Montalivet to Tournon, 10 January 1814: BG 3.132.
98 De Gérando to Camuccini, February 1810: ASL 171.63.
99 The date of 6 November is confirmed by the Archives Nationales, Secrétaire
    d'Etat, AF IV 495, pl. 3805, n.8. The moderns usually give the correct date:
    Boyer, articles of 1932, 1943, 1957 (see bibliography); cf. 8 Nov., Jonsson,
    p. 78 and n.107. What is amazing is that the archives of the Accademia di
    S. Luca indicate 6 *October*: the minute of thanks to the Emperor, 98.89e;
    Canova to Daru, 85.30; Daru to the Accademia, 169.78. Madelin completely
    confuses this decree with that for the Crown's excavations, implying that the
    Accademia had 200,000 frs, of which 50,000 for restoration and excavation
    (p. 376; cf. p. 537). My best thanks to the Archives de France.
        Histories of the Accademia by Misserini, pp. 347ff., Arnaud, pp. 88ff, and
    a collection, *L'Accademia di S. Luca*, 1974, pp. 22ff. pass over the period with
    a minimum of detail. Misserini says nothing about work on the monuments,
    Arnaud is interested only in Canova's relations with Napoleon, and the last
    work devotes two paragraphs to the French period! The fullest treatment is
    in Marita Jonsson's book, which devotes more attention to the Accademia
    than to any other organisation under the French.
100 By 2 February 1811 the Minister of Finances, the Duc de Gaète, was writing
    to Comte Daru, the Intendant, saying that they and the Minister of the Interior
    were *all* in charge of the Accademia by article 3 of the decree, and asking
    who should take possession of the properties in the endowment (O 2 1074).
    Daru the Elder replied that the Accademia was to hold the property and that
    the Intendant at Rome was only to supervise the restoration of monuments
    and had nothing to do with the administration of the Accademia or the insuffi-
    ciency of the funds.
101 Most professors received 1500 frs a year, beadles 500, models 450, making a
    total of 25,000 frs.

102 Daru to Canova, 8 May 1811: ASL 169.111; Valadier's report: 56.119; the Accademia's vote: 169.112.
103 Daru to Canova, 4 June: ASL 169.114; 17 June: 169.118; 24 June: 169.118. Resignations of Valadier and Camporese, 23 June: 169.119.
104 A copy in vol. 89.
105 See chapter 3, under those monuments.
106 Report of Camporese and Valadier, 3 August: ASL 169.133.
107 ASL 56.122; 173.119.
108 Meeting of 25 August: ASL 56.123.
109 Daru to Canova, 2 October: ASL 169.140, with Canova's reply; meeting of 17 November: 56.129.
110 Meeting of 17 November: ASL 56.129; Camporese and Valadier to Canova, 30 December: 171.53.
111 Accounts August–December 1811: ASL 173.34. Marita Jonsson, p. 78, is thus misleading in suggesting that the Accademia's income made it 'relatively independent of the finances of the regime', implying that Daru's supervision was nominal, and in stating that the Accademia did not pay for embellisements or excavations (p. 79).
112 See chapter 3, under these monuments. Meetings of 22 November, 23 December: ASL 59.21-3.
113 Daru to Canova, 15 April 1812: ASL 170.39.
114 Daru to Canova, 26 November: ASL 169.78.
115 Tournon to Montalivet, 6 October; Neuville to Montalivet, 19 November; Montalivet to Cadore, 26 November; Cadore to Montalivet, 4 December: all F 17 1091.
116 Cadore to Daru, 4 December: O 2 1074.
117 Daru to Canova, 22 January 1813: ASL 85.15.
118 Tournon to Canova, 28 January: ASL 85.20, 89.41. An investigation by the Accademia of its endowment exists in the Paris archives (F 17 1091). In the column of 'observations', seven times appears the note: 'il n'existe point ce local'! Errors in rent are also noted: increases (493 scudi) are outweighed by decreases (722 scudi), a loss of 229 scudi or 1,225 frs. Many revenues, moreover, had been counted twice: 448 scudi or 2,400 frs. One must admire the Academicians: for a group of despised intellectuals, they were not easily deceived.
119 Daru to Canova, 13 February: ASL 85.103, 89.41; 13 March: 85.30.
120 Canova's reply: ibid. On the Arch, see chapter 3, p. 99.
121 Daru to Canova, 9 July: ASL 85.63.
122 Valadier and Camporese's report, 28 July: ASL 85.56.
123 Braschi to Canova, 23 July: ASL 85.68.
124 Meeting of 25 July: ASL 59.31; Valadier to Canova, 12 August: 85.91; 25 August: 85.90.
125 Montalivet to Daru, 28 September: ASL 85.102.
126 Canova to Daru, 4 November: ASL 85.116.
127 Daru to Montalivet, 4 November: F 13 1646A; Daru to Canova, 17 November: ASL 85.127.
128 Daru to Canova, 30 November: ASL 85.143.

129 Antonio d'Este, *Memorie di Antonio Canova*, p. 164.

130 See above, p. 79.

131 The letter, in the archives of the Louvre, and dated 21 March 1811 was published in part by F. Boyer, 'Napoléon, Vivant Denon et les promenades publiques', p. 250–1.

132 His instructions, dated 22 March, and numbering twelve pages, may be found in O 2 1069. Suzanne d'Huart, 'Martial Daru, intendant militaire de l'Empire', adds nothing on this vital period of Daru's career, referring to Boyer's article in *Studi ... Trompeo*. The main sources for Daru's work are O 2 1069–70, 1074, 1076, 1079–81.

133 Pierre to Martial, 15 May: O 2 1069.

134 Martial to Pierre, 2 May: O 2 1081.

135 Martial to Pierre, 20 May: ibid.

136 See chapter 3.

137 Daru to Gérard, 16 June: O 2 1081.

138 One should also note Daru's spirited intervention for Raffaele Stern, whose salary of 2,400 frs was declared 'proper' by de Gérando, until it was raised in September 1811 to 6,000 frs: O 2 1069, 1074, 1080.

139 Salaries list: O 2 1076, 1080; Valadier replaces Camporese, o 2 1079.

140 Daru to Gérard, 22 June: O 2 1081.

141 Martial to Pierre, 12 July: ibid.

142 O 2 1081, 1079.

143 Martial to Pierre, 17 July: O 2 1074.

144 Pierre to Martial, 19 July: ibid.

145 Martial to Pierre, 21 July: O 2 1081.

146 Cadore to de Gérando, 5 December: O 2 1069.

147 Daru to Cadore, 1 December: O 2 1081.

148 See chapter 3, on these monuments.

149 O 2 1074. Minor errors in Giardini's French have been corrected.

150 F. Boyer studied the finds of 1811 and had to admit that, although this year saw the establishment of 'official, methodical and controlled' excavations, it was only in 1812 with the move to the Forum of Trajan that important objects were found: 'La campagne de fouilles à Rome en 1811'. We have seen, however, that not even that site, for which such great hopes were held at the time, produced very much of note.

151 Amelung, *Die Sculpturen des Vaticanischen Museums*, vol. 1, pp. 151–2 (Dacian head), vol. 1, p. 8 (woman's bust), vol. 1, p. 42 (head of Medusa), vol. 2, 303-4 (statue of Atlantis).

152 Comm. Emb. reg. 9.

153 F le 137.

3 THE MONUMENTS CLEARED AND RESTORED BY THE FRENCH

1 Valadier, 25 May 1812: BG 3.132.

2 Guattani *et al.*, 22 June: ibid.

3 30 August 1812: ASL 59.16; 13 September: 59.18; 169.83; 17 October: 169.82.

4 Vasi, *Itinerario istruttivo di Roma*, vol. 2, p. 398; Nibby, *Roma nell'anno 1838*, vol. 1, p. 470; Tournon, *Etudes statistiques*, vol. 2, p. 252.

5 Tournon to Montalivet, 4 August 1811: BG 3.132.

6 Commission, 26 September: Comm. Emb. reg. 1.

7 Camporese and Valadier to Fortuna, 28 September: BG 3.132, Comm. Emb. reg. 6.

8 Tournon to Montalivet, 19 October: F 13 1568B.

9 Comm. Emb. reg. 6. Identical figures are given on 31 December (F 13 1568B) and 31 March 1813 (Comm. Emb. reg. 9).

10 Valadier, 20 July 1812: BG 3.132.

11 Uggeri, *Journées pittoresques*, vol. 23, pp. 47ff. It is strange that Moulard in his biography of Tournon (vol. 2, p. 326) claims that this vegetation was removed.

12 Nibby, *Roma nell'anno 1838*, vol. 1, p. 470.

13 See also Vasi, *Itinerario istruttivo di Roma* vol. 1, pp. 102ff., and the drawings of Auguste Guénepin, *Roma antiqua*, Rome 1809, pp. 292ff.

14 Rossini, *Raccolta di cinquanta principali vedute*, plates 12–13.

15 Tournon, *Etudes statistiques*, vol. 2, p. 249.

16 Fea, *Indicazione del Foro Romano*, p. 3.

17 Valadier and Camporese to Canova, 15 February 1813: ASL 85.23.

18 Gisors' report, 31 March 1813: F 13 1646A; Montalivet to Tournon, 28 September: Comm. Emb. reg. 9. We may note that there is no evidence for the judgement of Madelin, *La Rome de Napoléon*, p. 545 that the mission of 1813 was 'dangerous', since it was based on the principle of 'putting a few stones of Augustus in a lot of Napoleonic marble', a view rightly rejected by F. Boyer, 'La conservation des monuments antiques'. Gisors' restraint is nowhere better illustrated than here, along with his strictures on Stern's Colosseum buttress (see above, p. 40).

19 Tournon, *Etudes statistiques*, vol. 2, p. 243.

20 Vasi, *Itinerario istruttivo*, vol. 1, pp. 100ff.

21 Nibby, *Roma nell'anno 1838*, vol. 2, p. 248; Lanciani, *Sulle vicende edilizie di Roma*, p. 50.

22 Tournon to Montalivet, 6 March 1812: F 13 1568B. Yet its only mention in La Padula, *Roma e la regione nell'epoca napoleonica* is p. 166, where the work's initiation is dated erroneously to 30 December 1811. Boyer, *Le monde des arts* mentions the basilica intermittently (pp. 307, 308, 309, 312). Best of the modern works is Marita Jonsson, *La cura dei monumenti*, pp. 87ff.

23 Tournon to Montalivet, 4 August: BG 3.132.

24 Camporese and Valadier to Fortuna, 28 September: ibid.

25 Fortuna to Gabrielli, 30 September: Comm. Emb. reg. 6.

26 Camporese and Valadier to Fortuna, 30 September: ibid.

27 Tournon to Montalivet, 19 October: F 13 1568B.

28 Tournon to Montalivet, 8 January 1812: ibid.

29 Comm. Emb. 14 January: Comm. Emb. reg. 1.

30 We should note the discovery on 29 April 1812 of a famous brick-stamp which was to cause so much controversy: 'ex fig Domitianis minor Opus doliare ex

praed. DDNN' (*CIL* 15.180). See Guattani, *Memorie enciclopediche 1817*, pp. 109–20. It was found in the external buttress ('contraforte esteriore') (Fea, *Frammenti de' fasti consolari*, p. 109), and, moreover, in the presence of Fea, Clemente Giardini, Daru's Inspector, and Luigi Valadier, the famous architect's son (Fea, *La Basilica di Constantino*). In his *Varietà di notizie*, p. 73 (a reprint of an article in the *Diario di Roma*, Saturday, 4 August 1818), Fea mentioned finding brick-stamps in almost all pieces of the great vault of the basilica when they were being broken to clear the site. He actually saved them! They read OFFSRFDOM (*CIL* 15.1569): i.e. Officina summae rei fisci Domitiana.

31 Visit of 13 April 1812: ASL 59.7; report, 24 April: 171.61; 14 June: 59.9.

32 ASL 169.65, 68, 82, 83, 87; 170.2; 59.18; 85.25, 26, 49, 47.

33 I have not come across either of these views. Tournon to Montalivet, 2 June: F 13 1568A.

34 Fragments given to the Vatican Museum, August and September: O 2 1081.

35 Valadier's report: Comm. Emb. reg. 1.

36 Tournon to Montalivet, 6 January 1813: F 13 1568B; Braschi to Tournon, 13 January: Comm. Emb. reg. 9; Tournon to Montalivet, 4 February: F 13 1568A; Camporese's plan, 10 February: Comm. Emb. reg. 8.

37 Gisors' report, 31 March: F 13 1646A. Uggeri, *Journées pittoresques*, vol. 23, pp. 7ff. also mentions these intrusions: the walling in of windows, the great supporting pylons, the leaving of only three niches in the upper windows. When he wrote, the garden of the Mendicanti was still in existence, and some building still occupied the western apse.

38 Fragments given to the Vatican Museum, April: O 2 1081.

39 Tournon to Montalivet, 8 June: F 13 1568B; 5 July: 1568A.

40 Comm. Emb. reg. 6.

41 Comm. Emb. reg. 5.

42 Comm. Emb. reg. 9.

43 Tournon, *Etudes statistiques*, vol. 2, p. 243.

44 Tournon, *Mémoire*, p. 46. For illustrations of the Basilica in 1814, by Pierre Martin Gauthier, see *Roma antiqua*, pp. 209ff.

45 Camporese and Valadier to Fortuna, 11 October: BG 3.132.

46 Comm. Emb. reg. 1 (21 October).

47 Ibid. (23 October).

48 Giulio Camporese to Braschi, 22 October: Comm. Emb. reg. 6.

49 Norvins to Tournon, 24 October: Comm. Emb. reg. 9.

50 Daru to the secretary of the Prefecture, 25 October: ibid.

51 Marita Jonsson, p. 87, alone of the modern accounts mentions this affair – in a few lines.

52 Above, pp. 39–41.

53 Tournon, *Etudes statistiques*, vol. 2, p. 243.

54 69 scudi 70 bajocchi, 1 September (decree no. 653); 12.75, 20 September (859); 28.65, same date (861); 23.30, 10–25 September (942); 24. 25, 12–18 November (1,356). Further payments appear under 1810: at the Colosseum and other unspecified monuments, 29 January–10 March: 921 frs (2,754); in the arena under Lucangeli, 23 November, 64 frs (4,623).

55 Braschi to de Gérando, 17 February: F le 156.

56 Olivetti to de Gérando, 24 February: ibid.

57 De Gérando to Tournon, 19 July: BG 3.132; de Gérando to Consulta, 2 November (decree no. 4472).

58 De Gérando to Tournon, 19 July: F le 147; 13 August: BG 3.132.

59 De Gérando to Tournon, 12 September: BG 3.132; Tournon to the colonel at the fort, 26 September: F le 156. Lucangeli's models still exist: *Roma antiqua*, p. xxv.

60 Stern to Tournon, 29 October: BG 3.132; Valadier to Braschi, 15 November: ibid.; Tournon to the Consulta, 28 December: F 13 1568A.

61 13 February 1811: BG 3.132.

62 Probably Daru's surveyor, Giuseppe Bernasconi, who retired after an apopleptic attack in November 1811 (see p. 88).

63 Report on the Colosseum, 31 May: O 2 1081.

64 Daru's report, 1 December: ibid.

65 Daru the Elder to Daru, 13 July: O 2 1069.

66 Material given to the Vatican Museum: O 2 1081.

67 Daru's report, 10 November: ibid.

68 Daru's report, 1 December: ibid.

69 ASL 169.129; 89.115; 169.137, 139, 141, 143, 144, 148, 150; 173.34; 169.103.

70 Valadier and Camporese, 13 November: BG 3.132.

71 Comm. Emb. reg. 6.

72 Tournon to Montalivet, 16 April: F 13 1568A.

73 Comm. Emb. reg. 1: 28 April.

74 ASL 59.11, 17.

75 ASL 59.18.

76 Comm. Emb. reg. 1 (22 September).

77 See above, p. 82.

78 Valadier and Camporese, 19 November: ASL 169.75; Daru to Camporese, 26 November: 169.80; Daru to the Accademia: 169.78; work on the pylons and arches: 169.65, 67; 85.2, 23.

79 State of demolitions, 31 March 1813: F 13 1646A.

80 Daru to Gisors, 3 April: F 13 1568B

81 Daru to Gisors, same date: F 13 1646A.

82 Fea, *Notizie degli scavi nell'Anfiteatro Flavio*, p. 5.

83 Fea, *Fasti*, p. 65.

84 Camporese and Valadier to Canova, 24 July: ASL 85.59; 31 July: 85.61.

85 Daru to Canova, 9 September: ASL 85.107; report of Valadier, Giardini and Bianchi: 85.109.

86 Bianchi, Giardini and Valadier to the Commission, 14 September: Comm. Emb. reg. 1; Daru to Tournon, 20 October: Comm. Emb. reg. 9.

87 Daru to Canova, 27 October: ASL 85.121; Valadier to Canova, 30 October: 85.120.

88 ASL 85.114.

89 Daru to Canova, 11 November: ASL 85.131.

90 Comm. Emb. reg. 1 (4 January 1814).

91 Daru to Gisors, 3 April: F 13 1568B.
92 Tournon, *Etudes statistiques*, vol. 2, pp. 249ff.
93 *Giornale del Campidoglio*, 7 November 1810: clearing the imperial entrance;
    14, 28 November, 9 January 1811: the porticoes; 19 March: northern retaining
    wall; 20 April: outer steps, paving, drain to Tiber, arena; 3 June: internal
    excavations complete; *Giornale politico*, 2 January 1812, 1 April: piazza begun,
    arena continuing; 20 February 1813: substructures of the arena; 3, 5, 10, 19
    May: the great Colosseum debate (see below, pp. 217–37) 15 November 1813.
        The contemporary French archaeologist, Petit-Radel, who visited Rome in
    1811 or 1812 ascribed the clearing of the porticoes to Pius VII! The periphery
    had been cleared and the steps found 'some years ago'. Now the arena was
    being cleared, so that the interior was accessible, and in fact a basin for *nauma-
    chiai* – which did not improve the health of the quarter (*Voyage historique*,
    vol. 2, p. 346). The French expert was hardly complimentary to one of the
    greatest of the administration's undertakings.
94 Uggeri, *Journées pittoresques*, vol. 23, pp. 21ff.
95 Charlotte Eaton, *Rome in the nineteenth century*, vol. 1, p. 132. In the next
    volume (vol. 2, p. 71) she credits the French with cleaning the Augean stable
    that was the amphitheatre – and claims that they shot the hermit who lived
    in the arena!
        Other accounts, contemporary and later, add nothing of substance or detail:
    Fea, *Nuova descrizione*, vol. 2, pp. 298ff.; Nibby, *Del Foro Romano*, p. 235,
    Itinerario di Roma, vol. 1, pp. 221ff., *Roma nell'anno 1838*, vol. 1, p. 408
    (misdating the finding of Lampadius' inscription to 1814, and Basilius' to 1813);
    Ciampi, *Vita di Giuseppe Valadier*, p. 34 (claiming that Valadier excavated
    the arena); Gori, *Le memorie storiche ... dell'Anfiteatro Flavio*, pp. 105ff.
    (with the same claim); Colagrossi, *L'Anfiteatro Flavio*, pp. 231ff. (and again).
    The same author preserves the bizarre note that in 1832 the Secretary of State,
    Cardinal Bernetti, proposed that the Colosseum be used as a cemetery. The
    plan was abandoned on the grounds that it was too wet for quick decomposition
    and that the hills around would prevent the dissipation of effluvia!; La Padula,
    Roma e la regione, pp. 92ff. (most perfunctory); Boyer, *Le monde des arts*,
    pp. 282, 297, 303, 309 (the same); Michela di Macco, *Il Colosseo*, pp. 99–101
    (some commendable use of S. Luca archives; Valadier and Camporese planned
    the excavations, but Camporese revealed the arena); Marita Jonsson, *La cura
    dei monumenti*, pp. 90ff. (the best recent account).
96 BG 3.132.
97 Fea to Tournon, 18 March 1811: ibid.
98 ASL 59.9.
99 Comm. Emb. reg. 9.
100 F 13 1568B.
101 Fea, *Iscrizioni di monumenti*, p. 3.
102 Guattani, *Memorie enciclopediche 1817*, pp. 37–52.
103 Nibby, *Del Foro Romano*, p. 163 (no precise date in his *Itinerario di Roma*,
    vol. 1, p. 190 or *Roma nell'anno 1838*, vol. 2, p. 152) and Fea, *Nuova descrizione*,
    vol. 2, p. 271.

104 *Diario di Roma*, Wednesday, 5 March 1817 (reprinted in his *Varietà di notizie*, p. 66); Lanciani, *Ruins and excavations*, p. 260; Moulard, *Tournon*, vol. 2, p. 237.

105 Tournon to Montalivet, 5 April: F 13 1568A.

106 Platner-Ashby, *Topographical dictionary*, p. 133, dates nothing except the removal of the steps in 1903! G. Lugli, *Roma antica*, Rome 1946, p. 154, incredibly mentions only the partial uncovering of the inscription in 1553. E. Nash, *Pictorial dictionary*, 1968, vol. 1, p. 280 dates the find only to 1813.

107 Bianchi to Daru: Comm. Emb. reg. 9.

108 See Visconti's obituary by L. Cardinali in *Atti Accad. Arch.* 6, 1836, 415ff. Petit-Radel, *Voyage historique*, vol. 2, p. 331 attributes the identification to the researches of Visconti.

It will not be amiss here to note that the subsequent excavations by the Duchess of Devonshire are also incredibly confused by modern references, being dated 1816 (Valadier, *Raccolta*, 5 bis, 1818; Nibby, *Del Foro Romano*, p. 163, *Itinerario di Roma*, vol. 1, p. 190), 1817 (Nibby, *Roma nell'anno 1838*, vol. 2, p. 156), and 1818 (Fea, *Nuova descrizione*, vol. 2, p. 271). The truth can easily be found by consulting the letters in the *Diario di Roma* by the director of the work, the Swedish orientalist, Johann David Akerblad, on 18 and 25 July 1818. The excavations began, he explains, on 19 December 1816 and found the pyramid of eleven marble steps on which the column rested at 35 palms (7.7m) depth, on the ancient travertine paving of the Forum. It is notable that Fea also took a leading hand in the reports in the *Diario*: 5 March, 27 September 1817 and 4 August 1818. Charlotte Eaton, *Rome in the nineteenth century*, vol. 1, p. 294 credits the Duchess with finding the inscription!

Dorothy Stuart's otherwise admirable biography of the Duchess, *Dearest Bess*, 1955, p. 244 talks of the 'discovery' of the column. It did not have to be discovered at all, having, of course, always stood out from the debris of the Forum.

109 De Fredis is buried in S. Maria in Aracoeli: his tombstone mentions the find.

110 Lanciani, *Storia degli scavi*, vol. 1, p. 222, vol. 2, p. 228.

111 Zorzi, *I disegni delle antichità di Andrea Palladio*, 1959, figs. 89–95.

112 Giovanni Bellori, *Le pitture antiche delle grotte di Roma ... intagliate ... da Pietro Santi Bartoli ... et descritte da Giovanni Bellori*, Rome 1706; Comte de Caylus, *Recueil de peintres antiques*, Paris 1757; Charles Cameron, *Les bains des romains*, Paris 1772.

113 Ludovico Mirri (1747–1824) was born at Forli, where he practised as an architect, building the church of La Madonna del Fuoco, and the palazzi Orselli and Romagnoli. For the early history of the monument, see Nibby, *Roma nell'anno 1838*, vol. 2, pp. 807ff. and Weege, 'Das Goldene Haus des Nero'.

114 Weege, p. 139. Of works on the French excavations, only Marita Jonsson, *La cura dei monumenti*, pp. 89ff., gives any account, because of her interest in the Accademia di S. Luca.

115 Visconti's report, 27 March 1810: F le 157.

116 Consulta, decree no. 2978.

117 Valadier's report, F le 157.

118 Perhaps to about this time belongs an undated report by Giuseppe Radici, Inspector of Antiquities at Tivoli, who had been appointed by Fea to clear the rooms. He had found new ones unknown to Mirri, and noted that Miollis, Valadier, Fea and Visconti had visited the ruins. Work had stopped because of the long distance to the dump, but a new site, closer to the work, had been found. Radici concluded by asking de Gérando for ten convicts to complete the task (F le 157).

119 Consulta, decree no. 4472.

120 Report of 16 June 1811: O 2 1082.

121 Report of 1 October: O 2 1074.

122 Daru to Daru the Elder, 1 December: O 2 1082.

123 O 2 1078–9. Guattani, *Memorie enciclopediche 1817*, p. 131 stated that the architect in 1812 and 1813 was Tancioni, who is unknown to Thieme Becker's *Lexikon*.

124 ASL 59.21, 23, 25, 26; Valadier to Canova: 85.117, 120; Daru to Canova: 59.35; 85.143.

125 Daru to Gisors, 13 April 1813: F 13 1568B.

126 Comm. Emb. reg. 1 (meetings of May and December 1814).

127 *Giornale politico*, 2 January 1812: new pictures; 1 April: work almost finished; 18 April: Fea's lecture to the Accademia on the Christian oratory; 20 February 1813.

128 Tournon, *Etudes statistiques*, vol. 2, p. 251.

129 Guattani, *Memorie enciclopediche 1817*, pp. 131–5; echoed by Uggeri, *Journées pittoresques*, vol. 23, pp. 65ff.

130 Tournon, *Etudes statistiques*, vol. 2, p. 252.

131 See below, pp. 205–16.

132 BG 3.132.

133 Tournon to Collicola, 4 January 1811: ibid.

134 Decree of 11 January 1811: ibid.

135 Ibid.

136 Ibid.

137 Camporese and Valadier, October: ibid.; Tournon to the Consulta, 28 December: F le 1568B.

138 Comm. Emb. reg. 6.

139 Comm. Emb. reg. 7; F le 1658B. The total counts odd centesimi!

140 Principe Gabrielli was, of course, assistant to the Mayor, Duca Braschi.

141 Valadier's report, 12 July: BG 3.132.

142 Uggeri, *Journées pittoresques*, vol. 23, pp. 49ff.

143 Nibby, *Roma nell'anno 1838*, vol. 2, p. 668 mentions only his own excavations in 1830; Lanciani, *Ruins and excavations*, p. 514 notes only the excavations of 1551! A. Muñoz, *Il restauro del tempio della Fortuna Virilis*, Rome 1925, p. 5 reminds his readers that the Commission des Embellisements achieved only the smallest part of its aims; La Padula, *Roma e la regione* makes only the barest mention, pp. 92, 93, 94, 117; Boyer, *Le monde des arts* does the same, pp. 307, 310, 312; Marita Jonsson, *La cura dei monumenti* has only one page (55), relying on newspapers.

For the Fascist clearances, see my 'Augusti manes volitant per auras', 20ff.

144 Uggeri, *Journées pittoresques*, Supplement vol. 1, pp. 53ff.; Nibby, *Roma nell-'anno 1838*, vol. 2, p. 33; R. Delbruck, *Die drei Tempel am Forum Holitorium*.

145 Bildt, 'Die Ausgrabungen C. F. von Fredenheim auf den Forum Romanum'.

146 Eustace, *Classical tour through Italy*, vol. 1, pp. 369, 373.

147 Tournon, *Etudes statistiques*, vol. 2, pp. 237ff.

148 Tournon to de Gérando, 24 October 1810: F le 139.

149 Tournon to de Gérando, 17 November: F le 137.1.

150 On 21 March, Vivant Denon had declined the offer to direct excavations in Rome (see above, p. 86). Incorporated in this refusal was a lengthy proposal for a garden of the Capitol, Forum and Palatine (Paris, Archives des Musées du Louvre, Correspondance des Directeurs 1808–11, reproduced by Boyer, *Le monde des arts*, p. 305). Since Tournon had already made such a proposal to de Gérando in October the previous year, the Prefect must be given some credit for the plan. The great detail and technicality of the project, however, prove that professional architects lay behind it. Thus Marita Jonsson, *La cura dei monumenti*, p. 54 convincingly suggests Valadier and Camporese.

The question of the supervision of the project, raised by La Padula, *Roma e la regione*, p. 116 is linked but different. La Padula begins by claiming that Camporese was entrusted with this, but he goes on to admit that the documents show him and Valadier 'almost always summoned as colleagues'. The archives do indeed show them working in tandem.

151 De Gérando to Tournon, 19 November: F le 137.1.

152 BG 3.132 (6 November); Ferrari to Gabrielli, 5 November: ibid. These are the buildings marked FF and GG on the plan. Tournon to Braschi, 12 November: ibid.

153 Monati's valuations, 30 November: Comm. Emb. reg. 6.

154 Valadier to Collicola, 8 December: BG 3.132. This list progresses from the Arch of Titus to the Arch of Severus and then along the foot of the Capitol and that of the Palatine. The Università (or Confraternità) dei Falegnami had the church of S. Giuseppe in the Forum next to SS. Luca e Martina. I cannot identify any church of S. Cecilia save the famous one in Trastevere, nor the church of S. Chiara di Gallese.

155 BG 3.132.

156 Attached to Consulta decree no. 5182, 28 December.

157 BG 3.128.

158 Ibid.

159 Director General of the Comptabilité des Communes to Tournon, 16 February: Comm. Emb. reg. 9; Tournon to Braschi, 1 March: BG 3.132, informing him of the new grant.

160 Tournon to Montalivet, April: F 13 1568B. The 'Confraternité des Serruriers' must be the Confraternità de' Ferrari, already mentioned. The Olivetani (Benedettini di Monte Oliveto) have held S. Francesca Romana since 1352. The Blasi foundry in August 1800 was casting a bell for S. Maria in Aracoeli weighing 3,000 pounds! (ASR Camerlengato I.4.37).

161 Tournon to Montalivet, 19 October: F 13 1568B.

162 Camporese and Valadier to Braschi, 23 October: BG 3.132.

163 Tournon to Montalivet, 12 November: F 13 1568B; Comm. Emb., 26 November: BG 3.132; Camporese and Valadier's valuation, 30 November: ibid.

164 Comm. Emb. reg. 6.

165 Fea, *Fasti*, p. 32. The great historian, Barthold Georg Niebuhr was in Italy in 1826. In a letter to the Berlin Academy, 20 November, he wrote: 'Bey den 3 Säulen, angeblich vom T. Iovis Statoris, graben zehn Galeerensklaven, jede fünf Minuten einen Spatenvoll Schutterde aussteckend (sic). Hier was zur Zeit des sehr fleissigen Grabens in der Zeit der Franzosen ein neues Bruckstück der Capitolinischen Fasten gefunden worden.' (A. Harnack, *Geschichte des Preussischen Akademie*, vol. 2, p. 392). In his standard edition of the Fasti, Attilio Degrassi commented that it was uncertain whether this was the fragment possessed by Bartolomeo Pinelli (147–142 BC) or that discovered by P. Mingazzini in the Palazzo Origo in 1925 (297–267 and 214–208 BC) (Degrassi, *Inscriptiones Italiae*, vol. 13, pt 1, p. 4). Degrassi's circumstantial discussion, mentioning leading figures of the time of the French occupation, lends credence to the Niebuhr reference. The main problem is that no scholar of the time, notably Fea in his *Fasti*, refers to such a fragment, and it surely could not have gone unnoticed. It seems, indeed, most likely that careless reference to the list of the augurs as 'fasti' misled Niebuhr: a very easy misunderstanding.

166 Tournon to Montalivet, 1 February 1812: F 13 1568A; 12 February: F 13 1568B; 2 March, 21 March: ibid.

167 Comm. Emb. meeting 28 April: Comm. Emb. reg. 1.

168 Valadier's report, 20 July: BG 3.132. This document occupies most of La Padula's account of the Jardin du Capitole (*Roma e la regione*, pp. 116ff.).

169 Comm. Emb. reg. 7.

170 Camporese and Valadier to Commission, 28 September: BG 3.132.

171 Comm. Emb. reg. 1. The round sums paid to Pereyre, Pianetti and Blasi were only instalments (see below, p. 147).

172 Berthault to Tournon, 13 February: Comm. Emb. reg. 9.

173 Gisors to Montalivet, 8 March: F 13 1568B.

174 23 March: Comm. Emb. reg. 9.

175 Berthault's report, 25 March: F 13 1568A.

176 For immoderate praise of this project, see P. Pinon in *Forma*, 1985, 31. For Berthault's plan for the Palatine, see below, p. 170.

177 Tournon to Montalivet, 1 June: F 13 1646A.

178 Tournon to Montalivet, 8 June: F 13 1568B.

179 Bianchi's report, 30 September, 2 December: BG 3.132.

180 Charlotte Eaton, *Rome in the nineteenth century*, vol. 1, p. 284, and cf. p. 122.

181 In November 1814 the Olivetani monks attempted to regain the land resumed from S. Francesca Romana. Cardinal Rivarola, head of the Papal Commission, admitted that this would excite 'universal criticism' and that it would be vandalism to hide again such interesting discoveries made at considerable public expense. Some compensation from the treasury was therefore proposed. The

monks, however, were not satisfied. Rivarola decided on 'una limitata precinzione' – obviously giving in to the monks – and the well-known Lezzani won the contract (Comm. Emb. reg. 1).

182 Nibby, *Roma nell'anno 1838*, vol. 2, pp. 183ff.

183 Cerasoli, 'La Colonna Traiana e le sue adiacenze nei secoli XVI e XVII'. Fea states that most of the expenses for the column by Sixtus went on the gilded statue of St Peter (!) and that the Roman people paid 6,000 of the 10,000 scudi for the demolitions (*Miscellanea*, vol. 2, pp. 9–11).

184 Ricci, *Il mercato di Traiano*.

185 Forsyth, *Remarks on antiquities*, p. 124. The only sign of activity in 1810 was Fea's use of the antiquities tax to clear grass and plants from the pedestal and top of the column at a cost of 3.5 scudi (BG 3.132).

186 Comm. Emb. reg. 6: 1 October 1811.

187 BG 3.132.

188 Comm. Emb. reg. 1: 26 November.

189 Comm. Emb. reg. 1: 3 December.

190 The plans were identified by La Padula, 'Lavori francesi' pp. 456ff. as S. Luca folio 236, signed by Valadier. Elise Debenedetti, *Valadier*, p. 63, gives S. Luca 2,680–2. Comm. Emb. reg. 1: 14, 21 January 1812.

191 Tournon to Montalivet, 24 February: F 13 1568A.

192 Comm. Emb. reg. 6: 15 March.

193 Tournon to Montalivet, 21 March: F 13 1568B; 24 March: F 13 1568A. On 10 April, the Council of the Prefect, on the advice of Valadier and Camporese, accepted the tender of Lezzani for the construction of the surrounding wall: BG 3.132.

194 Daru to Daru the Elder, 14 May: O 2 1081.

195 Comm. Emb. reg. 6.

196 Tournon to Montalivet, 2 June: F 13 1568A; Comm. Emb. reg. 1: 28 July.

197 F 13 1568B.

198 Tournon to Montalivet, 5 September: F 13 1568A.

199 Valadier and Camporese's report, 3 October: BG 3.132; Comm. Emb. reg. 1: 6 October; Montalivet, 28 November: Comm. Emb. reg. 9, F 13 1568B.

200 Comm. Emb. reg. 1: 22 December.

201 Tournon to Montalivet, 1 January: F 13 1568A; 6 January: 1568B.

202 Gisors' report, 23 February: Comm. Emb. reg. 1; F 13 1568A.

203 Camporese to Tournon, 13 April: BG 3.132; F 13 1646A.

204 Tournon to Montalivet, 5 April: F 13 1568A.

205 Unsigned report to Montalivet, 1 June: Comm. Emb. reg. 9.

206 Tournon to Montalivet, 5 July: F 13 1568B.

207 Canova to Tournon, 15 July: Comm. Emb. reg. 9.

208 Comm. Emb. reg. 8.

209 Fauchat, Head of the Second Division of the Ministry, to Montalivet, 21 August: F 13 1568B.

210 Tournon to Montalivet, 6 September: Comm. Emb. reg. 9. Bianchi's report, 30 September: BG 3.132.

211 Valadier's report, 4 October: BG 3.132.

212 Bianchi's report, 6 November: ibid. There is a strange note that it was his plan for the Forum which was unanimously approved by the Commission des Embellisements on 7 December 1813 (Comm. Emb. reg. 1). La Padula, 'Lavori francesi' pp. 456ff. suggests that it was the Accademia di S. Luca which forced the Commission to re-examine the project. He further identified Bianchi's plans with the one in Comm. Emb. reg. 8, published by Tournon in his *Etudes statistiques*, vol. 2, p. 285. Since the essential change was the preservation of Nome di Maria, this was rather the result of Austrian intervention (see above).

Marita Jonsson further objects (recte) that Bianchi was hardly in a position to have played such an influential part in such an important piece of planning and that he only advised Camporese and Valadier (*La cura dei monumenti*, p. 78.)

213 Daru to Daru the Elder, 3 April: F 13 1568B.

214 Biographies of Valadier, as usual, give him the sole credit: Ciampi, *Vita di Giuseppe Valadier*, p. 76; Visconti, *Biografia del cavaliere Giuseppe Valadier*, p. 8. Valadier's connection was partly inherited from his father, Luigi, who had made a silver model of the column for the Elector of Bavaria (Guattani, *Roma descritta*, vol. 1, p. 4).

215 This seems to have been correctly noted by Gasparoni, *Biografia di Giuseppe Camporese*, p. 11, who mentions the uncovering of the basilica and the replacing of the remains of the columns; see also Guattani, *Memorie enciclopediche 1817*, pp. 135ff.

216 This is in contrast to his unappreciative remarks to Montalivet, above, p. 156.

217 Tournon, *Etudes statistiques*, vol. 2, pp. 244, 253.

218 Tournon, *Mémoire*, p. 51. For accounts in the *Giornale politico*, see 2 January, 1 April 1812, 22 February, 15 November 1813. For other references, see Fea, *Notizie degli scavi nell'Anfiteatro Flavio e nel Foro Traiano*, pp. 13ff.; Uggeri, *Journées pittoresques*, vol. 23, pp. 30ff.; Guattani, *Memorie enciclopediche 1817*, pp. 135ff., calling the work 'strepitoso' (clamorous); Nibby, *Itinerario*, vol. 1, pp. 310ff., *Roma nell'anno 1838*, vol. 2, pp. 183ff. More recently, Boyer, *Le monde des arts*, pp. 299ff.; La Padula, *Roma e la regione*, pp. 119ff.; Jonsson, *La cura dei monumenti*, pp. 63ff., 74ff.; Amici, *Foro di Traiano*, pp. 3ff. It is striking that no mention is made of the French excavations in any work on the column (Lehmann-Hartleben, Florescu, Rossi) or in Petit-Radel, *Voyage historique*, vol. 2, p. 287.

219 Stendhal, *Vie de Rossini* (works ed. Martineau, vol. 11, p. 264); *Rome, Naples et Florence*, 1826. See also *Promenades dans Rome*, under 4 March and 15 June.

220 Amici, *Foro di Traiano*, pp. 3ff.

221 Comm. Emb. reg. 1.

222 Fea, *Fasti*, p. 111.

223 Fea, *Iscrizioni di monumenti pubblici*, pp. 7ff.; *Varietà di notizie*, pp. 48ff., 65.

224 Fea, *Notizie degli scavi nell'Anfiteatro Flavio e nel Foro Traiano*, pp. 13ff.

225 Guattani, *Memorie enciclopediche 1817*, pp. 135ff.

226 Uggeri, *Journées pittoresques*, vol. 23, p. 42.

227 Ritterling, *Real Encyclopädie*, ed. Pauly-Wissowa, 1893–, vol. 12, p. 1,776.

228 See the illustration in Lanciani, *Ruins and excavations*, p. 463.

229 Goethe, *Italienische Reise*, 16 July 1787.

230 Consulta decree no. 1391.

231 F 17 1091. The story is told in detail, for once (because of its conciseness?), at least by Boyer, *Le monde des arts*, pp. 290ff. La Padula, *Roma e la regione* ignores it. See also Boyer, 'Projets napoléoniens pour le Mausolée d'Auguste'.

232 Tournon, *Mémoire*, p. 50.

233 Visconti's report, 25 November 1809: F le 156. From this meagre description, the 'baths' seem to be the cellar under the lararium of Domitian's palace: see Lanciani, *Ruins and excavations*, p. 159.

234 Tournon's decree, 4 August: Comm. Emb. reg. 1, F 13 1568B.

235 Tournon to Montalivet, 6 March 1812: ibid; accounts: ibid.

236 Berthault's report, 25 March 1813: F 13 1568A.

237 Gisors' report, 7 April: ibid.

238 F 13 1568B.

239 See above, pp. 41ff.

240 Consulta decree no. 186, which La Padula, *Roma e la regione*, p. 121 dates to 1809; Stern to Tournon, 29 October: BG 3.132. His earlier appeals he dates 5 September and 14 November 1809 and 3 April 1810.

241 Commission des Monuments, 30 October: BG 3.132; de Gérando to Braschi, 15 November: Comm. Emb. reg. 6; Commission, 11 December: BG 3.132.

242 Daru to Canova, 17 July 1811: ASL 169.124.

243 Valadier to Tournon, 27 May: ASL 169.117.

244 Accademia, 25 August: ASL 56.123; September: 169.135, 137; October: 169.142; December: 171.52. Costs: 173.34.

245 Comm. Emb. reg. 1: 21 January 1812.

246 Tournon to Montalivet, April: F 13 1646A.

247 Valadier's report, 20 July: Comm. Emb. reg. 8.

248 Montalivet to Tournon, 13 November: F 13 1568B; Comm. Emb. reg. 1: 8 December. Tournon to Montalivet, 13 December: F 13 1568B.

249 ASL 59.11, 13.

250 ASL 59.18, 169.3.

251 Gisors' report, 23 February 1813: Comm. Emb. reg. 9, F 13 1646A.

252 Comm. Emb. reg. 1: 23 February.

253 Valadier's estimates: F 13 1646A. It is interesting to find that while Gisors was reporting on the Romans, someone was reporting on him. An unsigned note to Montalivet, dated 1 June 1813, sets the estimates for the demolition at 338,805 frs and for the enlargement of the square at about 360,000 frs, far beyond Gisors' estimates. The author admits that this is very expensive, but claims that the work is very important (Comm. Emb. reg. 9).

254 ASL 85.45, 49; 59.35.

255 Montalivet to Tournon, 13 November: Comm. Emb. reg. 9.

256 Tournon, *Etudes statistiques*, vol. 2, p. 254. Nothing is said of any French work in Fea, *Nuova descrizione*, vol. 2, pp. 490ff. (but he had carried out

excavations himself previously: see above, p. 42). The French are said to have had many plans but achieved little in Bartocetti, *S. Maria ad Martyres*. There is incredibly nothing of the French in Licht, *The Rotonda in Rome*, pp. 242ff. Boyer, *Le monde des arts*, pp. 287ff. devotes some pages to the Pantheon plans. La Padula, *Roma e la regione*, pp. 121ff. gives the main story with ample quotation from documents. Marita Jonsson, *La cura dei monumenti*, pp. 72, 89 is interested in Gisors.

257 Lanciani, *Ruins and excavations*, p. 486; Licht, *The Rotonda in Rome*, p. 243.

258 Tournon, *Etudes statistiques*, vol. 2, p. 244.

259 Reported in Uggeri, *Journées pittoresques*, Supplement, pp. 51ff. and plate 12. The survey was carried out by the architect Boara of Milan (unknown to Thieme Becker's *Lexikon*): 'fouille accidentale, occasionée par la restauration nécessaire'.

260 Undated report by Visconti: F le 156.

261 De Gérando to Valadier, 9 February 1810: F le 147.

262 Valadier's report, 27 February: F le 156.

263 Tournon to de Gérando, 24 October: F le 139.

264 Tournon's report, 5 December: F 20 102.

265 ASL 59.7; de Marchis' report: 170.13.

266 Rossini, *Cinquanta principali vedute*, plate 29.

267 *Notizie degle scavi*, 1878, pp. 93ff.; 1883, pp. 420ff.; 1888, pp. 276ff.

268 Rossini, *Cinquanta principali vedute*, plates 20, 27.

269 Tournon to Montalivet, 5 September 1812: F 13 1568A; 7 October, 4 November.

270 Comm. Emb. reg. 5; F 13 1568B.

271 Comm. Emb. reg. 7.

272 Tournon to Montalivet, 6 January 1813; 18 May (?): F 13 1568A.

273 F 13 1568B.

274 Moulard, in his biography of Tournon, vol. 2, pp. 313ff., states that 2,000 cu m of earth were removed, in an excavation 30 feet deep, 30 feet wide and 60 feet long, citing Tournon's *Etudes statistiques*. I cannot find any such figures there for any monument. There is nothing in Boyer, *Le monde des arts*; only an allusion in La Padula, *Roma e la regione*, p. 92.

275 For Menager's excavations and drawings, see *Roma antiqua*, pp. 93ff.

276 Ottaviani, 31 July 1809: F le 156.

277 Valadier to de Gérando, 15 August: ibid.

278 Visconti, 6 November: ibid.

279 De Gérando to the President of the Administrative Commission, 21 November: F le 148.

280 Visconti and Martorelli, 30 November: F le 156.

281 De Gérando to Valadier, April 1810: F le 148. It is undoubtedly the plan for these restorations which still exists in the Istituto di Archeologia in Rome (Coll. Lanciani 11.100, vol. 2, no. 41), reproduced in Elisa Debenedetti, *Valadier*, fig. 105 and there dated '*c.* 1815'.

282 Tournon to Olivetti, 29 September: BG 3.132.

283 Report to Olivetti, 1 October: ibid.

284 Tournon to de Gérando, 18 October: F le 148.

285 Tournon to Braschi, 19 November: BG 3.132; Orlandi's petition: F le 149.12.

286 De Gérando to Tournon, 29 December: ibid.

287 Braschi to Tournon, 30 April 1813: BG 3.132.

288 Collicola to Tournon, 7 January 1811: ibid.

289 Decree of 11 January: ibid.

290 Daru to Canova, 23 September: ASL 169.13.

291 Tournon to Montalivet, 8 January 1812: F 13 1568B.

292 Comm. Emb. reg. 6.

293 Tournon, *Mémoire*, p. 48. Otherwise, in his *Etudes statistiques*, vol. 2, pp. 242, 247, he complained of the poor taste of the façade in contrast to the elegance of the portico, whose columns had been buried above their bases. They were now clear and the Via Sacra lay exposed, along which conquerors had marched to the Capitol and prisoners had been dragged to the Mamertine.

There were short notes in the newspapers: *Giornale del Campidoglio*, 2 May 1810, announcing the proposed restoration; 7 November, the intention to employ the poor; 14 and 28 November, rapid progress; 9 January, 1811, the uncovering of the steps; *Giornale politico*, 2 January 1812, clearing down to the Via Sacra.

Valadier's *Raccolta*, vol. 1 is mainly concerned with comparison with Vitruvius' canons (confirming his early interest in restoration); Fea, *Prodromo*, p. 19 is anxious to state that Palladio's suggested cortile with Aurelius' equestrian statue has been shown to be an invention. In his *Nuova descrizione*, vol. 2, p. 277 he ignores the French work. Nibby is slightly more generous, noting the discovery of the steps and Via Sacra: *Del Foro Romano*, p. 185; *Roma nell'anno 1838*, vol. 2, pp. 634ff. Pinon in *Forma*, pp. 24ff. is excellent on the Académie's work.

294 Tournon, *Etudes statistiques*, vol. 2, pp. 242, 247.

295 Valadier to de Gérando, 6 April 1810: F le 156.

296 De Gérando to Valadier, 13 April: F le 147.

297 De Gérando to Tournon, 18 December: BG 3.128. Tournon to Montalivet, 4 February 1813: F 13 1568A.

298 Valadier and Camporese to Canova, 23 May: ASL 85.49; Daru to Canova, 14 July: 85.70; Camporese to Canova, 23 July: 85.58.

299 Comm. Emb. reg. 9.

300 F 13 1568B. Petit-Radel, *Voyage historique*, vol. 2, p. 329 knows nothing of these excavations. Guattani, *Memorie enciclopediche 1817*, pp. 101ff and Fea, *Nuova descrizione*, vol. 2, p. 273 are interested only in the later excavations (see next note). La Padula, *Roma e la regione*, p. 93 notes de Gérando's interest in the foundations.

301 'The monuments of the Roman Forum: the struggle for identity', pp. 72ff.

302 Tournon, *Etudes statistiques*, vol. 2, p. 246. Moulard, *Camille de Tournon*, vol. 2, p. 314 notes that the Prefect thought that Cicero had spoken here against Catiline: this must have been a powerful stimulus to the clearing.

303 Braschi to Gabrielli, 19 November 1810: Comm. Emb. reg. 6. Toniazzi is unknown to Thieme Becker's *Lexikon*.

304 Collicola to de Gérando, 6 December: F le 137.1.

305 Tournon to Montalivet, 5 April 1813: F 13 1568A.

306 Comm. Emb. reg. 9; F 13 1568B.

307 Rossini, *Cinquanta principali vedute*, plate 26. The same impression is given by the engraving in Fea's *Nuova descrizione*, vol. 1, pp. 253ff.

308 Fea, ibid.; Nibby, *Itinerario*, vol. 1, p. 170; *Roma nell'anno 1838*, vol. 1, p. 531.

309 Uggeri, *Journées pittoresques*, vol. 23, pp. 52ff. For other illustrations, by Jean-Louis Provost, see *Roma antiqua*, pp. 76ff.

310 Bianchi's report: BG 3.132.

311 A. Caristie, *Plan et coupe d'une partie du forum romain et des monuments sur la voie sacrée*, without pagination.

312 Fea, *Indicazione del Foro Romano* dated it 1810–. A. Muñoz says the work began in March 1814 (so after the French left!) with 700 men, 90 women and 90 boys: 'Il tempio di Venere e Roma', *Capitolium*, 1935, 215–34, at p. 223.

313 Uggeri, *Journées pittoresques*, vol. 23, pp. 61ff.

314 Tournon, *Etudes statistiques*, vol. 2, p. 248. Contemporary sources were more interested in later work: that of the French architect, Henri Landon in December 1819, who made small soundings in the *ambulacrum* and cella, and in the intention of the French ambassador, le comte de Blacas, to make an exact plan of the building (Fea, *Notizie del giorno*, 30 April 1820, reprinted in his *Varietà di notizie*, pp. 137ff.) and in the completion of the clearing by Nibby, 1827–9 (Nibby, *Roma nell'anno 1838*, vol. 2, p. 724).

315 Fea, *Fasti*, p. 110.

316 'Augusti manes volitant per auras', p. 36.

317 Tournon, *Etudes statistiques*, vol. 2, p. 246.

318 BG 3.128. The work got off to a serious start, for on 10 December, General Miollis fined the superintendents half a day's pay for not being at work by 7.45 a.m. (ibid.).

319 Collicola to de Gérando, 12 December: F le 137.1.

320 BG. 3.128.

321 Daru to Canova, 9 July 1811: ASL 169.125.

322 Daru to Daru the Elder, 13 July: O 2 1069.

323 Camporese's report: O 2 1081.

324 Daru the Elder to his younger brother, 19 July (O 2 1069) tried to sort out the confusion that had already arisen over who was to pay for the work. Daru the Younger had specified that the Accademia di S. Luca was to pay for the excavations, and that it was not to be charged against the 200,000 frs for the Crown's work. He had, however, kindly offered to lend the Accademia 4,500 frs to pay the labourers until its funds were granted. His brother warned him against such involvement with a 'learned society' and told him the payment should be by the Crown.

325 ASL 169.125: report of 19 July.

326 The reports to the Accademia are in the name of both architects, since they were reporting on *all* projects in progress. The situation was also so serious that Camporese was doubtless glad to have his colleague's support.

327 Valadier and Camporese to Canova, 22 July: ASL 169.126.

328 ASL 169.125: cf. above, n. 325.

329 Camporese and Valadier to Canova, 10 August: ASL 169.131; 31 August: 89.115; 169.135.

330 ASL 169.141, 142.

331 ASL 169.125.

332 ASL 169.148, 151, 150.

333 ASL 173.34.

334 Report of 27 February 1812: ASL 169.125.

335 Daru to Canova, 24 March: ASL 170.19.

336 Camporese to Tournon, 31 March: BG 3.132.

337 Tournon to Montalivet, 20 August: F 13 1568A.

338 Ibid.

339 F 13 1568A, Comm. Emb. reg. 5.

340 Tournon to Montalivet, 6 January 1813: F 13 1568B. *Mémoire*, pp. 49ff.

341 Tournon, *Etudes statistiques*, vol. 2, p. 246. An interesting commentary on the unexpected difficulties is provided by the *Giornale del Campidoglio*. On 14 November 1810 it announced that the work would be completed during the winter, and on 9 January 1811 that it was virtually completed. On 9 March the columns were declared cleared, and by 2 January 1812 the temple was said to be 'restored with great skill'. It was, however, only on 27 June that the real achievement was told, the restoration of the columns, and only on 22 February 1813 was it proudly announced that visitors could walk on the steps, whereas once they had been able to touch the frieze.

342 Uggeri, *Journées pittoresques*, vol. 23, p. 50 and Gasparoni, *Vita di Giuseppe Camporese*, p. 11. There is a drawing by Valadier of the project for the arrangement of the remains in the Istituto di Archeologia in Rome (Coll. Lanciani 11.100, vol. 2, no. 38) showing a retaining wall dividing the three columns from the Tabularium (reprinted in Debenedetti, *Valadier*, fig. 105).

343 Jonsson, *La cura dei monumenti*, p. 82 rightly points this out.

344 Uggeri, *Journées pittoresques*; Fea, *Nuova descrizione*, vol. 1, p. 256 says not a word about the French; Nibby, *Del Foro Romano*, p. 142; *Itinerario*, vol. 1, p. 174; *Roma nell'anno 1838*, vol. 1, pp. 541, 545.

  Even Valadier in his famous *Raccolta delle più insigni fabbriche di Roma antica*, fascicule 5, devoted to the temple, has a very unexcited description of the complex undertaking.

345 Boyer, *Le monde des arts*, pp. 282, 308 has the briefest allusions and the wrong date; La Padula, *Roma e la regione* ignores it; best is Jonsson, *La cura dei monumenti*, pp. 80ff., who gives full credit to the Accademia. Pinon in *Forma*, pp. 26–7, supposedly about the temple, relies for his main sources on the newspaper accounts, and devotes much space to the Arch of Titus!

346 Biondo, *Roma instaurata*, book 2, chapter 56; Fea, *Nuova descrizione*, vol. 3, pp. 609ff.

347 Tournon, *Etudes statistiques*, vol. 2, pp. 244, 252.

348 All these dates are quite misleading as usual, a trap for the unwary modern writers who rely on such sources instead of on the archives. Relying, for exam-

ple, on the *Giornale del Campidoglio*, Madelin, *La Rome de Napoléon*, p. 537, claimed that the work was finished by May 1810. Marita Jonsson, *La cura dei monumenti*, p. 51 accepts the same date.

349 Almost all the documents for this temple are in the Archives Nationales F le 157. Where no reference is given, this is the location. Marita Jonsson makes the extraordinary assertion that no documents survive to reconstruct the progress of the work.

350 Fea to de Gérando, 27 August 1809: F le 148.

351 F le 147.

352 The two undated reports by Visconti, F le 148.1.

353 By the standard rate, 5.35 frs = 1 scudo, Valadier's conversion is erroneous: 1,184 scudi would be 6,275 frs.

354 Jean-Baptiste Dagincourt (1730–1814), archaeologist and numismatist (*NBG*, vol. 1, p. 390). Pierre Paris (1747–1819), architect, Dessinateur du cabinet du Roi, dismissed by the Revolution, came to Italy for the third time in 1806. Works such as 'L'amphithéâtre flavien' remain in manuscript. *NBG*, vol. 39, pp. 209–10.

355 Giambattista Ottaviani, an elusive figure not found in any of the standard biographical dictionaries, known to me only as an architect who was a member of the Commission des Monuments in 1810 (above, p. 286).

356 Andrea Vici (1743–1817), chief engineer of the Département de Rome, twice president of the Accademia di S. Luca, member of the Commission des Monuments, 1810. See the obituary in Guattani, *Memorie enciclopediche 1816*, p. 167.

357 Attached to Consulta decree no. 4472.

358 BG 3.128.

359 BG 3.132.

360 Uggeri, *Journées pittoresques*, vol. 23, pp. 44ff.; Fea, *Nuova descrizione*, vol. 3, pp. 607ff.; Stendhal, *Promenades dans Rome*, under 15 June 1828. Another French observer, Petit-Radel, *Voyage historique*, vol. 2, p. 371 talks of the columns still walled in, although the steps were being uncovered and the abutting walls removed. Nibby, *Roma nell'anno 1838*, vol. 2, p. 740.

361 The temple is barely mentioned in Madelin, *La Rome de Napoléon*, p. 537; La Padula, *Roma e la regione*, pp. 92, 94; or Boyer, *Le monde des arts*, p. 295. There is no mention of French work in Platner and Ashby, *Topographical dictionary*, p. 430 (under Portunium). Lanciani, *Ruins and excavations*, p. 516 is, however, more informative than usual: 'At the beginning of this century the intercolumniations were reopened, the building was restored and protected by railings, and the roof was repaired. At the same time, the accumulation of soil between the two temples ... was removed, and the steps were exposed to view.' There is, however, the characteristic diffidence: no date, and no hint of the architect or antiquarian who proposed or directed the work.

362 Tournon's report, 5 December 1811: F 20 102.

363 'Augusti manes volitant per auras', pp. 23ff.

4 THE GREAT COLOSSEUM DEBATE

1 'Osservazioni sull'arena e sul podio dell'Anfiteatro Flavio' (note that it was

not published for ten years). The heavily polemical tone, indeed, makes one suspect, as with so many other lectures of this Academy not published until much later, that there are some additions from hindsight.

2 In Guattani, *Memorie enciclopediche*, vol. 5 (*c.* 1810), p. 142.

3 Bianchi and Re were aware that some claimed that Calpurnius was talking of a wooden structure. They understood the wood as the *pegmata* or stage machinery; Calpurnius meant the Colosseum because he mentioned a marble wall, 1.49. Calpurnius Siculus was a Neronian bucolic poet.

4 Martial Daru to Pierre Daru, 18 January 1813: O 2 1081.

5 A paper on the Domus Aurea was published in 1832; he had already written much on the Forum Trajanum; the Temple of Vespasian appeared in various works on the Forum; the last, as far as I can see, never appeared.

6 Among his sources are Plautus, *Persa* 3.3.31, and Suetonius, *Tiberius* 73, who obviously can have nothing to do with the Colosseum. Historia Augusta, *Gallienus* 12 mentions a bull in the arena. Ammianus 31.10.19 describes one hundred lions sent simultaneously 'in amphitheatrali circulo'. Historia Augusta, *Probus* 19 mentions one thousand ostriches, stags, and boars sent into the amphitheatre 'per omnes aditus'.

7 Today the text is regarded as corrupt, and the reference is to an obscene gladiator sent out of the arena; 'de ruina' is obelised now by editors: 'derisum' (Fraenkel), 'de ruma' (Housman), or perhaps just a misreading of 'harena' (Warmington).

8 We now know the identity of the author. In the collected works of Luigi Martorelli, *Opere*, appears the work in question (vol. 1, pp. 345–58). Martorelli (1760– 1831) was author of various antiquarian works such as *De' cani*, 1814, *De' medici*, 1815, *Dell'usura*, 1809, *Dissertazione sugli odori usati dagli antichi Romani*, 1812, *Dissertazione sull'orologio e sull'ore degli antichi Romani*, 1812, *Degli Ebrei*, 1826.

9 Juan Francisco Masdeu (1744–1817) was born at Palermo and died at Valencia. He was a Jesuit. His main works were *Historia critica de España y de la cultura española*, 20 vols., 1783–1805, a criticism of chronicles and historians especially to destroy the poetical traditions; *Arte poetica facil*, 1801; and *Memorial*, 1806, a satire on the French Republic.

10 The novelties seem perfectly clear in this source: rope-walkers, 'wall-climbers', acting bears, trick musicians, one thousand mimes and gymnasts, and a *pegma* which burst into flames!

11 This last I cannot trace in any bibliography or dictionary of anonymous writers, especially Melzi, *Dizionario di opere anonime e pseudonime*, 1848 (the work does not appear in the index of authors or in the main text under 'Lettera').

12 Platner and Ashby, p. 10.

13 Ward-Perkins, *Roman imperial architecture*, p. 224.

14 Colagrossi, *L'Anfiteatro Flavio*, p. 235.

15 Platner and Ashby.

16 Sear, *Roman architecture*, p. 141.

CONCLUSION

1 Comm. Emb. reg. 1.

2 Valadier, *Opere di architettura e di ornamento*, p. 7.

3 D. Angeli, *Storia romana di trent'anni 1770–1800*, Rome 1931, pp. 131, 136. See also Madelin, *La Rome de Napoléon*, pp. 676ff.

4 *Diario di Roma*, 7 May 1817; Lanciani, *Ruins and excavations*, p. 287.

5 Nibby, *Roma nell'anno 1838*, vol. 2, pp. 238ff.

6 Ibid., vol. 2, pp. 723ff.

7 Lanciani, *Ruins and excavations*, p. 338.

8 L. Canina and O. Jahn, 'Sepolcro di Marco Vergilio Eurisace', *Ann. Ist.*, 10, 1838, 202–48.

9 Lanciani, *Ruins and excavations*, p. 302.

10 Canina, 'Ultime scoperte del Foro Romano', *Ann. Ist.*, 21, 1849, 257–64.

11 A. Pellegrini, 'Orti di Asinio Pollione', *Bull. Ist.*, 1867, 109–19.

12 Lanciani, *Ruins and excavations*, p. 164.

13 Ibid., p. 525.

14 Ibid., p. 136.

15 G. Perrot, 'Les peintures du Palatin', *Rev. Arch.*, 21, 1870, 387–95; 22, 1871, 47–53, 152-8, 193–202.

16 Rosa, *Relazione*, 1873; G. Fiorelli, 'Notizie degli scavi', *NS* 1878, p. 66; G. Gatti, 'Notizie degli scavi', *NS* 1893, pp. 31, 70, 117–18, 162-3.

17 Pellegrini, 'Escavazione della basilica Giulia', *Bull. Ist.*, 1871, 225–33.

18 Lanciani, *Ruins and excavations*, p. 411.

19 Lanciani, 'Notizie degli scavi', *NS*, 1881, 255–69, 1882, 340-5.

20 Lanciani, *Ruins and excavations*, p. 188.

21 H. Jordan, *Der Tempel der Vesta*, 1886.

22 H. Jordan, 'Gli edifici antichi fra il tempio di Faustina e l'atrio di Vesta', *RM*, 1, 1886, 94–111; G. Hülsen, 'Der Regia', *JDAI*, 4, 1889, 228–53.

23 Lanciani, 'Il foro di Augusto', *BCAR*, 1889, 26ff., 73ff.

24 C. Guillaume, 'Le Panthéon d'Agrippa à propos des découvertes récentes', *Revue des deux mondes*, 112, 1892, 562–81; Licht, *The Rotonda in Rome*, pp. 247ff.

25 Lanciani, *Ruins and excavations*, p. 521.

26 C. Hülsen, *Das Forum Romanum*, pp. 41–4. One might also consult Bunsen, 'Scavi romani, escavazione del Foro Romano e delle sue adjacenze', *Bull. Ist.*, 1829, 26–36 on the resumption of work in 1827: the article is full of carelessness and adulation of Fea.

27 Folchi, 'Elogio di G. Valadier', *Atti Accad. Arch.*, 10, 1842, 508ff.

28 Eva Brues, *Raffaele Stern*, pp. 134ff.

29 Many contemporaries date the completion to 1822: Fea, *Indicazione* 1827; Nibby, *Roma nell'anno 1838*, vol. 1, p. 491; followed by Lanciani, *Ruins and excavations*, p. 201; Platner and Ashby, *Topographical dictionary*, p. 46. Other suggestions are 1821: Bunsen, *Bull. Ist.*, 1829, 32; 1823: Nash, *Pictorial dictionary*, vol. 1, p. 134. The correct dates are given by Marita Jonsson, *La cura dei monumenti*, pp. 99–116, as well as the authoritative account. For the archival sources, see ASR Camerlengato 1.4.40.106.

30 For a defence of the restoration, see, for example, Nibby, *Roma nell'anno 1838*, vol. 1, p. 491.

31 See above, p. 39. The relative costs were 21,560 scudi for Stern's buttress,

and 18,430 for Valadier's: Ciampi, *Vita di Giuseppe Valadier*, p. 54, quoting
Valadier's papers.

32 L. Canina, 'Sul ristabilmento e riparazione . . . del Anfiteatro Flavio', 169–94;
also ASR Camerlengato I.4.37 (Valadier).

33 Again, modern dates are everywhere: 1820: Ciampi, p. 54; 1822: Michele di
Macco, *Il Colosseo*, pp. 38ff.; 1825: P. Quennell, *The Colosseum*, 1981, p. 126;
1828: Nibby, *Roma nell'anno 1838*, vol. 1, p. 420, Colagrossi, *L'Anfiteatro
Flavio*, pp. 215ff. See Jonsson, pp. 117ff. for the authoritative account.

34 Valadier, *Opere di architettura e di ornamento*, p. 17.

35 Tournon, *Mémoire*, p. 43.

36 Ibid., p. 54.

37 Tournon, *Etudes statistiques*, vol. 2, p. 238.

38 Ibid., p. 242.

39 Lanciani, *Le vicende edilizie di Roma*, Rome 1878, p. 48.

40 Boyer, *Le monde des arts*, p. 312.

41 For example, the destruction of the road under the Arch of Severus, of the
steps of the Temple of the Dioscuroi, and as late as 1936 of the Meta Sudans.

42 Fiorella Bartoccini, *Roma nell'Ottocento*, pp. 322–4.

43 Tournon, *Lettres inédites*, vol. 1, p. 277.

Select Bibliography

1. ARCHIVAL SOURCES

Paris, Archives Nationales
F le 137, 139, 147, 148, 149, 156
F 13 1568, 1646
F 17 1091
F 20 102
O 2 1069, 1070, 1074, 1076, 1079, 1080, 1081

Rome, Archivio dello Stato (ASR)
Buon Governo (BG)
Camerale
Camerlengato
Commissione degli Abbellimenti (Commission des Embellisements) (Comm. Emb.)
Consulta Straordinaria

Rome, Accademia di S. Luca (ASL)

2. PUBLISHED SOURCES

Abbott, Henry, *Antiquities of Rome*, London 1818
Académie de France à Rome, *Correspondance des directeurs*, Paris 1887–
L'Accademia Nazionale di S. Luca, Rome 1974
Aite, Livia, *I tre templi del Foro Olitorio*, Rome 1981
Amelung, W., *Die Sculpturen des Vatikanischen Museums* (4 vols.), Berlin 1903–8
Amici, Carla, *Il Foro di Traiano*, Rome 1982
Angelio, P., *de privatorum publicorumque aedificorum urbis Romae eversoribus epistola*, Florence 1587
Arnaud, J., *L'Académie de S. Luc*, Rome 1886
Ashby, T., *Forty drawings of Roman scenes by British artists 1715–1850*, London 1911
    'Thomas Jenkins in Rome', *PBSR*, 6, 1913, 487–511
Aureas, H., *Un général de Napoléon: Miollis*, Paris 1961
Bartocetti, V., *S. Maria ad Martyres*, Rome 1960

Bartoccini, Fiorella, *Roma nell'Ottocento*, Bologna 1985

Bartolomeo Pinelli e il suo tempo, Rome 1983

Becattini, F., *Storia di Pio VI*, Venice 1801–2

Berlia, G., *Gérando, sa vie et son œuvre*, Paris 1942

Bertaut, J., *L'Italie vue par les Français*, Paris 1913

Bianchi, P. and Re, L., 'Osservazioni sull'arena e sul podio dell'Anfiteatro Flavio', *Mem. Accad. Arch.*, 1(2), 1823, 127–54 with three figures

Bildt, C., 'Die Ausgrabungen C. F. von Fredenheim auf den Forum Romanum', *RM*, 16, 1901, 3–20

Biondo, Flavio, *Roma instaurata*, 1446 (published Rome 1471)

Biver, Marie Louise, 'Rome, seconde capitale de l'Empire', *Rev. Inst. Napoléon*, 109, 1968, 145–54.

Bollettino delle leggi e decreti imperiali pubblicati dalla Consulta Straordinaria negli Stati Romani, Rome 1809

Boyer, F., 'La campagne des fouilles à Rome en 1811', *Bull. Soc. Nat. Antiq. Fr.*, 1957, 179–183

'La conservation des monuments antiques', *CRAIBL.*, 1943, 101–8

'Les embellisements de Rome, *Rev. Etudes Nap.*, 34, 1932, 216–29

Le monde des arts, en Italie et la France de la Révolution à l'Empire, Paris 1969

'Napoléon, Vivant Denon et les promenades publiques à Rome', *Rev. Inst. Napoléon*, 76, 1960, 249ff.

'Le Panthéon et la fontaine de Trevi dans les projets de Napoléon', *Rev. Etudes Ital.*, 1931, 210–16

'Projets napoléoniens pour le Mausolée d'Auguste et le pont d'Horatius Cocles', *Strenna dei Romanisti*, 24, 1963, 96–102

'Rome sous Napoléon et le projet d'un jardin du Capitole', *Bull. Soc. Hist. Art. Fr.*, 1932, 201–15

'Stendhal, Martial Daru et les fouilles à Rome en 1811', *Studi sulla litteratura dell' Ottocento in onore di Pietro Paolo Trompeo*, Naples 1959, pp. 145–56

Bracciolini, Poggio, *de varietate fortunae*, Paris 1723

Bracco, V., *L'archeologia classica nella cultura occidentale*, Rome 1979

Brues, Eva, *Raffaele Stern* (Doct. Diss, Bonn), 1958

Bunsen, C, 'Scavi romani: escavazioni del Foro Romano e delle sue adjacenze', *Bull. Ist. Arch.*, 1829, 26–37

Burda, H., *Die Ruinen in den Bildern Hubert Roberts*, Munich 1967

Burton, E., *Description of the antiquities and other curiosities of Rome*, Oxford 1821

Byron, Lord, *Letters and journals*, ed. Marchand (12 vols.), London 1973–82

Canina, L., *Sterramento del Foro Romano*, Rome 1818 (plan in Uggeri, *Journées pittoresques*, vol. 26)

'Sul ristabilmento e riparazione … del Anfiteatro Flavio', *Atti. Accad. Arch.*, 14, 1860, 169–94

'Sui tre templi antichi esistenti nella chiesa di S. Nicola in Carcere', *Ann. Ist.*, 7, 1850, 347–56

Carettoni, G., 'Il Foro Romano nel medio evo e nel rinascimento', *Studi Romani*, 11, 1963, 406–16

Caristie, A., *Plan et coupe d'une partie du Forum Romain et des monuments sur la Voie Sacrée indiquant les fouilles qui ont été faites dans cette partie de Rome depuis l'an 1809 jusqu'en 1819*, Rome 1821

Casiello, Stella, 'Aspetti della tutela dei beni culturali nell'Ottocento e il restauro di Valadier per l'Arco di Tito', *Restauro*, 2, 1973, 77–111

Cerasoli, F., 'La Colonna Traiana e le sue adiacenze nei secoli XVI e XVII', *BCAR*, 29, 1901, 300–8

   'Nuovi documenti sulle vicende del Colosseo dal secolo XIII al XVIII', *BCAR*, 30, 1902, 300–15

   'I restauri del Pantheon dal secolo XV al XVIII', *BCAR*, 28, 1900, 280-9

Chateaubriand, François René, *Mémoires d'outre tombe*, Paris 1849–50

Ciampi, I., *Vita di Giuseppe Valadier*, Rome 1870

Cicognara, L., *Biografia di Antonio Canova*, Venice 1823

Colagrossi, P., *L'Anfiteatro Flavio*, Rome 1913

Cole, H., *Fouché, the unprincipled patriot*, London 1971

Colonna, G. B., *Roma napoleonica, interpretazioni*, Florence 1929

Consalvi, E. (Cardinal), *Mémoires*, Paris 1864

   See also *Nel primo centenario della morte del Cardinale Consalvi*

Corbo, Annamaria, 'Gli scavi nello stato pontificio nella seconda metà del secolo XVIII', *Archeologia medioevo*, 1981, 88–103

Debenedetti, Elisa, *Valadier, segno e architettura*, Rome 1985

   'Valadier e Napoleone: diario architettonico', in *Ville et territoire pendant la période napoléonienne* (Ecole Française), Rome 1987

Delbruck, R., *Die drei Tempel am Forum Holitorium*, Rome 1903

Dictionary of national biography, London 1885–

Dictionnaire de biographie française, Paris 1933–

Dizionario biografico degli italiani, Rome 1960–

Douglas, S., *Diaries of Sylvester Douglas, Lord Glenbervie* (2 vols.), London 1928

Driault, E., *Napoléon et l'Europe*, vol. 4, *Le grand empire 1809–1812*, Paris 1924

Eaton, Charlotte, *Rome in the nineteenth century*, London 1826 (4th edn)

Emiliani, A., *Leggi bandi e provvedimenti per la tutela dei beni artistici e culturali negli antichi stati italiani 1571–1860*, Bologna 1978

Este, A. d', *Memorie di Antonio Canova*, Florence 1864

Eustace, J., *A classical tour through Italy* (4 vols.), 1815 (3rd edn)

Fauno, L., *de antiquitatibus urbis Romae*, Venice 1549

Fea, C., *Ammonizioni critico-antiquarie*, Rome 1813

   La Basilica di Costantino, Rome 1819

   Dei diritti del Principato sugli antichi edifici publici, Rome 1806

   'Dissertazione sulle rovine di Roma', in Winckelmann, *Storia dell'arte del disegno presso gli antichi*, 1783, vol. 3, 267–416

   Frammenti de' fasti consolari, Rome 1820

   L'integrità del Pantheon, Rome 1807

   Indicazione del Foro Romano, 1827 (in Bunsen)

   Iscrizioni di monumenti pubblici, Rome 1813

   Miscellanea filologica critica e antiquaria (2 vols.), Rome 1790, 1836

   Notizie degli scavi nell'Anfiteatro Flavio e nel Foro Traiano, Rome 1813

Nuova descrizione di Roma antica e moderna (3 vols.), Rome 1820

Nuove osservazioni di Carlo Fea intorno all'arena dell'Anfiteatro Flavio, Rome 1813

Prodomo di nuovi osservazioni e scoperte, Rome 1816

Relazione di un viaggio ad Ostia, Rome 1802

Varietà di notizie, Rome 1820

Folchi, C., 'Elogio di G. Valadier', *Atti. Accad. Arch.*, 10, 1842, 499–512

Ford, B., 'Thomas Jenkins', *Apollo*, 1974, 416–25

Forma, la città antica e il suo avvenire, Rome 1985

Forsyth, J., *Remarks on antiquities, arts and letters*, London 1813

Les Français à Rome, Rome 1961. There is also an Italian edition, *I francesi a Roma*, Rome 1961

Fugier, A., *Napoléon et l'Italie*, Paris 1947

Gasparoni, F., *Biografia di Giuseppe Camporese*, Rome 1836

Gelli, I., *I terramoti di Lazio*, Rome 1906

Gendry, J., *Pie VI, sa vie, son pontificat* (2 vols.), Paris 1907

Gibbon, E., *The decline and fall of the Roman Empire* (6 vols.), London 1776–88

Giornale del Campidoglio, Rome 1809–11

Giornale politico del dipartimento di Roma, Rome 1812–14

Giovannoni, G. and Patrizi, M., 'Il programma edilizio del prefetto di Roma, conte di Tournon', *Nuova antologia*, 1,322, 1927, 446–59

Giucci, G., *Storia della vita e del pontificato di Pio VII*, Rome 1857

Gloton, N., 'Transformation et réemploi des monuments du passé dans la Rome du XVI siècle', *MEFR*, 74, 1962, 705–58

Goethe, J. W., *Italian journey*, trans. by W. Auden and Elizabeth Mayer, London 1962

Gori, F., *Le memorie storiche . . . del Anfiteatro Flavio*, Rome 1875

Gregorovius, F., *Rome in the Middle Ages (400–1534)*, trans. by Annie Hamilton (8 vols.), London 1894–1902

Guattani, G., *Memorie enciclopediche romane sulle belle arti, antichità* (5 vols.), Rome 1806–*c.* 1810

Memorie enciclopediche sulle antichità e belle arti di Roma per il 1816, Rome 1817

Memorie enciclopediche sulle antichità e belle arti di Roma per il 1817, Rome 1819

Roma descritta ed illustrata, Rome 1805

I tre archi di Costantino, Severo e Tito, Rome 1815

Hautecœur, L., *Histoire de l'architecture classique en France*, vol. 5, Paris 1953

Rome et la Renaissance de l'antiquité à la fin du XVIII siècle, Paris 1912

'La vente de la collection Mattei et les origines du Musée Pio Clementino', *Mel. Arch. Hist.*, 30, 1910, 57–75

Highet, G., *The classical tradition*, Oxford 1949

Huart, Suzanne d', 'Martial Daru, intendant militaire de l'Empire', *Rev. Inst. Napoléon*, 103, 1967, 57–66

Hülsen, C., *Das Forum Romanum*, Rome 1904

Irwin, D., 'Gavin Hamilton', *Art Bulletin*, 44, 1962, 87–102

Jonsson, Marita, *La cura dei monumenti*, Stockholm 1986 (Italian trans. of *Monumentvardens Begynnelse*, 1976)

Ladolini, A., 'Scavi nel Foro Romano dal 1800 al 1836', *Notizie degli archivi di Stato*, 13, 1953, 138–55

Lamartine, A., *Mémoires inedits 1790–1815*, Paris 1909

Lanciani, R., *Ancient Rome in the light of recent discoveries*, London 1888
   The destruction of ancient Rome, London 1899
   Golden days of the Renaissance in Rome, London 1906
   'Notizie inedite sull'Anfiteatro Flavio', *RAL*, 5(5), 1896, 3–8
   Ruins and excavations of ancient Rome, London 1897
   Storia degli scavi (1000–1605) (4 vols.), Rome 1902–12 (a reprint with illustrations is in progress)
   Sulle vicende edilizie di Roma, Rome 1878
   MSS and collections of illustrations in the Istituto di Archeologia in Rome

La Padula, A., *Contributo alla storia dell'urbanistica, Roma 1809–1814*, Rome 1958
   'Lavori francesi di abbellimento a Roma 1809–1814: la chiesa del Nome di Maria e la Piazza della Colonna Traiana', *Fede ed Arte*, 1958, 456–63.
   Roma e la regione nell'epoca napoleonica, Rome 1969

Lapauze, H., *Histoire de l'Académie de France à Rome* (2 vols.), Paris 1924

Leggi, decreti, ordinanze e provvedimenti generali emanati dai Governi d'Italia per la conservazione dei monumenti, Rome 1881

Lenormant, Amélie, *Mme Récamier, les amis de sa jeunesse et sa correspondance*, Paris 1872

Leto, Pomponio, *de antiquitatibus urbis Romae*, Basle 1538

Liber Pontificalis, ed. L. Duchesne, Paris 1886

Licht, K. de Fine, *The Rotonda in Rome*, Copenhagen 1966

Logica, see Martorelli

Luigi Rossini, incisore, Rome 1982

Mabillon, J., *Museum italicum* (2 vols.), Paris, 1687

Macco, Michela., *Il Colosseo*, Rome 1971

Madelin, L., *La Rome de Napoléon*, Paris 1909

Marconi, P., *Giuseppe Valadier*, Rome 1964
   'Roma 1806–1829, un momento critico per la formazione della metodologia del restauro architettonico', *Ricerche di storia dell'arte* 8, 1978/9, 63–72

Marconi, P. and Cipriani, A., *Disegni architettonici dell'Archivio Storico dell'Accademia di S. Luca*, Rome 1975

Marino, Angela, 'Cultura archeologica e cultura architettonica a Roma', in *Ville et territoire pendant la période napoléonienne*, Rome 1987 (Coll. Ecole Française 96)

Mariotti, F., *La legislazione delle Belle Arti*, Rome 1892

Marshall, R., *Italy in early English literature 1775–1815*, New York 1934

Martorelli, L., *La logica nel Colosseo*, Rome 1813

Marucchi, O., *The Roman Forum and Palatine*, Rome 1906

Masdeu, J., *Lettere sette al Fea sulle antiche iscrizioni romane ne' recenti scavi rinvenute*, Rome 1813
   Riflessioni pacifiche dirette a conciliare le contrarie opinioni de' chiarissimi antiquarii Lorenzo Re e Carlo Fea intorno all'arena del Colosseo, Rome 1813

Mayne, J., *Journal during a tour on the Continent*, London 1909

Michaelis, A., *Ancient marbles*, Cambridge 1882

'Storia della collezione capitolina di antichità', *RM*, 6, 1891, 3–66

Mirabilia urbis Romae (the medieval guidebook to Rome) ed. and trans. F. Nichols, London 1889

Mirri, L. and Carletti, G., *Le pitture delle Terme di Tito*, Rome 1776

Misserini, M., *Storia dell'Accademia di S. Luca*, Rome 1823

Montaigne, M., *Journal de voyage*, ed. C. Dedeyan, Paris 1946

Moulard, J., *Le comte de Tournon 1778–1833* (3 vols.), Paris 1927–32

Muñoz, A., *Roma nel primo Ottocento*, Rome 1961

Müntz, E., *Les antiquités de la ville de Rome aux 14–16 siècles*, Paris 1886

Les arts à la cour des Papes pendant le XV et le XVI siècle (3 vols.), Rome 1878–82

'Les monuments antiques de Rome au xv siècle', *Rev. Arch.*, 2(32), 1876, 158–75

'Les monuments antiques de Rome à l'époque de la Renaissance', *Rev. Arch.*, 3(3), 1884, 296–313; 3(4), 1884, 38–53; 3(5), 1885, 350–63; 3(6), 1885, 26–41; 3(7), 1886, 124–340; 3(8), 1886, 33–9

Napoleone e l'Italia, Rome 1973 (Quaderno 179 dell'Accademia Nazionale dei Lincei)

Nel primo centenario della morte del Cardinale Consalvi, Rome 1924

Nibby, A., *Del Foro Romano, della Via Sacra e dell'Anfiteatro Flavio*, Rome 1819

Itinerario di Roma (2 vols.), Rome 1827

Roma nell'anno 1838 (4 vols.), Rome 1838

Nogara, B., 'Il cardinale Ercole Consalvi e le antichità e le belle arti', in *Nel primo centenario della morte del Cardinale Consalvi*, 1924, pp. 84–101

Nouvelle biographie générale (46 vols.), Paris 1855–66

Onofrio, C. d', *Gli obelischi di Roma*, Rome 1965

Ossat, G. de Angelis d', 'Carlo Fea e lo studio dei monumenti romani', *Bolletino della R. deputazione di storia patria per la Liguria*, 2, 1936, 315–28

Ozzola, L., *Gian Paolo Panini, pittore*, Rome 1921

Pacca, Cardinal Bartolomeo, *Memorie storiche del ministero*, 1835 (Eng. trans. *Historical memoirs*, London 1850)

Parker, H., *The cult of antiquity and the French revolutionaries*, Chicago 1937

Pastor, L. von, *History of the Popes* (1305–1800), trans. Antrobus *et al.* (40 vols.), London 1891–1953

Perkins, J. Ward, *Roman imperial architecture*, Harmondsworth, 1970

Petit-Radel, *Voyage historique . . . dans les principales villes d'Italie en 1811 et 1812* (2 vols.), Paris 1815

Piale, S., *Delle Terme Traiane, della Domus Aurea di Nerone, e della Domus Titi*, Rome 1832

Pietrangeli, C., 'Archaeological excavations in Italy 1750–1850', in *The age of Neoclassicism*, London 1972, pp. xlvi–lii

'Il Museo Clementino Vaticano', *Rend. Accad. Arch.*, 27, 1951–2, 87–109

Il Museo Napoleonico, Rome 1950

'I Musei Vaticani al tempo di Pio VI', *Rend. Accad. Arch.*, 49, 1976–9, 195–233

'I Musei Vaticani dopo Tolentino', *Strenna dei Romanisti*, 36, 1975, 354–9

Scavi e scoperti di antichità sotto il pontificato di Pio VI, Rome 1958

Pinelli, see *Bartolomeo*

Pinelli, Orietta, 'Carlo Fea e il chirografo del 1802', *Ricerche e storia sull'arte*, 8, 1978–9, 27–41

Pinon, P., 'Comment fouillait-on au 18e et au début du 19e siècle', *Archeologia* (Fontaine-les–Dijon), Sept. 1981, 17–26

Piranesi, G. B., *Vedute di Roma* (137 plates), Rome *c.* 1746–78

Platner, E. and Ashby, T., *Topographical dictionary of ancient Rome*, Oxford 1929

The prosopography of the Later Roman Empire, edited by Jones, Martindale and Martin, Cambridge 1971–

Rabelais, F., *Lettres*

Real Encyclopädie der klassischen Altertumswissenschaften, ed. Pauly and Wissowa, Stuttgart 1893–1978

Récamier, Jeanne Françoise, *Souvenirs et correspondance*, ed. Mme Lenormant (2 vols.), Paris 1860

Ricci, C., *Il mercato di Traiano*, Rome 1929

Ridley, R., 'Augusti manes volitant per auras: the archaeology of Rome under the Fascists', *Xenia*, 11, 1986, 19–46

'The struggle for identity: the monuments of the Roman Forum in the nineteenth century', *Xenia*, 17, 1989, 71–90

Righini, Bici Stern, 'L'insigne architetto romano Raffaele Stern', lecture at the Circolo di Cultura Femminile, 16 Dec. 1920 (copy at Accademia di S. Luca)

Robinet, J., *Dictionnaire historique et biographique de la Révolution et de l'Empire* (2 vols.), Paris 1899

Robinson, J., *Cardinal Consalvi*, London 1987

Rodocanachi, E., *Le Capitole romain*, Paris 1904

Roma antica, envois degli architetti francesi 1788–1924, Rome (Académie de France), 1985

Romanis, A. de, *Le antiche camere esquiline*, Rome 1822

Rossini, L., *Le antichità romane divise in cento tavole*, Rome 1819–23

Raccolta di cinquanta principali vedute di antichità, Rome 1818

See also *Luigi Rossini*

Ruggiero, E. de, *Il Foro Romano*, Rome 1913

Sear, F., *Roman architecture*, London 1982

Servi, G., *Notizie alla vita del cav. Giuseppe Valadier*, Bologna 1840

Six, G., *Dictionnaire biographique des généraux et amiraux français de la Révolution et de l'Empire*, Paris 1934

Staël, Mme de, *Corinne*, Paris 1807

Correspondance générale, ed. Jasinski, Paris 1960–

Stendhal (Henri Beyle), *Correspondance*

Promenades dans Rome, Paris 1828

Rome, Naples et Florence, Paris 1826 (3rd edn)

Vie de Rossini, Paris 1823

see *Oeuvres*, ed. Martineau (79 vols.), Paris 1927–37

Thedenat, H., *Le forum romain*, Paris 1904 (3rd edn)

Thieme, U. and Becker, F., *Allgemeines Lexikon der bildenden Kunst* (38 vols.) Leipzig 1907–50

Tournon, C., *Etudes statistiques sur Rome* (3 vols.), Paris 1831

   Lettres inédites du comte Camille de Tournon, préfet de Rome 1809–1814, ed. J. Moulard, Paris 1914

   'Mémoire sur les travaux entrepris à Rome par l'administration française de 1810 à 1814', *Académie de Bordeaux*, 2, 1821, 39–54

Uggeri, A., *Journées pittoresques des édifices de Rome ancienne*, Rome 1800–, especially series 1, *Monuments de Rome* (6 vols.) and series 2, *Edifices antiques*, including *Edifices antiques réparés par les ordres de Pie VII de l'an 1804 à 1816*, 1817

Urlichs, C., *Codex urbis Romae topographicus*, Wirceburgh 1871

Valadier, G., 'Narrazione artistica sull'arco di Tito', *Diss. Accad. Arch.*, 1, 1821–3, 275–86

   Opere di architettura e di ornamento ideate e eseguite da G. Valadier, Rome 1833

   Raccolta delle più insigni fabbriche di Roma antica (7 parts), Rome 1810–26

Valentini, R. and Zuchetti, G., *Codice topografico di Roma* (4 vols.), 1940–53

Vasi, G., *Delle magnificenze di Roma antica e moderna* (200 plates in ten books), Rome 1747–61

   La raccolta delle più belle vedute antiche e moderne di Roma, Rome 1803

Vasi, M., *Itinerario istruttivo di Roma* (2 vols.), Rome 1804

Vercesi, E., *Pio VII.* Turin 1933

Visconti, F. A., *Lettera sopra la colonna dell'imperatore Foca*, Rome 1813

Visconti, P. E., *Biografia del cav. Giuseppe Valadier*, Rome 1839

Weege, F., 'Das Goldene Haus des Nero', *JDAI*, 28, 1913, 127ff.

Winckelmann, J., *Storia dell'arte del disegno presso gli antichi*, ed. C. Fea (3 vols.), Rome 1783

Index

Apart from some leading figures, identifying notes have been added only where I cannot discover a person's first name.